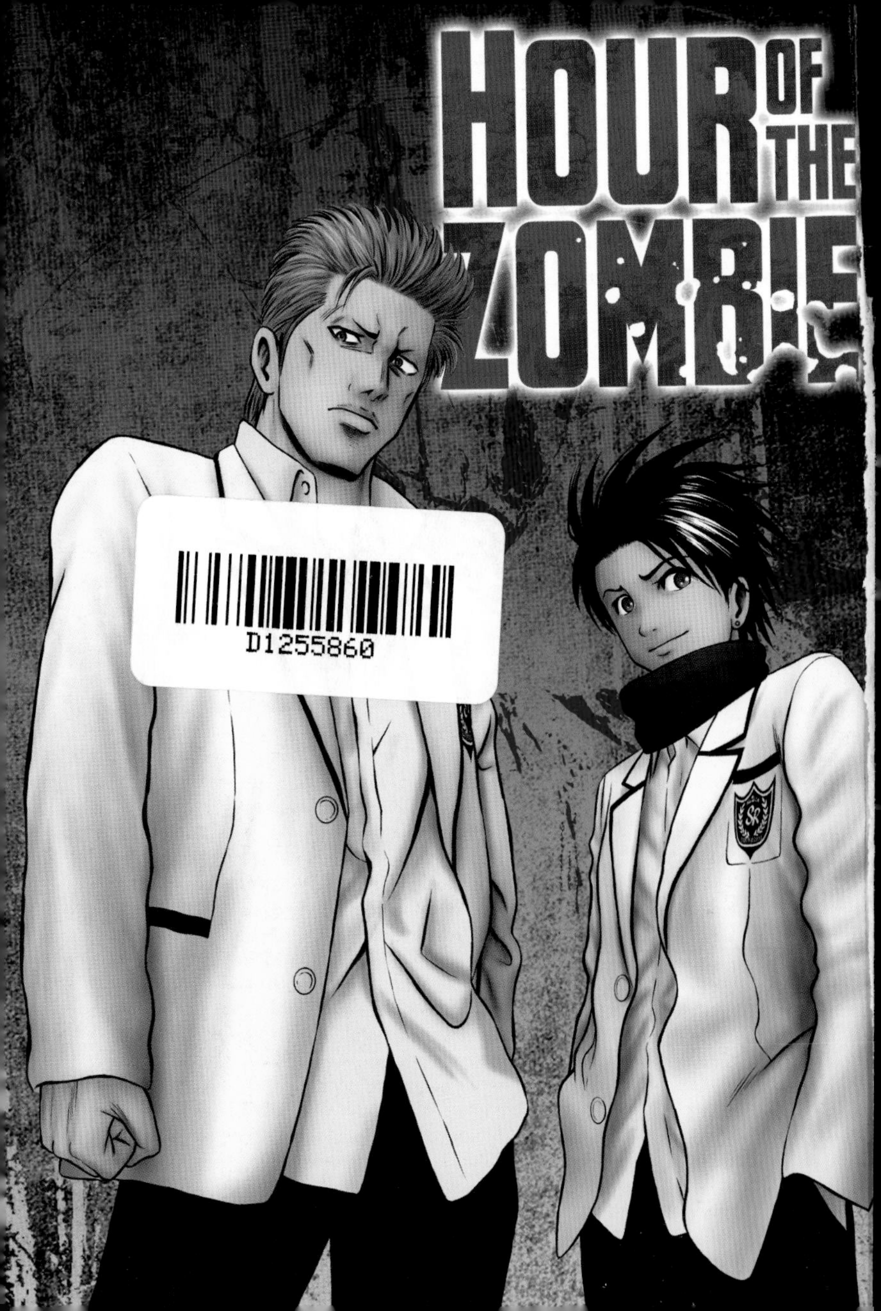
HOUR OF THE ZOMBIE

BOXING TEAM

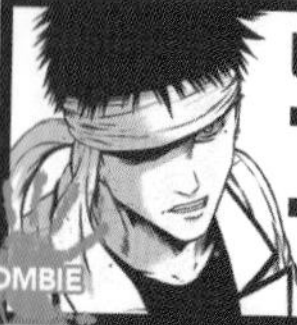
ZOMBIE

Umezawa Reiji

- Boxing Team member, second-year.
- Placed fourth in the Interhigh championship. Trusts Akira.

BEST FRIENDS

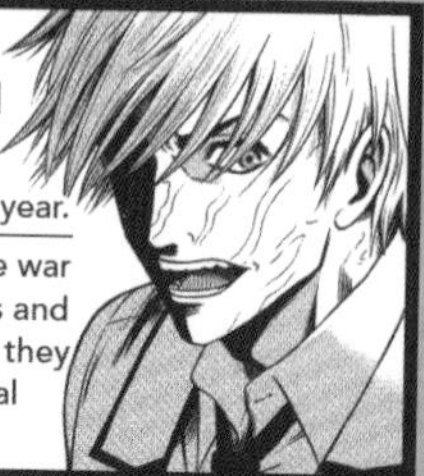

Nikaidou Akira

- Boxing Team member, second-year.
- Wants to stop the war between zombies and humans. Believes they can reach a mutual understanding.

CRUSH

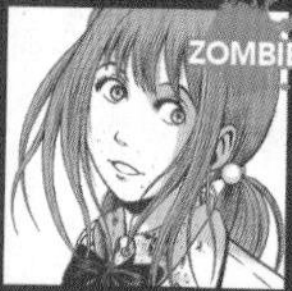
ZOMBIE

Akutsu Kurumi

- Second-year.
- Childhood friends with Akira.

CRUSH

RESPECTS

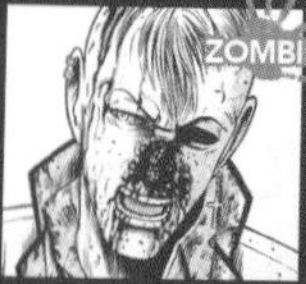
ZOMBIE

Usa Sadaharu

- Band, third-year.
- He was a hardliner...

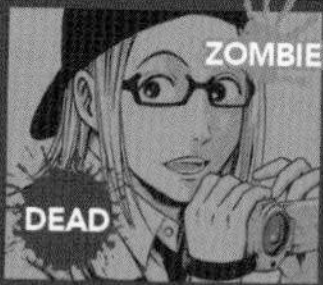
ZOMBIE
DEAD

Furuchi Madoka

- Film Club president, second-year.
- Realized he contracted the zombie virus and killed himself.

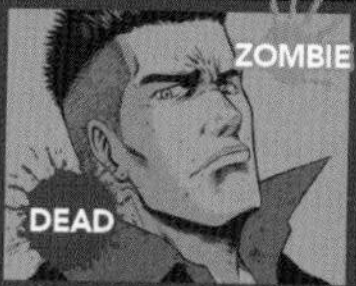
ZOMBIE
DEAD

Igarashi Kaoru

- Rugby Team captain, third-year.
- The supreme leader of the zombies. Died while shielding Umezawa.

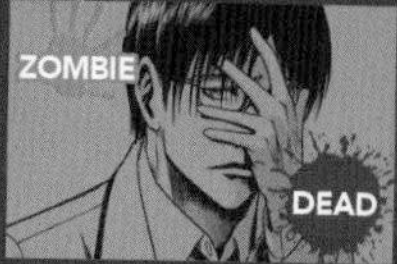
ZOMBIE
DEAD

Houjou Shunichi

- Shogi Team co-captain, Student Council President, third-year.
- Discovered the principles of zombification. Attempted to escape with his girlfriend, but died.

BASKETBALL TEAM

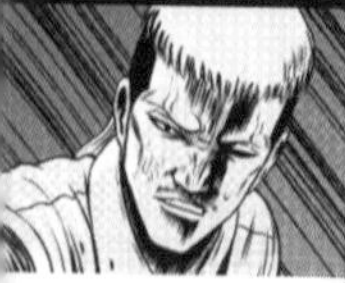

Muroya Masami

- Basketball Team member, second-year.
- A delinquent who went to the same junior high as Akira and Kurumi.

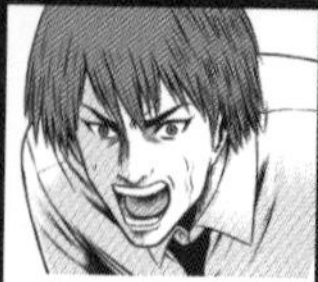

Makimura Tadanobu

- Basketball Team captain, third-year.
- Began to act on his belief of zombie annihilation.

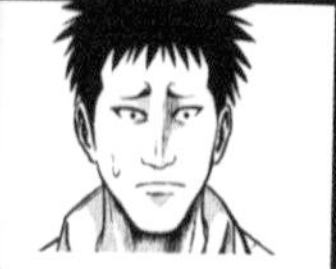

Kishi Kyousuke

- Basketball Team member, third-year.
- Worried about his little sister at home.

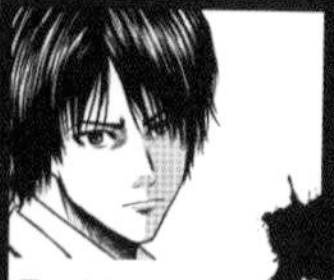

Ezaki Taiyou

- Basketball Team member, second-year.
- Trusts Makimura.

SOCCER TEAM

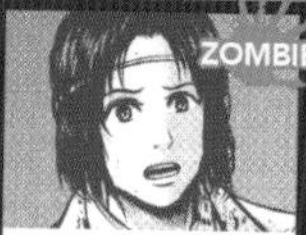
ZOMBIE

Asakura Yukie

- Girls' Soccer Team captain, third-year.
- Collaborates with Hino.

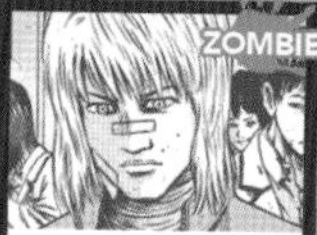
ZOMBIE

Hino Hideaki

- Boys' Soccer Team captain, third-year.
- Took Igarashi's place to rally the zombies together.

CRAFT CLUB

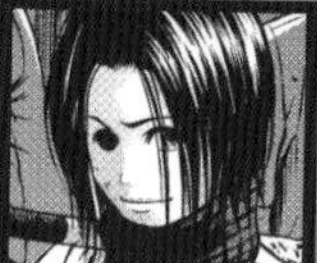

Kisaragi Takeru

- Craft Club member, first-year.
- Prefers to be a lone wolf in this hellish world.

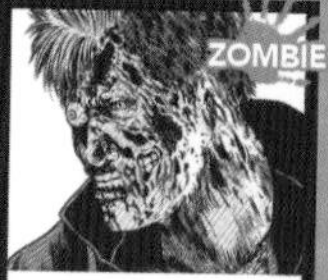
ZOMBIE

Kubo Ryuuhei

- Craft Club member, first-year.
- Was betrayed by his best friend, Kisaragi.

PHASE 37: The Precipice

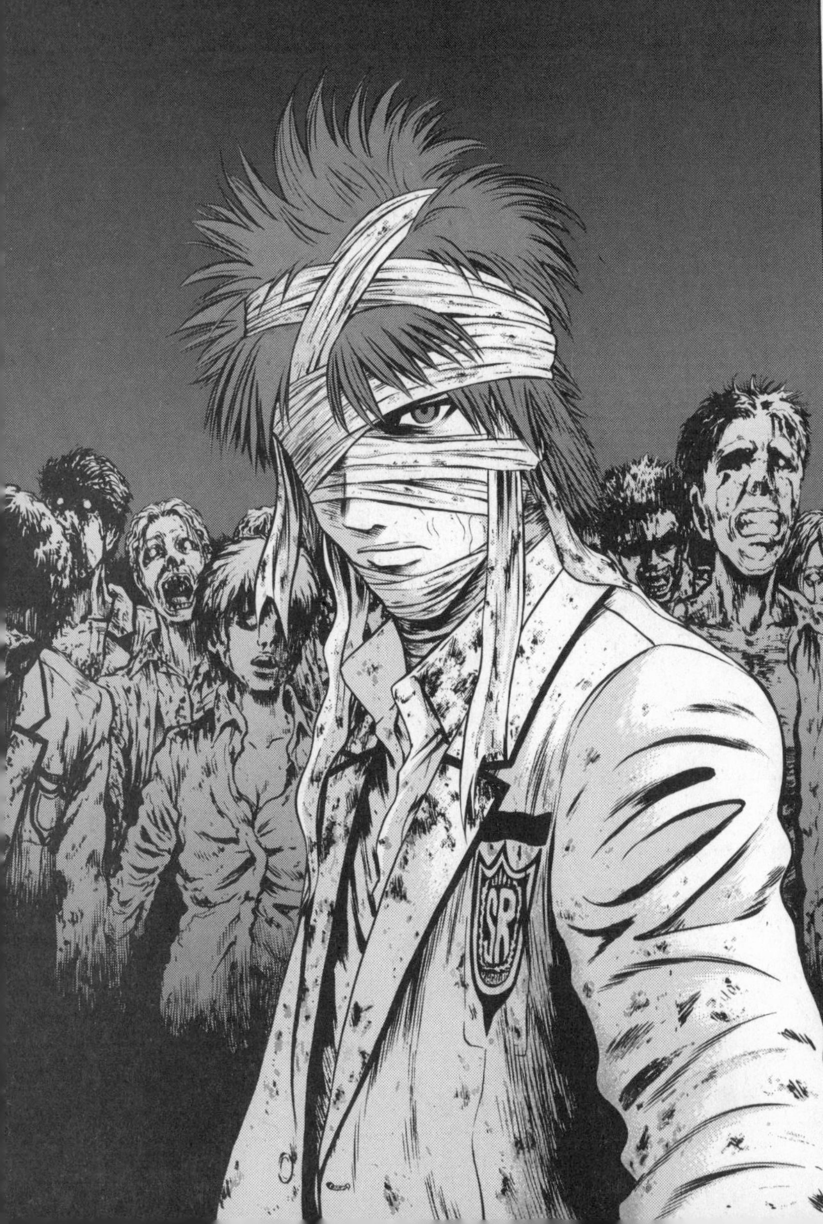

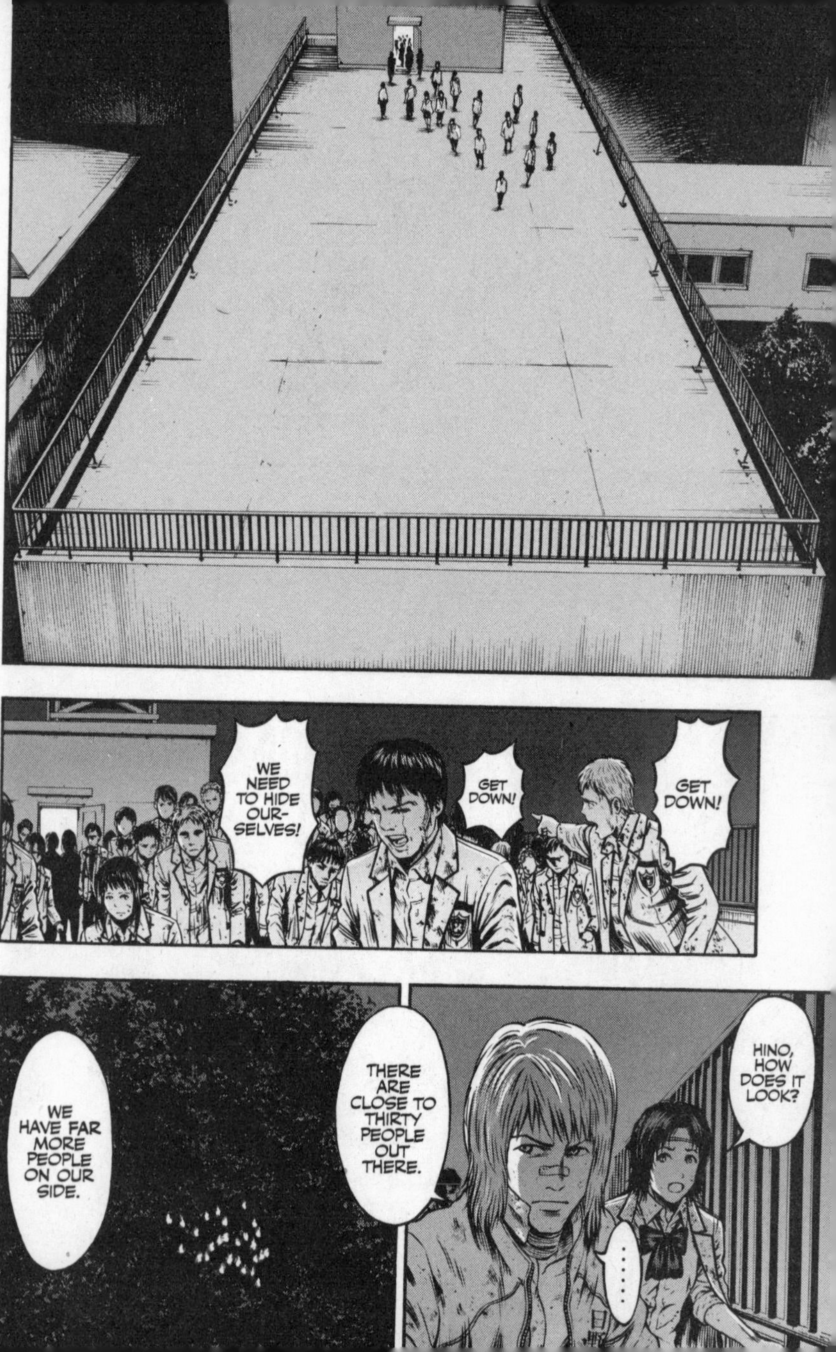
GET DOWN!
GET DOWN!
WE NEED TO HIDE OUR-SELVES!
HINO, HOW DOES IT LOOK?
THERE ARE CLOSE TO THIRTY PEOPLE OUT THERE.
......
WE HAVE FAR MORE PEOPLE ON OUR SIDE.

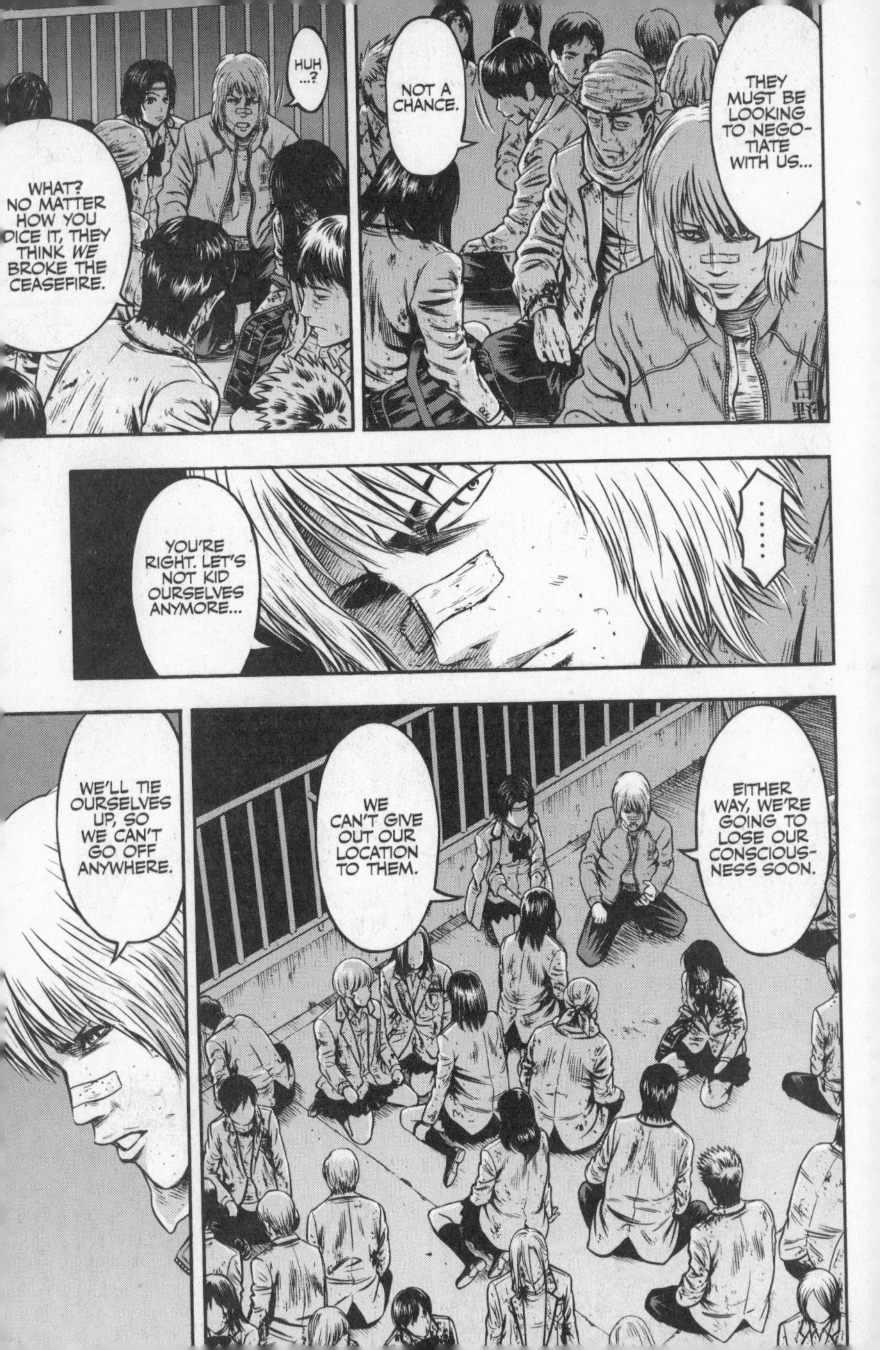
THEY MUST BE LOOKING TO NEGOTIATE WITH US...
NOT A CHANCE.
HUH ...?
WHAT? NO MATTER HOW YOU DICE IT, THEY THINK *WE* BROKE THE CEASEFIRE.
......
YOU'RE RIGHT. LET'S NOT KID OURSELVES ANYMORE...
EITHER WAY, WE'RE GOING TO LOSE OUR CONSCIOUSNESS SOON.
WE CAN'T GIVE OUT OUR LOCATION TO THEM.
WE'LL TIE OURSELVES UP, SO WE CAN'T GO OFF ANYWHERE.

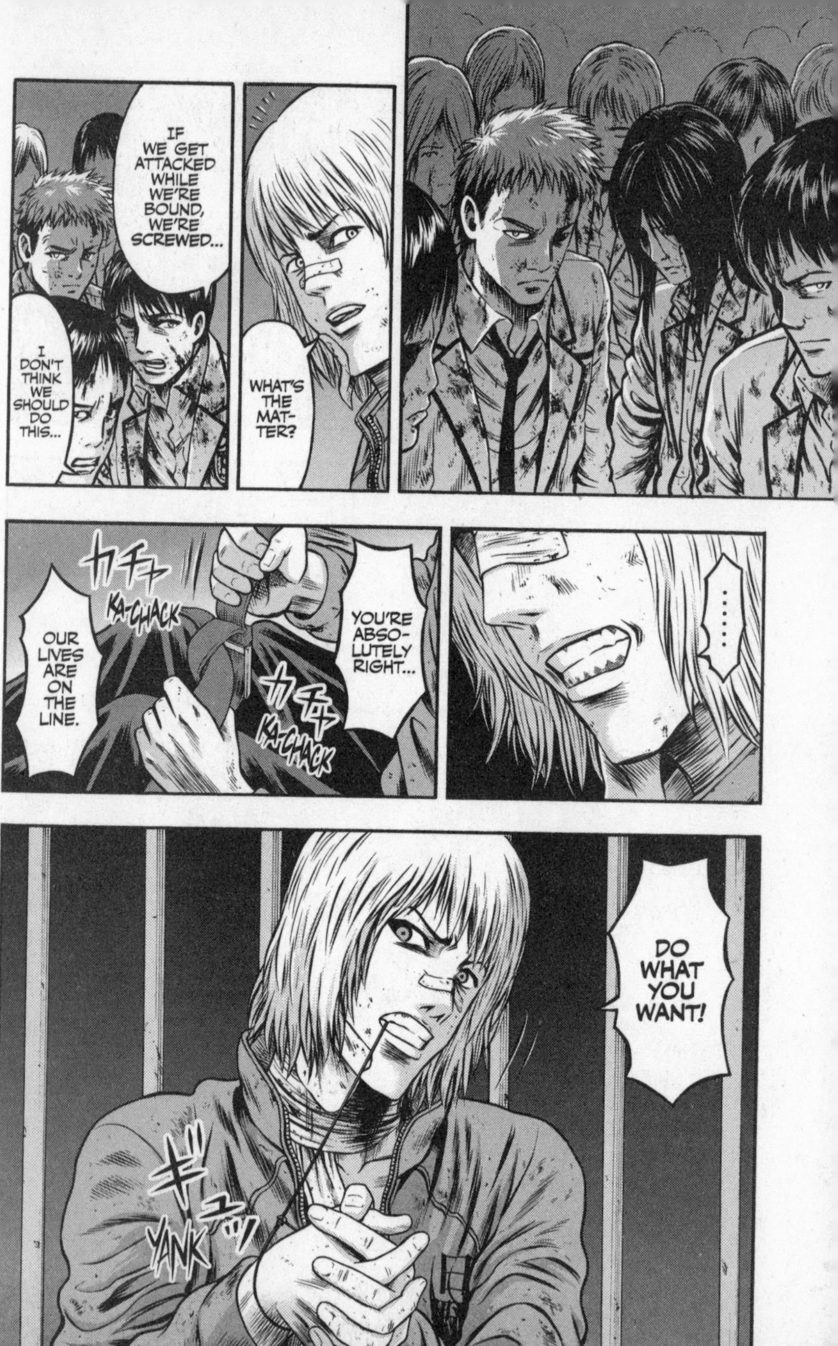
WHAT'S THE MATTER?
IF WE GET ATTACKED WHILE WE'RE BOUND, WE'RE SCREWED...
I DON'T THINK WE SHOULD DO THIS...
......
YOU'RE ABSOLUTELY RIGHT...
カチャ
KA-CHACK
OUR LIVES ARE ON THE LINE.
カチャ
KA-CHACK
DO WHAT YOU WANT!
ギュッ
YANK

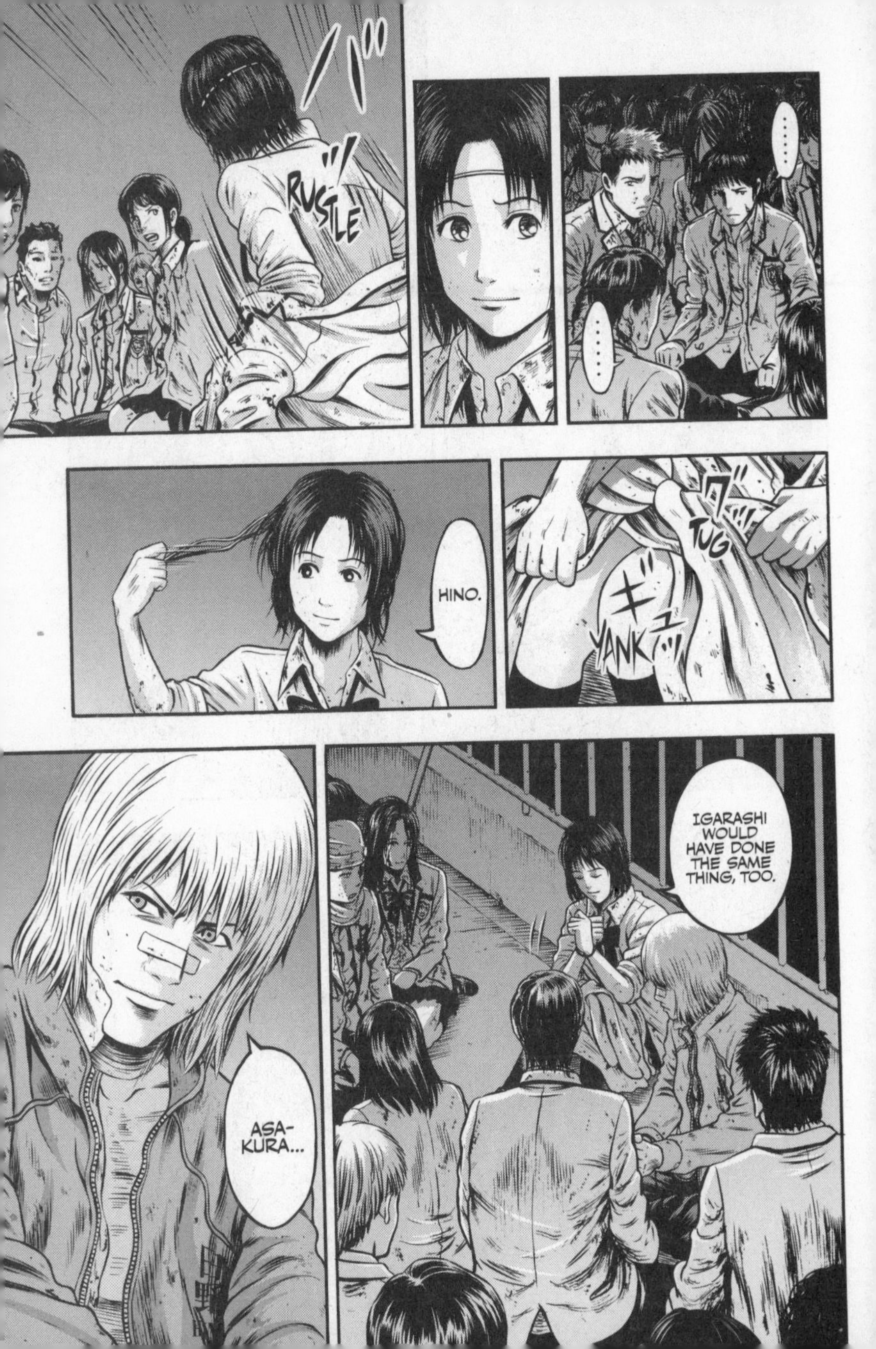
......
......
RUSTLE
TUG
YANK
HINO.
IGARASHI WOULD HAVE DONE THE SAME THING, TOO.
ASA-KURA...

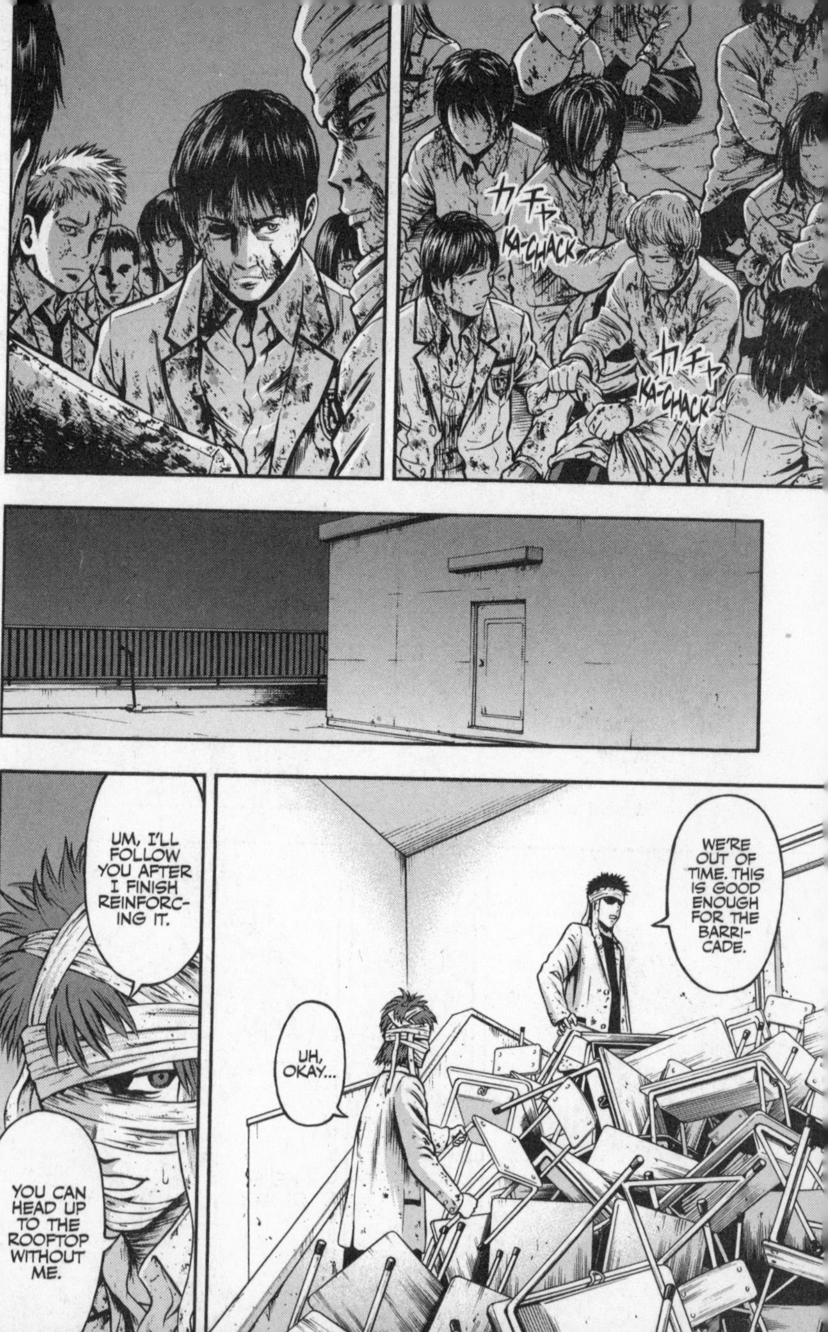
カチャ
KA-CHACK
カチャ
KA-CHACK
WE'RE OUT OF TIME. THIS IS GOOD ENOUGH FOR THE BARRI-CADE.
UH, OKAY...
UM, I'LL FOLLOW YOU AFTER I FINISH REINFORC-ING IT.
YOU CAN HEAD UP TO THE ROOFTOP WITHOUT ME.

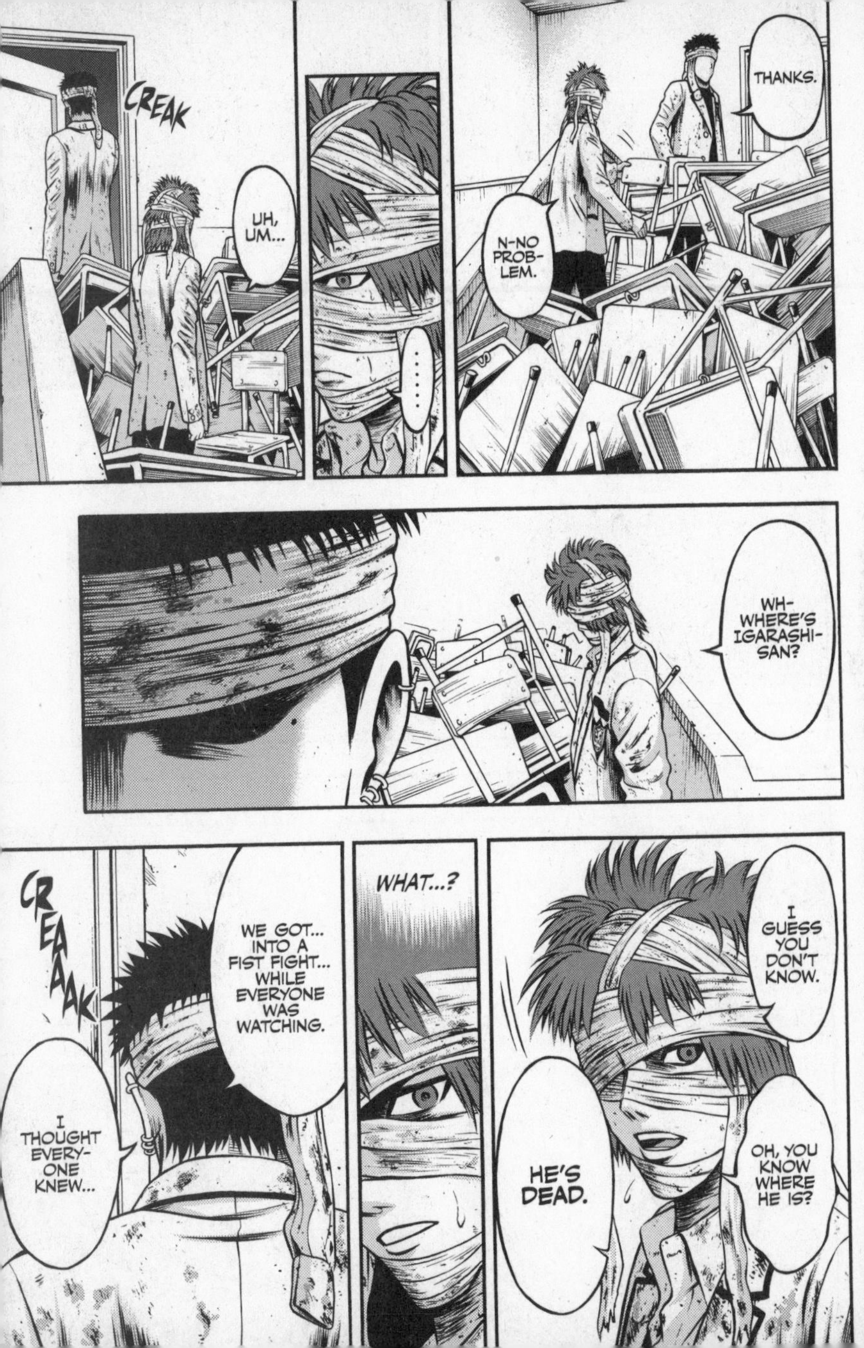
THANKS.
N-NO PROB-LEM.
......
CREAK
UH, UM...
WH-WHERE'S IGARASHI-SAN?
I GUESS YOU DON'T KNOW.
OH, YOU KNOW WHERE HE IS?
HE'S DEAD.
WHAT...?
CREAAAK
WE GOT... INTO A FIST FIGHT... WHILE EVERYONE WAS WATCHING.
I THOUGHT EVERY-ONE KNEW...

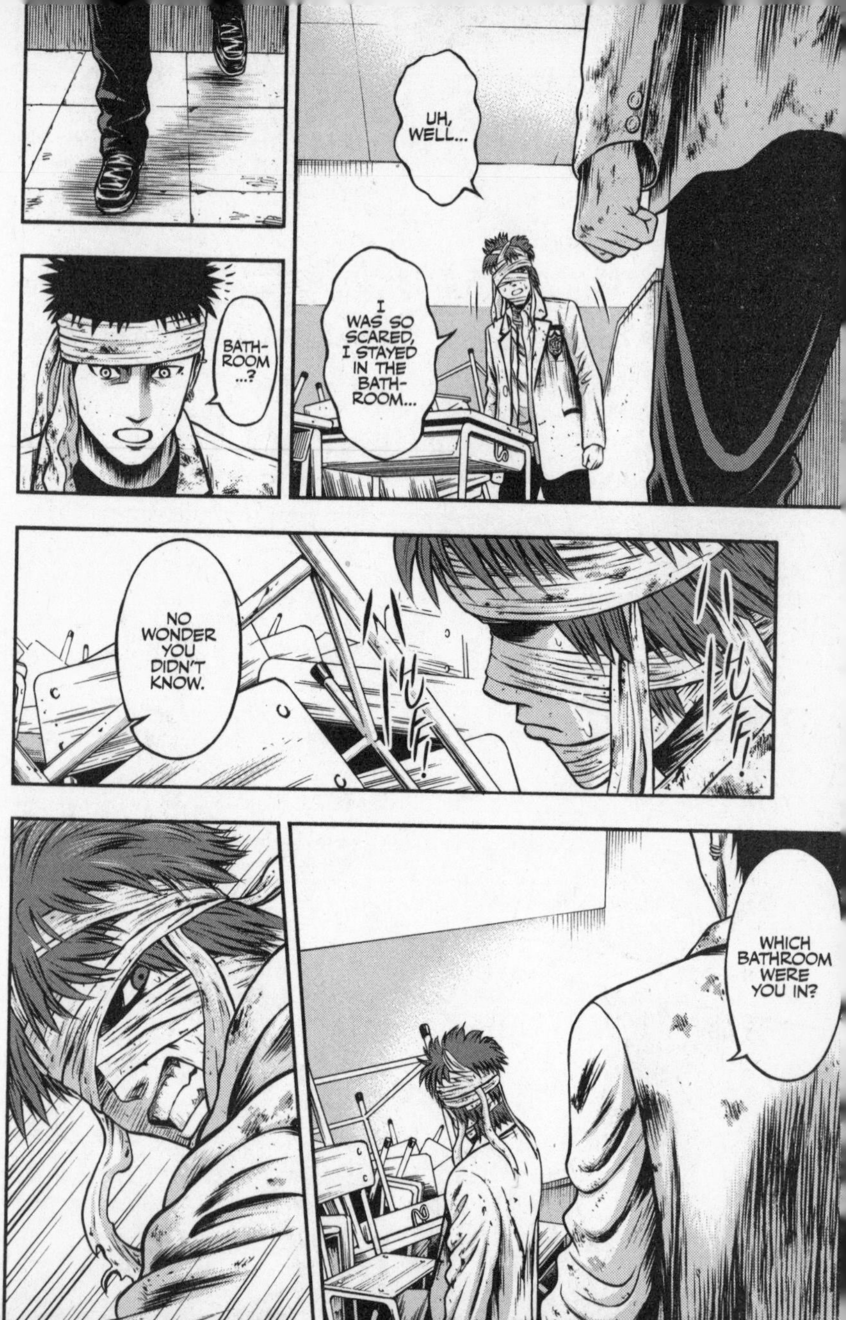
UH, WELL...
I WAS SO SCARED, I STAYED IN THE BATH-ROOM...
BATH-ROOM ...?
HUFF!
HUFF!
NO WONDER YOU DIDN'T KNOW.
WHICH BATHROOM WERE YOU IN?

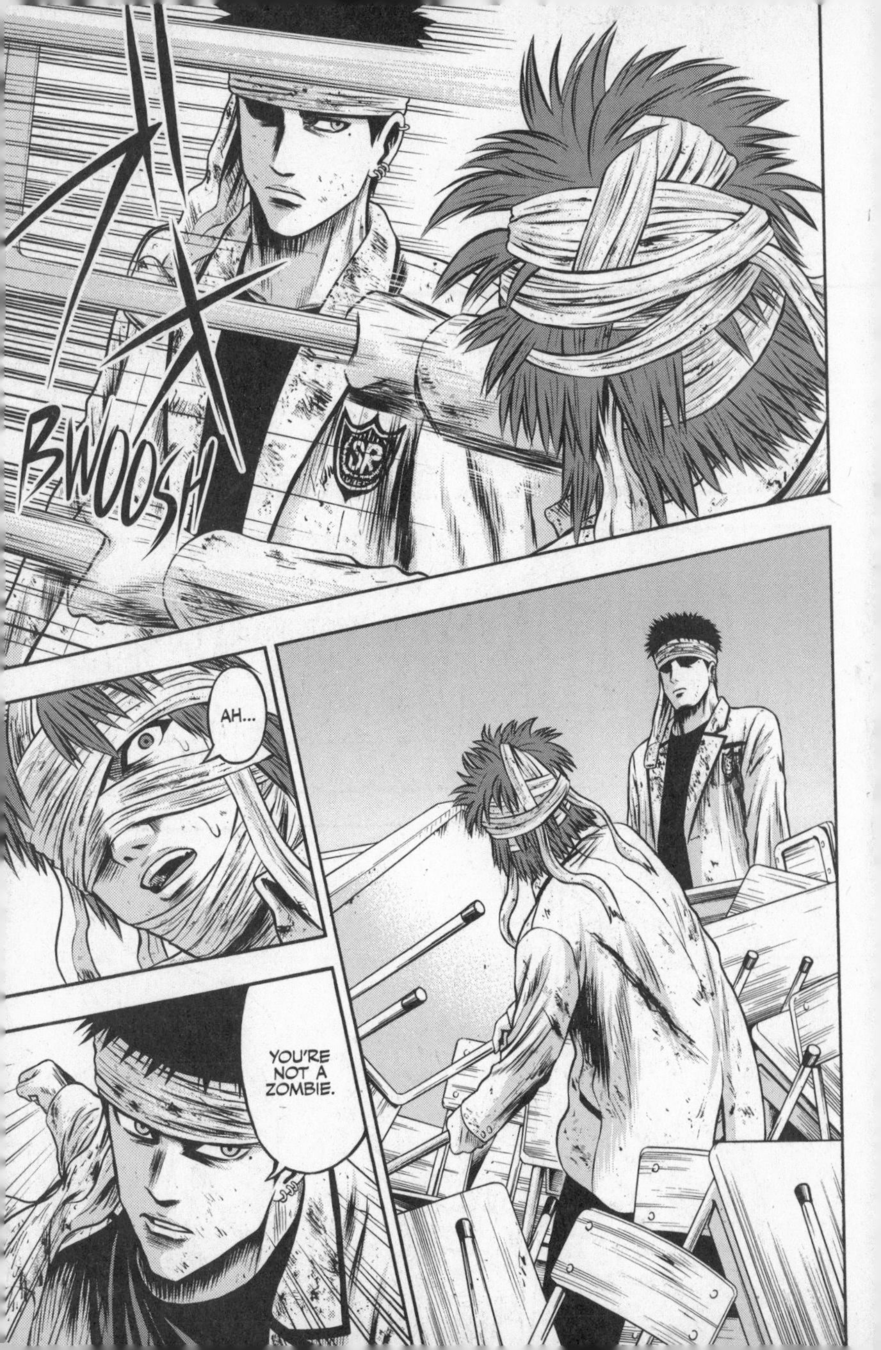
BWOOSH
AH...
YOU'RE NOT A ZOMBIE.

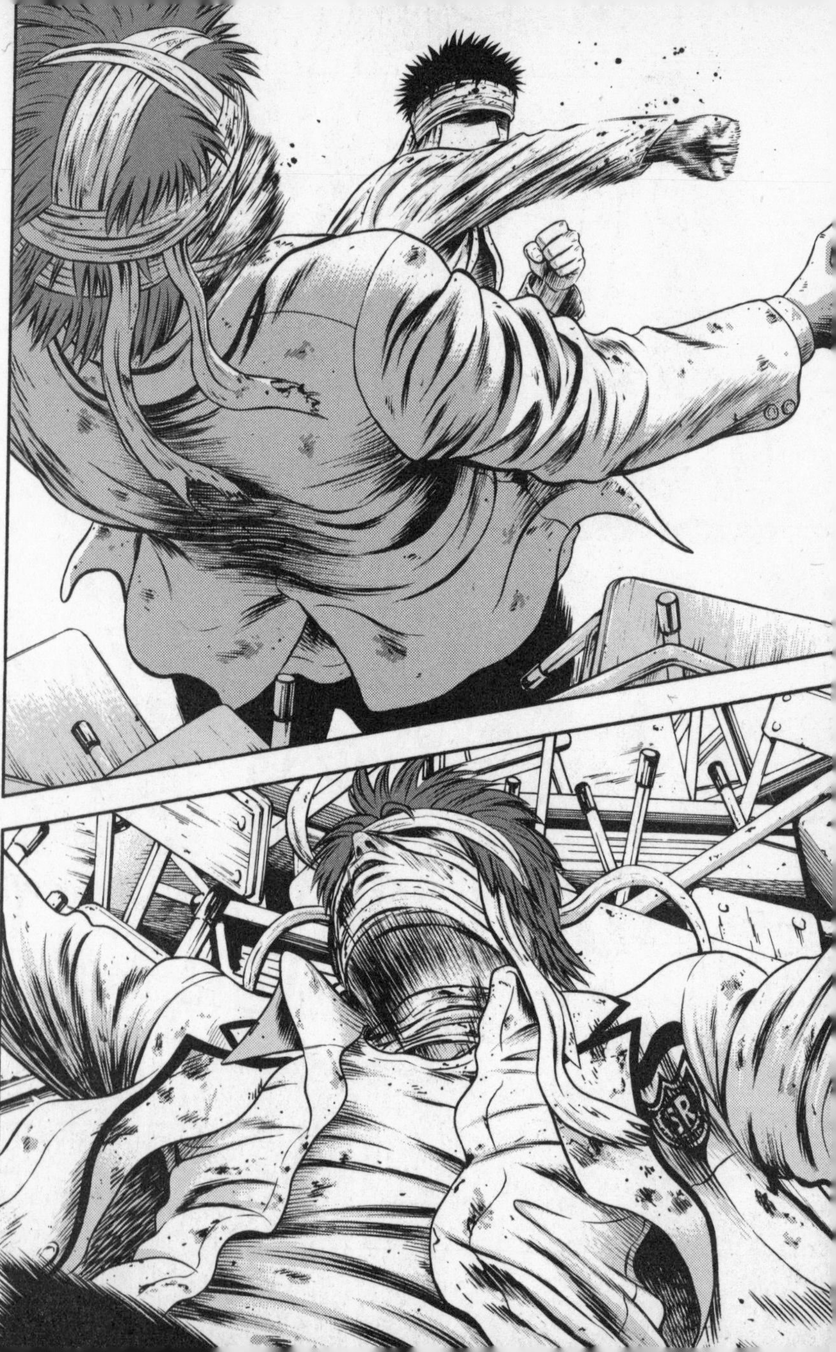

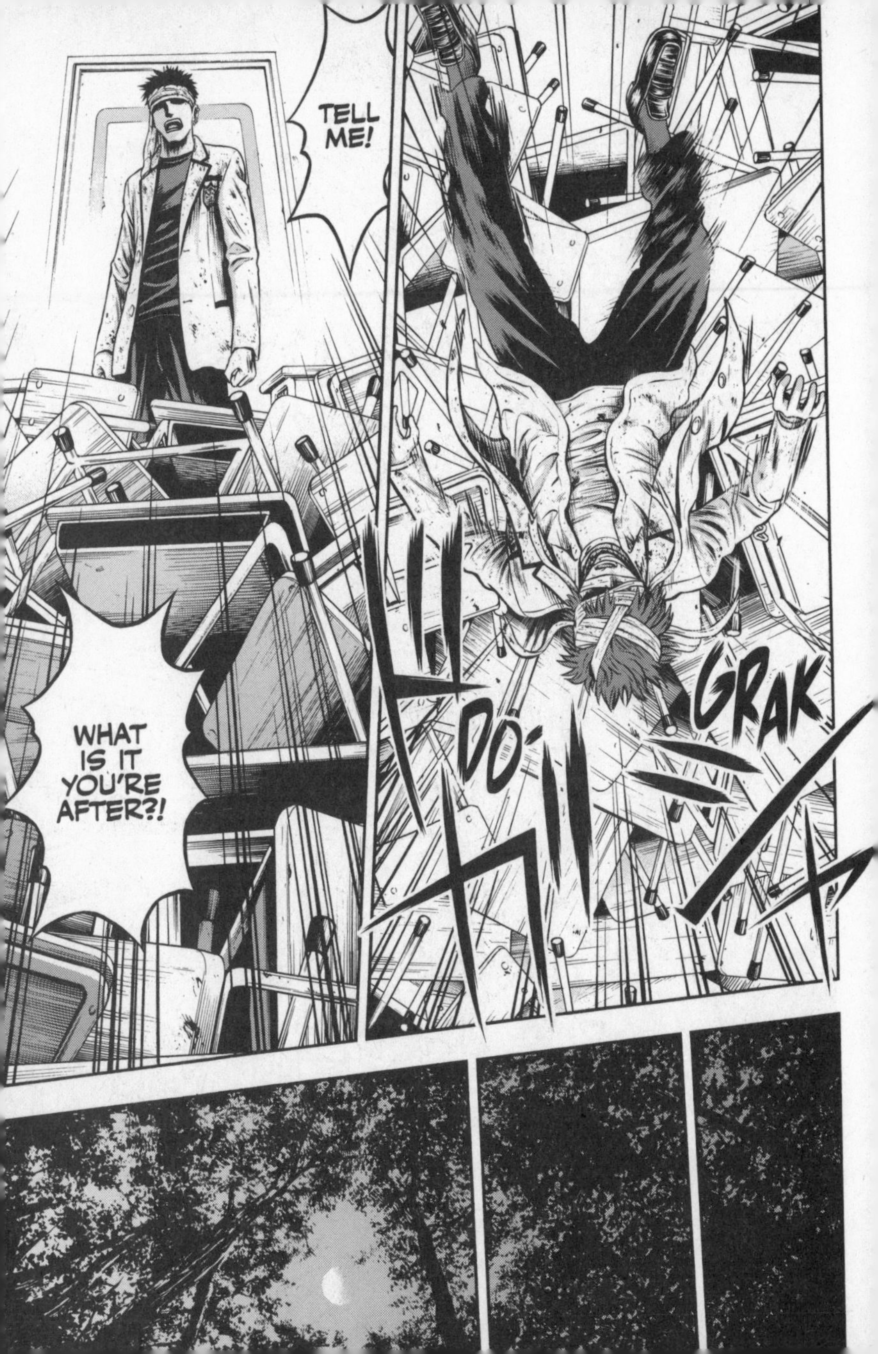
DO
GRAK
TELL ME!
WHAT IS IT YOU'RE AFTER?!

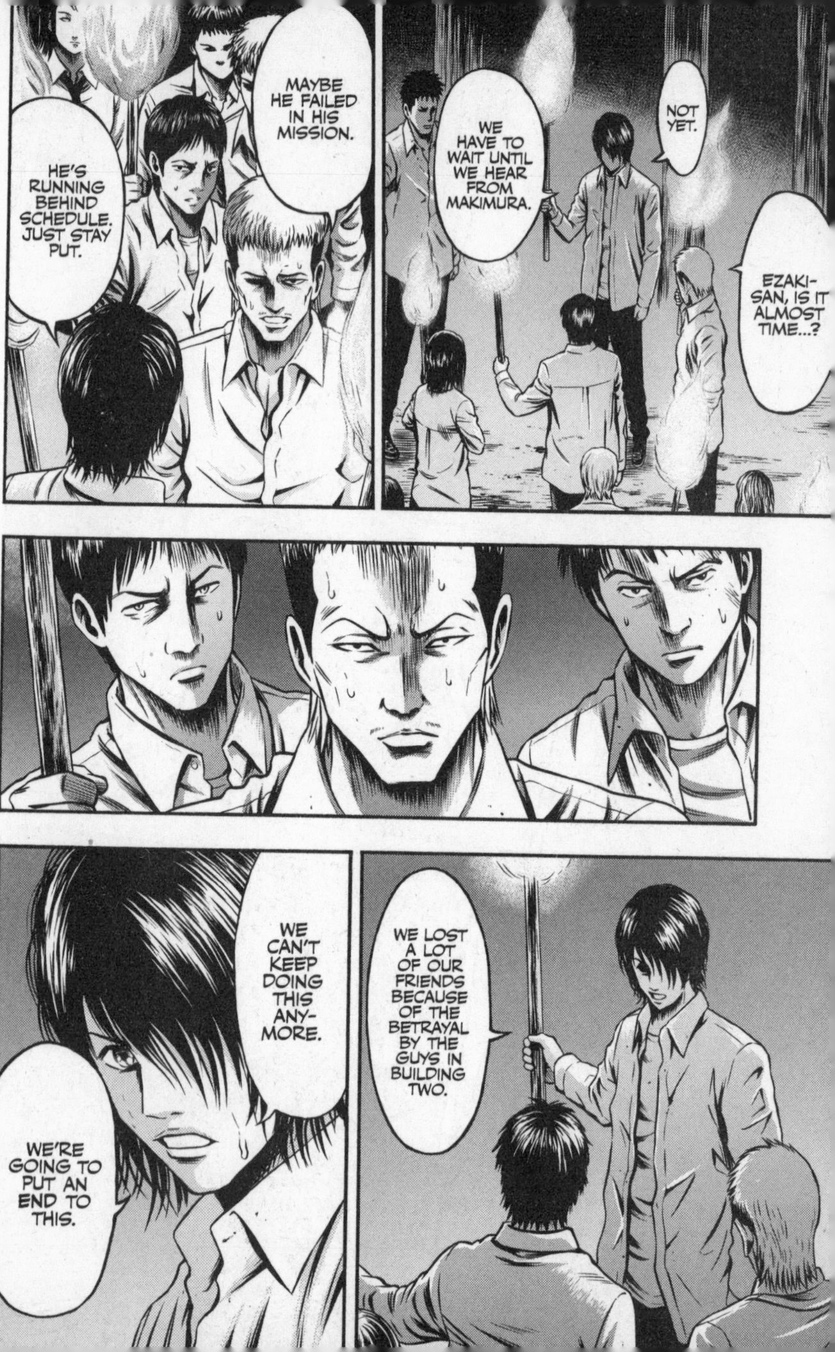
EZAKI-SAN, IS IT ALMOST TIME...?
NOT YET.
WE HAVE TO WAIT UNTIL WE HEAR FROM MAKIMURA.
MAYBE HE FAILED IN HIS MISSION.
HE'S RUNNING BEHIND SCHEDULE. JUST STAY PUT.
WE LOST A LOT OF OUR FRIENDS BECAUSE OF THE BETRAYAL BY THE GUYS IN BUILDING TWO.
WE CAN'T KEEP DOING THIS ANYMORE.
WE'RE GOING TO PUT AN END TO THIS.

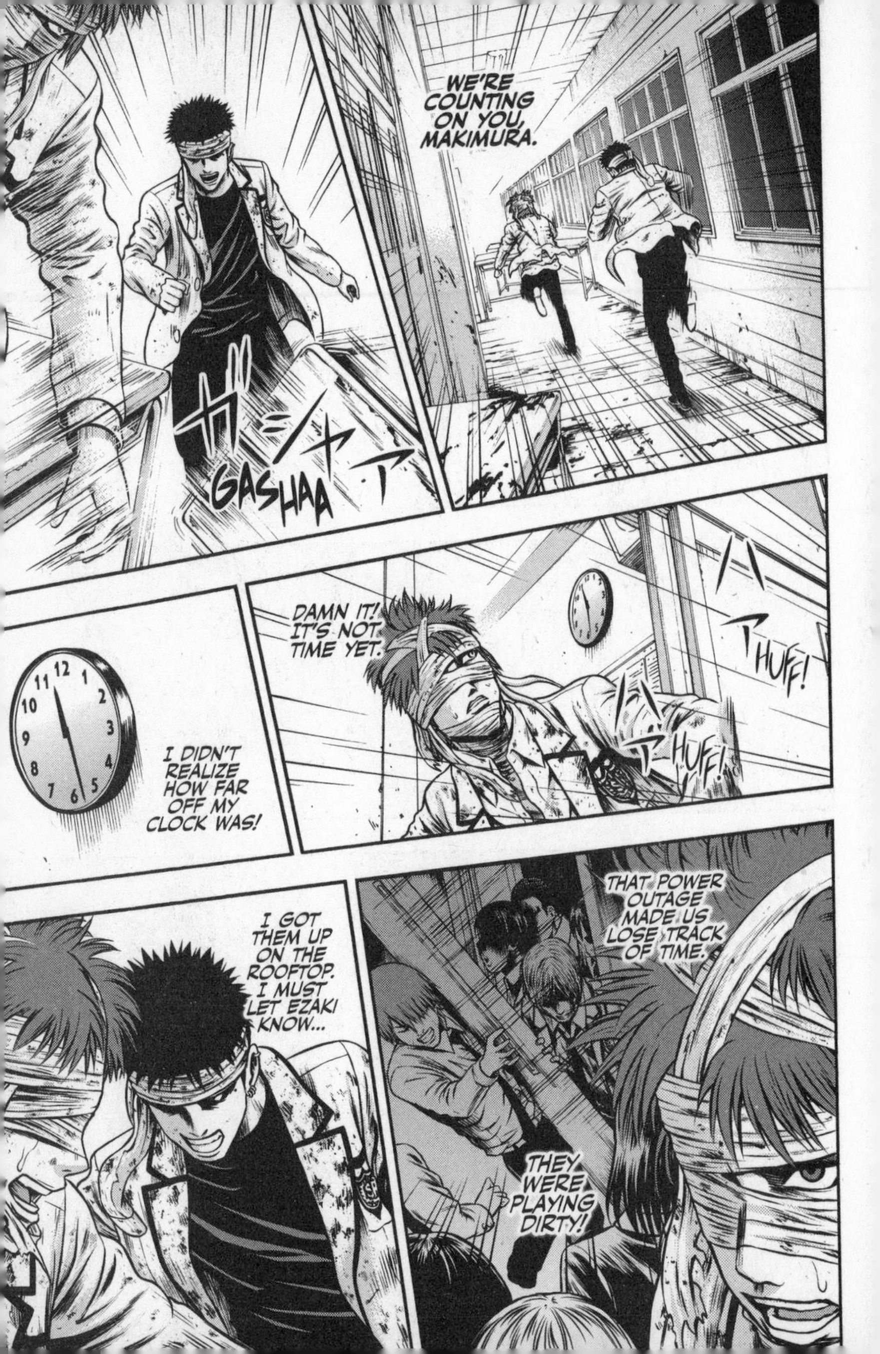
WE'RE COUNTING ON YOU, MAKIMURA.
GASHAA
DAMN IT! IT'S NOT TIME YET.
HUFF!
HUFF!
I DIDN'T REALIZE HOW FAR OFF MY CLOCK WAS!
THAT POWER OUTAGE MADE US LOSE TRACK OF TIME.
THEY WERE PLAYING DIRTY!
I GOT THEM UP ON THE ROOFTOP. I MUST LET EZAKI KNOW...

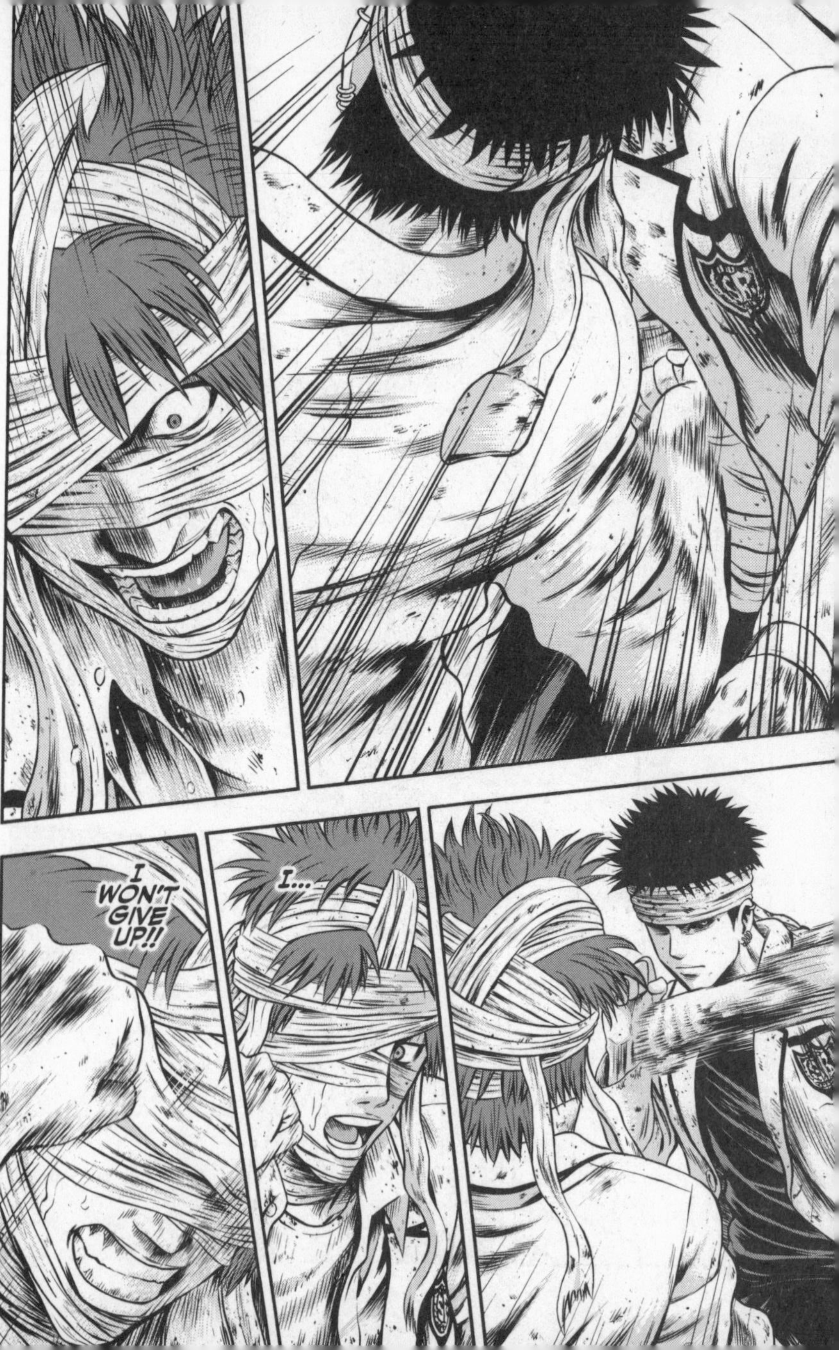
I...
I WON'T GIVE UP!!

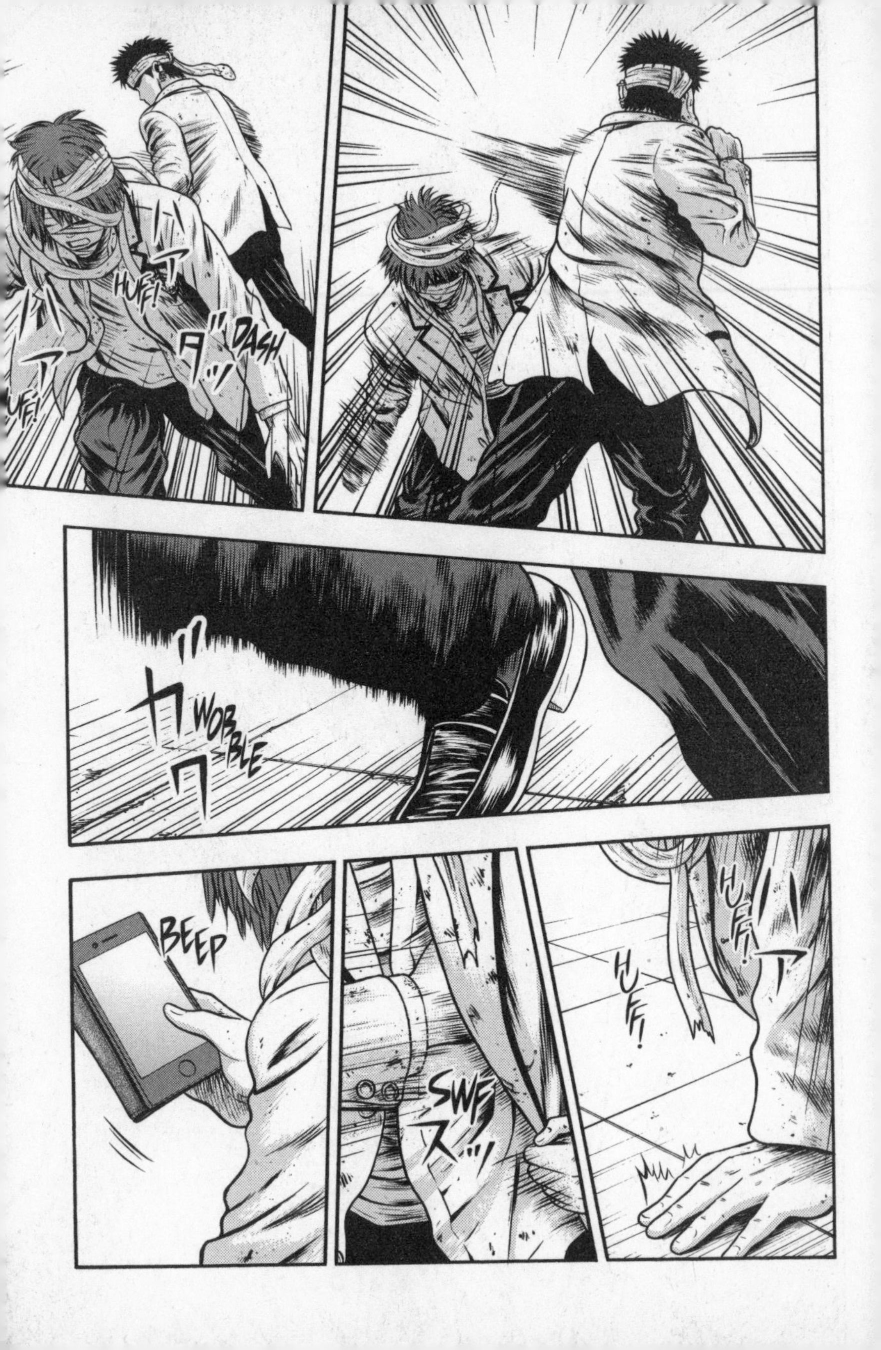
HUFF!
DASH
WOBBLE
HUFF!
HUFF!
SWF
BEEP

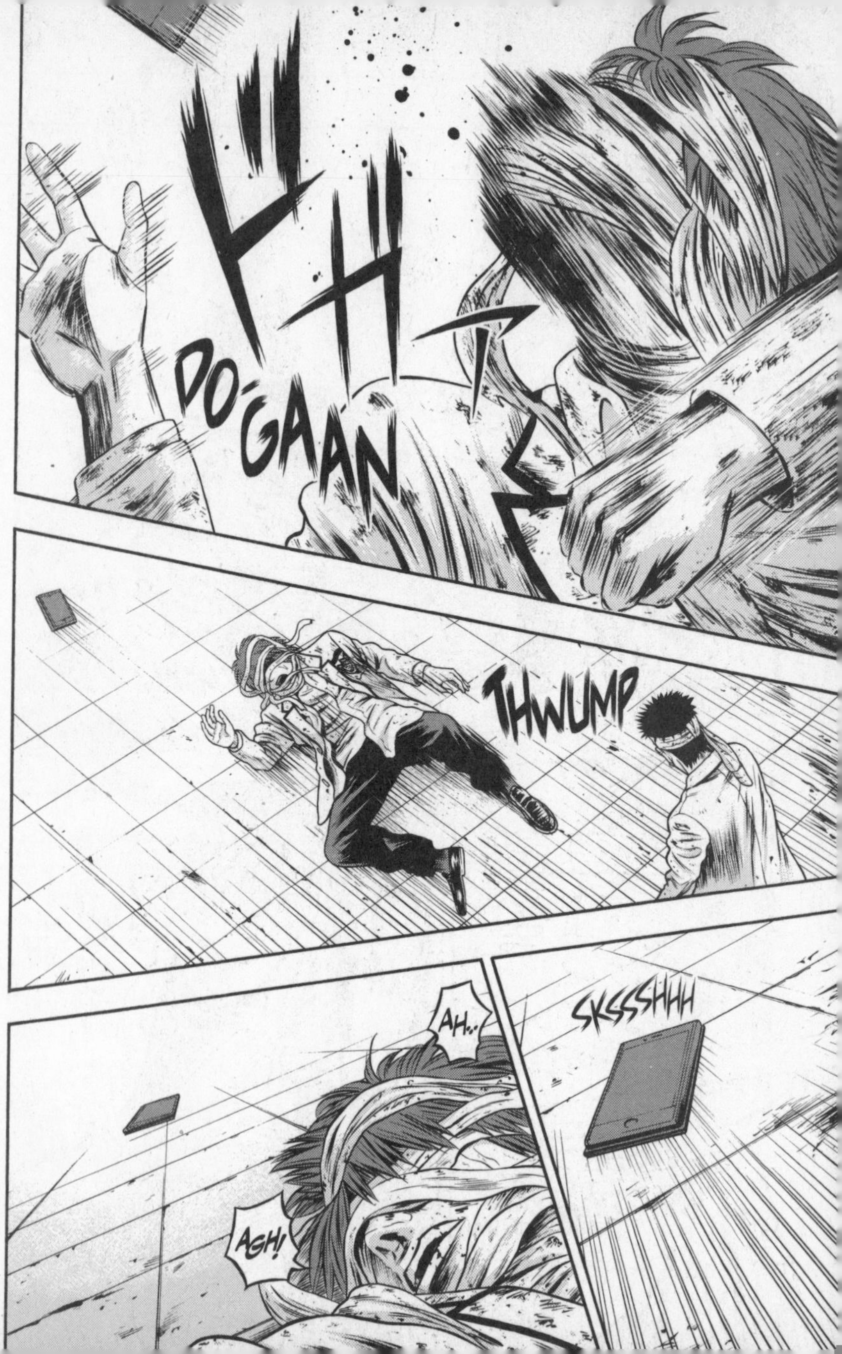
DO-GAAN
THWUMP
SKSSSHHH
AH...
AGH!

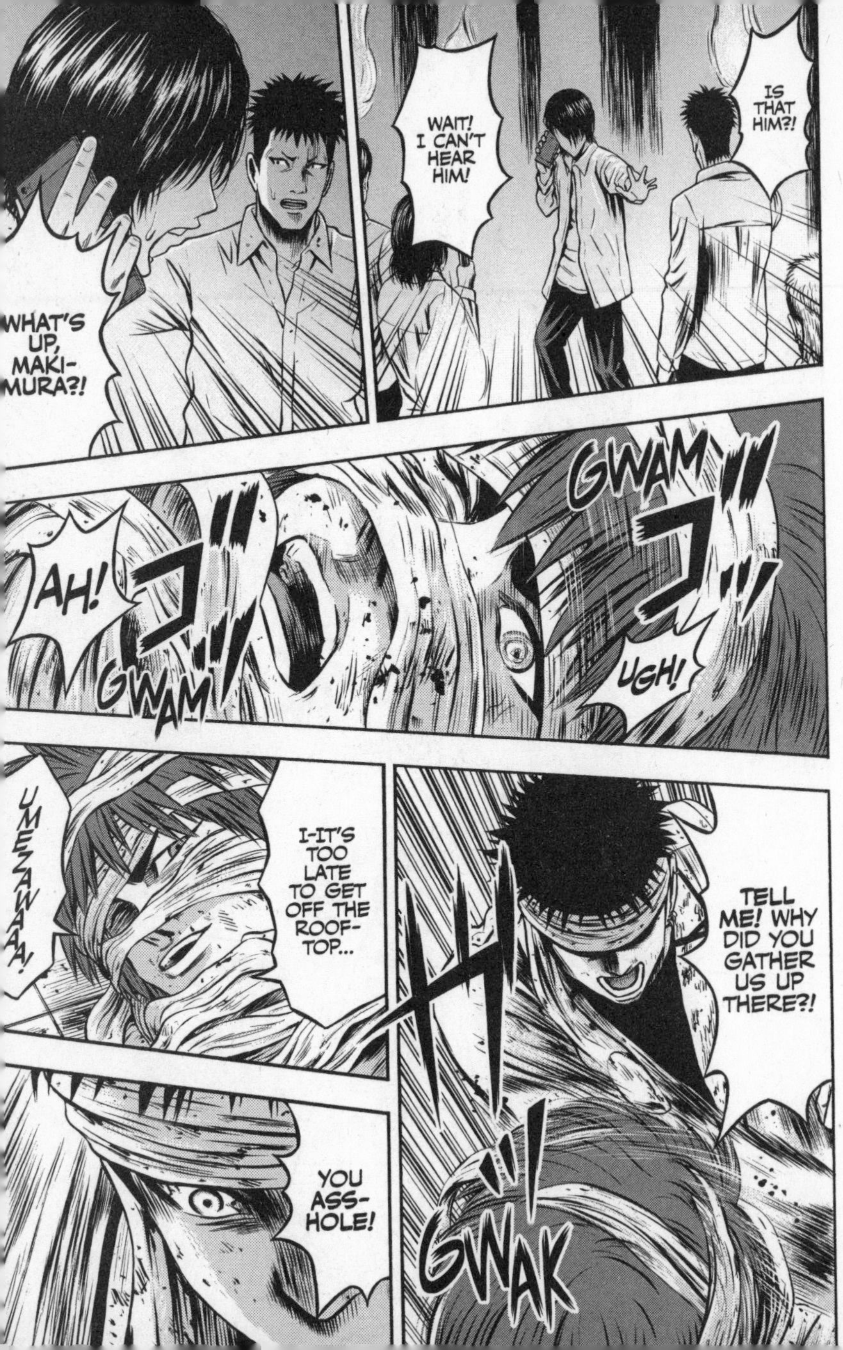
IS THAT HIM?!
WAIT! I CAN'T HEAR HIM!
WHAT'S UP, MAKIMURA?!
GWAM
ゴッ
UGH!
ゴッ
GWAM
AH!
TELL ME! WHY DID YOU GATHER US UP THERE?!
ガッ
GWAK
I-IT'S TOO LATE TO GET OFF THE ROOFTOP...
UMEZAWAAA!
YOU ASSHOLE!

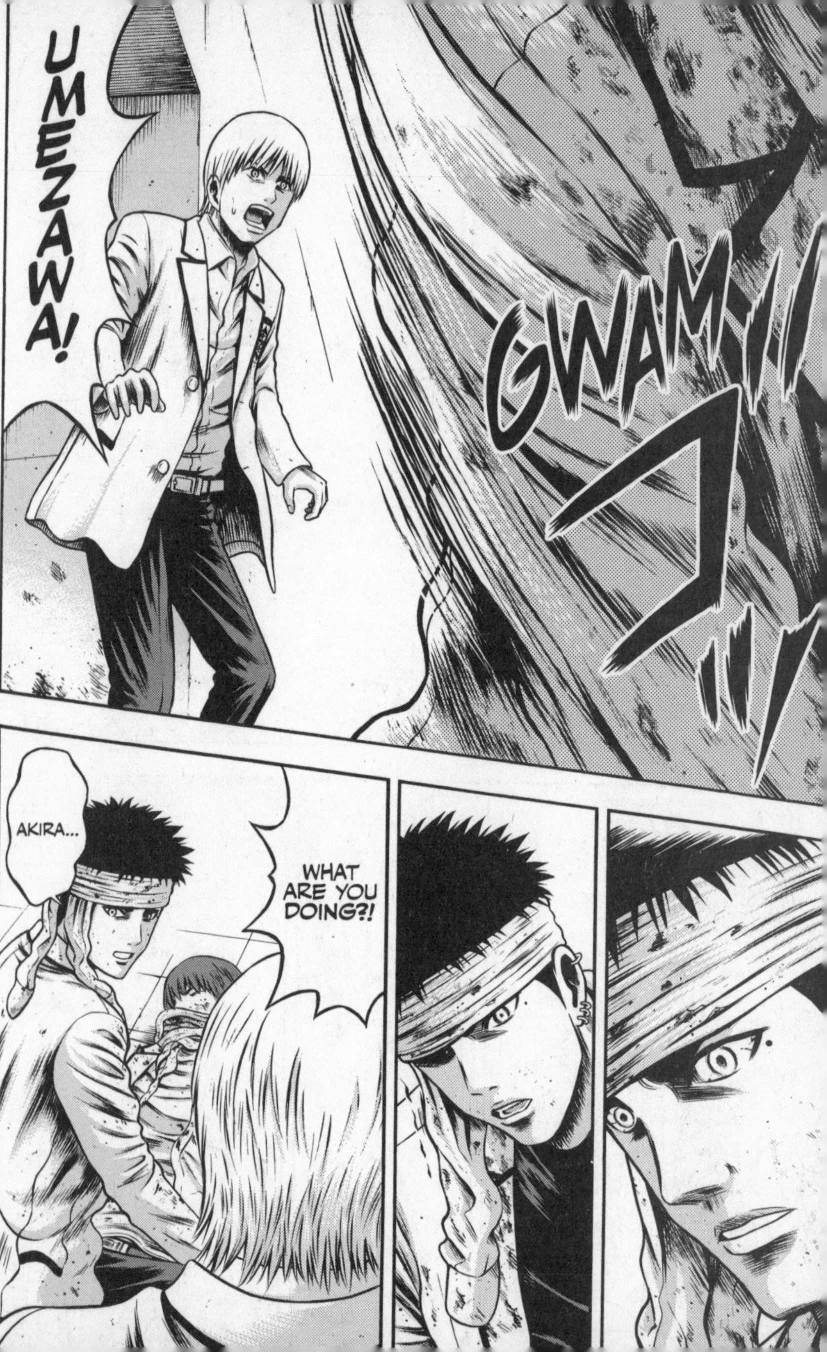
GWAM!!
UMEZAWA!
AKIRA...
WHAT ARE YOU DOING?!

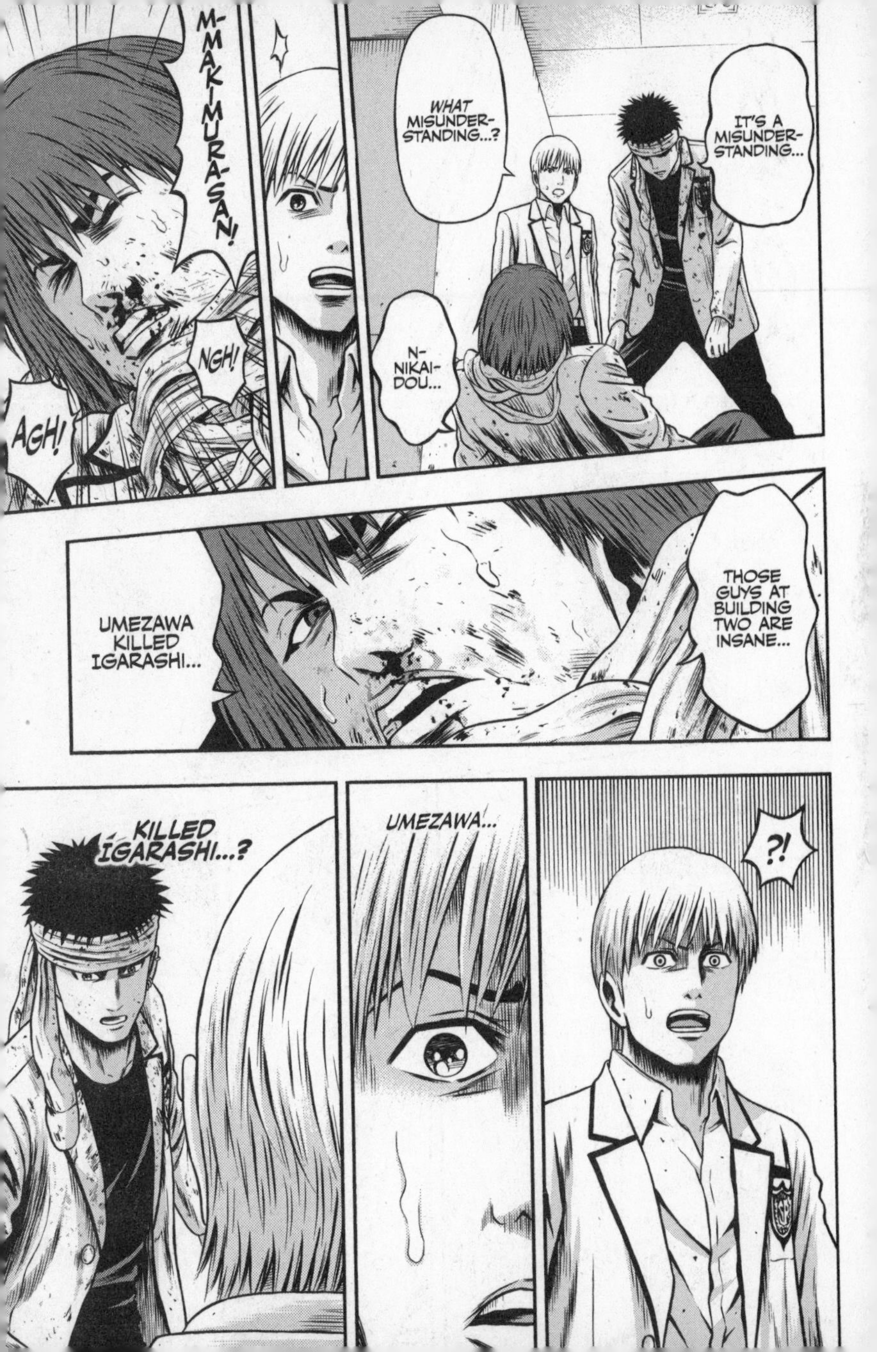
IT'S A MISUNDER-STANDING...
WHAT MISUNDER-STANDING...?
N-NIKAIDOU...
M-MAKIMURA-SAN!
NGH!
AGH!
THOSE GUYS AT BUILDING TWO ARE INSANE...
UMEZAWA KILLED IGARASHI...
?!
UMEZAWA...
KILLED IGARASHI...?

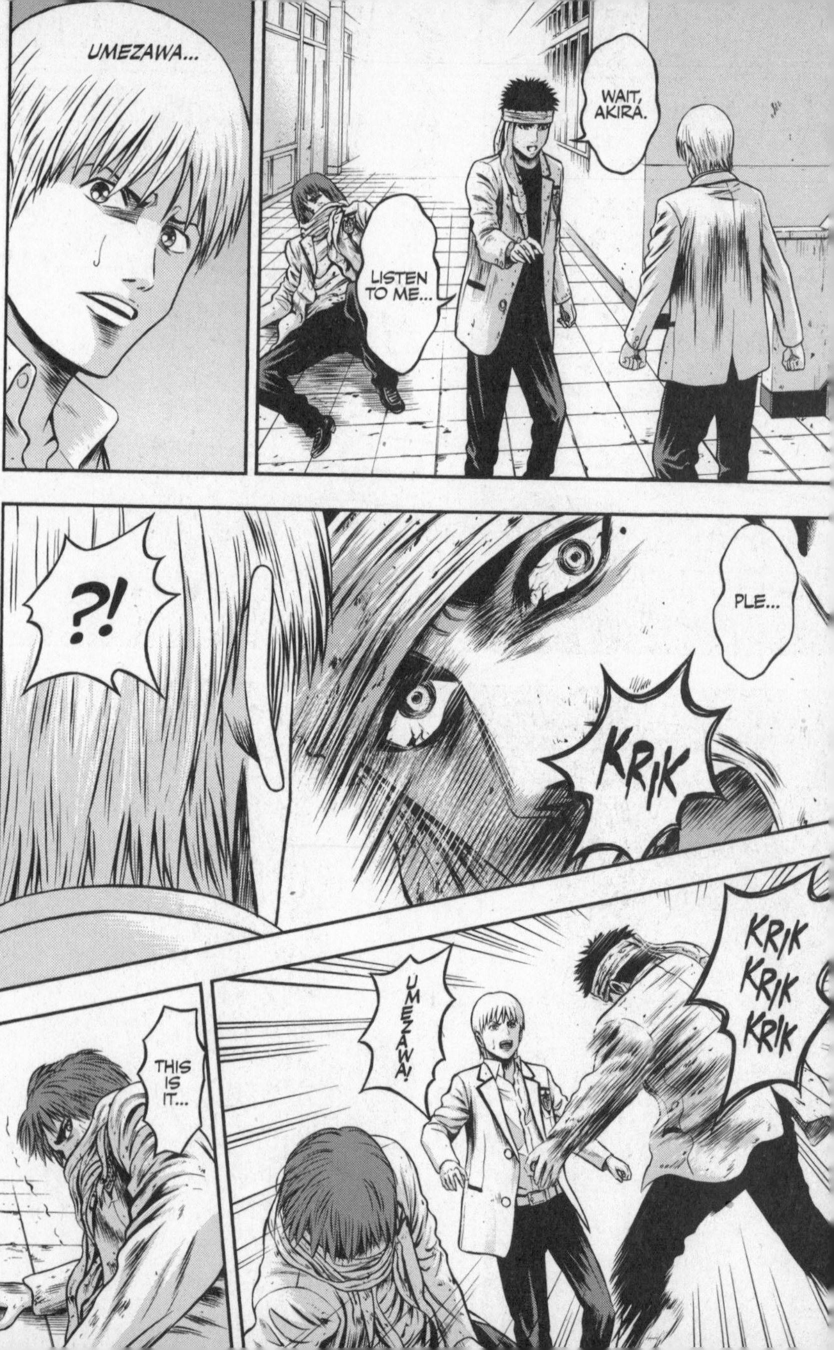
WAIT, AKIRA.
LISTEN TO ME...
UMEZAWA...
PLE...
KRIK
?!
KRIK KRIK KRIK
UMEZAWA!
THIS IS IT...

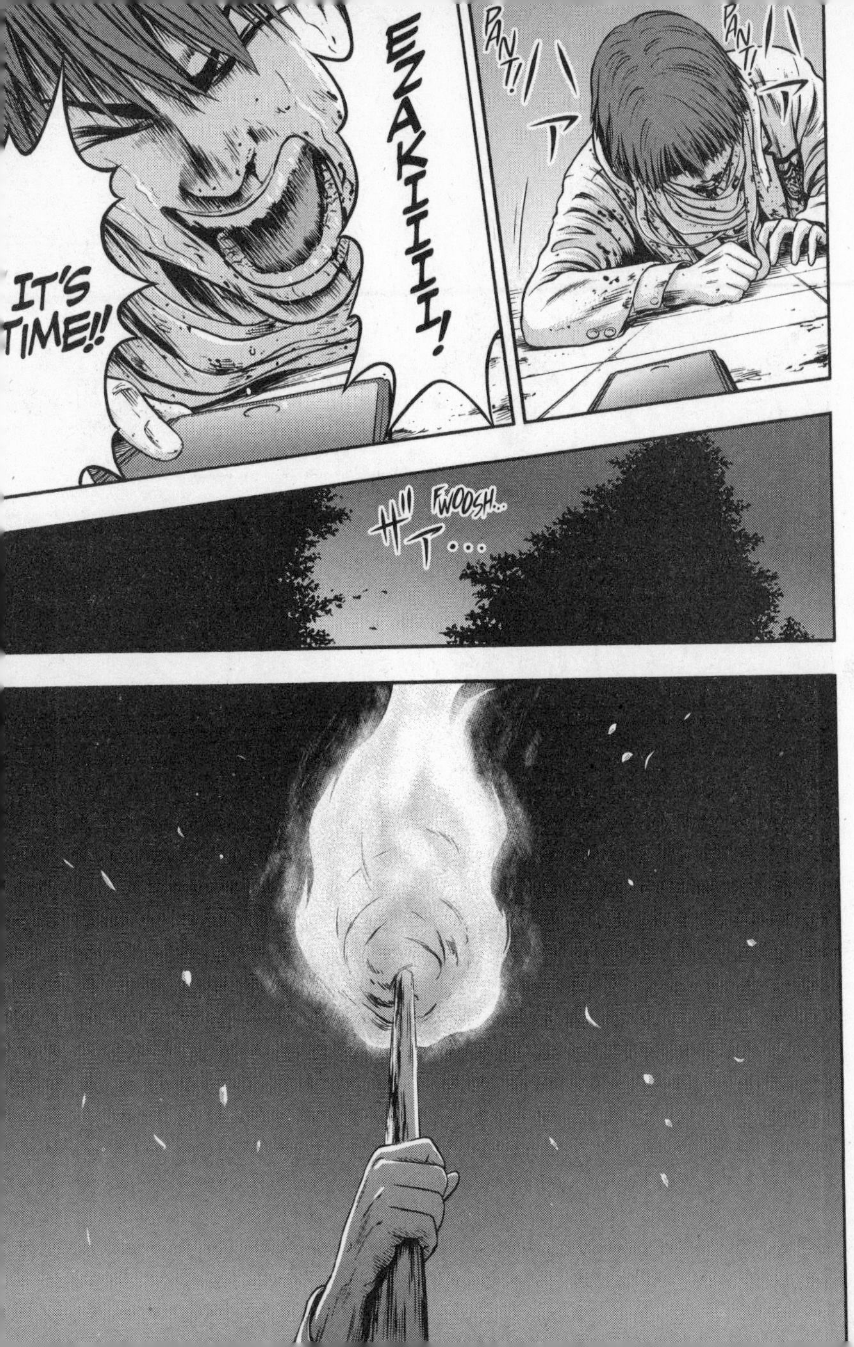
PANT!!
PANT!!
EZAKIIIII!
IT'S TIME!!
FWOOSH...

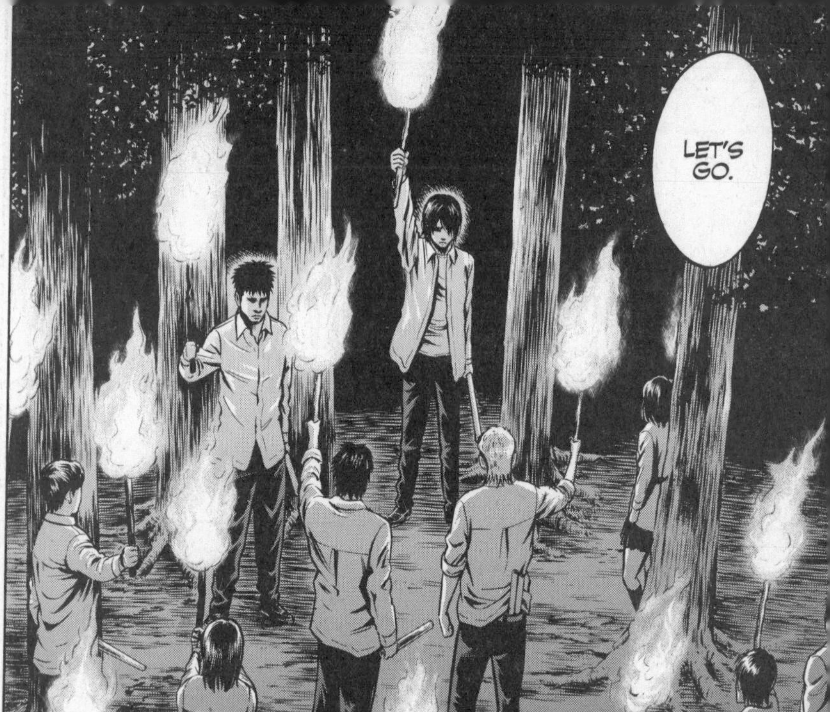
LET'S GO.
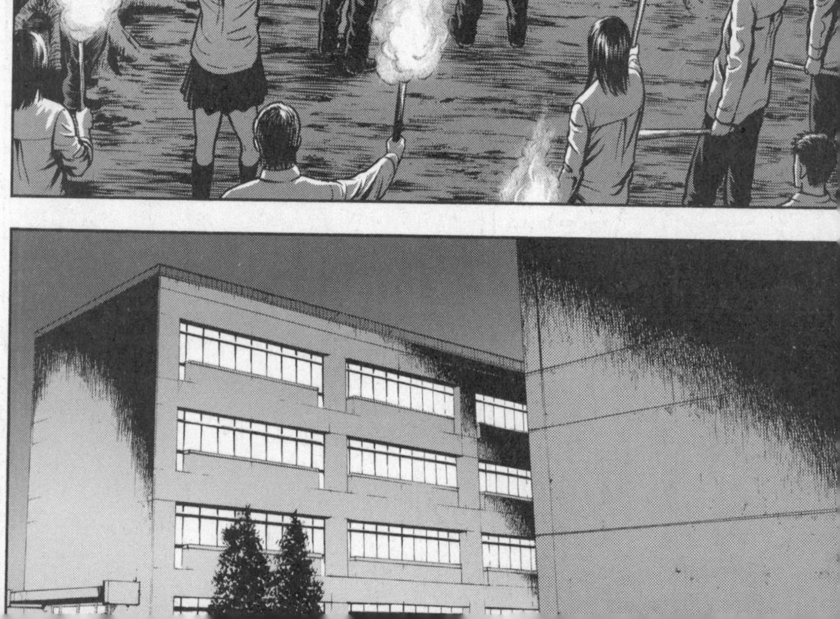

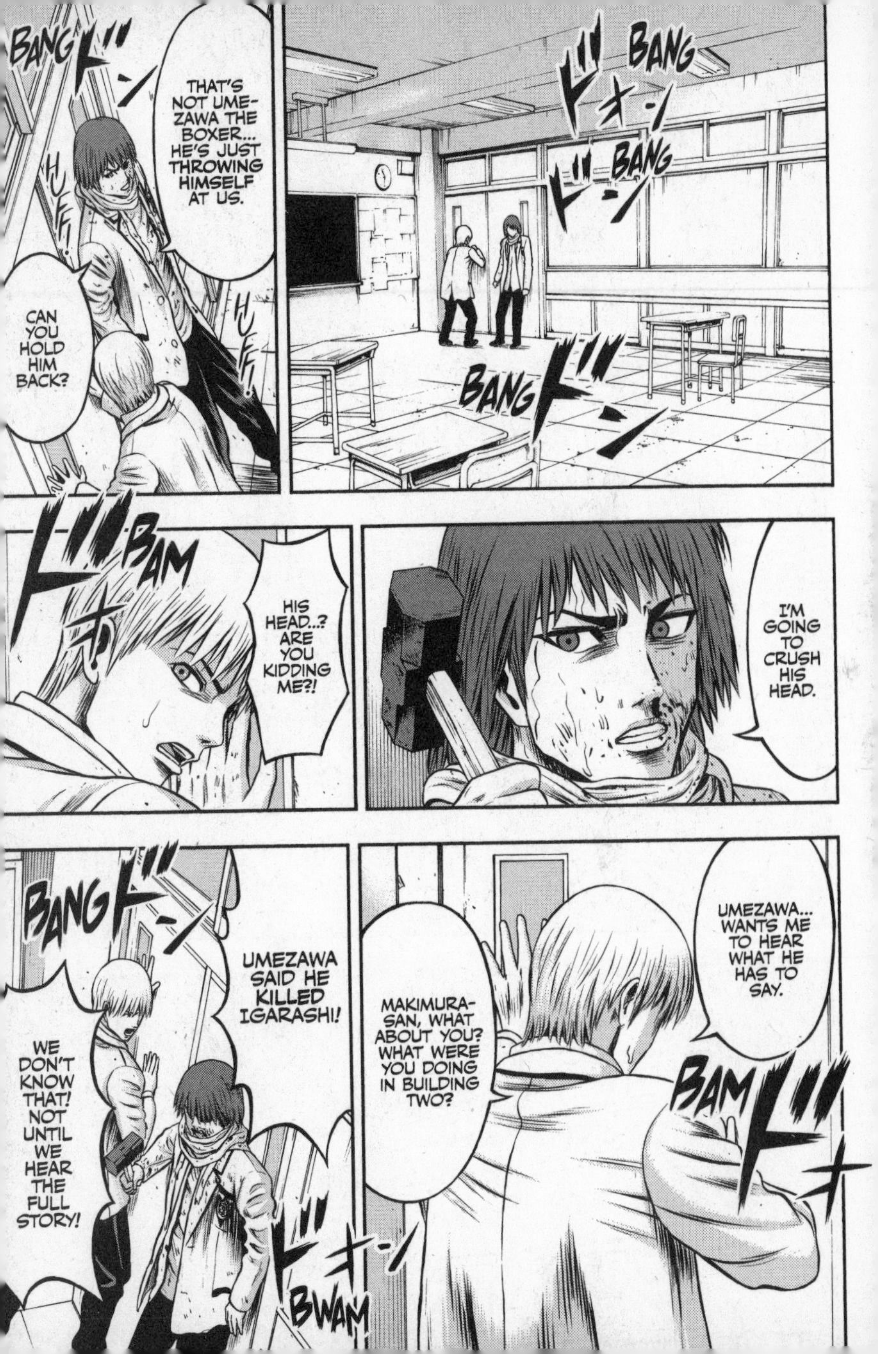
BANG
BANG
BANG
BANG
THAT'S NOT UMEZAWA THE BOXER... HE'S JUST THROWING HIMSELF AT US.
HUFF HUFF
CAN YOU HOLD HIM BACK?
I'M GOING TO CRUSH HIS HEAD.
BAM
HIS HEAD...? ARE YOU KIDDING ME?!
UMEZAWA... WANTS ME TO HEAR WHAT HE HAS TO SAY.
MAKIMURA-SAN, WHAT ABOUT YOU? WHAT WERE YOU DOING IN BUILDING TWO?
BAM
BANG
UMEZAWA SAID HE KILLED IGARASHI!
WE DON'T KNOW THAT! NOT UNTIL WE HEAR THE FULL STORY!
BWAM

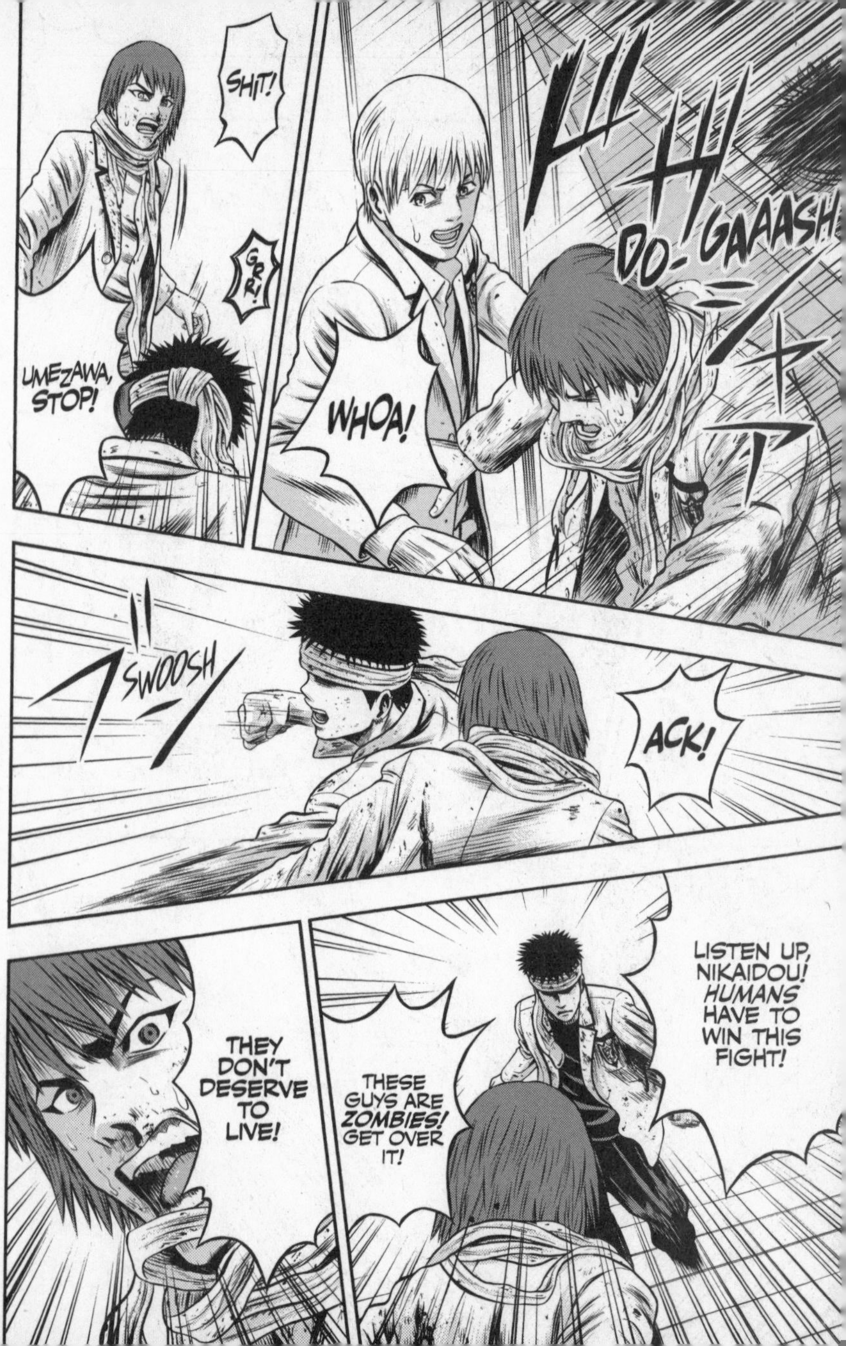
DO-GAAASH
WHOA!
SHIT!
GRR!
UMEZAWA, STOP!
ACK!
SWOOSH
LISTEN UP, NIKAIDOU! HUMANS HAVE TO WIN THIS FIGHT!
THESE GUYS ARE ZOMBIES! GET OVER IT!
THEY DON'T DESERVE TO LIVE!

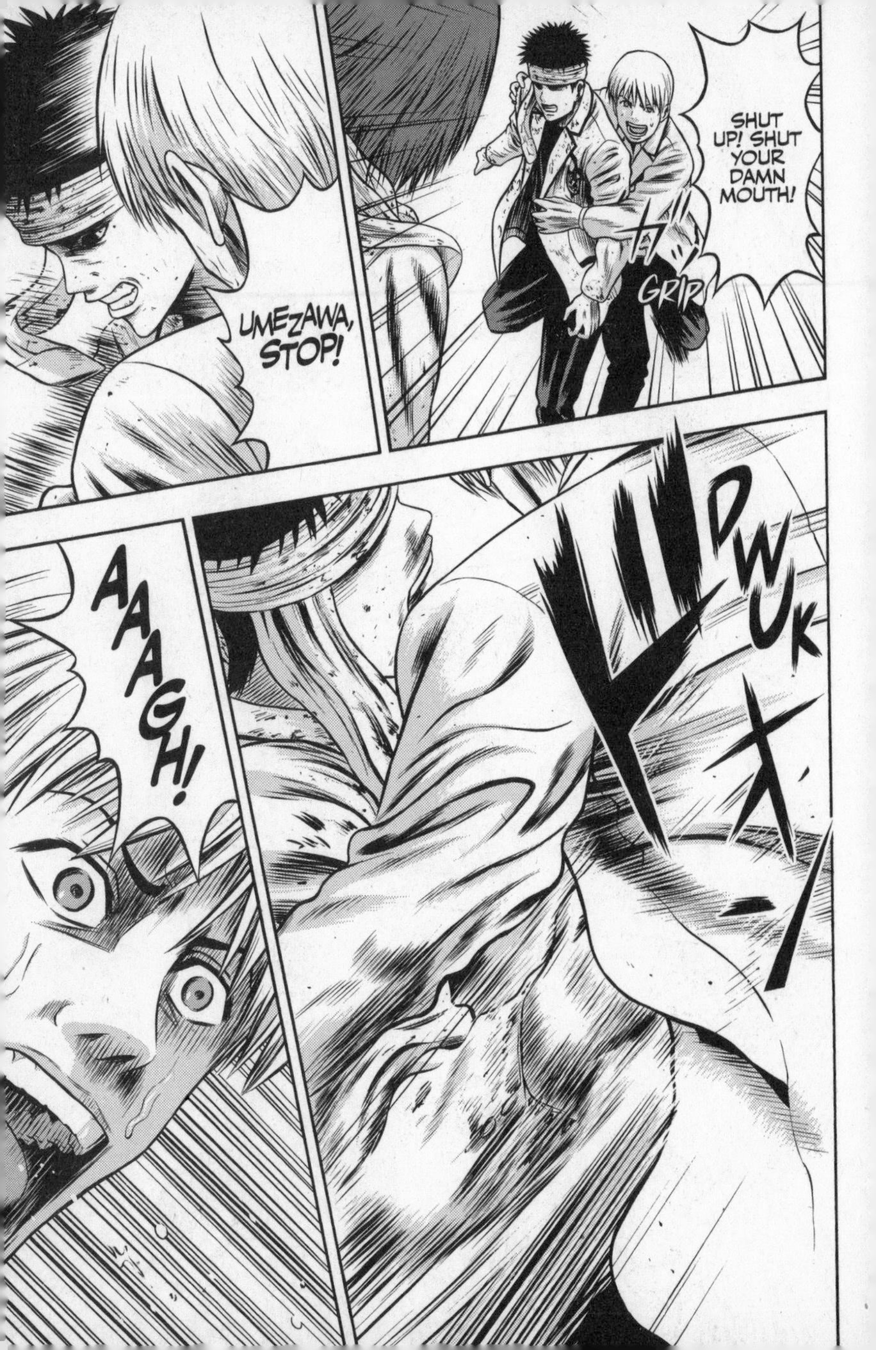
SHUT UP! SHUT YOUR DAMN MOUTH!
GRIP
UMEZAWA, STOP!
DWUK
AAAGH!

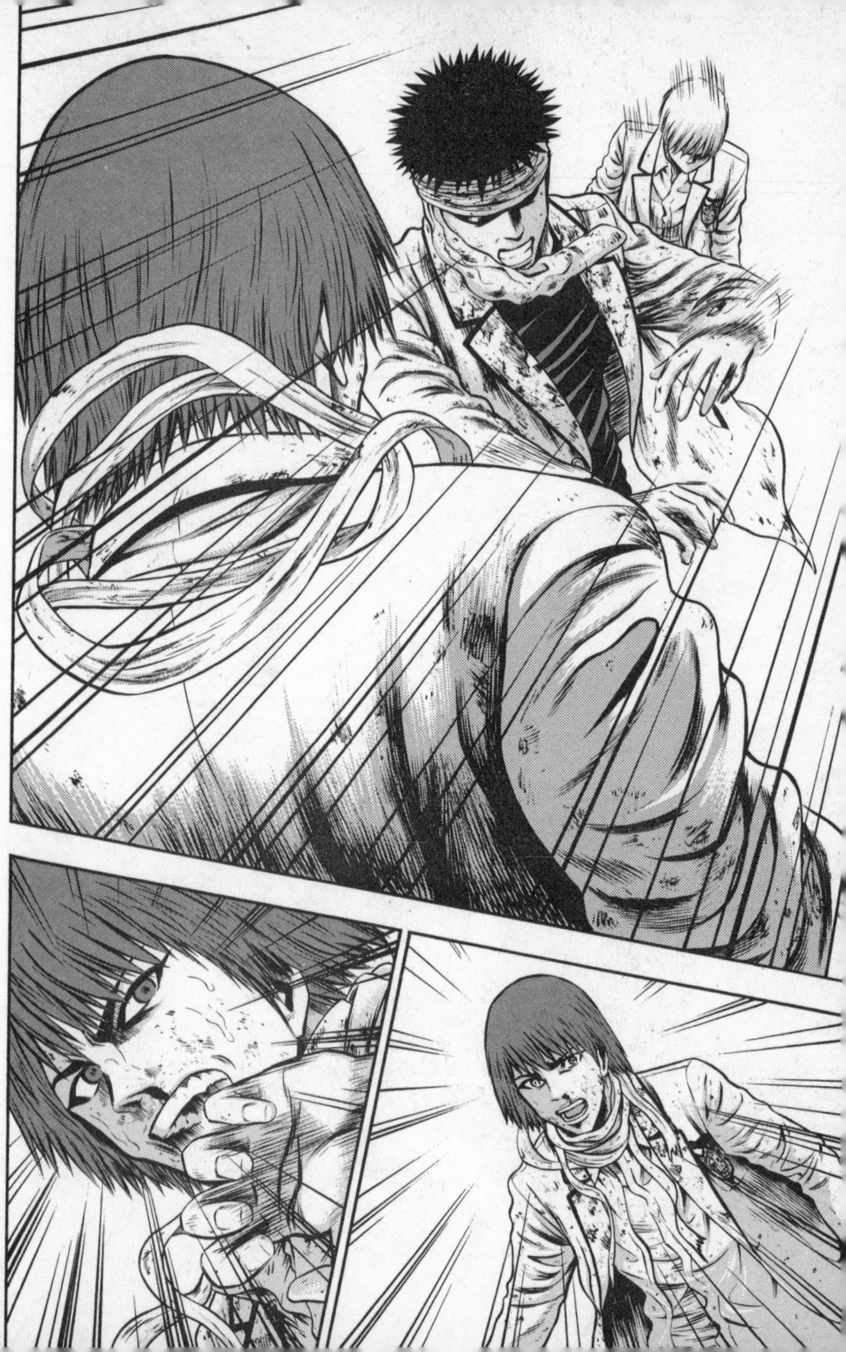

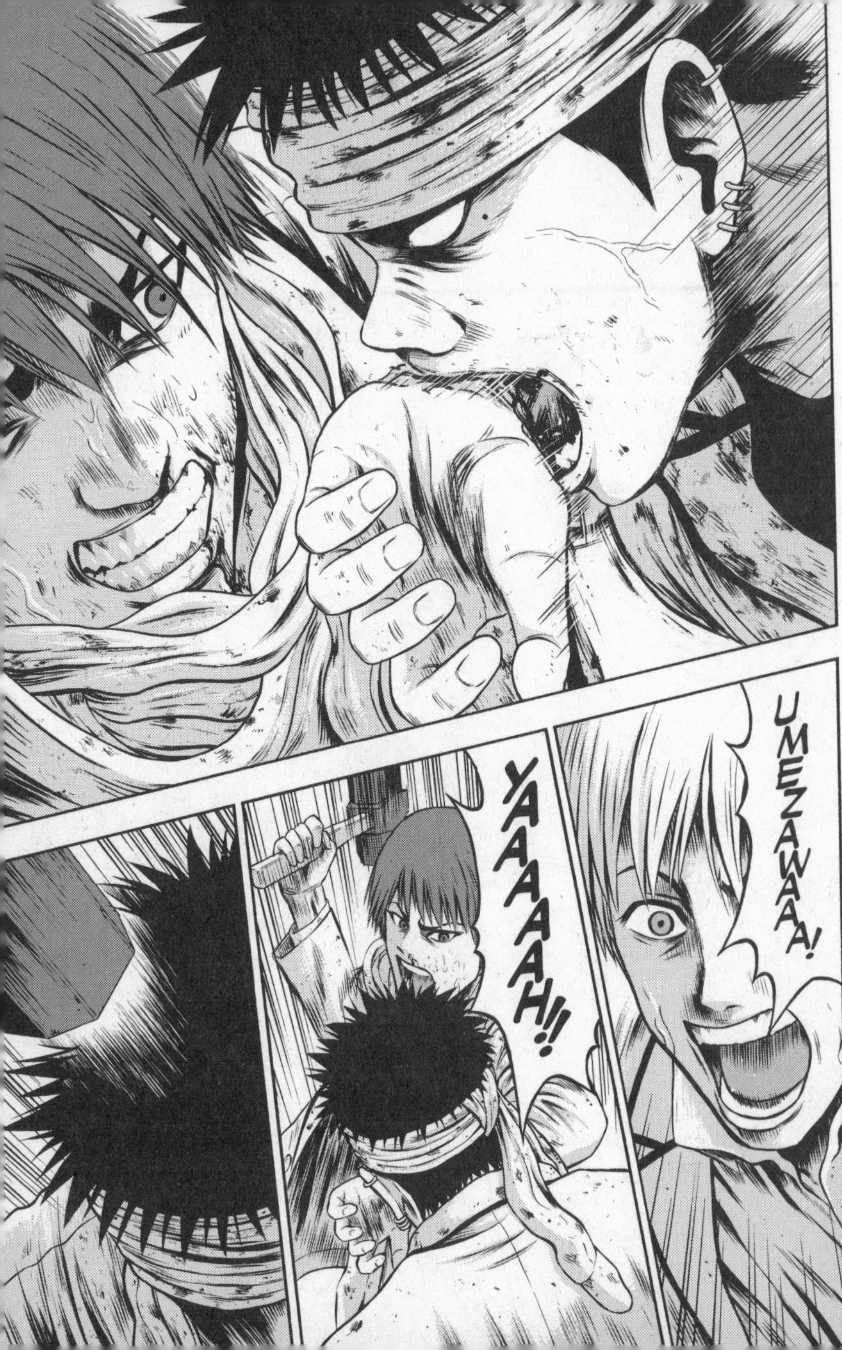
UMEZAWAAA!
YAAAAAH!!

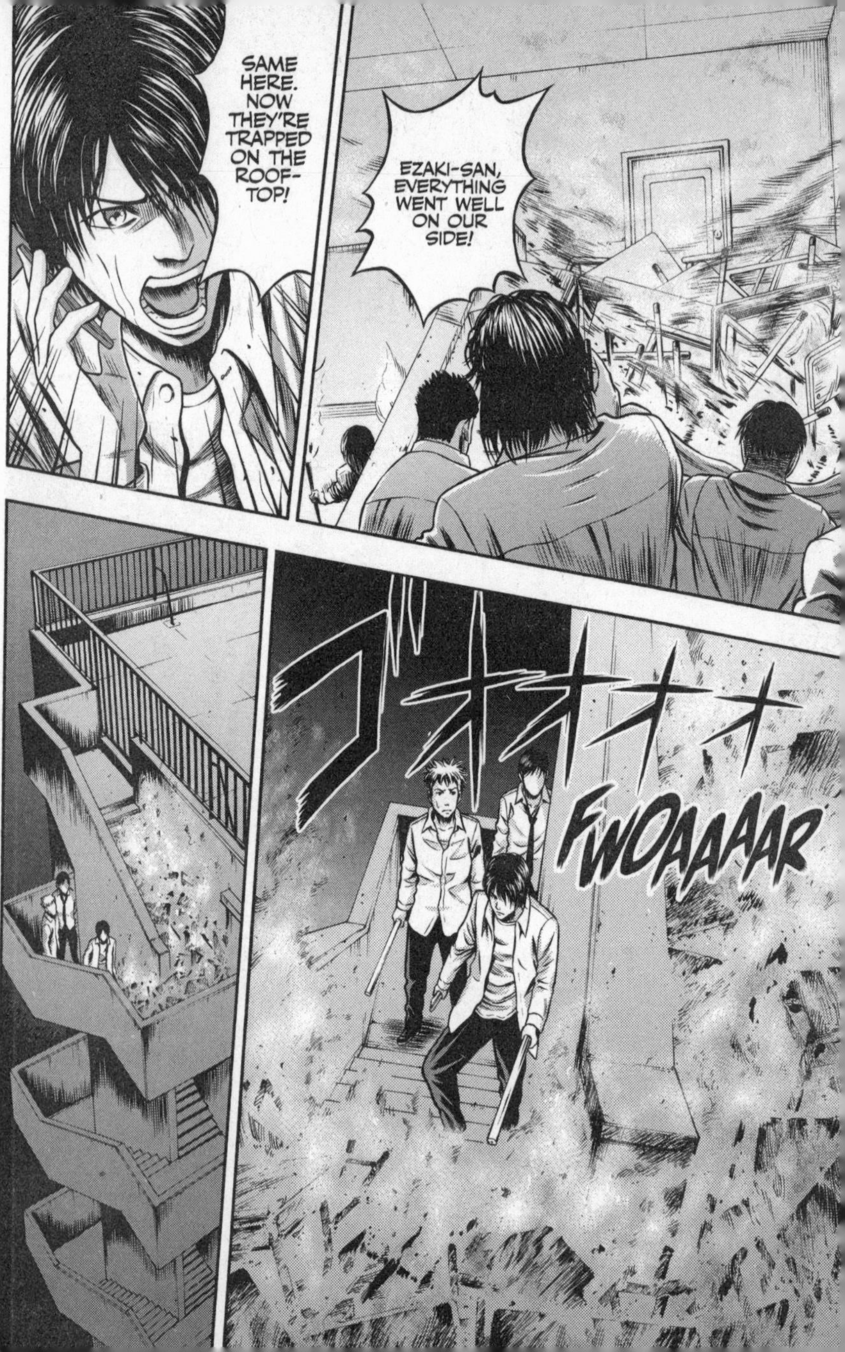
EZAKI-SAN, EVERYTHING WENT WELL ON OUR SIDE!
SAME HERE. NOW THEY'RE TRAPPED ON THE ROOF-TOP!
ゴオオオオ
FWOAAAAR

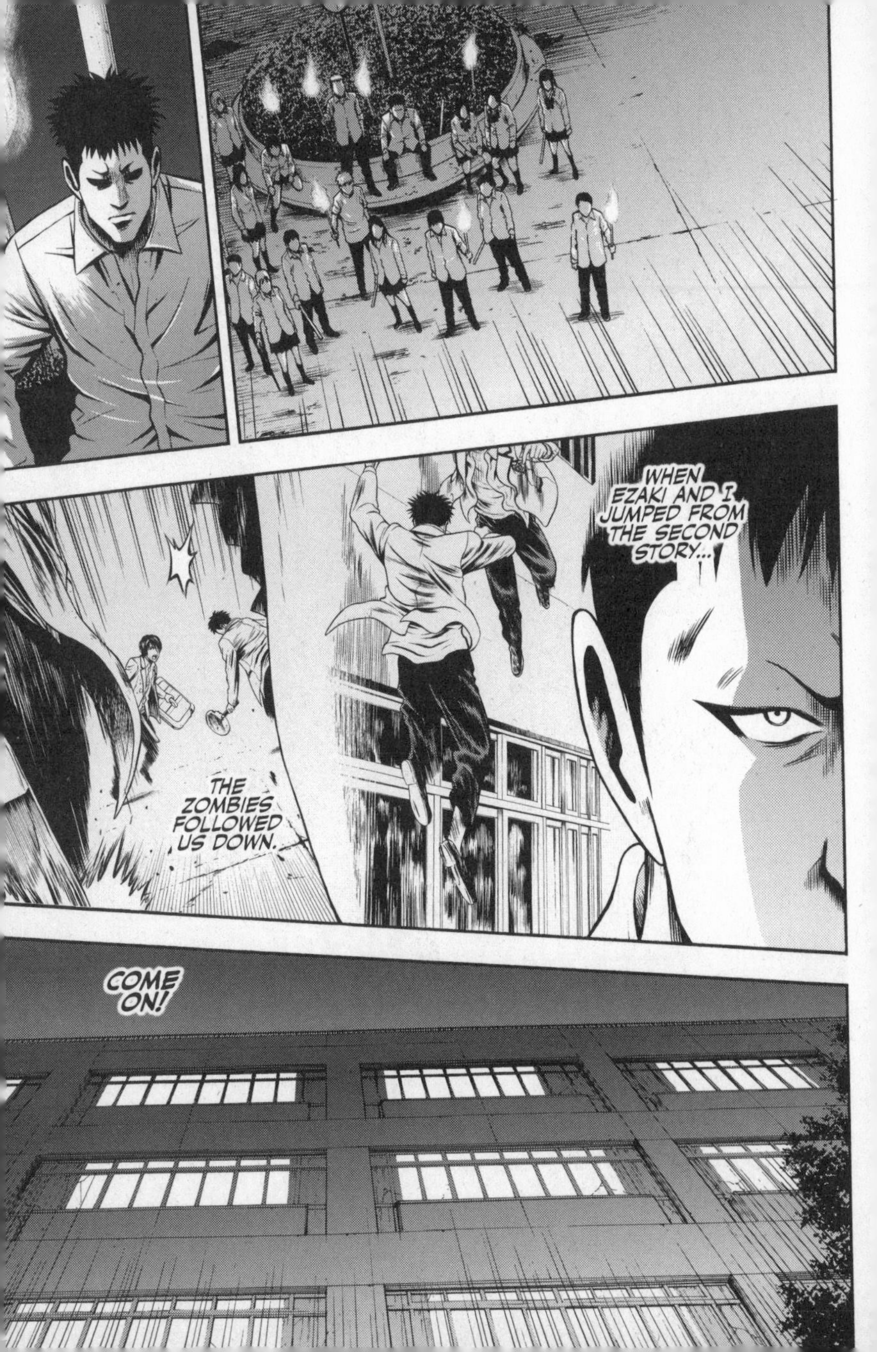
WHEN EZAKI AND I JUMPED FROM THE SECOND STORY...
THE ZOMBIES FOLLOWED US DOWN.
COME ON!

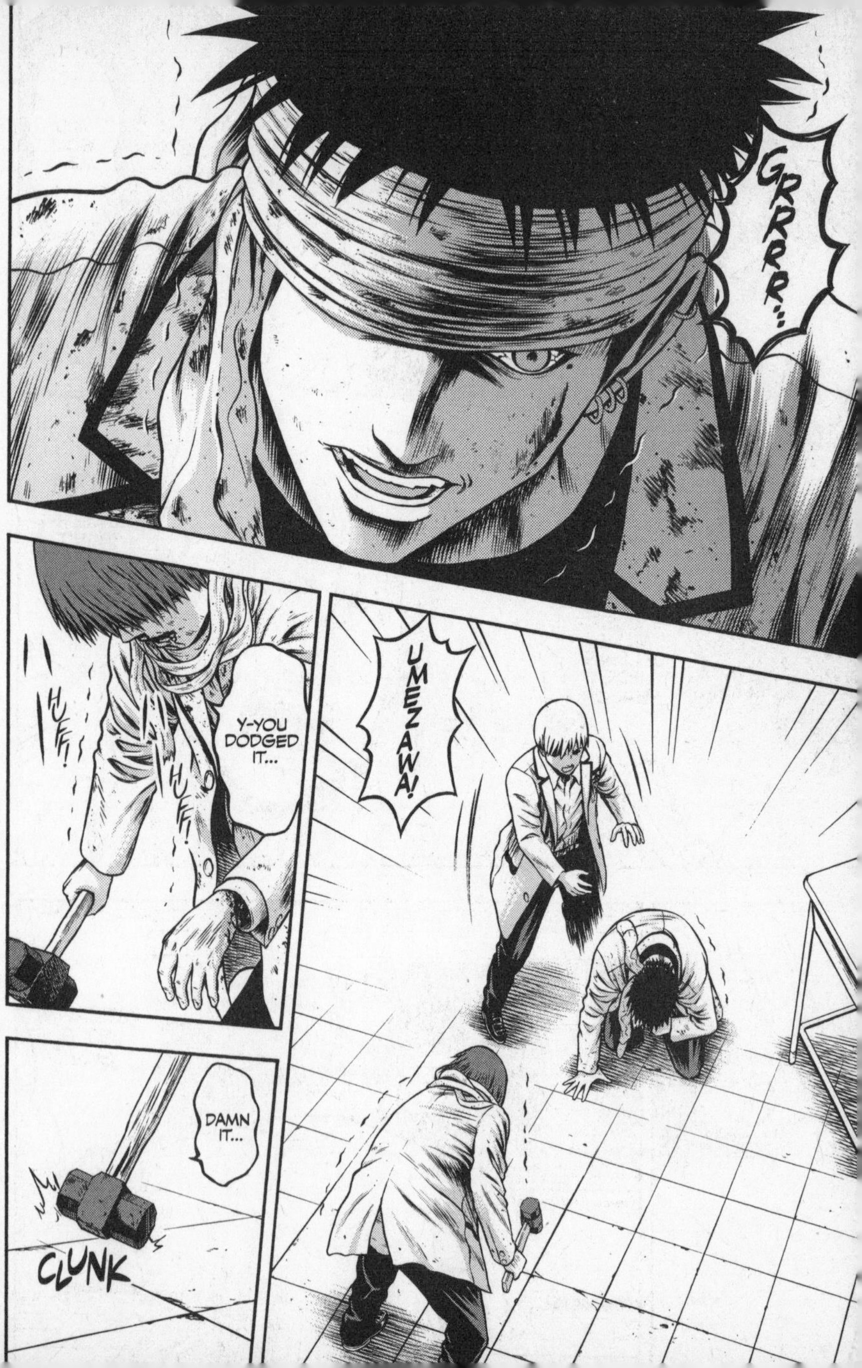
GRRRR...
UMEZAWA!
HUFF! HUFF!
Y-YOU DODGED IT...
DAMN IT...
CLUNK

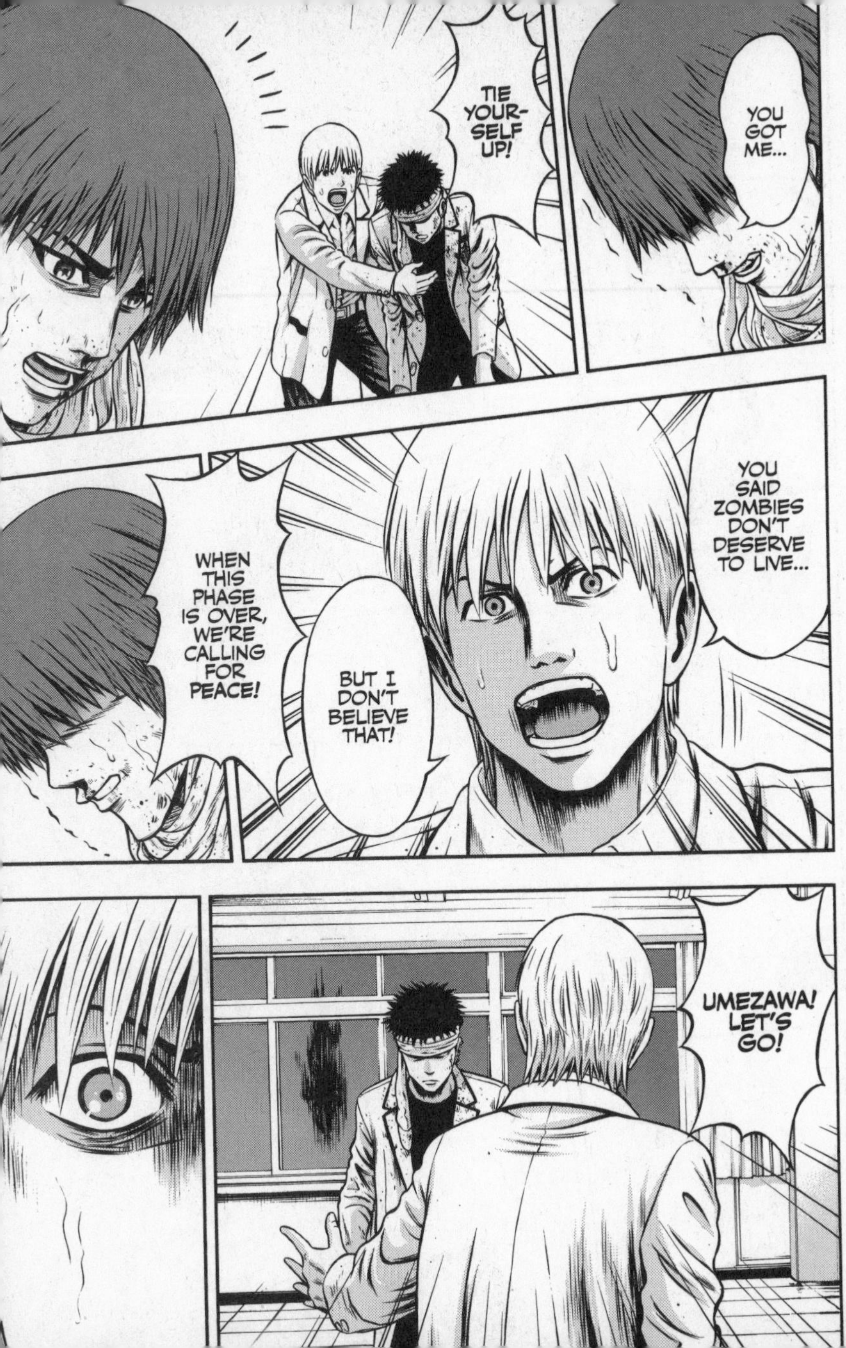
YOU GOT ME...
TIE YOUR-SELF UP!
YOU SAID ZOMBIES DON'T DESERVE TO LIVE...
BUT I DON'T BELIEVE THAT!
WHEN THIS PHASE IS OVER, WE'RE CALLING FOR PEACE!
UMEZAWA! LET'S GO!

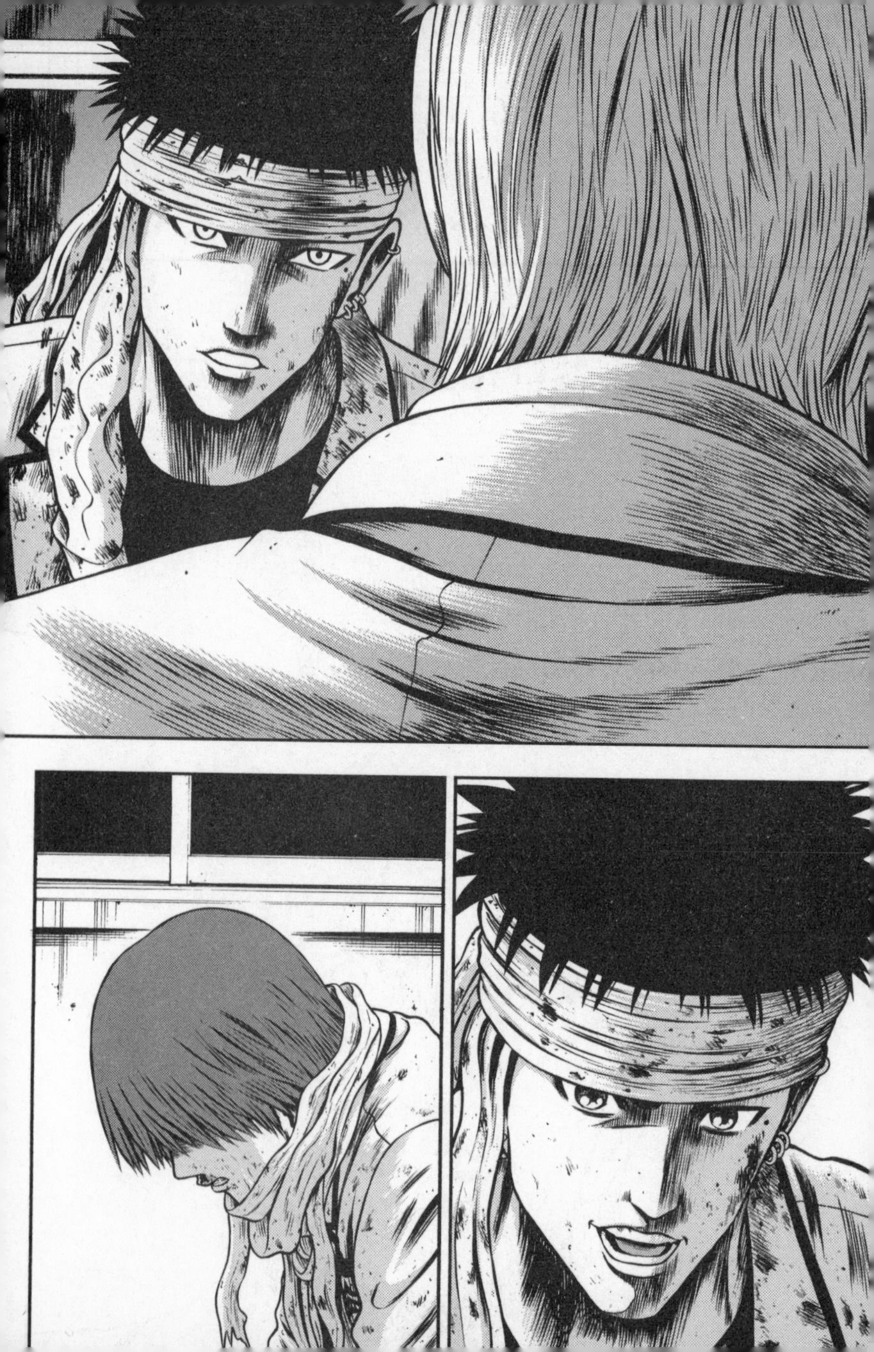

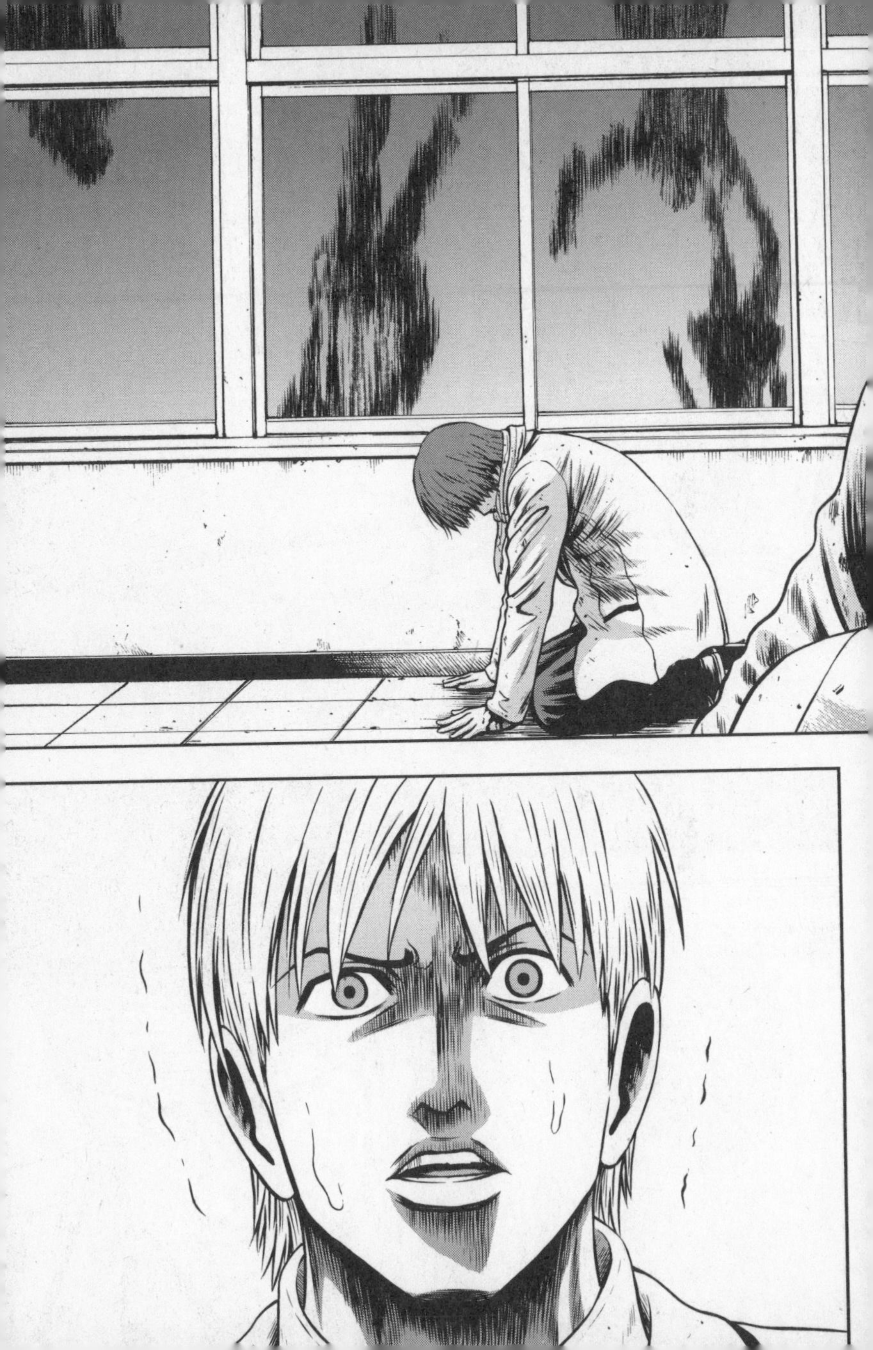

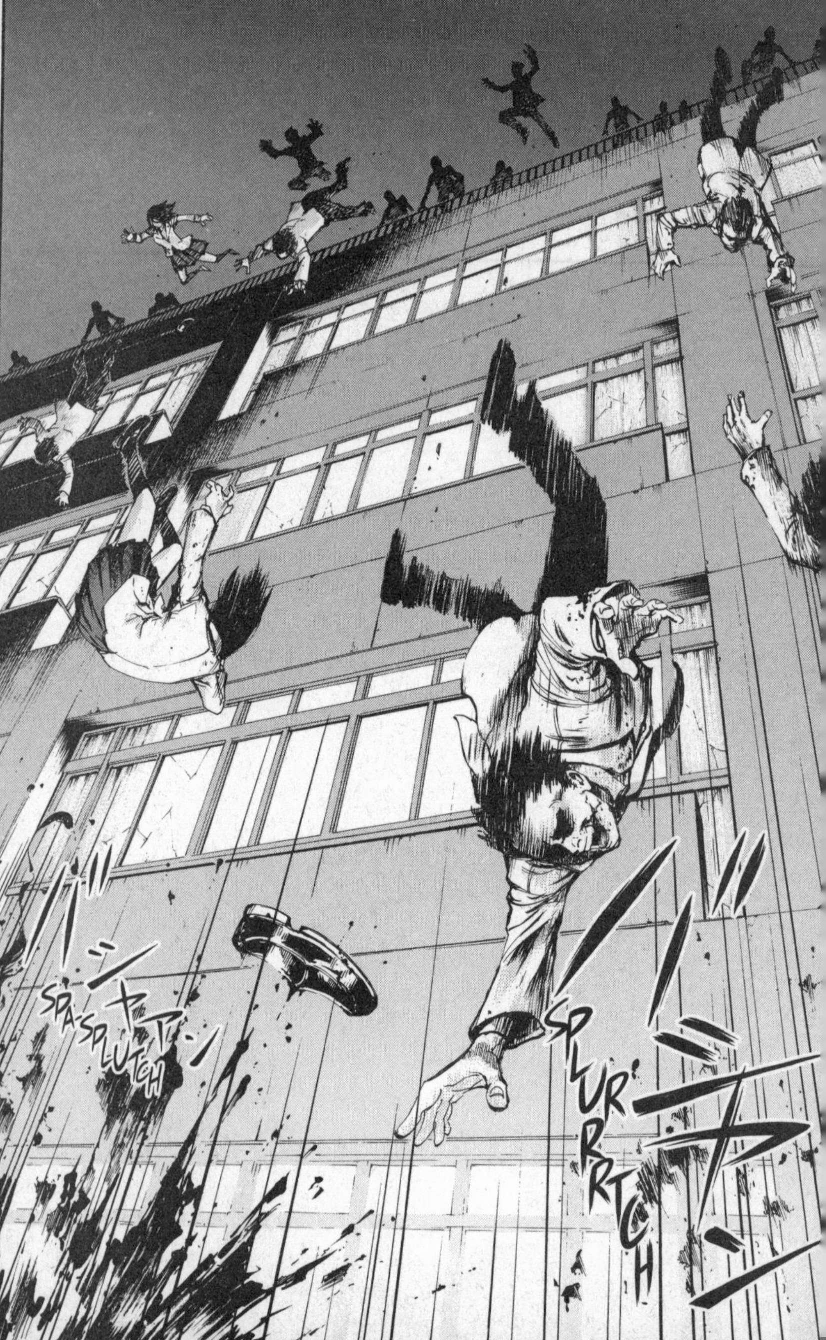
SPLURRRTCH
SPA-SPLUTCH

HOUR OF THE ZOMBIE

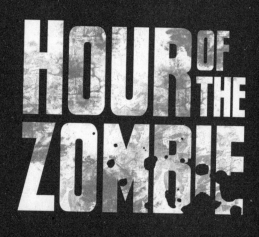

PHASE 38: A Life of Light and Shadow

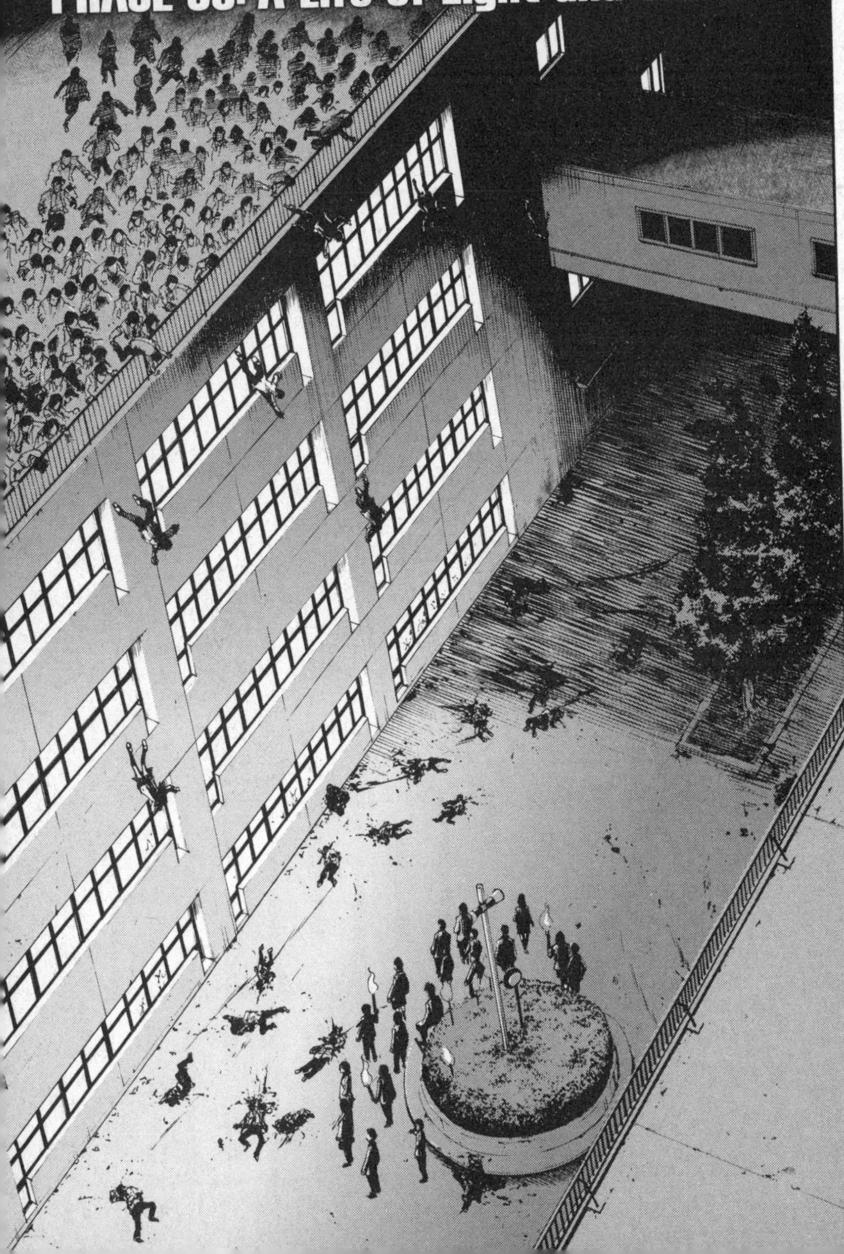

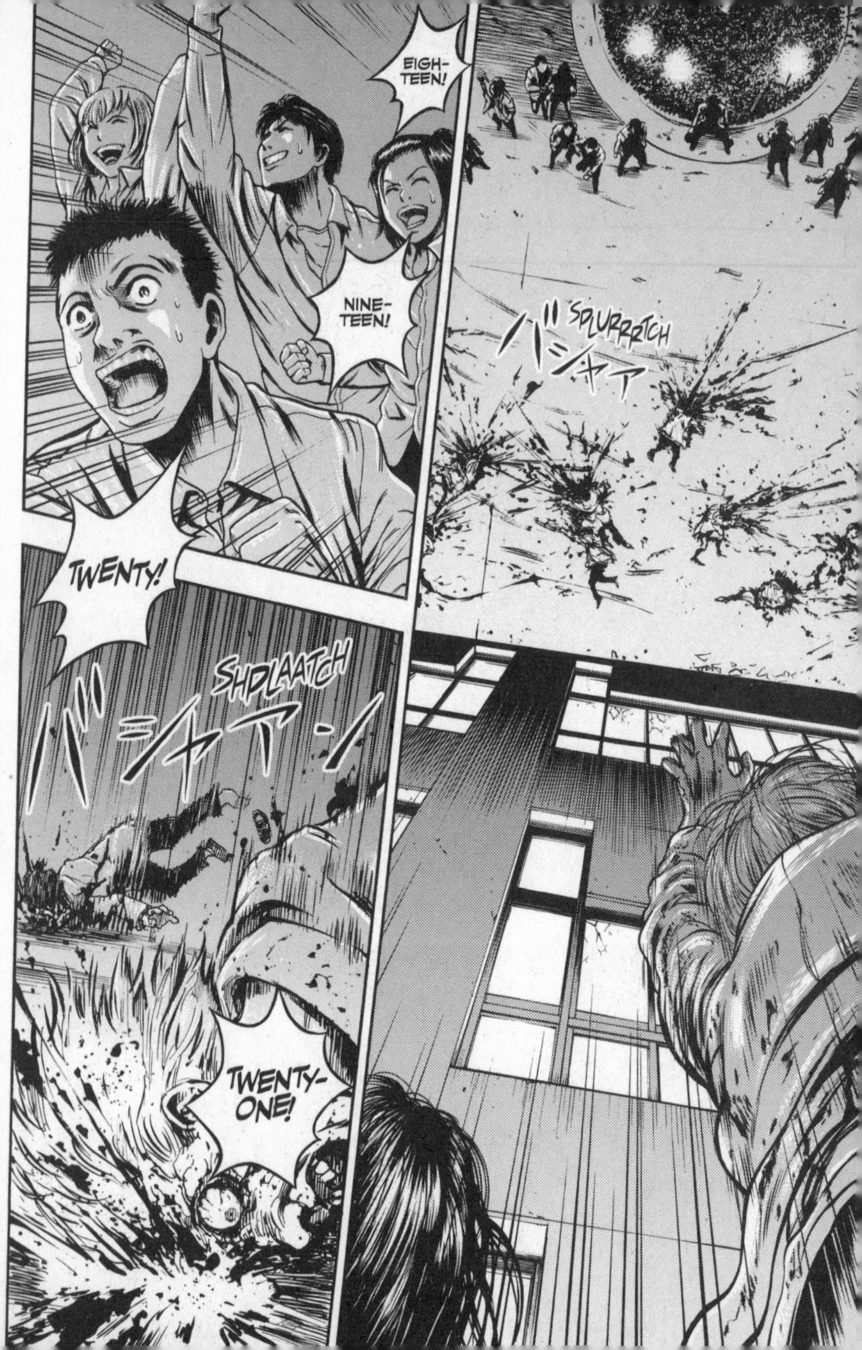
SPLURRRTCH
EIGH-TEEN!
NINE-TEEN!
TWENTY!
SHPLAATCH
TWENTY-ONE!

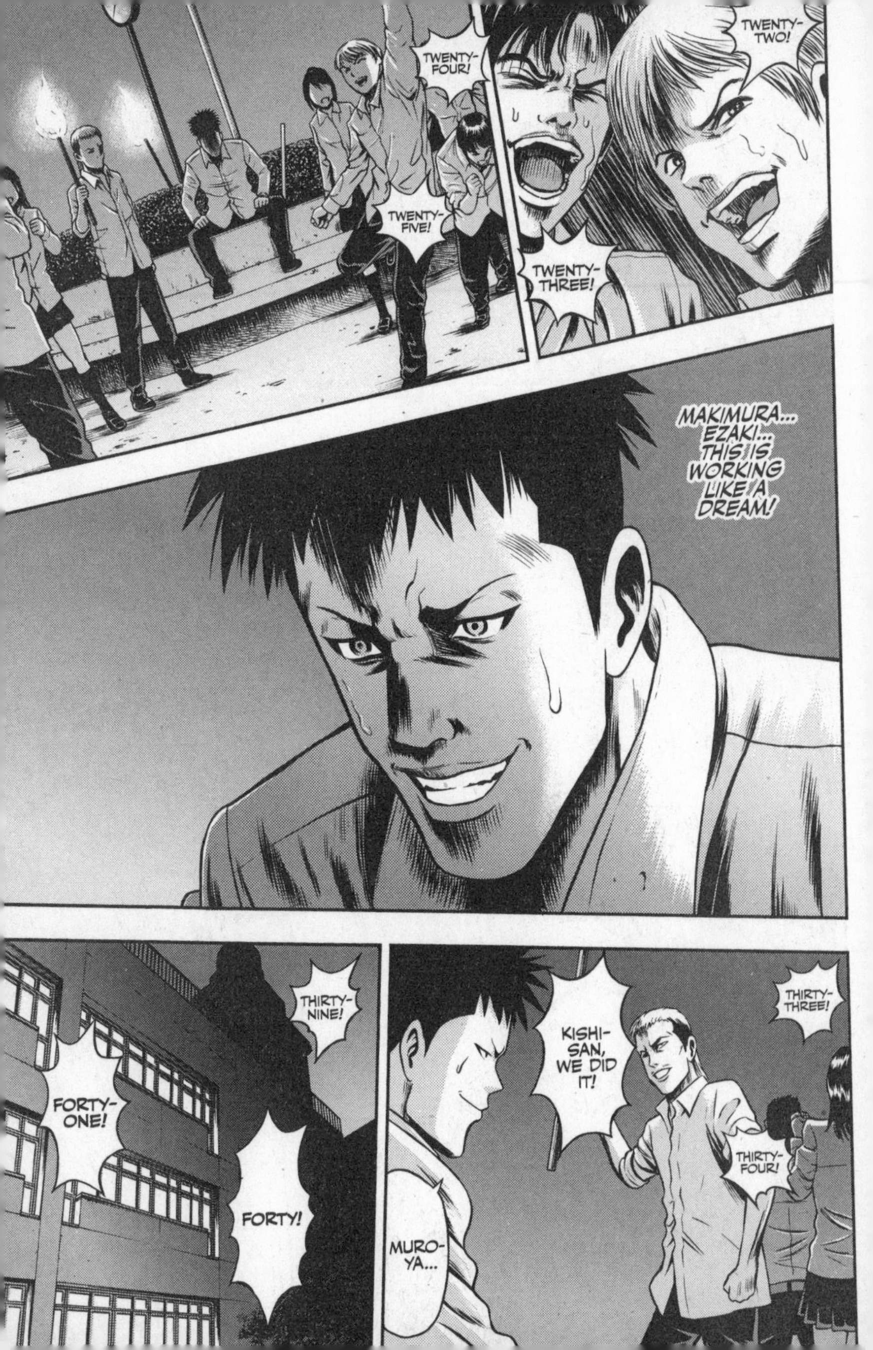
TWENTY-TWO!
TWENTY-THREE!
TWENTY-FOUR!
TWENTY-FIVE!
MAKIMURA... EZAKI... THIS IS WORKING LIKE A DREAM!
THIRTY-THREE!
KISHI-SAN, WE DID IT!
THIRTY-FOUR!
MURO-YA...
THIRTY-NINE!
FORTY!
FORTY-ONE!

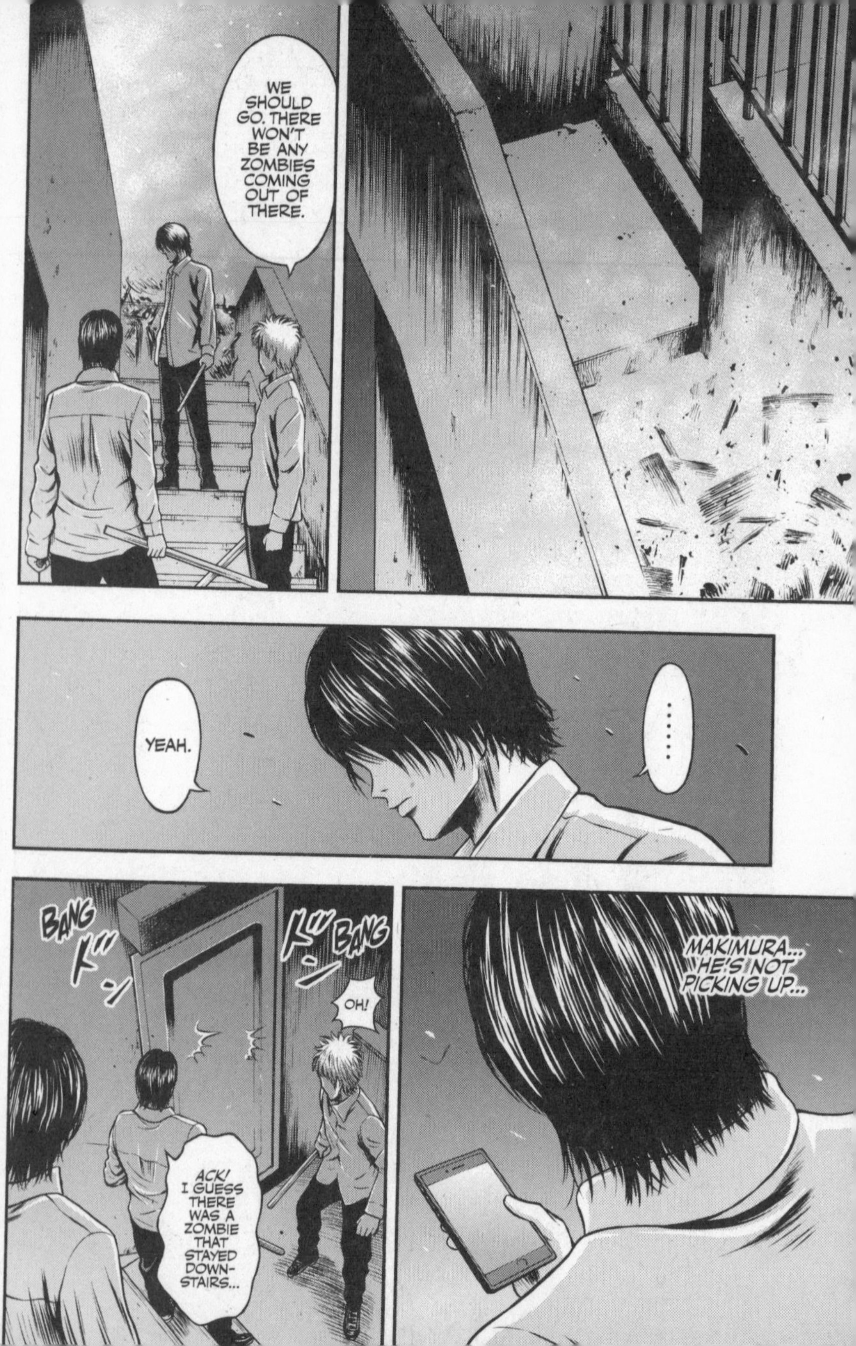
WE SHOULD GO. THERE WON'T BE ANY ZOMBIES COMING OUT OF THERE.
......
YEAH.
MAKIMURA... HE'S NOT PICKING UP...
BANG
BANG
OH!
ACK! I GUESS THERE WAS A ZOMBIE THAT STAYED DOWN-STAIRS...

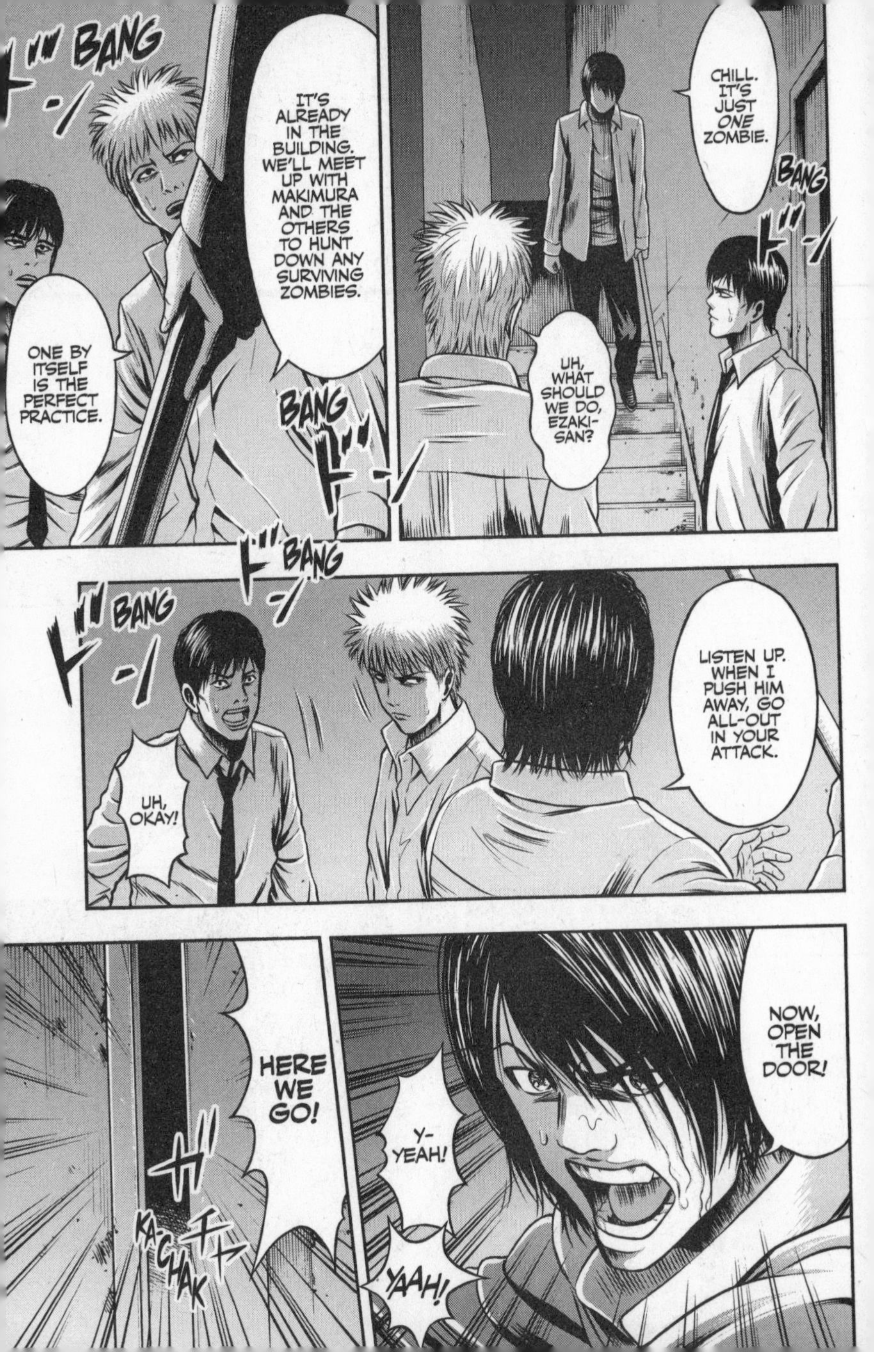
CHILL. IT'S JUST *ONE* ZOMBIE.
BANG
UH, WHAT SHOULD WE DO, EZAKI-SAN?
IT'S ALREADY IN THE BUILDING. WE'LL MEET UP WITH MAKIMURA AND THE OTHERS TO HUNT DOWN ANY SURVIVING ZOMBIES.
BANG
BANG
ONE BY ITSELF IS THE PERFECT PRACTICE.
LISTEN UP. WHEN I PUSH HIM AWAY, GO ALL-OUT IN YOUR ATTACK.
BANG
BANG
UH, OKAY!
NOW, OPEN THE DOOR!
Y-YEAH!
YAAH!
HERE WE GO!
KA-CHAK

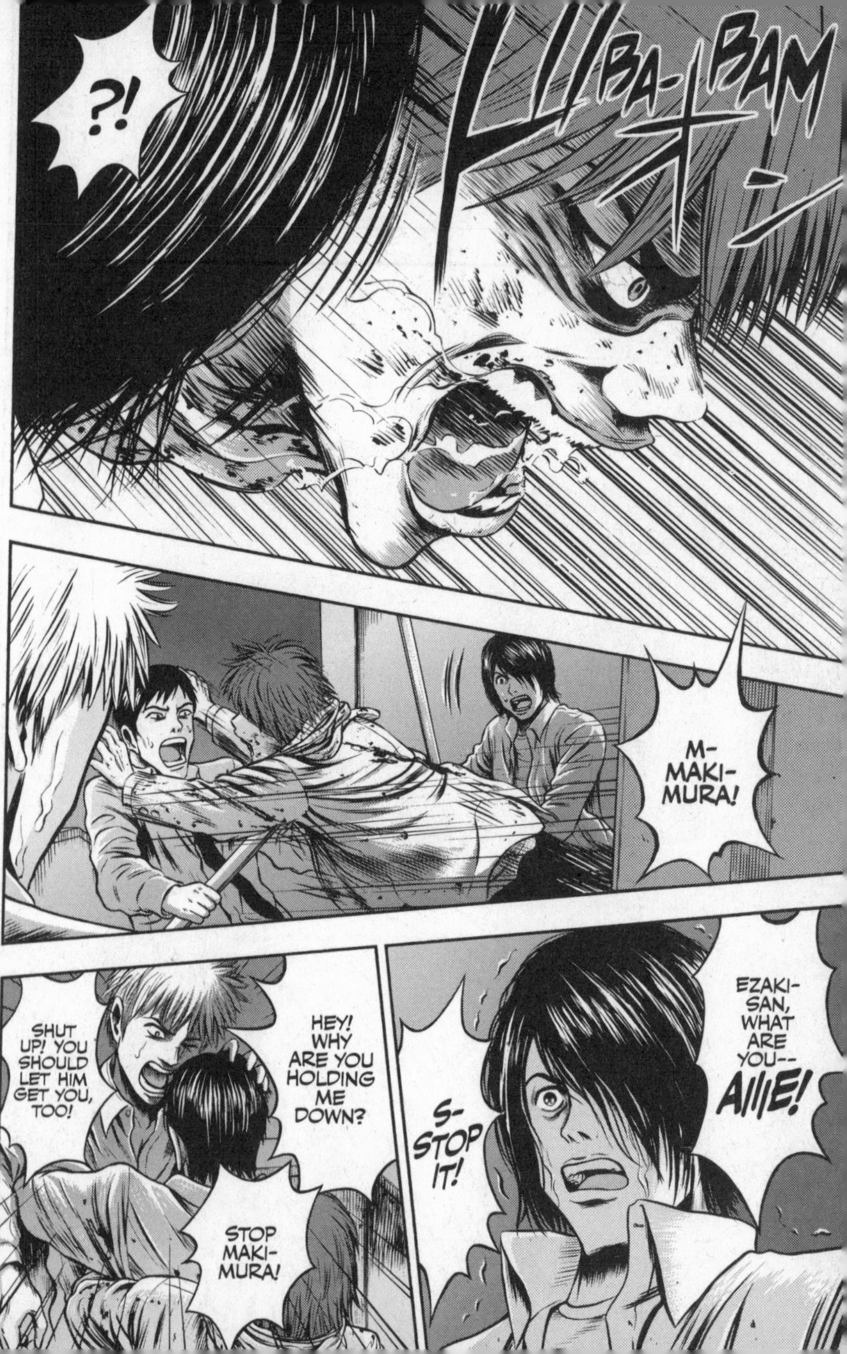
BA-BAM
?!
M-MAKI-MURA!
EZAKI-SAN, WHAT ARE YOU-- AIIIE!
S-STOP IT!
HEY! WHY ARE YOU HOLDING ME DOWN?
SHUT UP! YOU SHOULD LET HIM GET YOU, TOO!
STOP MAKI-MURA!

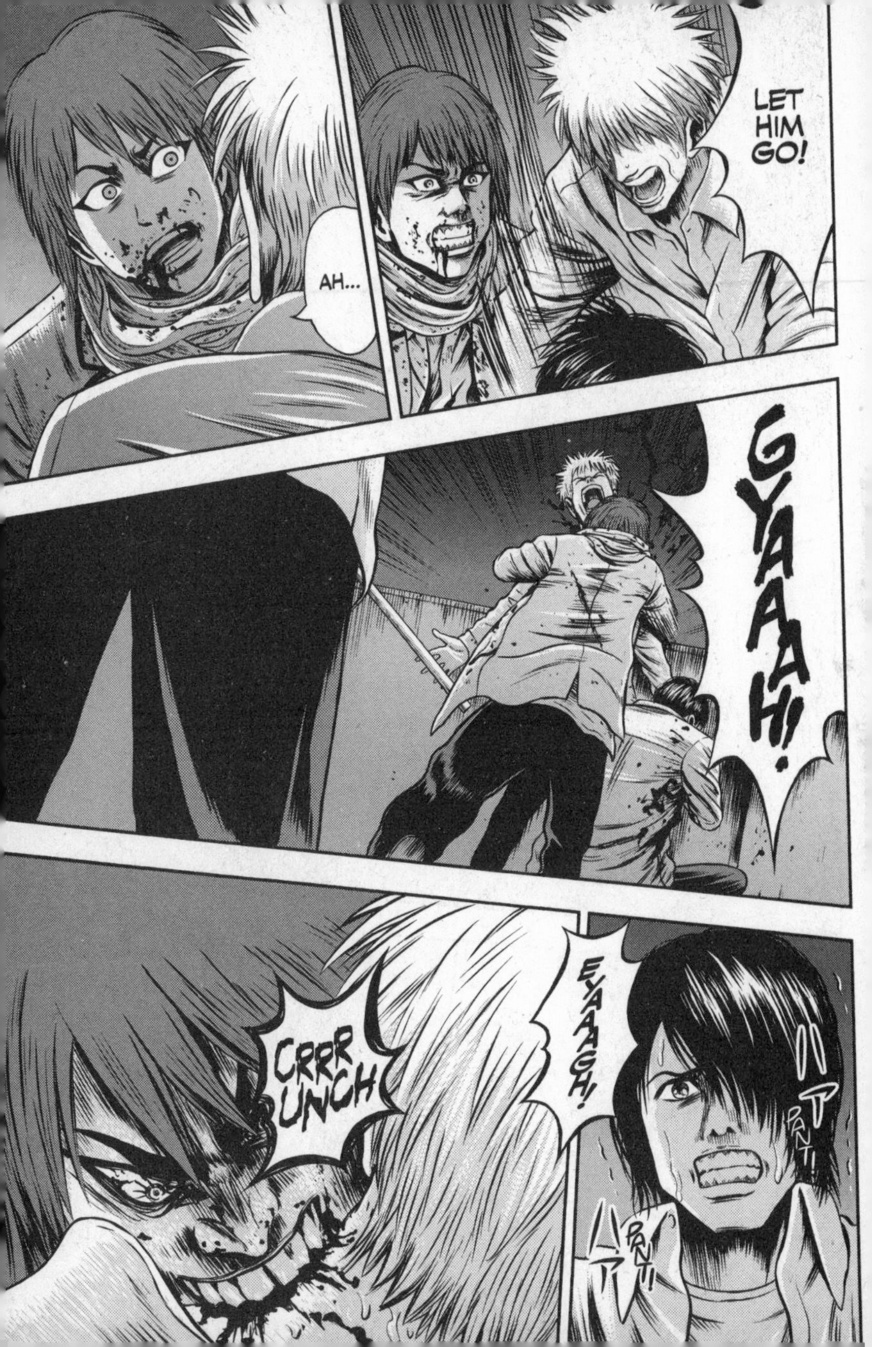
LET HIM GO!
AH...
GYAAAH!
PANT! PANT!
EYAAAGH!
CRRR UNCH

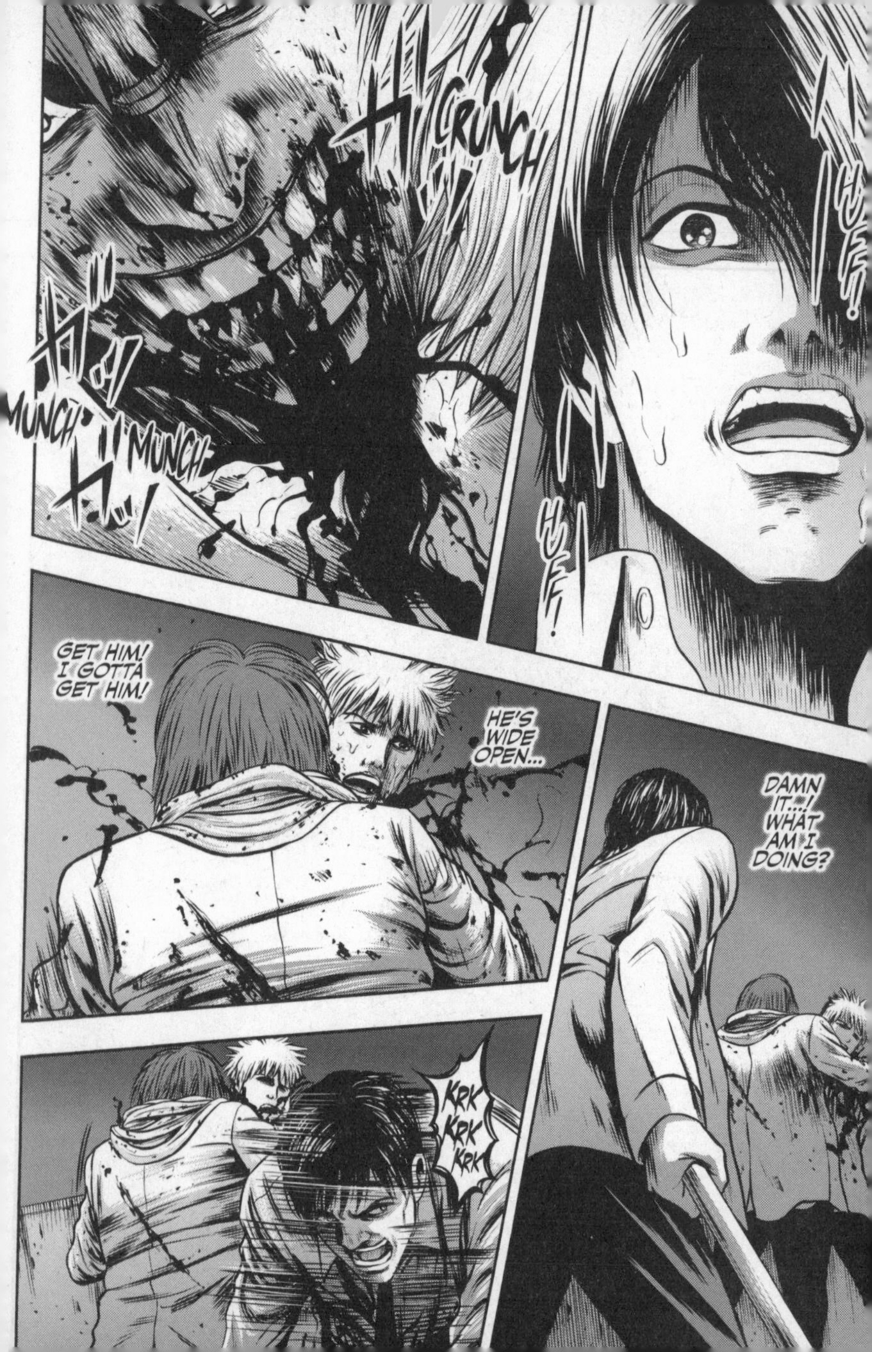
HUFF!
HUFF!
CRUNCH
MUNCH MUNCH
DAMN IT...! WHAT AM I DOING?
GET HIM! I GOTTA GET HIM!
HE'S WIDE OPEN...
KRK KRK KRK

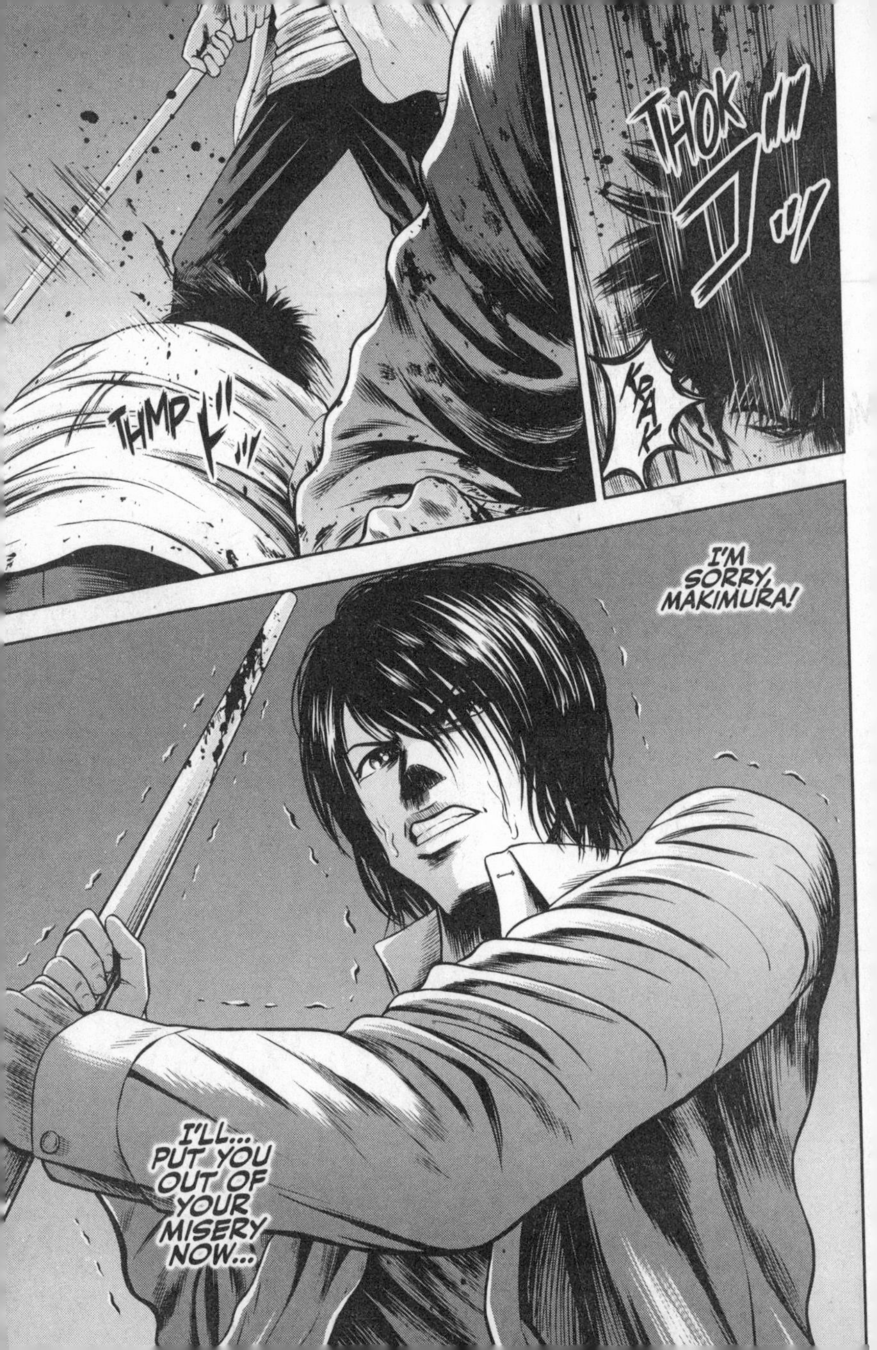
THOK
KRAK
THMP
I'M SORRY, MAKIMURA!
I'LL... PUT YOU OUT OF YOUR MISERY NOW...

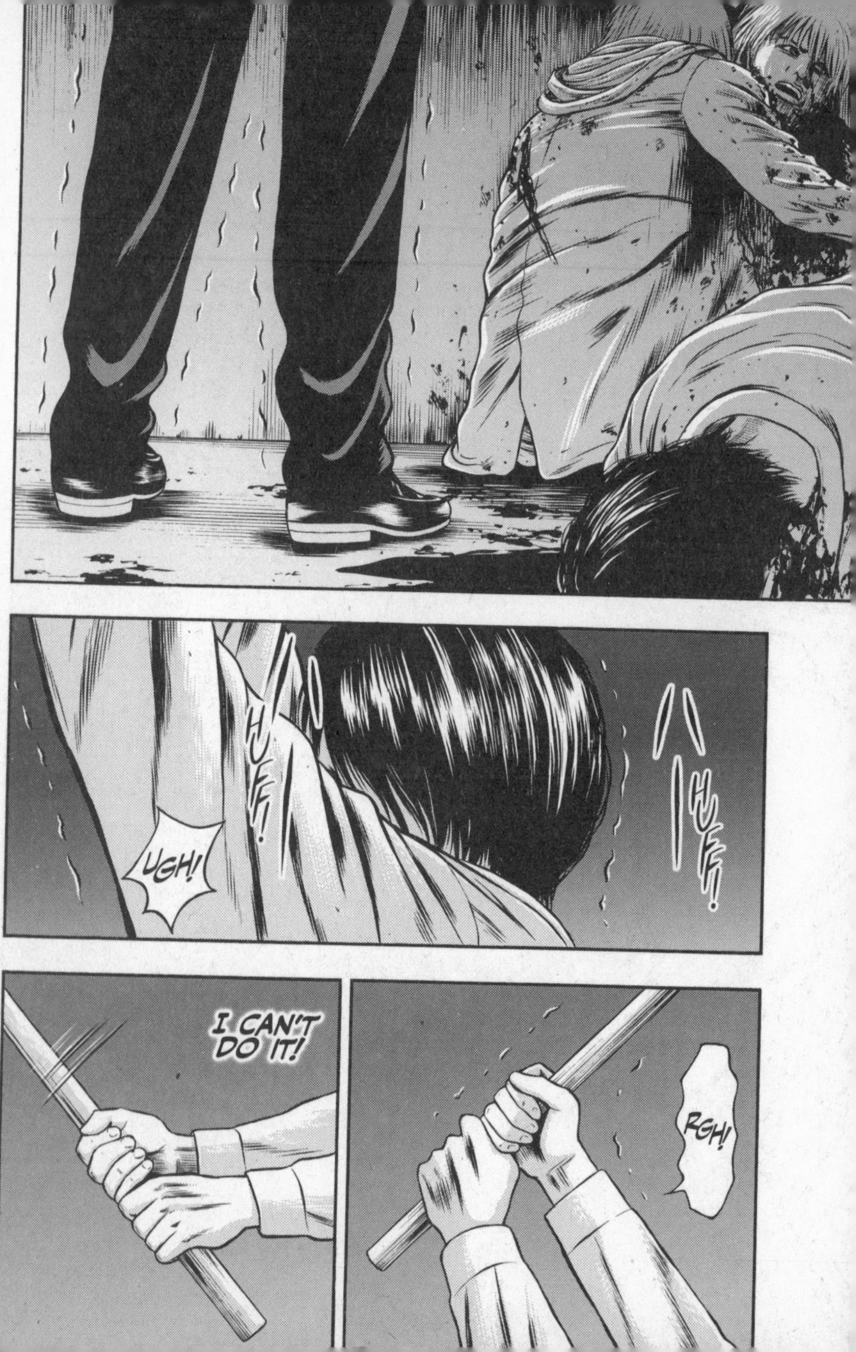
HUFF!
HUFF!
UGH!
RGH!
I CAN'T DO IT!

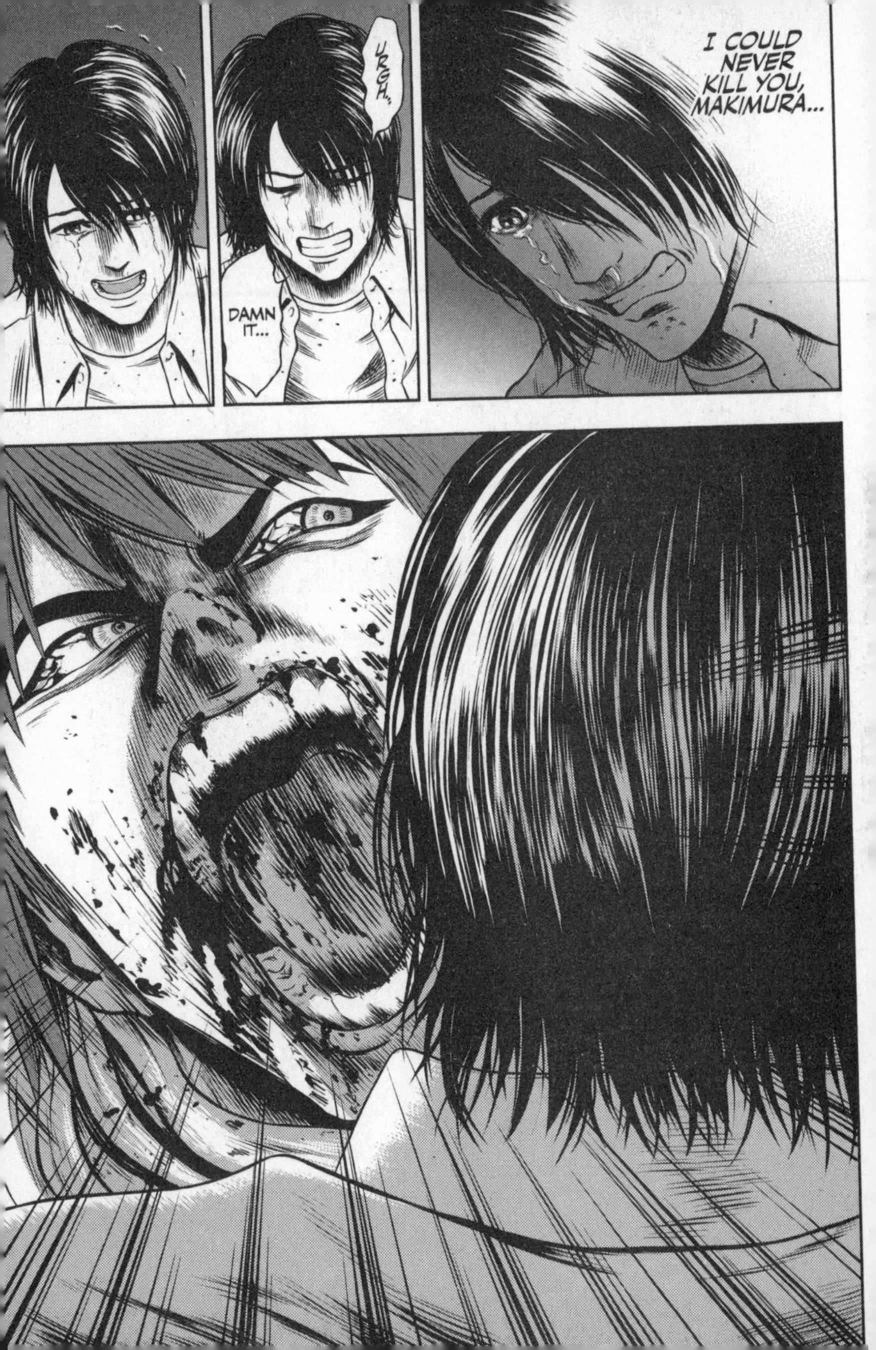
I COULD NEVER KILL YOU, MAKIMURA...
URGH...
DAMN IT...

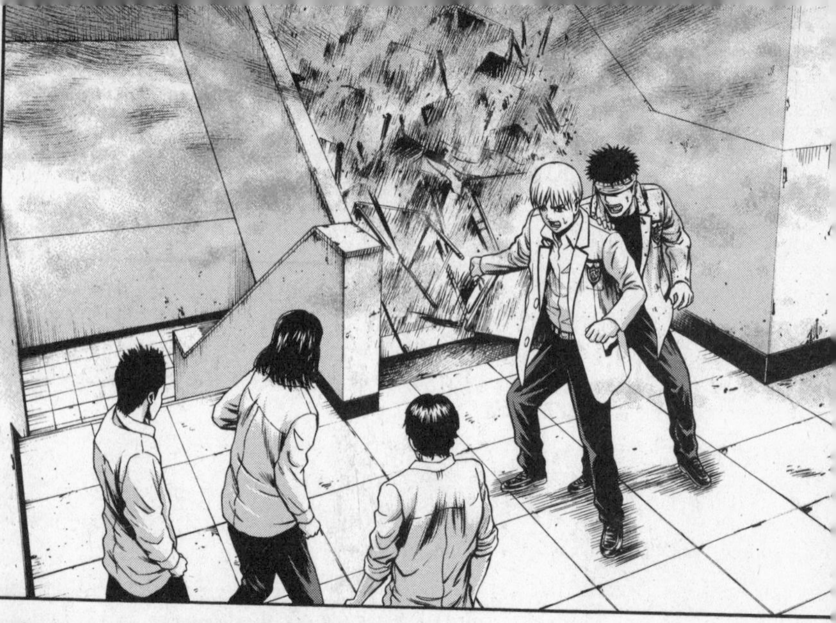

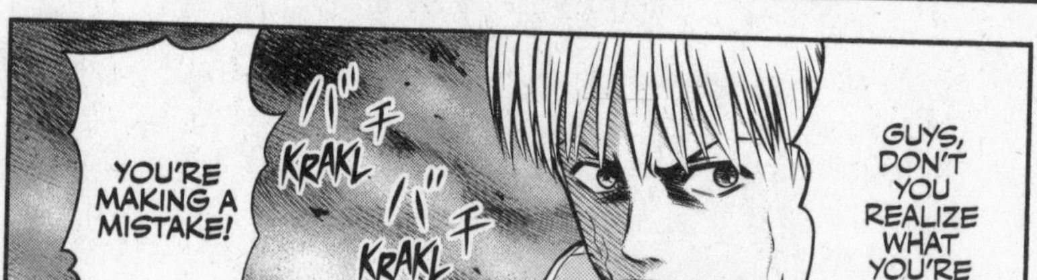
GUYS, DON'T YOU REALIZE WHAT YOU'RE DOING?!
バチ
KRAKL
バチ
KRAKL
YOU'RE MAKING A MISTAKE!

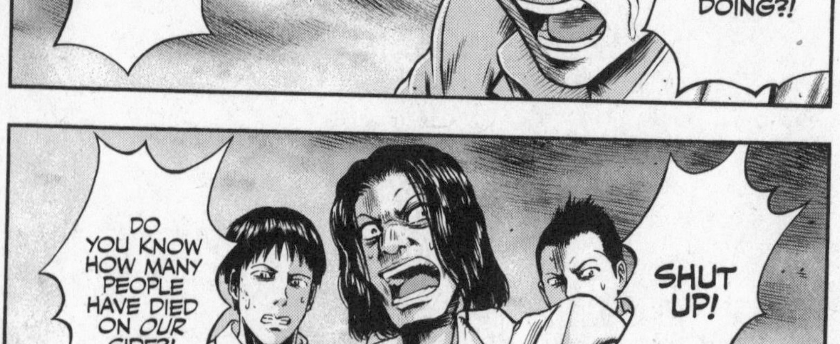
SHUT UP!
DO YOU KNOW HOW MANY PEOPLE HAVE DIED ON *OUR* SIDE?!

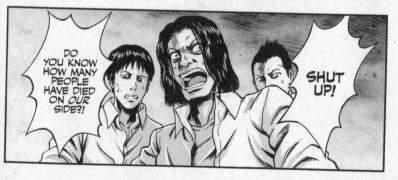

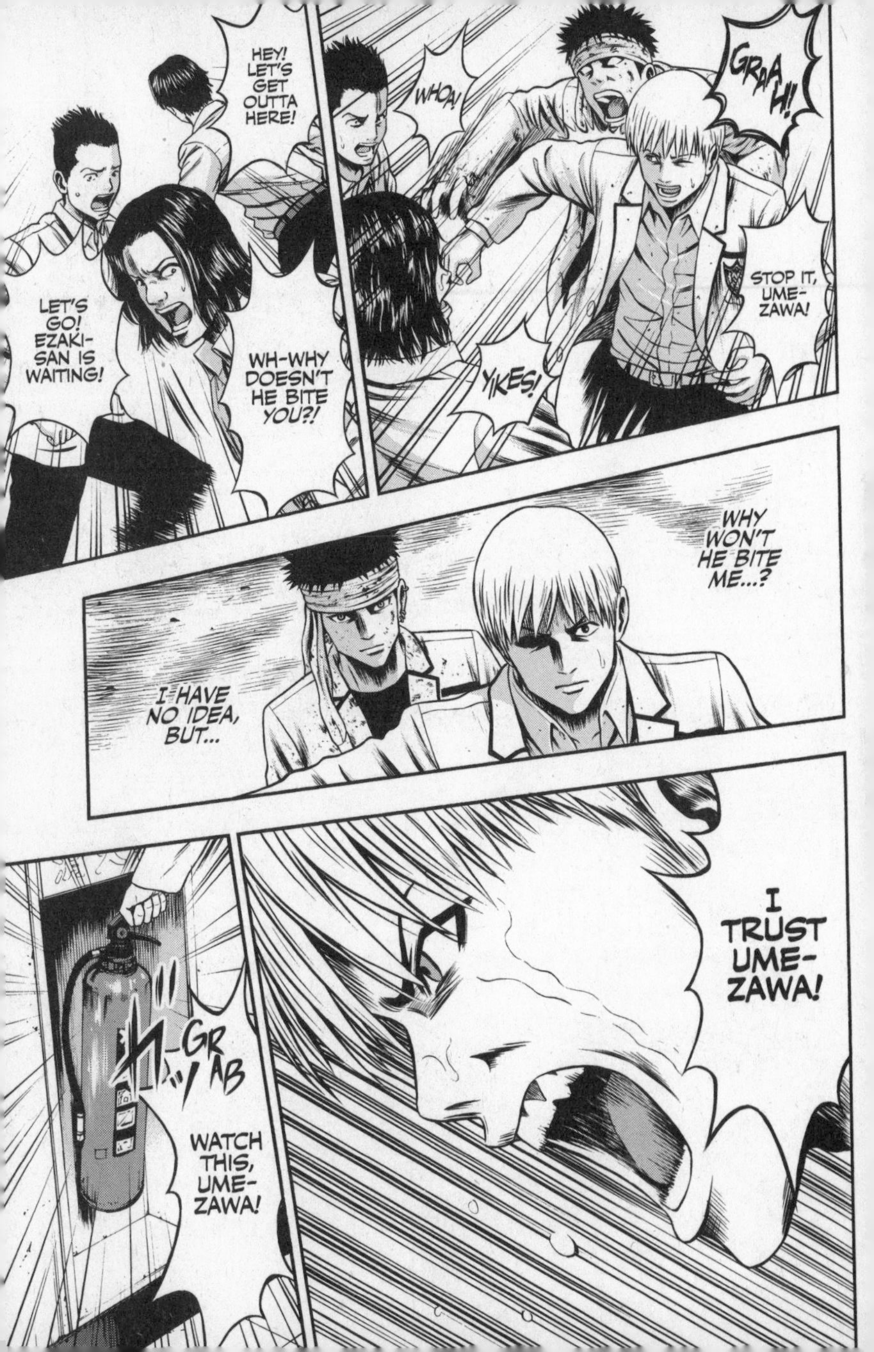
GRAAH!
WHOA!
STOP IT, UME-ZAWA!
YIKES!
HEY! LET'S GET OUTTA HERE!
WH-WHY DOESN'T HE BITE YOU?!
LET'S GO! EZAKI-SAN IS WAITING!
WHY WON'T HE BITE ME...?
I HAVE NO IDEA, BUT...
I TRUST UME-ZAWA!
GRAB
WATCH THIS, UME-ZAWA!

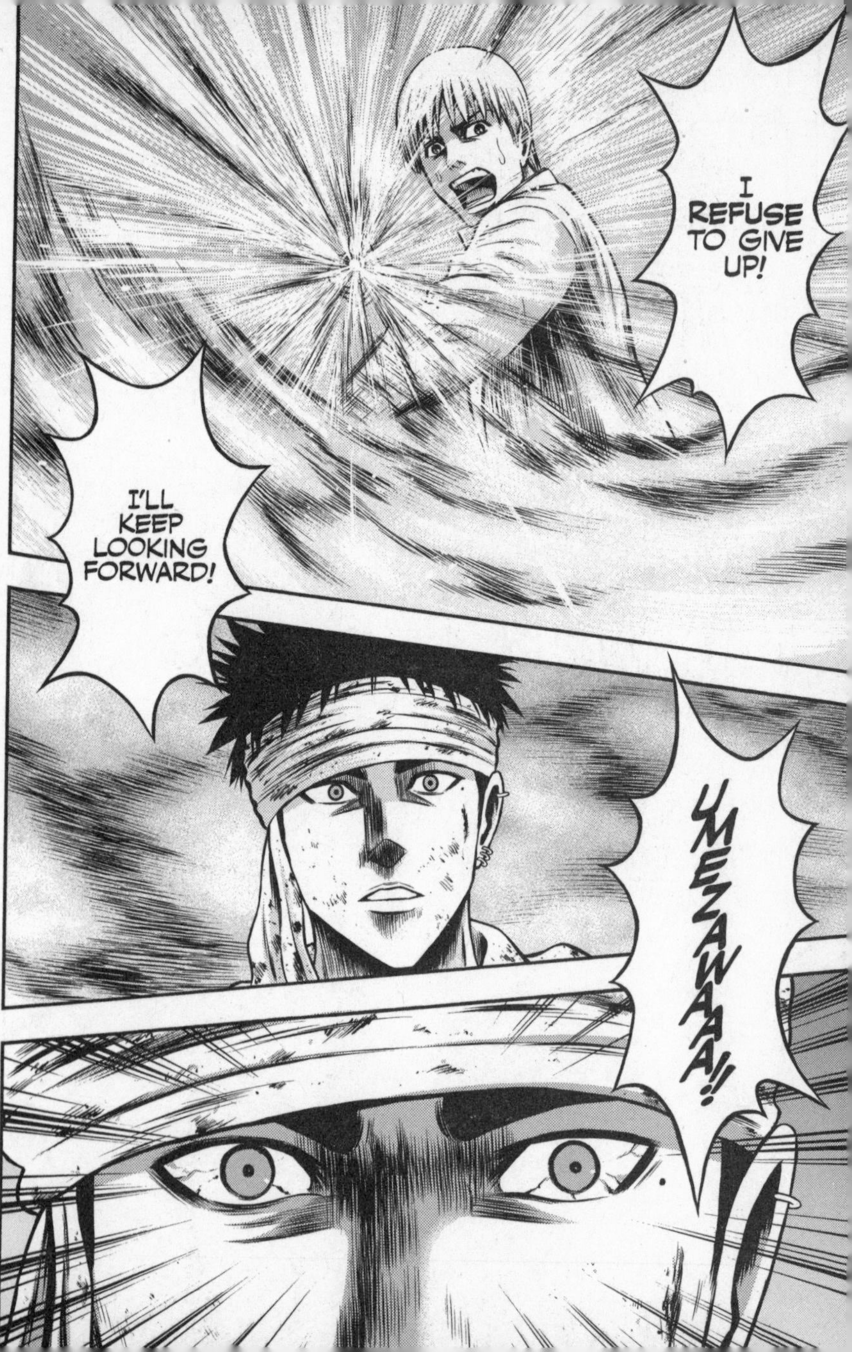
I REFUSE TO GIVE UP!
I'LL KEEP LOOKING FORWARD!
UMEZAWAAA!!

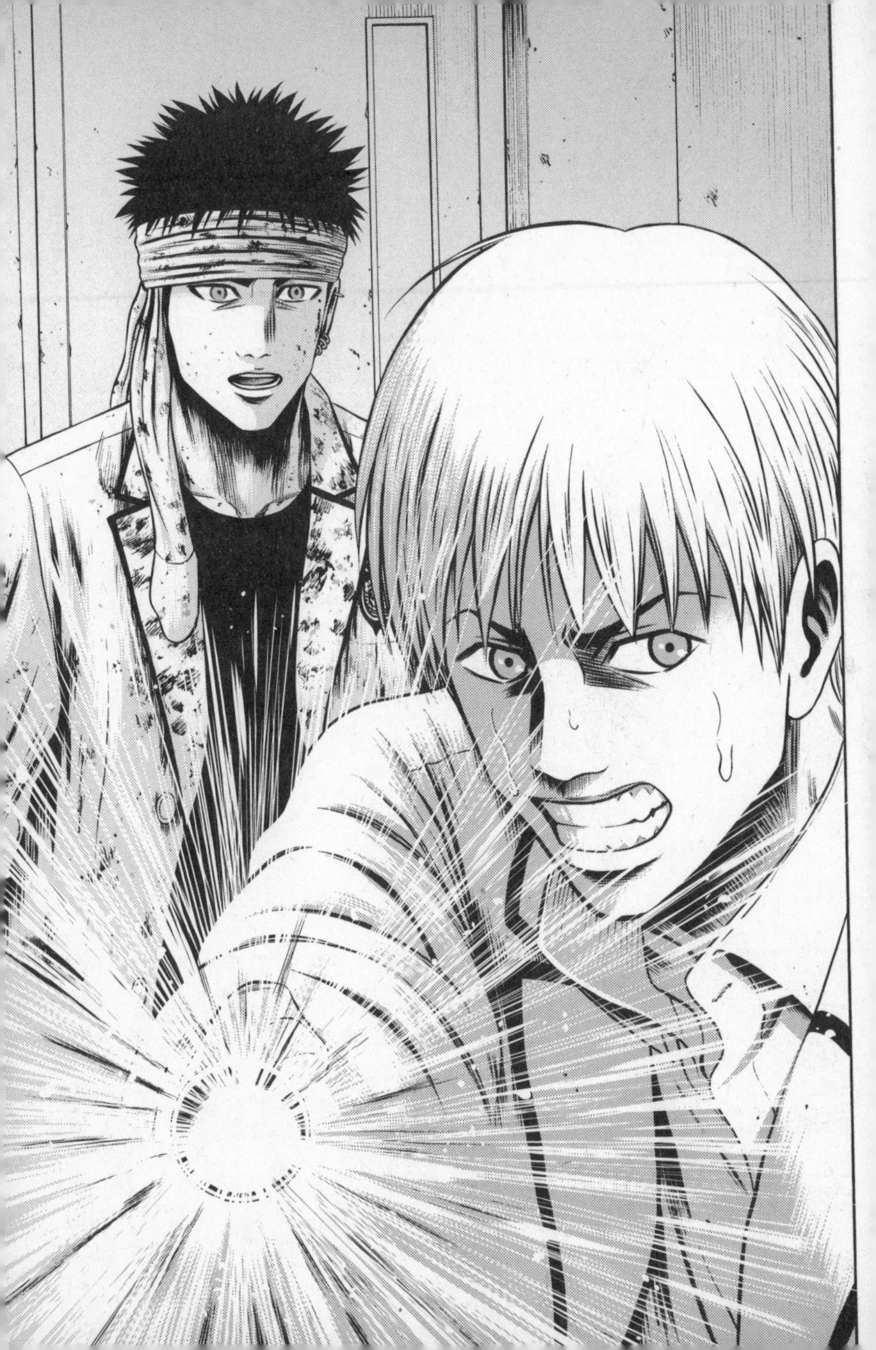

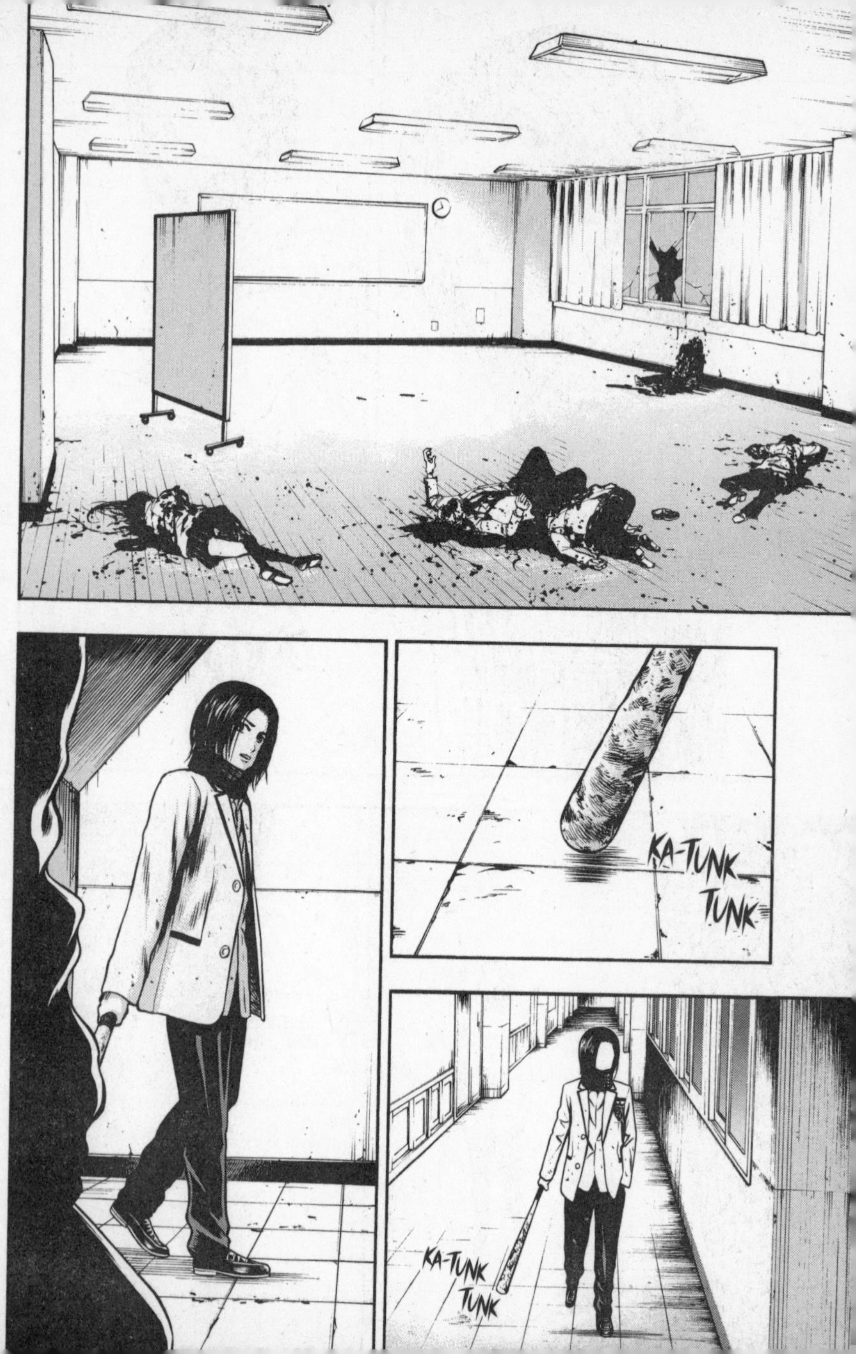
KA-TUNK
TUNK
KA-TUNK
TUNK

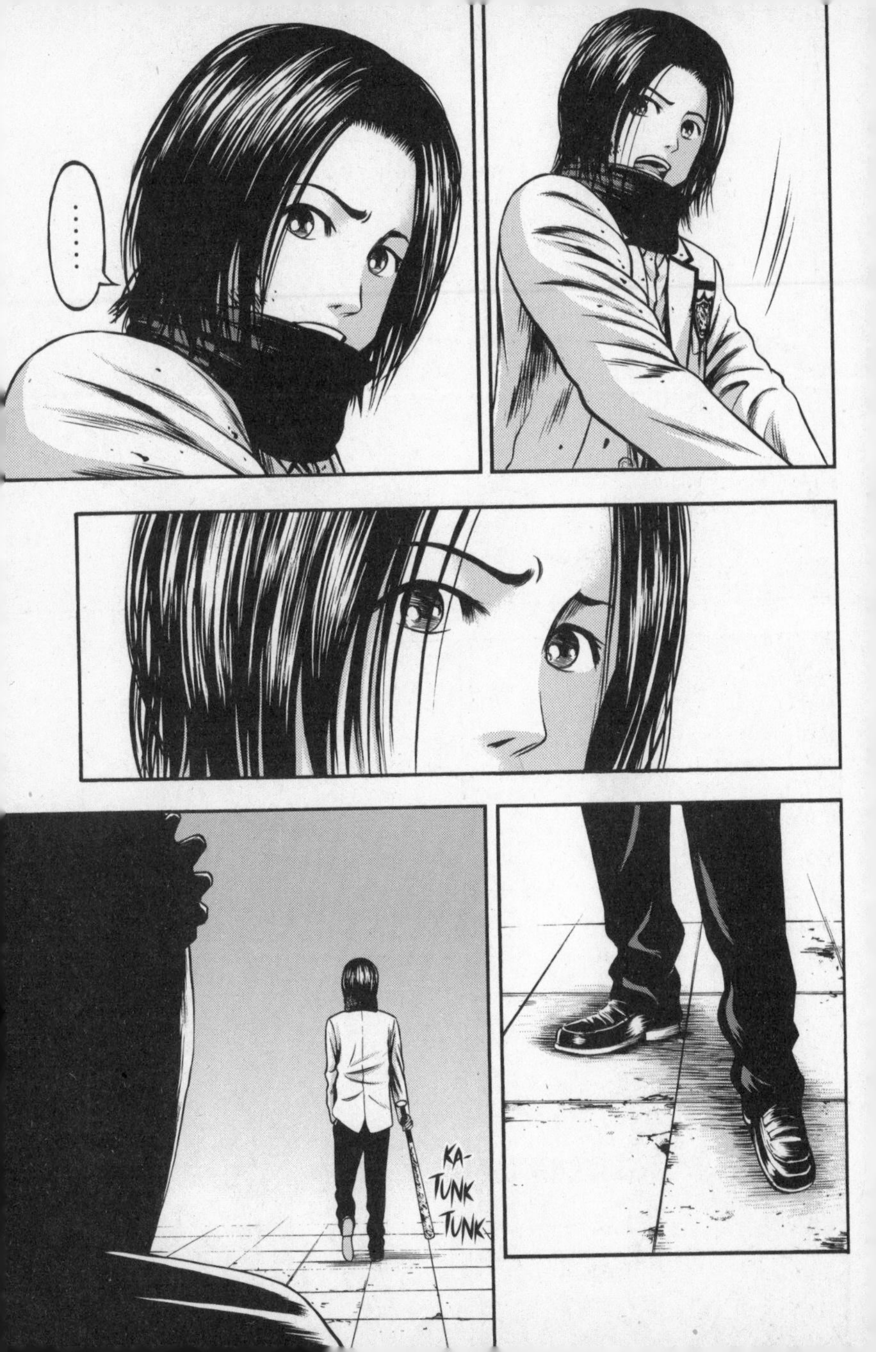
......
KA-TUNK TUNK

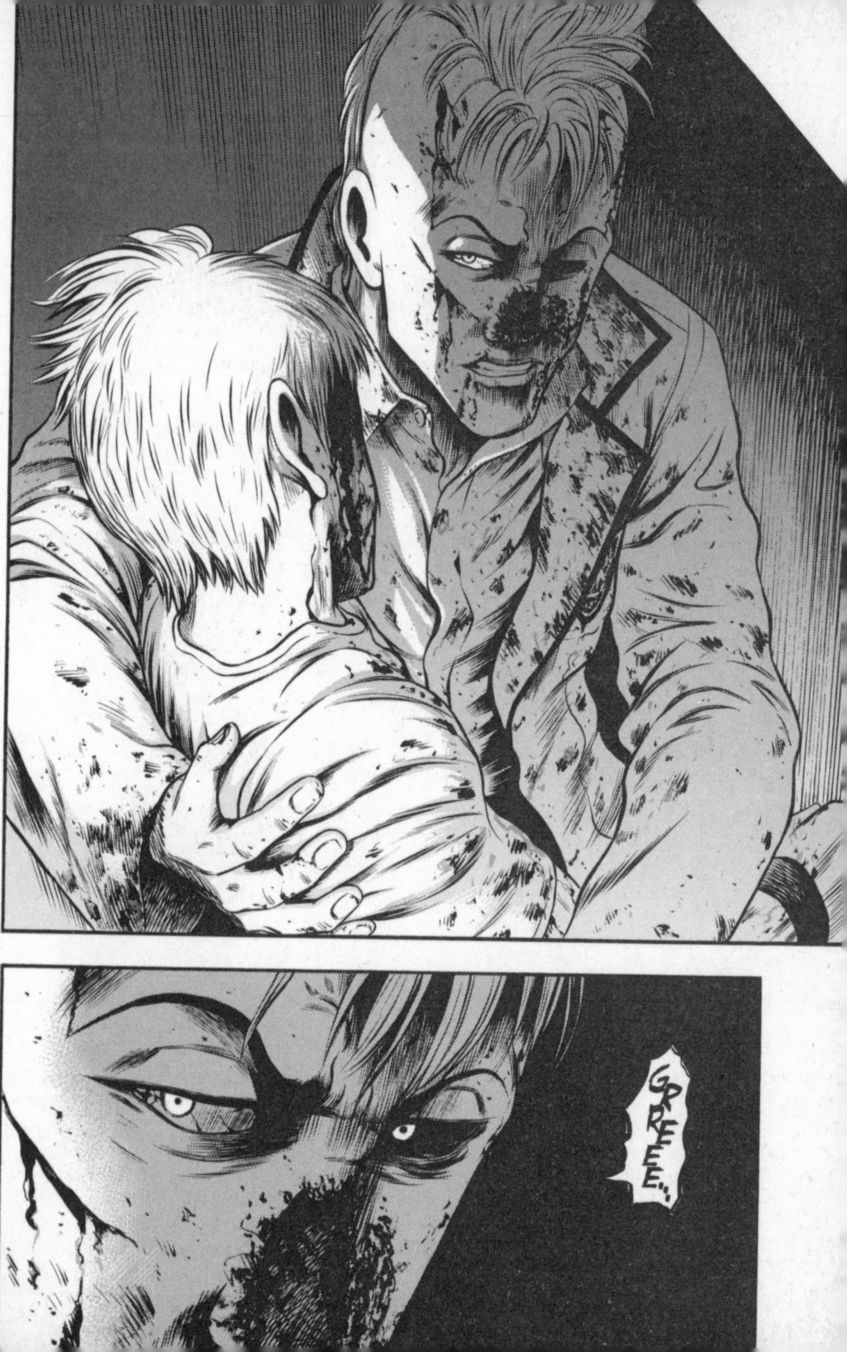
GRREEE...

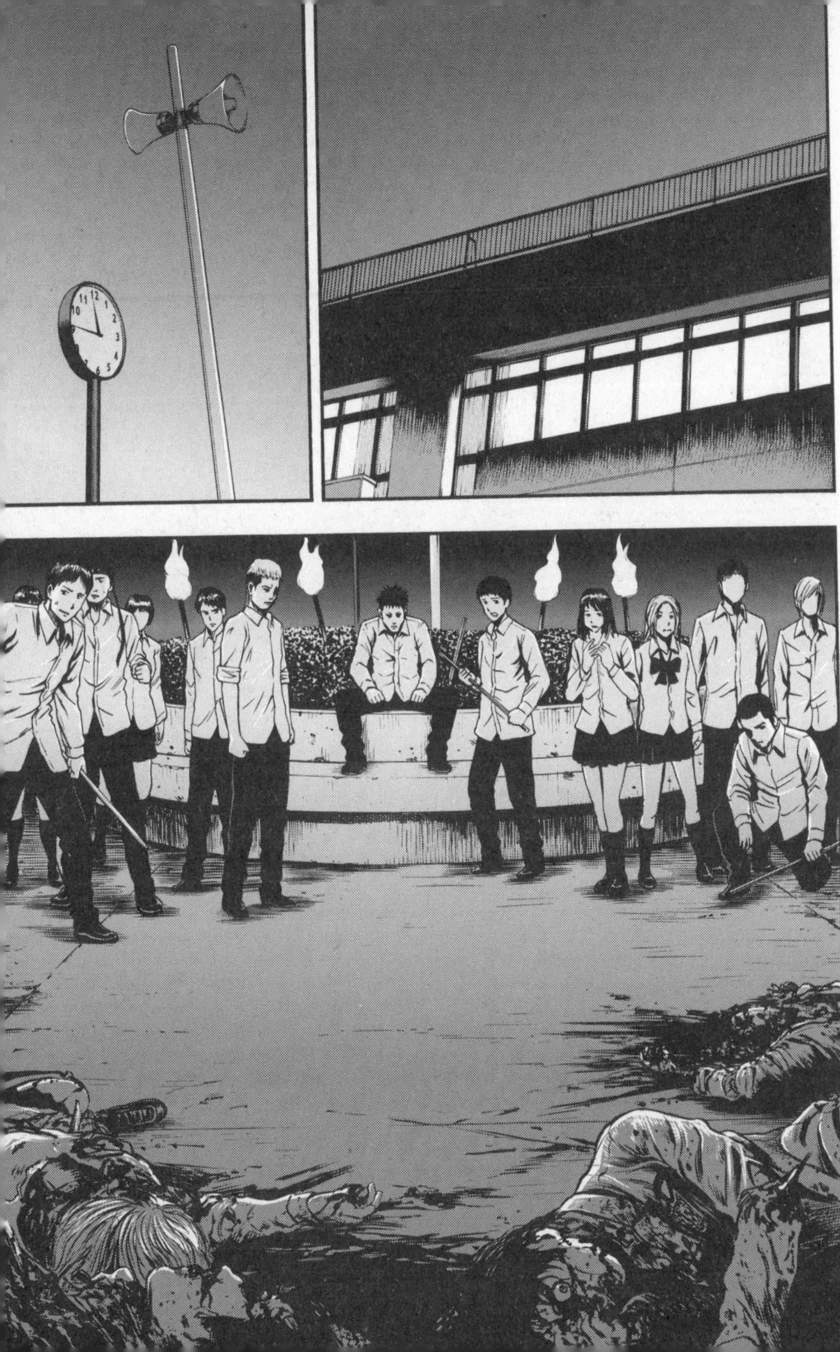

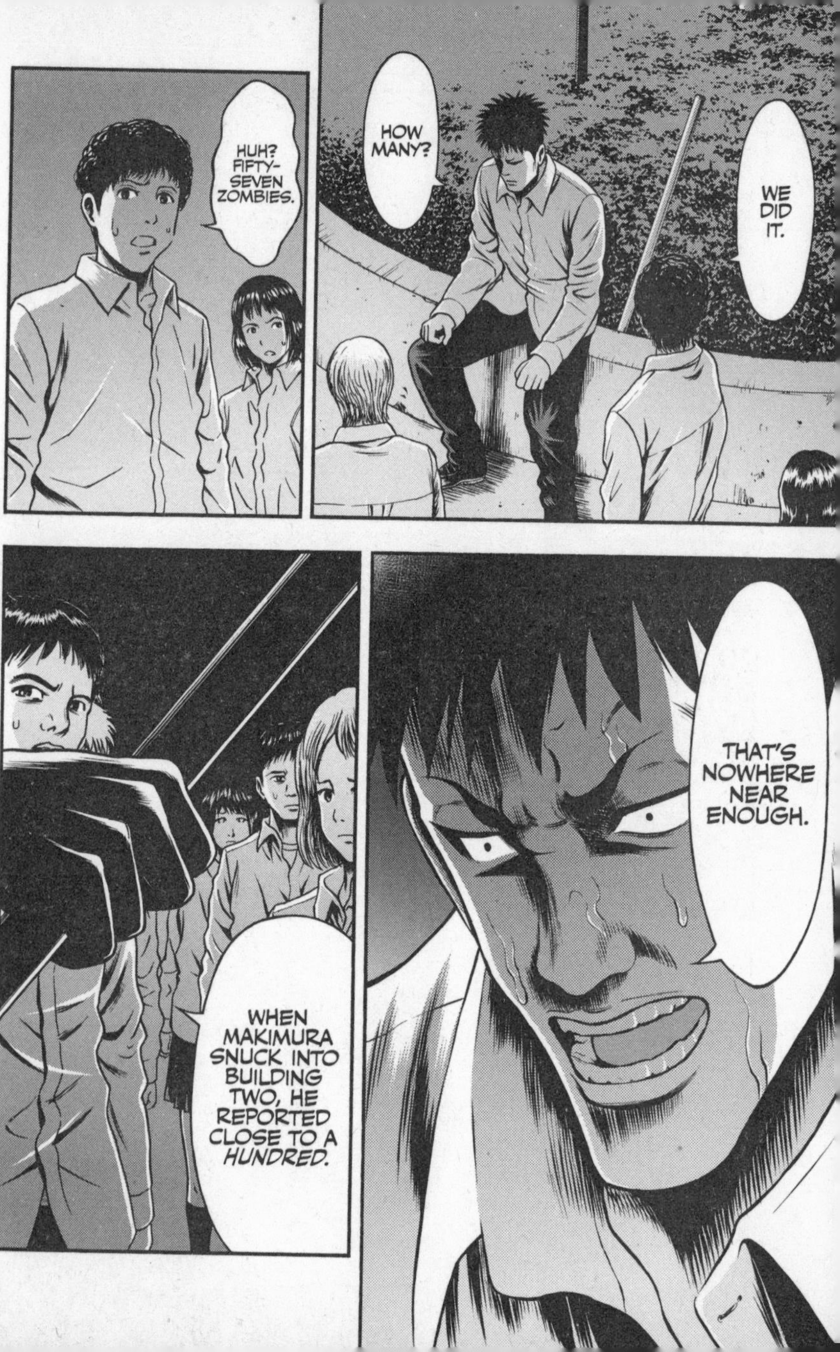
WE DID IT.
HOW MANY?
HUH? FIFTY-SEVEN ZOMBIES.
THAT'S NOWHERE NEAR ENOUGH.
WHEN MAKIMURA SNUCK INTO BUILDING TWO, HE REPORTED CLOSE TO A *HUNDRED*.

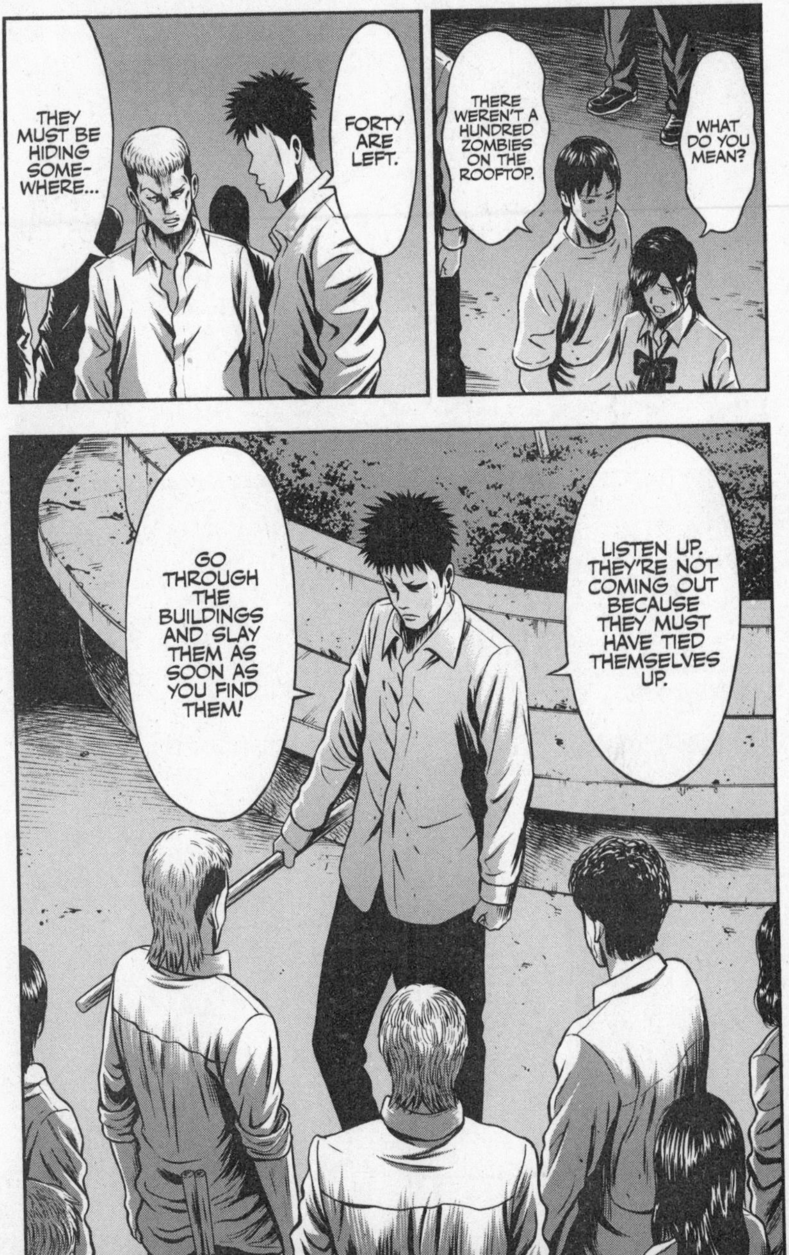
WHAT DO YOU MEAN?
THERE WEREN'T A HUNDRED ZOMBIES ON THE ROOFTOP.
FORTY ARE LEFT.
THEY MUST BE HIDING SOME-WHERE...
LISTEN UP. THEY'RE NOT COMING OUT BECAUSE THEY MUST HAVE TIED THEMSELVES UP.
GO THROUGH THE BUILDINGS AND SLAY THEM AS SOON AS YOU FIND THEM!

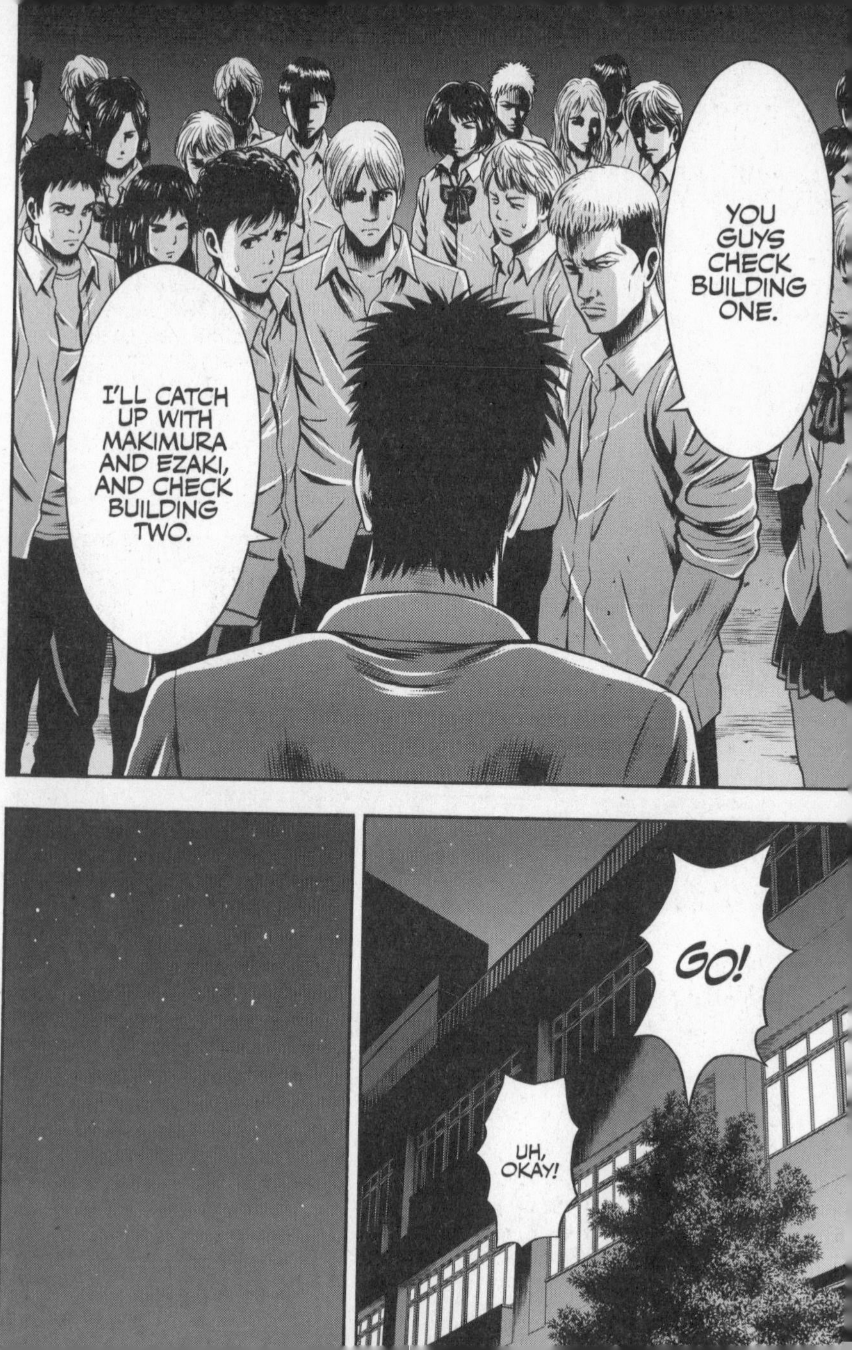
YOU GUYS CHECK BUILDING ONE.
I'LL CATCH UP WITH MAKIMURA AND EZAKI, AND CHECK BUILDING TWO.
GO!
UH, OKAY!

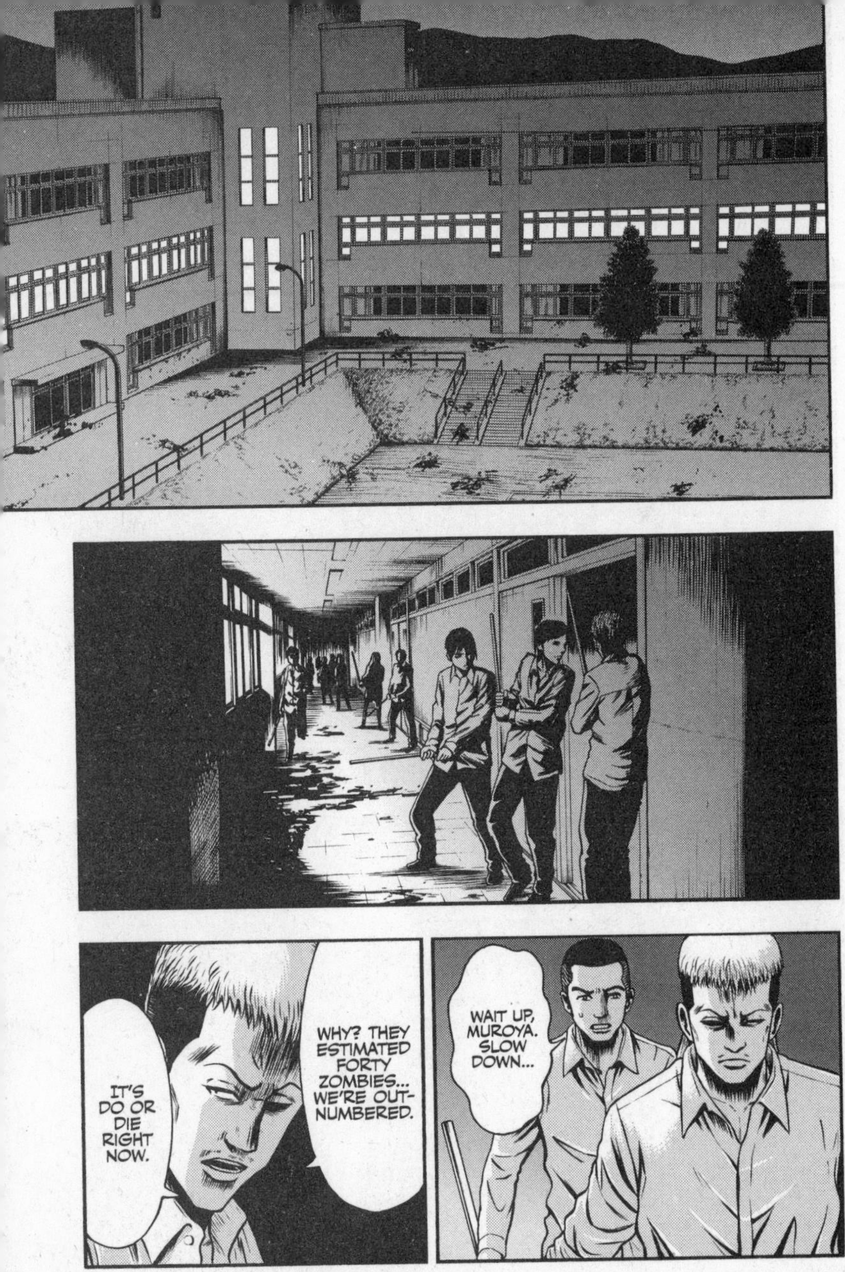
WAIT UP, MUROYA. SLOW DOWN...
WHY? THEY ESTIMATED FORTY ZOMBIES... WE'RE OUT-NUMBERED.
IT'S DO OR DIE RIGHT NOW.

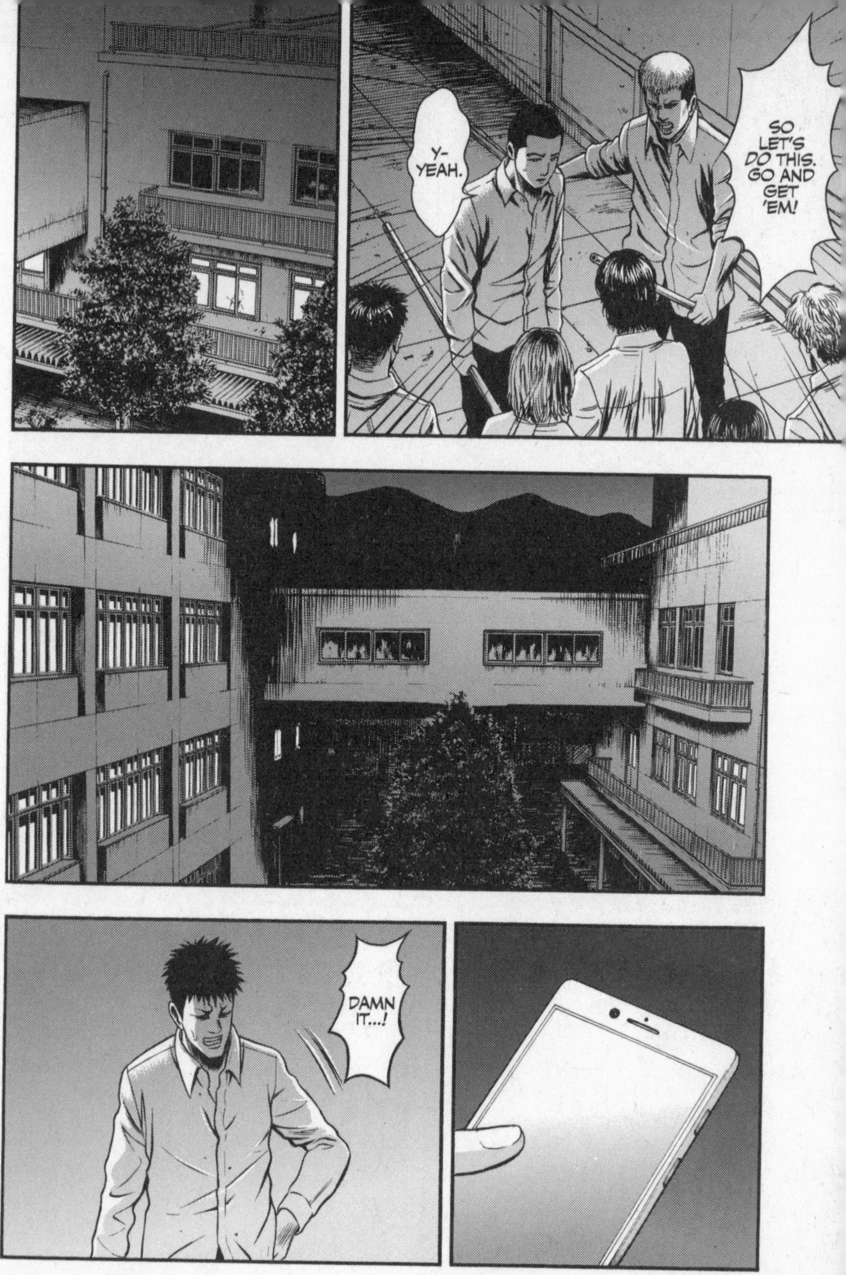
SO LET'S DO THIS. GO AND GET 'EM!
Y-YEAH.
DAMN IT...!

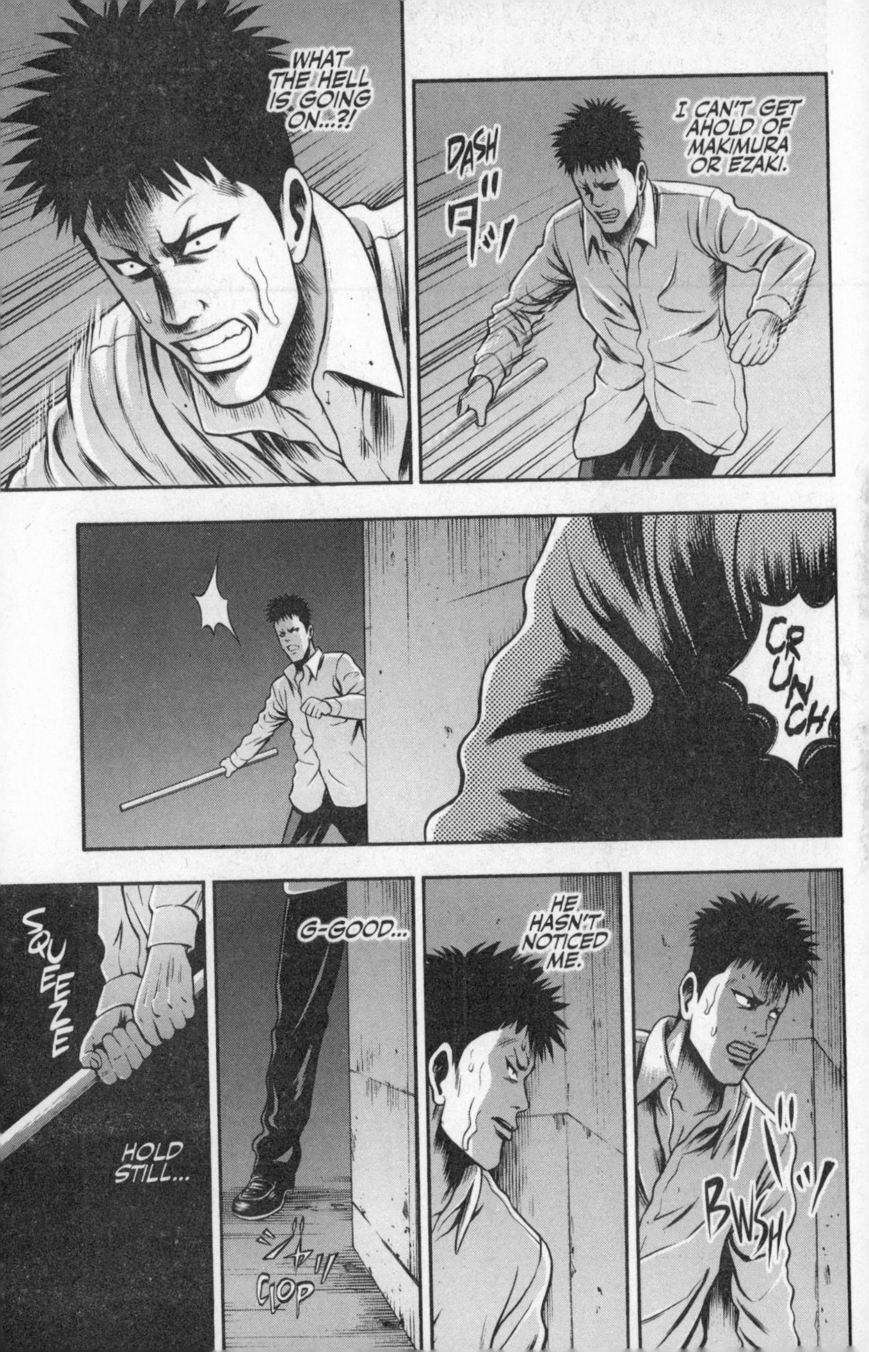
I CAN'T GET AHOLD OF MAKIMURA OR EZAKI.
DASH
WHAT THE HELL IS GOING ON...?!
CRUNCH
BWSH
HE HASN'T NOTICED ME.
G-GOOD...
CLOP
SQUEEZE
HOLD STILL...

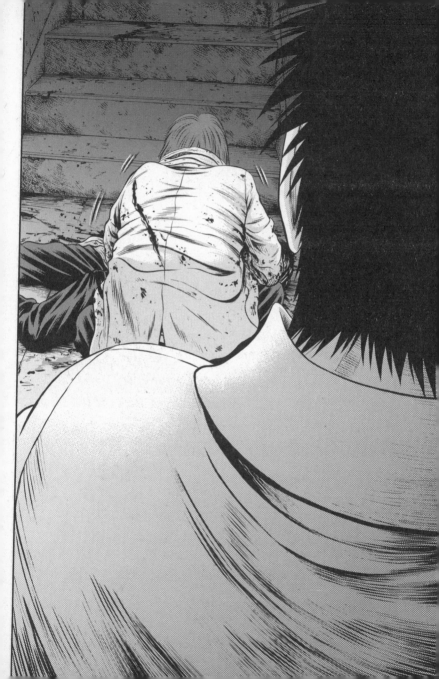

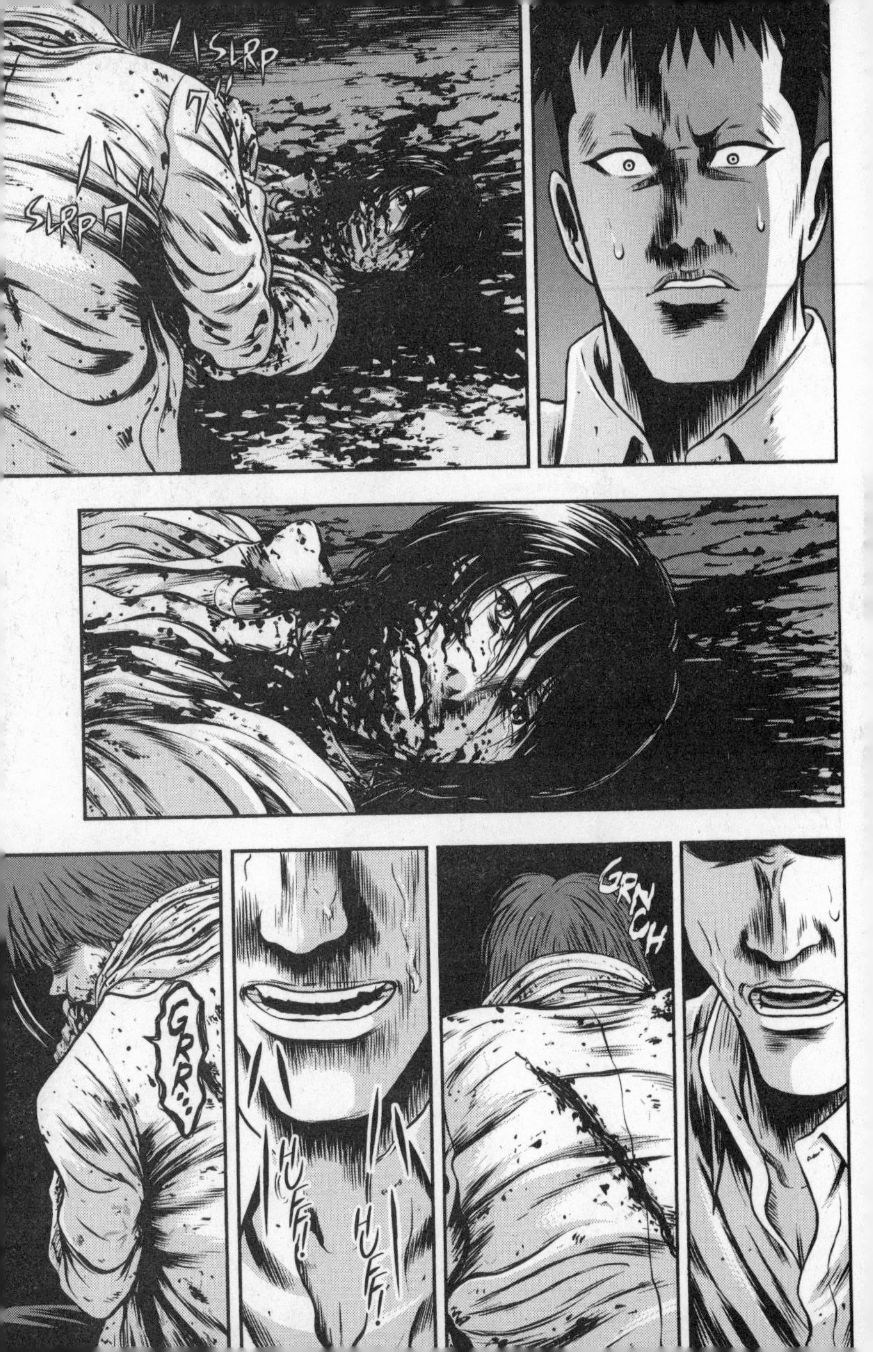
SLRP
SLRP
GRNCH
HUFF!
HUFF!
GRR...

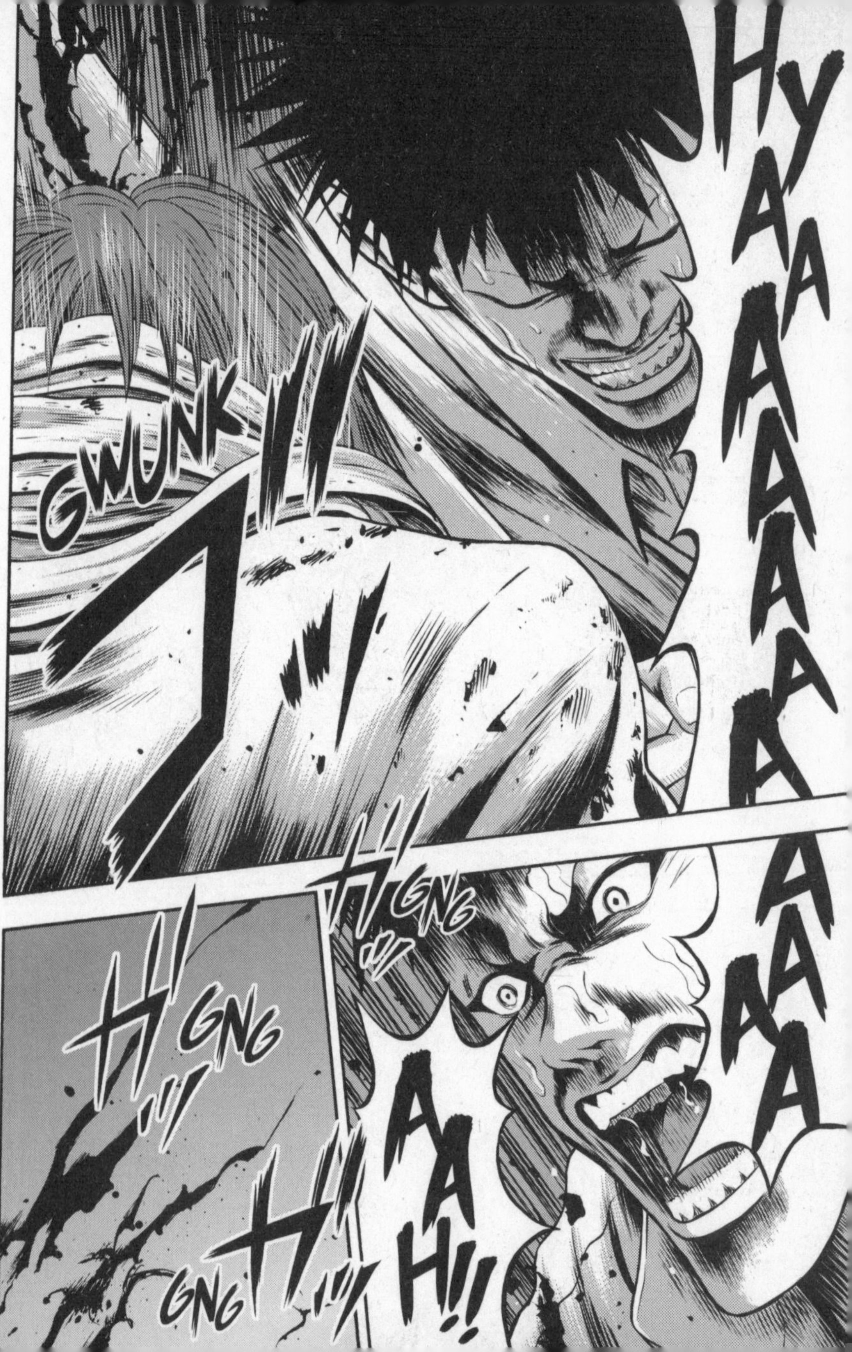

HYAAAAAAAAAAAAAA
GWUNK!!
HGNG!!
AAH!!
HGNG!!
HGNG!!

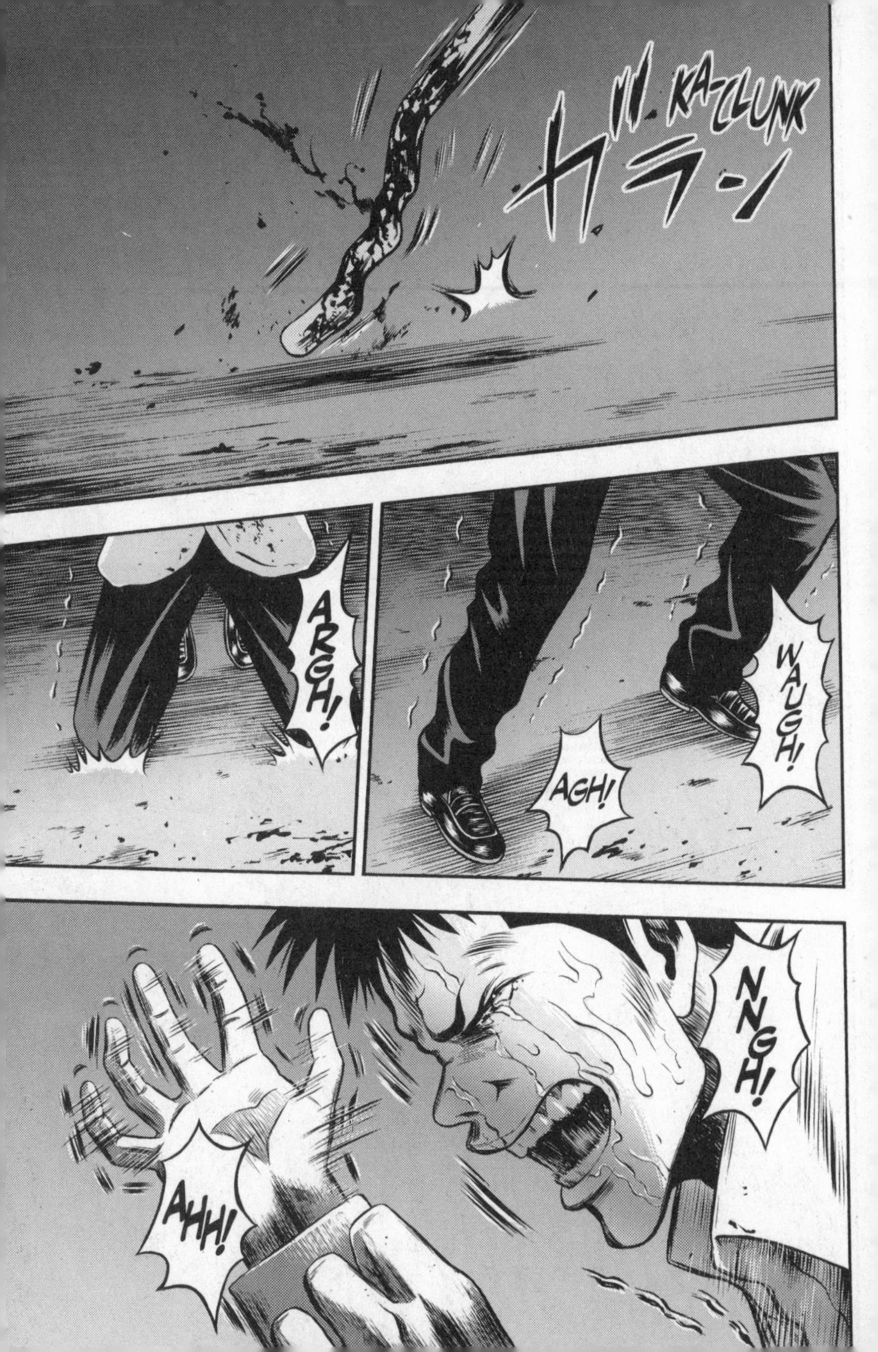
カラーン KA-CLUNK
WAUGH!
AGH!
ARGH!
NNGH!
AHH!

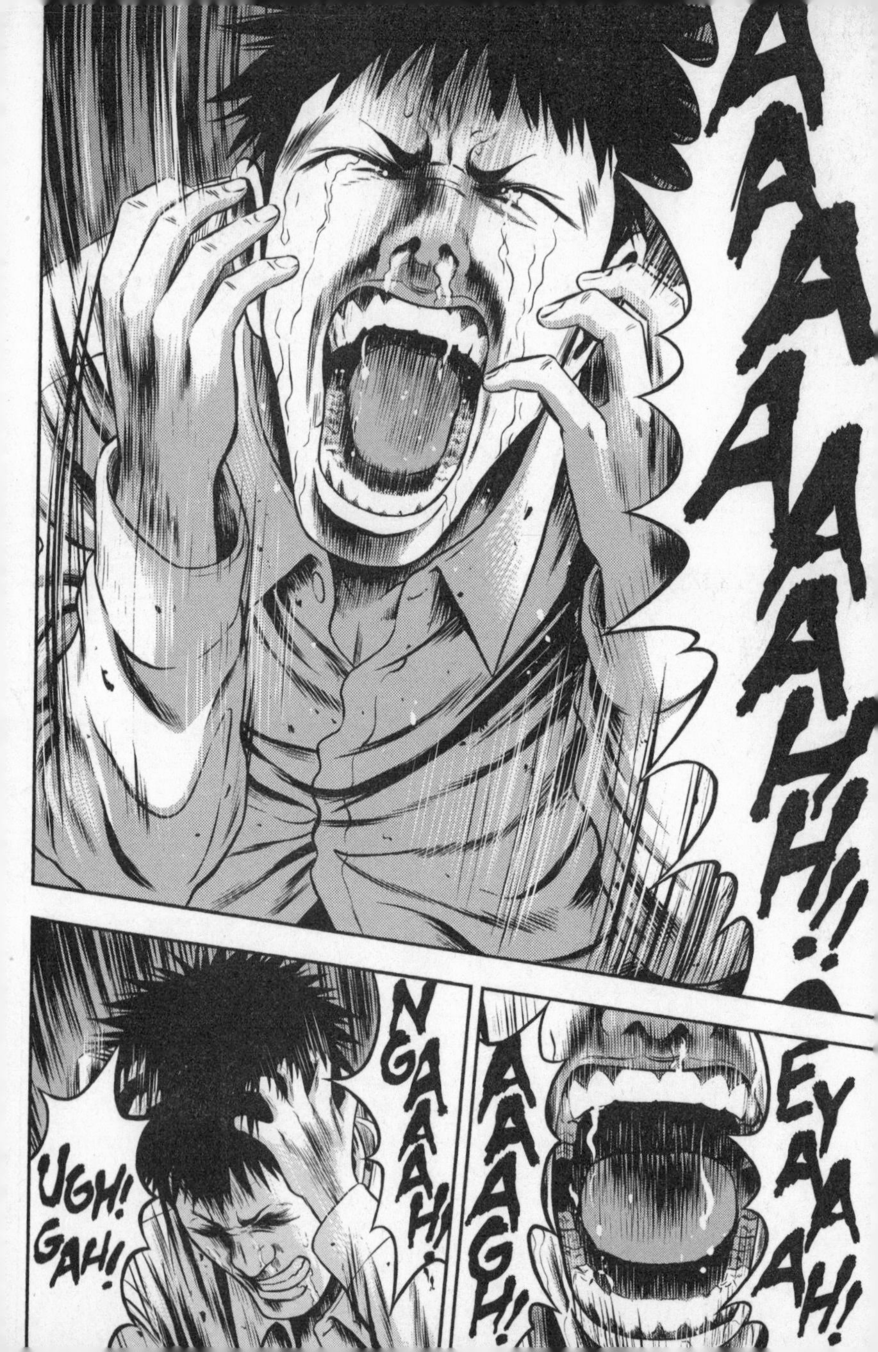

AAAAAAHH!!
EYAAAH!!
AAAAGH!!
NGAAAAH!!
UGH! GAH!

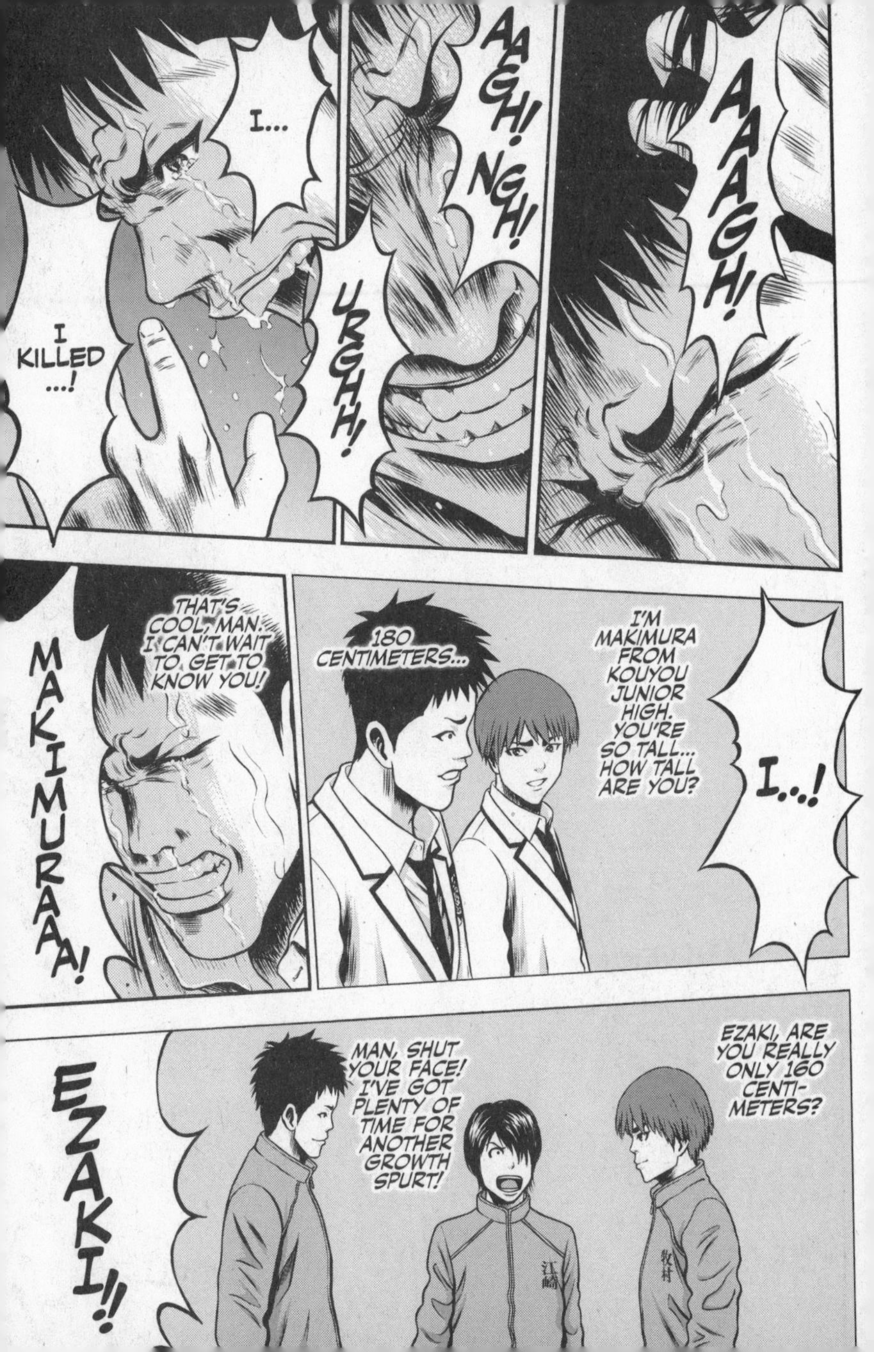
AAAAGH!
AAGH! NGH!
URGHH!
I...
I KILLED ...!
I...!
I'M MAKIMURA FROM KOUYOU JUNIOR HIGH. YOU'RE SO TALL... HOW TALL ARE YOU?
180 CENTIMETERS...
THAT'S COOL, MAN. I CAN'T WAIT TO GET TO KNOW YOU!
MAKIMURAAAA!
EZAKI, ARE YOU REALLY ONLY 160 CENTI-METERS?
牧村
MAN, SHUT YOUR FACE! I'VE GOT PLENTY OF TIME FOR ANOTHER GROWTH SPURT!
江崎
EZAKI!!

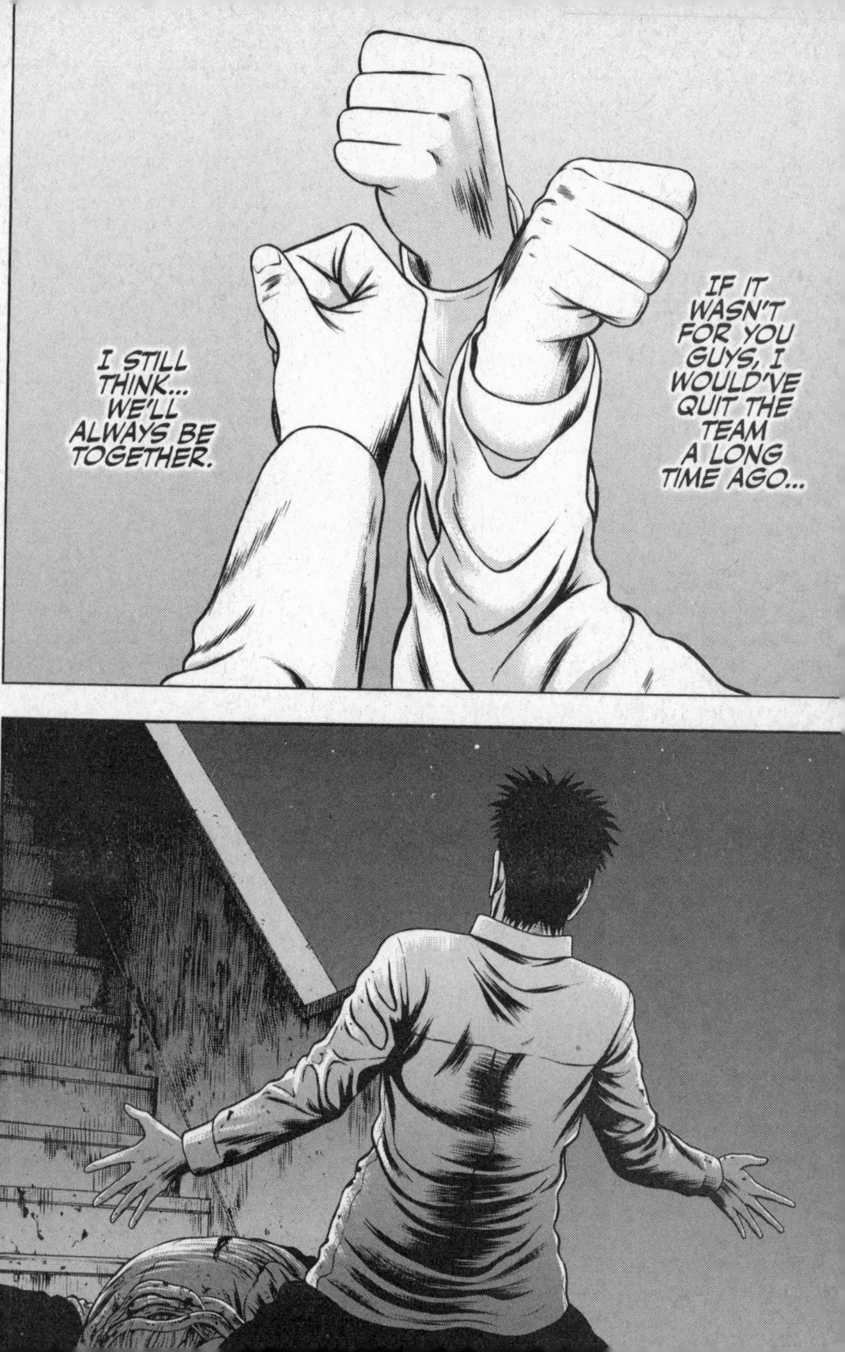
IF IT WASN'T FOR YOU GUYS, I WOULD'VE QUIT THE TEAM A LONG TIME AGO...
I STILL THINK... WE'LL ALWAYS BE TOGETHER.

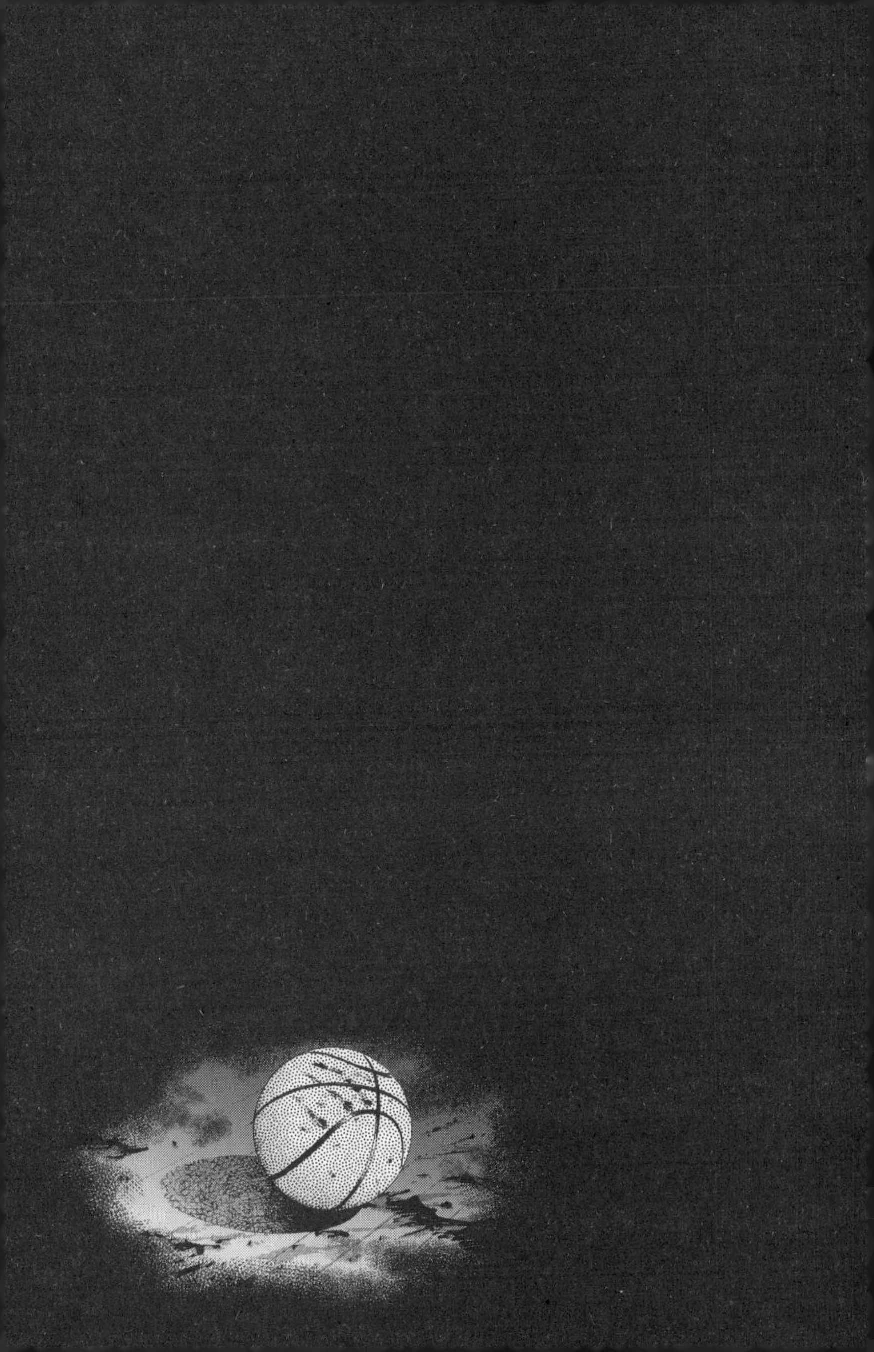

HOUR OF THE ZOMBIE

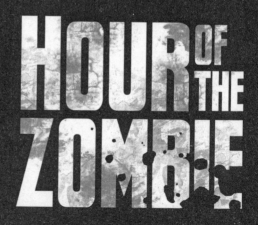

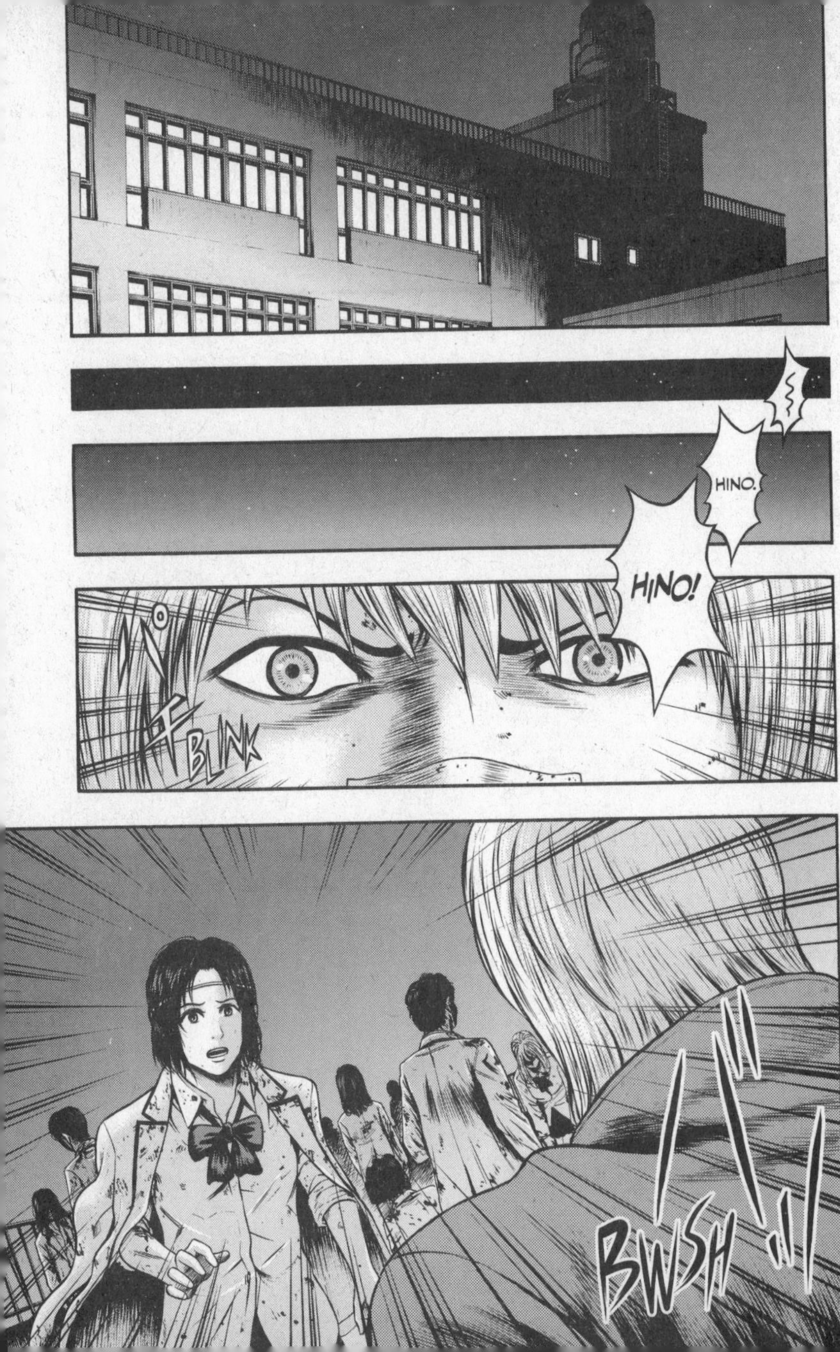
HINO.
HINO!
BLINK
BWSH

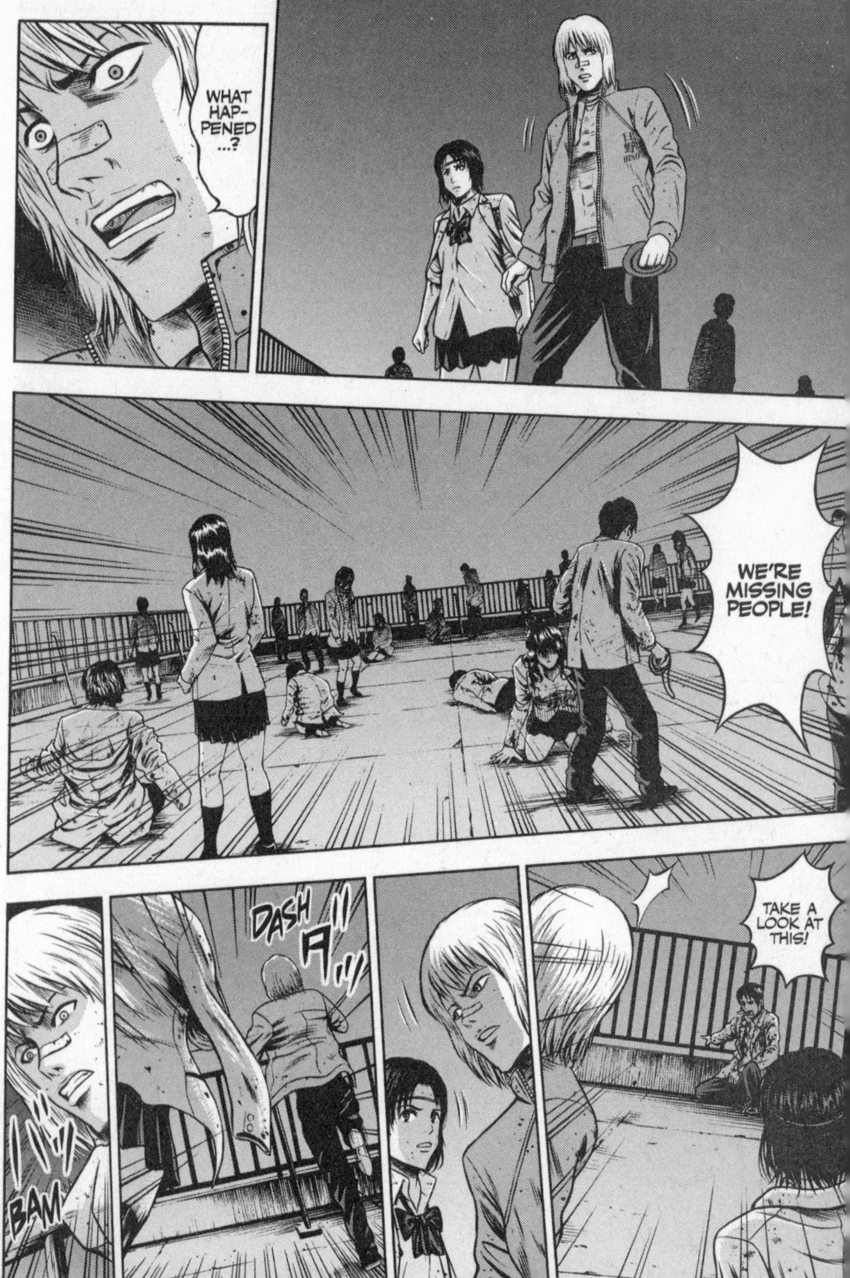
WHAT HAP-PENED ...?
WE'RE MISSING PEOPLE!
TAKE A LOOK AT THIS!
DASH
BAM

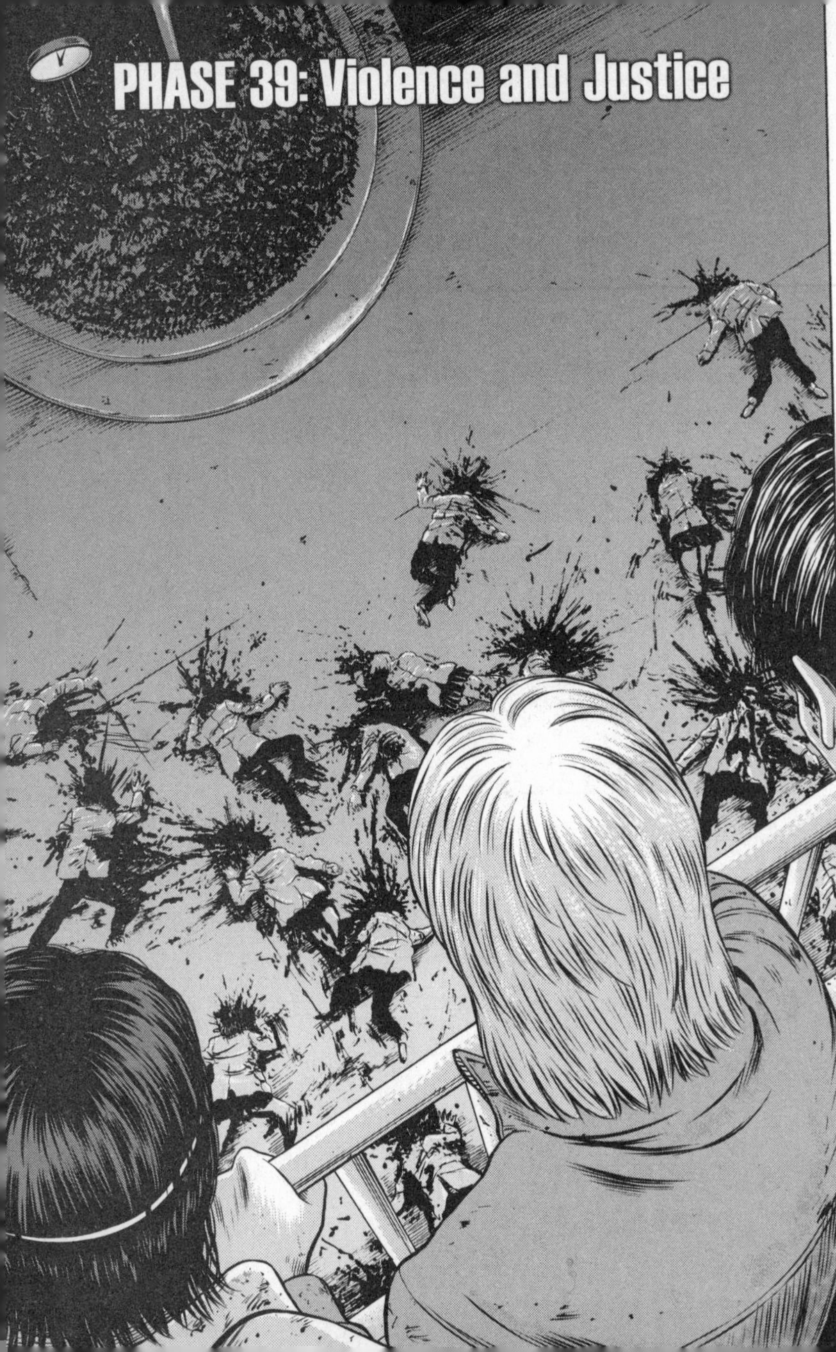
PHASE 39: Violence and Justice

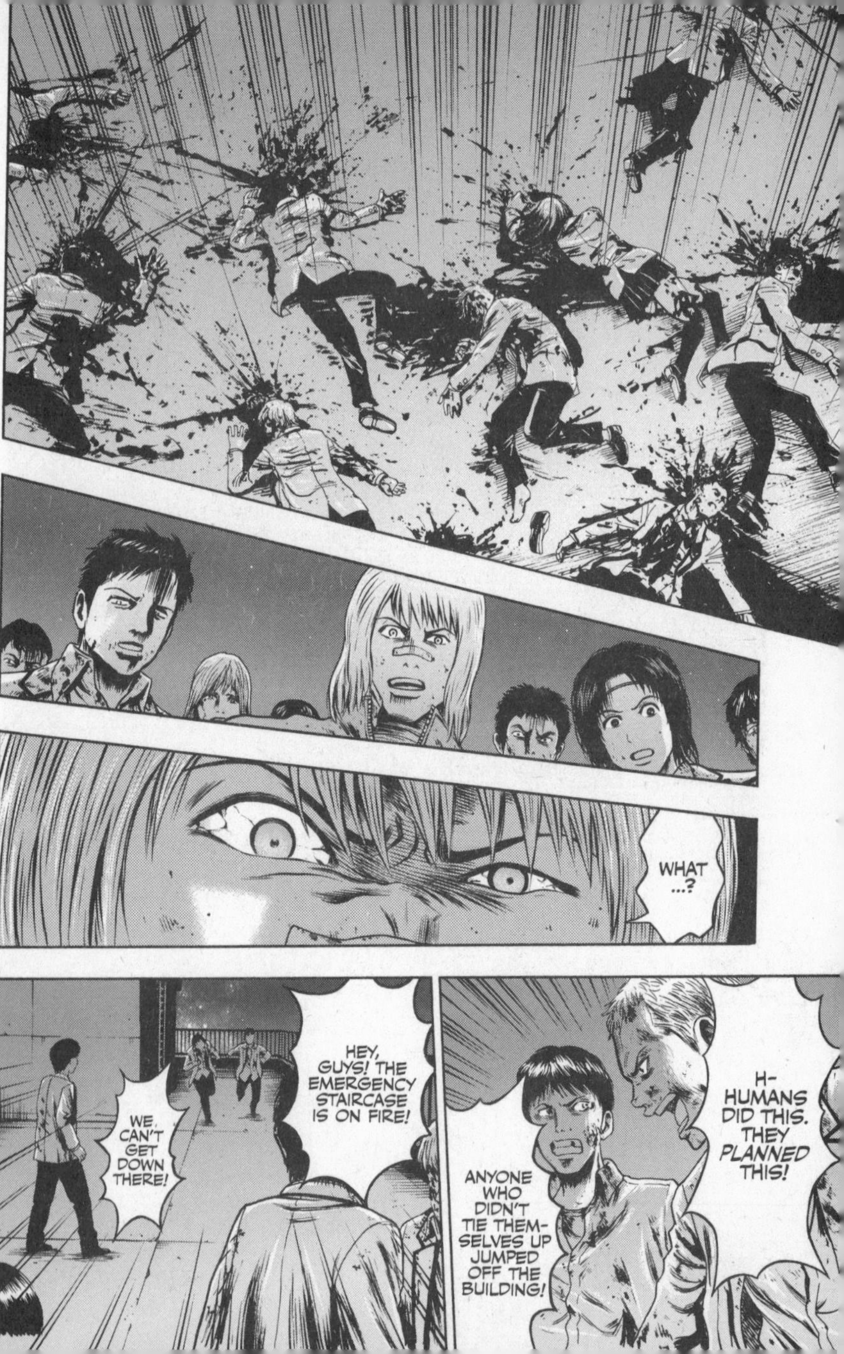
WHAT ...?
H-HUMANS DID THIS. THEY *PLANNED* THIS!
ANYONE WHO DIDN'T TIE THEM-SELVES UP JUMPED OFF THE BUILDING!
HEY, GUYS! THE EMERGENCY STAIRCASE IS ON FIRE!
WE CAN'T GET DOWN THERE!

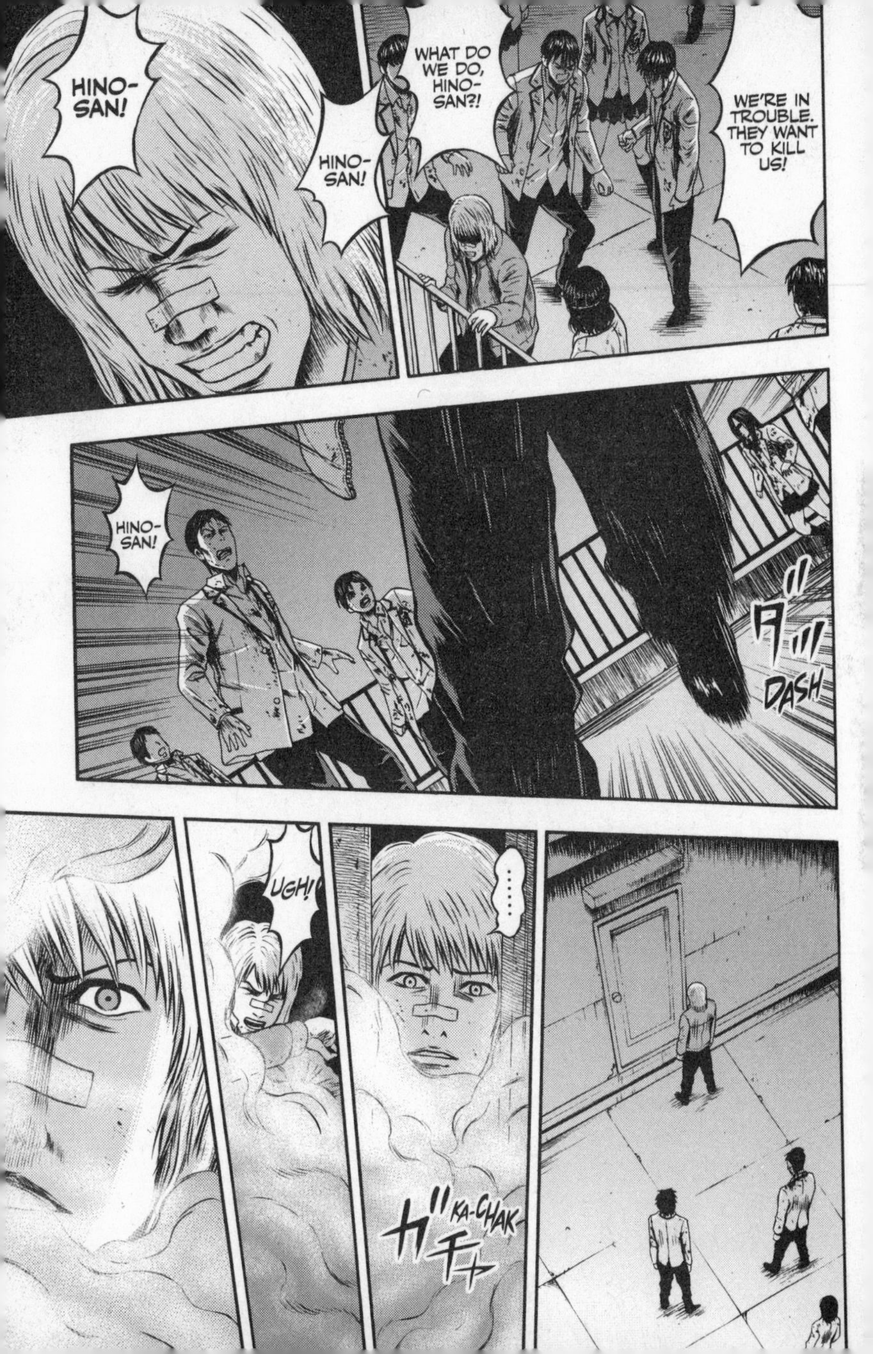
WE'RE IN TROUBLE. THEY WANT TO KILL US!
WHAT DO WE DO, HINO-SAN?!
HINO-SAN!
HINO-SAN!
DASH
HINO-SAN!
......
KA-CHAK
UGH!

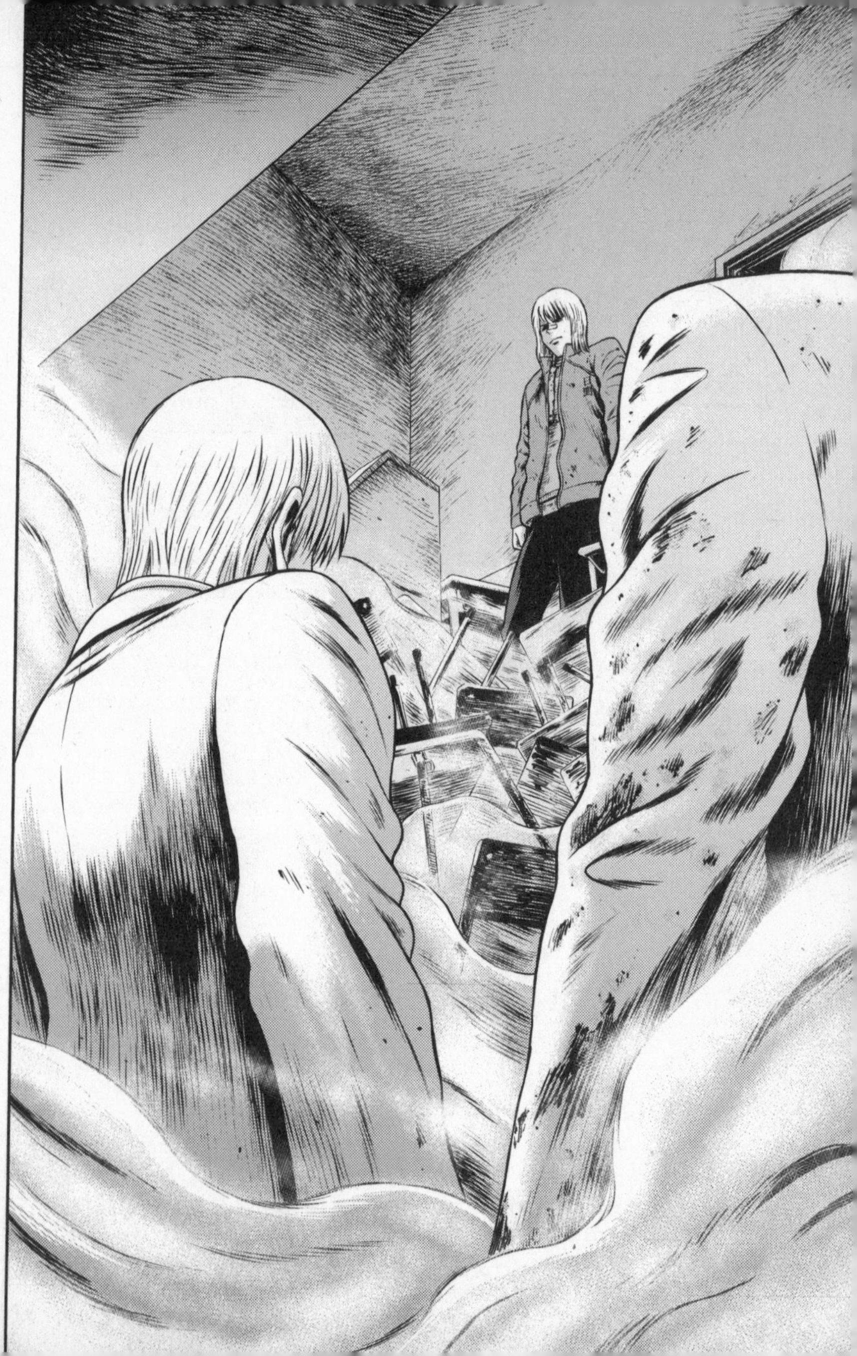

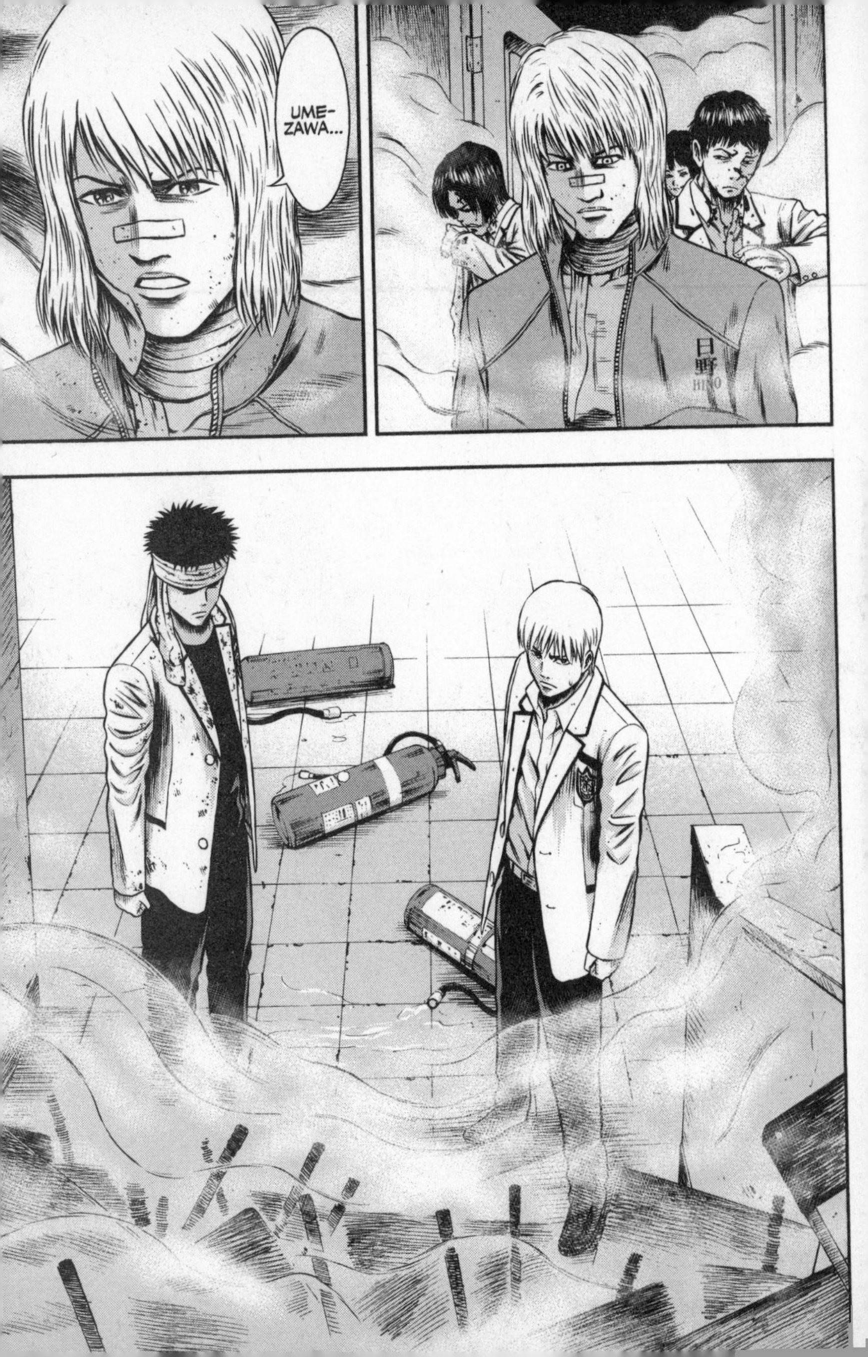
日野
HINO
UME-ZAWA...

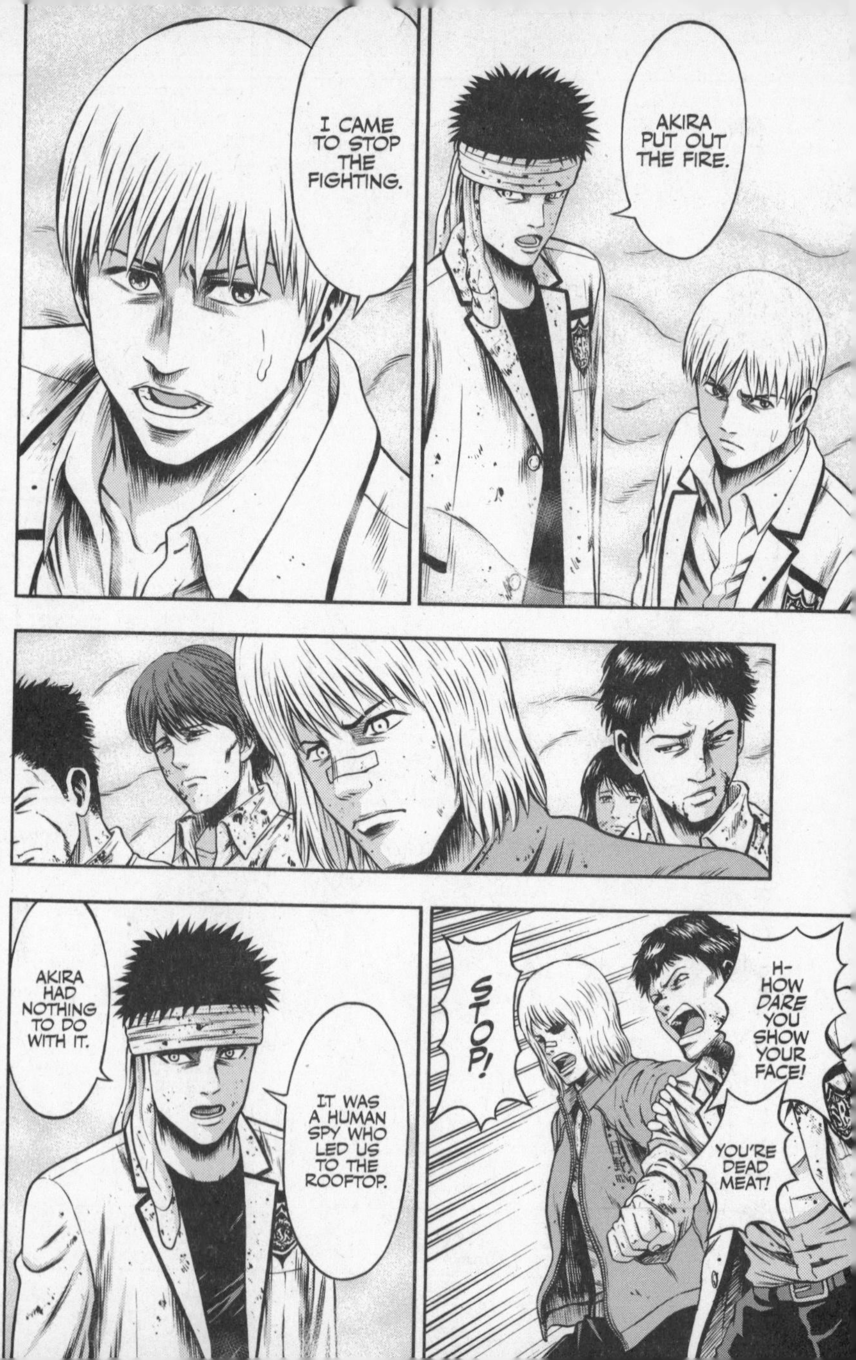
AKIRA PUT OUT THE FIRE.
I CAME TO STOP THE FIGHTING.
H- HOW DARE YOU SHOW YOUR FACE!
STOP!
YOU'RE DEAD MEAT!
AKIRA HAD NOTHING TO DO WITH IT.
IT WAS A HUMAN SPY WHO LED US TO THE ROOFTOP.

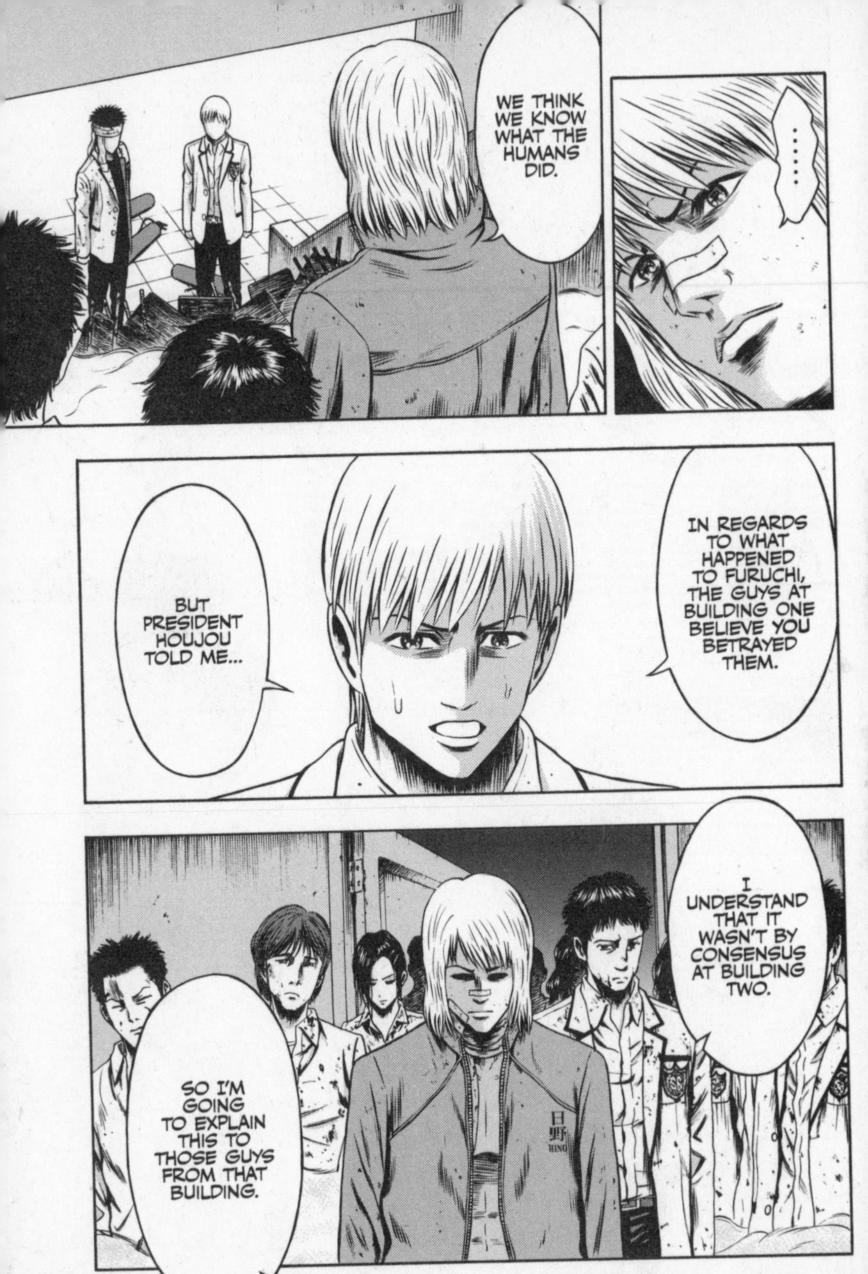
......
WE THINK WE KNOW WHAT THE HUMANS DID.
IN REGARDS TO WHAT HAPPENED TO FURUCHI, THE GUYS AT BUILDING ONE BELIEVE YOU BETRAYED THEM.
BUT PRESIDENT HOUJOU TOLD ME...
I UNDERSTAND THAT IT WASN'T BY CONSENSUS AT BUILDING TWO.
SO I'M GOING TO EXPLAIN THIS TO THOSE GUYS FROM THAT BUILDING.

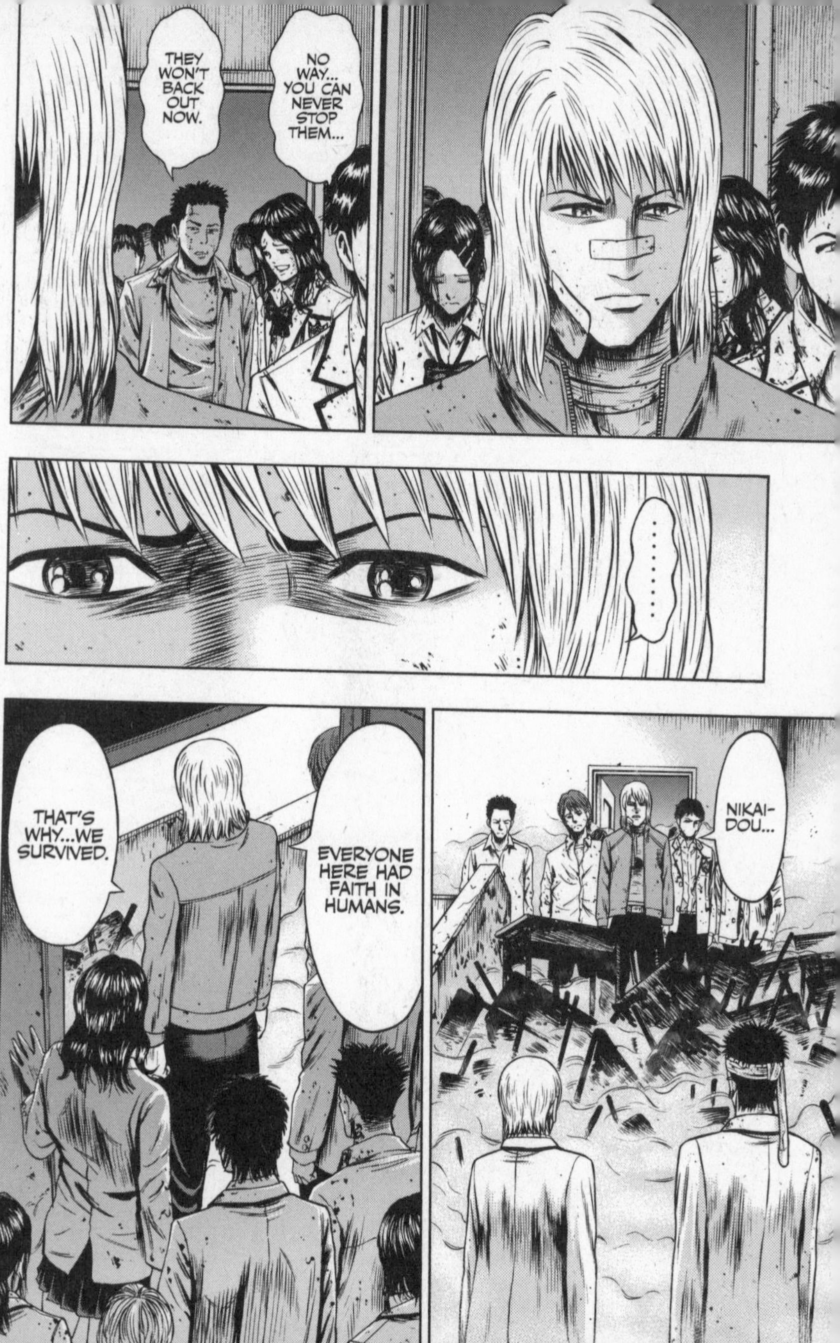
NO WAY... YOU CAN NEVER STOP THEM...
THEY WON'T BACK OUT NOW.
......
NIKAI-DOU...
EVERYONE HERE HAD FAITH IN HUMANS.
THAT'S WHY...WE SURVIVED.

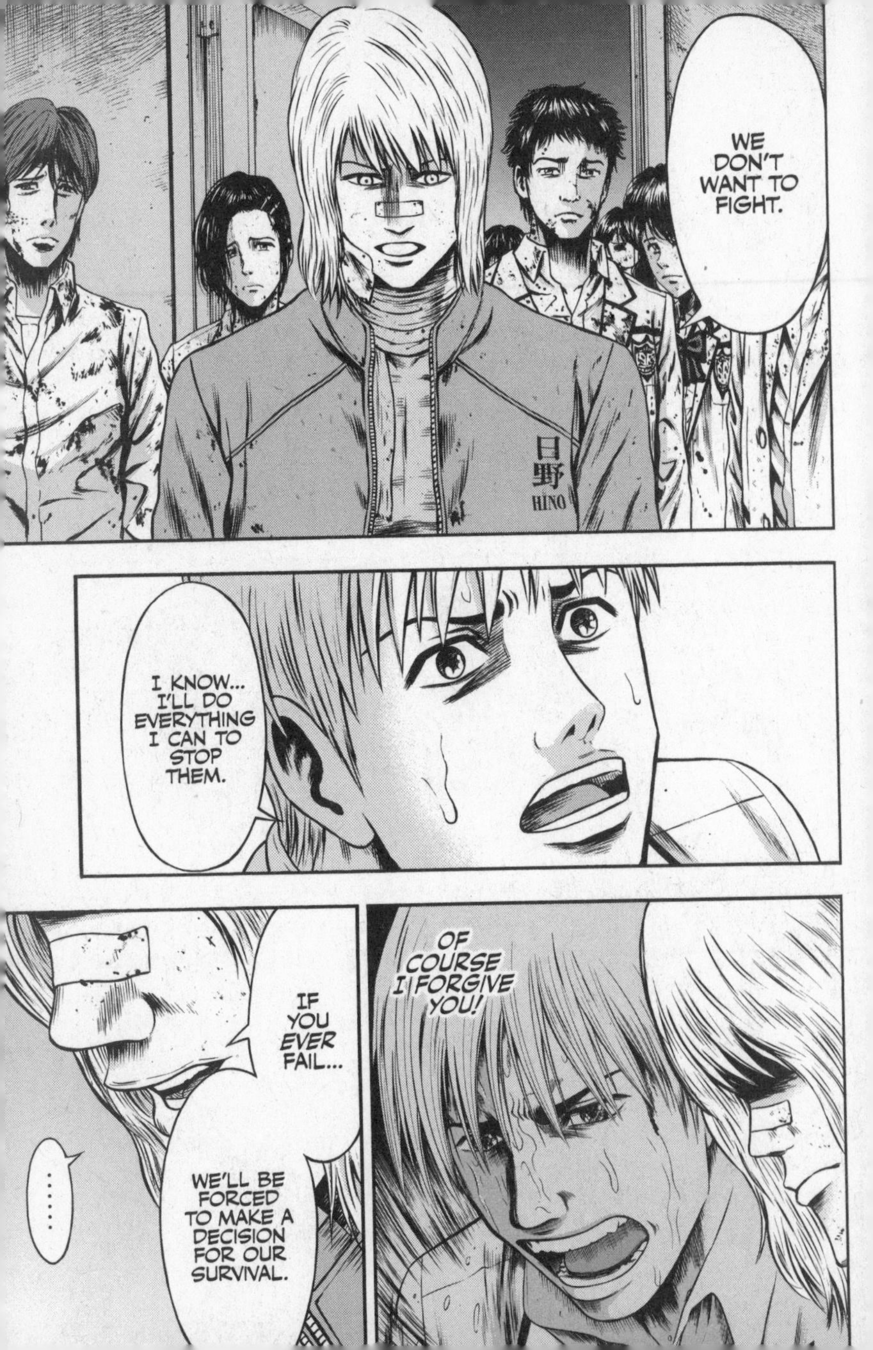
WE DON'T WANT TO FIGHT.
日野
HINO
I KNOW... I'LL DO EVERYTHING I CAN TO STOP THEM.
OF COURSE I FORGIVE YOU!
IF YOU EVER FAIL...
WE'LL BE FORCED TO MAKE A DECISION FOR OUR SURVIVAL.
......

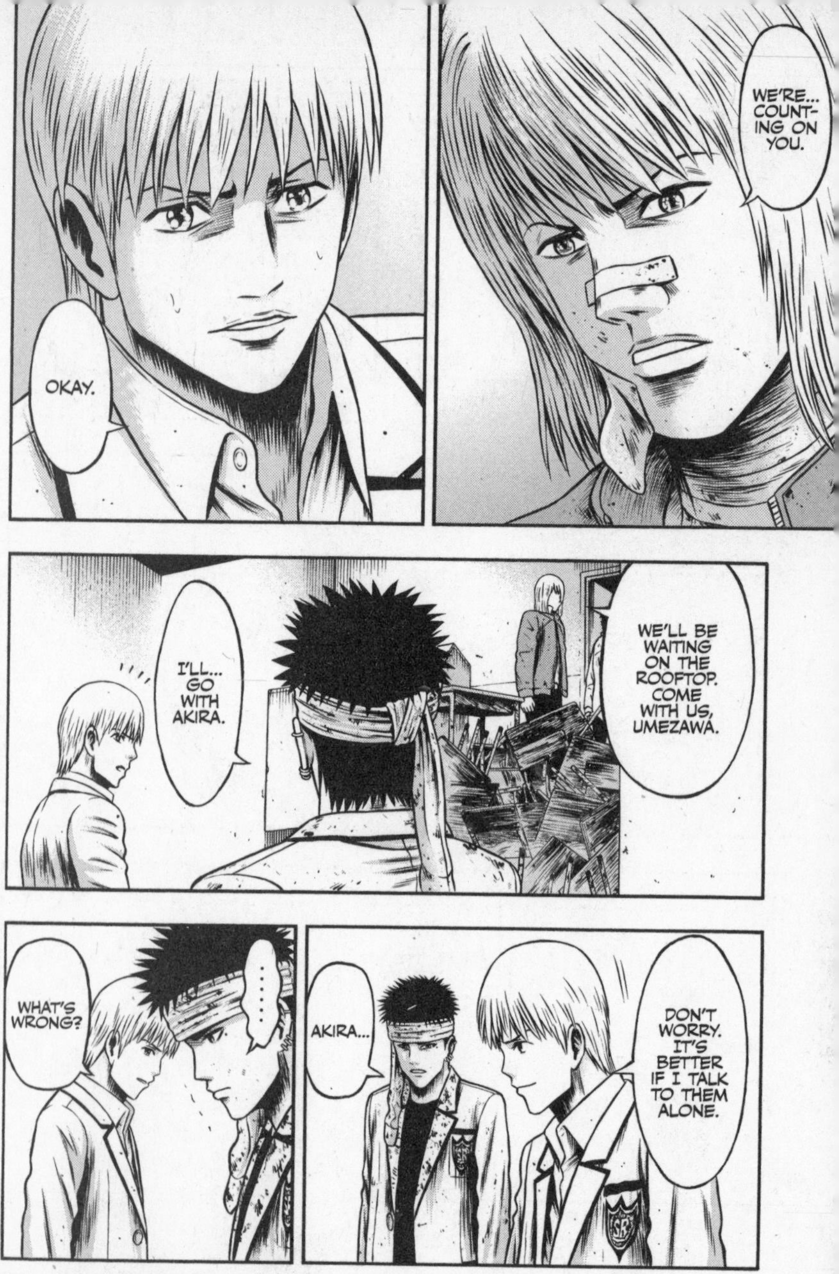
WE'RE... COUNT-ING ON YOU.
OKAY.
WE'LL BE WAITING ON THE ROOFTOP. COME WITH US, UMEZAWA.
I'LL... GO WITH AKIRA.
DON'T WORRY. IT'S BETTER IF I TALK TO THEM ALONE.
AKIRA...
......
WHAT'S WRONG?

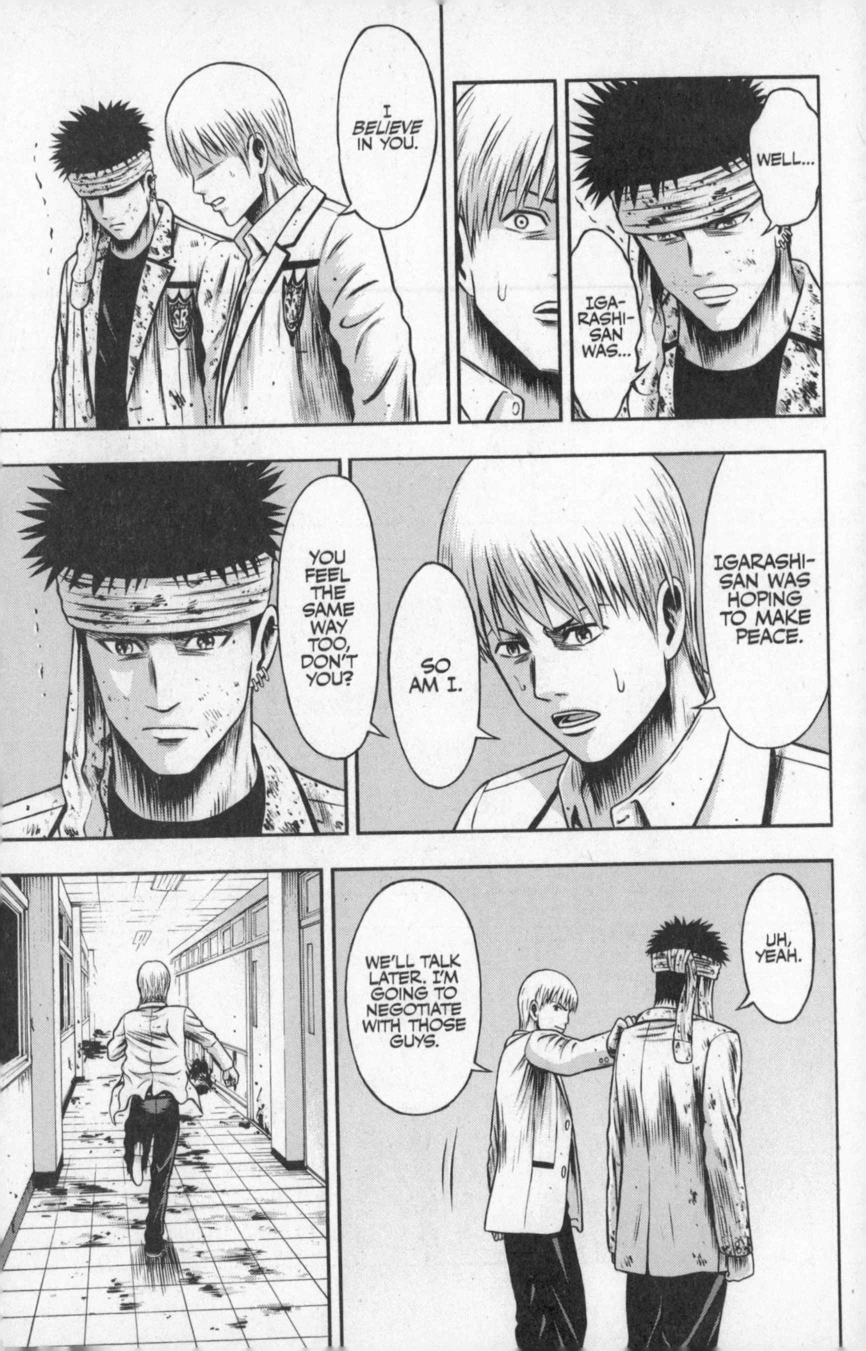
WELL...
IGARASHI-SAN WAS...
I BELIEVE IN YOU.
IGARASHI-SAN WAS HOPING TO MAKE PEACE.
SO AM I.
YOU FEEL THE SAME WAY TOO, DON'T YOU?
UH, YEAH.
WE'LL TALK LATER. I'M GOING TO NEGOTIATE WITH THOSE GUYS.

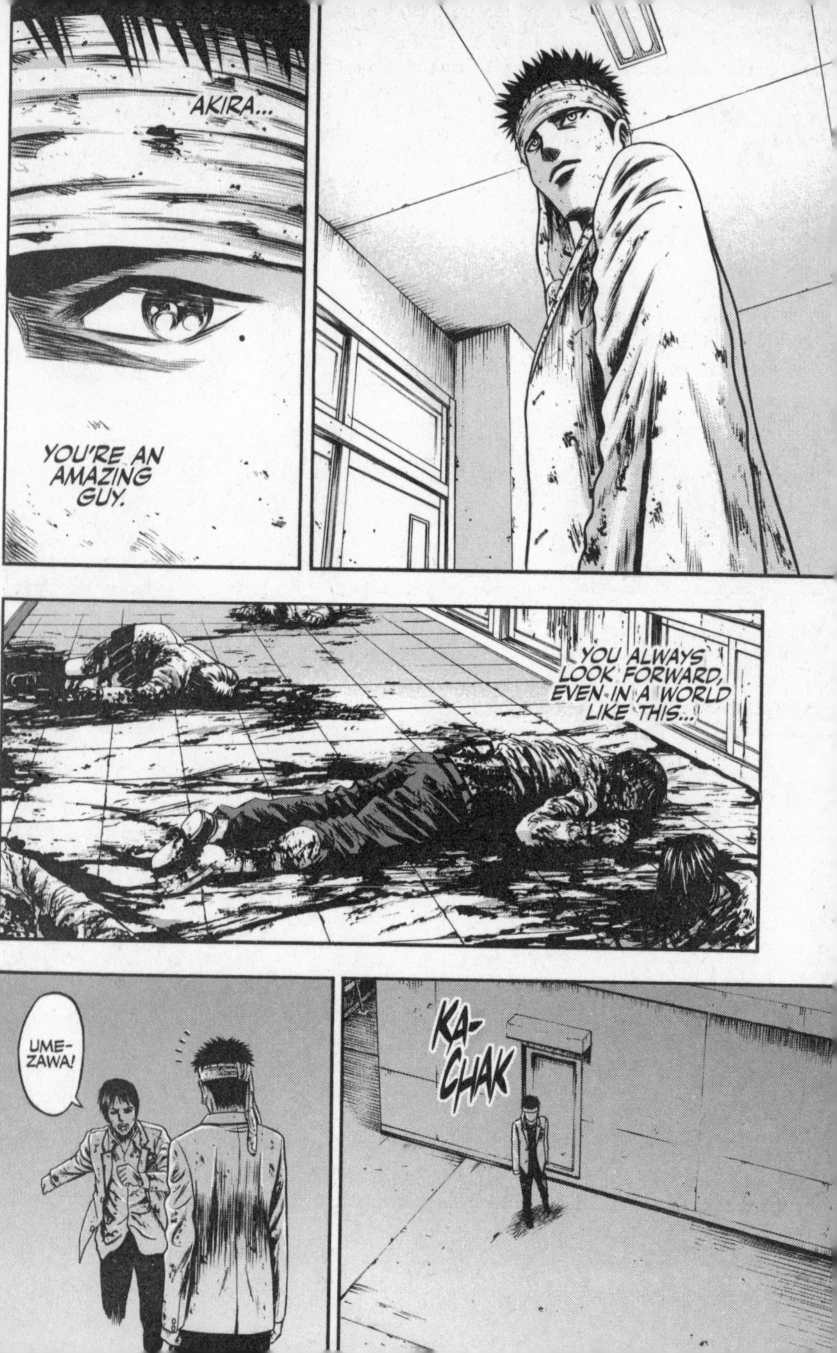
AKIRA...
YOU'RE AN AMAZING GUY.
YOU ALWAYS LOOK FORWARD, EVEN IN A WORLD LIKE THIS...
KA-CHAK
UME-ZAWA!

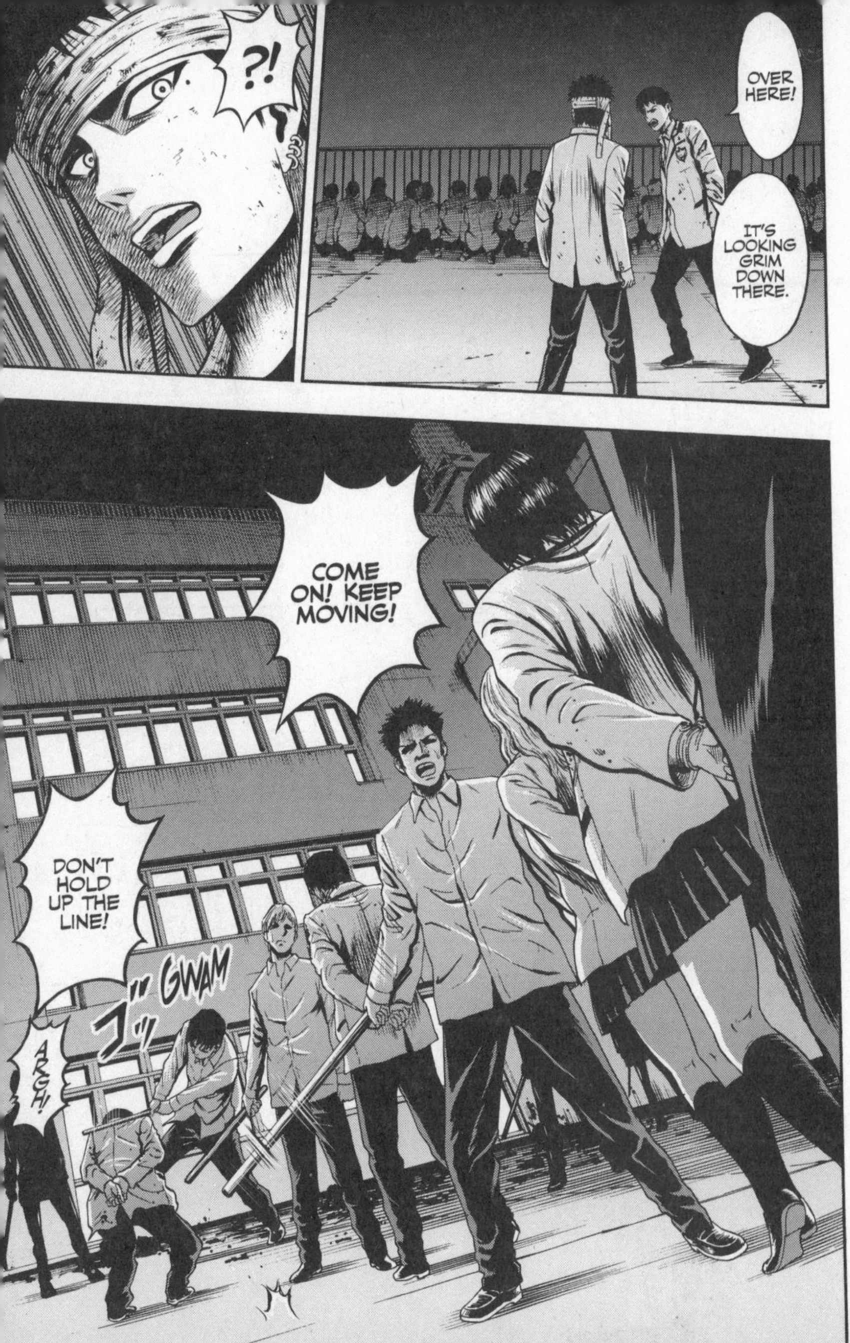
OVER HERE!
IT'S LOOKING GRIM DOWN THERE.
?!
COME ON! KEEP MOVING!
DON'T HOLD UP THE LINE!
GWAM
ARGH!

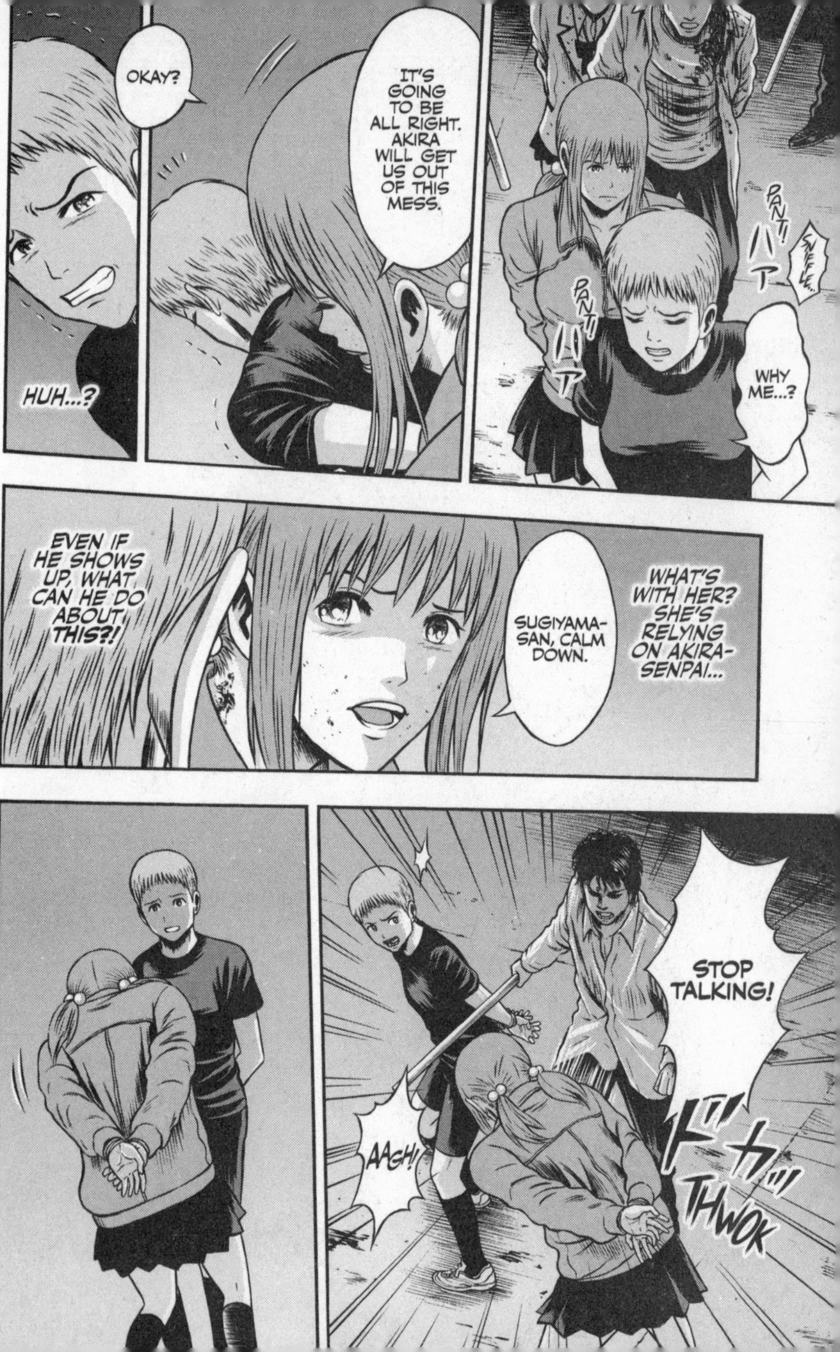
SNIFFLE...
PANT!
PANT!
WHY ME...?
IT'S GOING TO BE ALL RIGHT. AKIRA WILL GET US OUT OF THIS MESS.
OKAY?
HUH...?
WHAT'S WITH HER? SHE'S RELYING ON AKIRA-SENPAI...
SUGIYAMA-SAN, CALM DOWN.
EVEN IF HE SHOWS UP, WHAT CAN HE DO ABOUT THIS?!
STOP TALKING!
THWOK
AAGH!

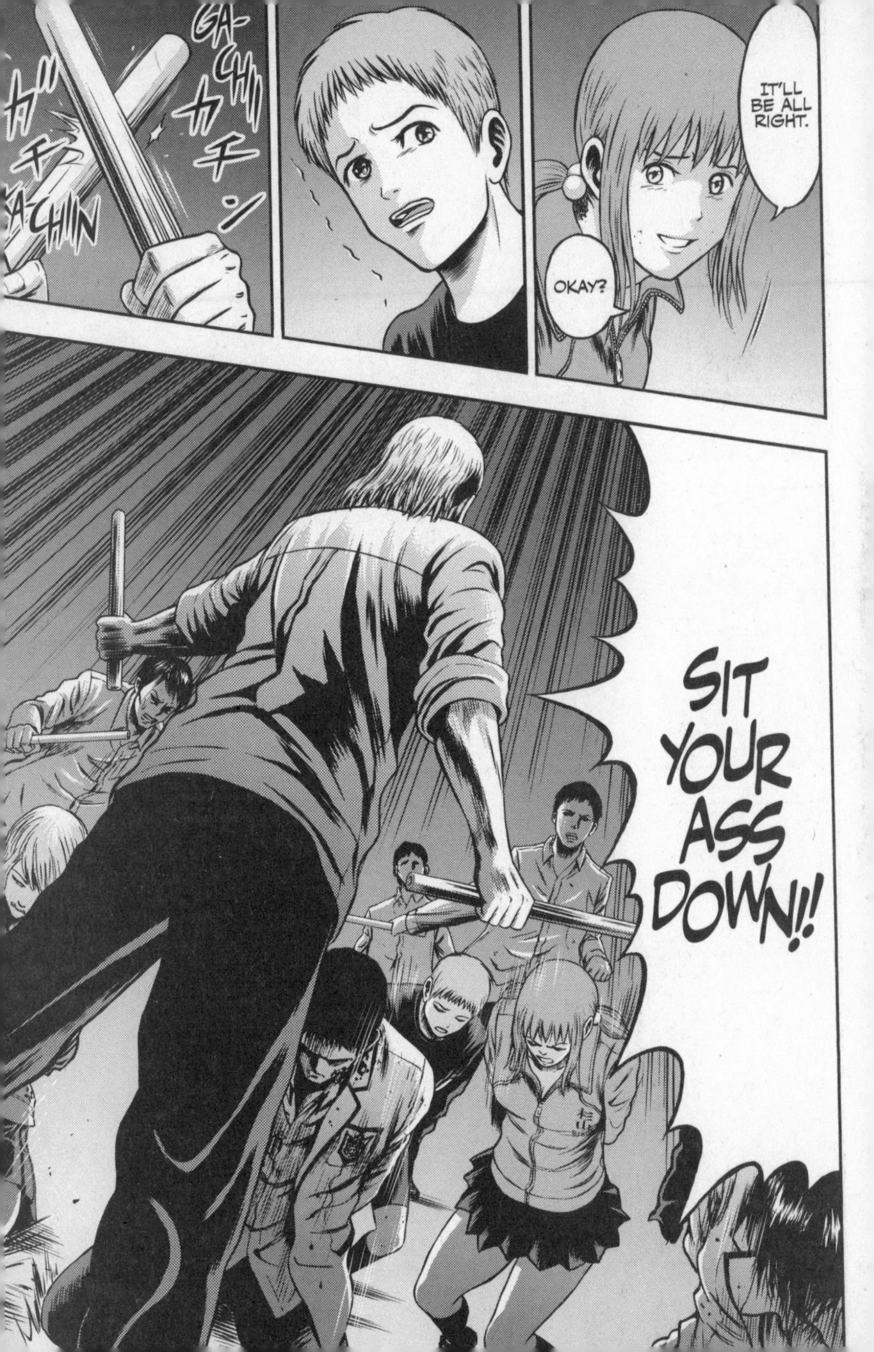
IT'LL BE ALL RIGHT.
OKAY?
GA-CHIIN
カチーン
ガチ
A-CHIN
SIT YOUR ASS DOWN!!

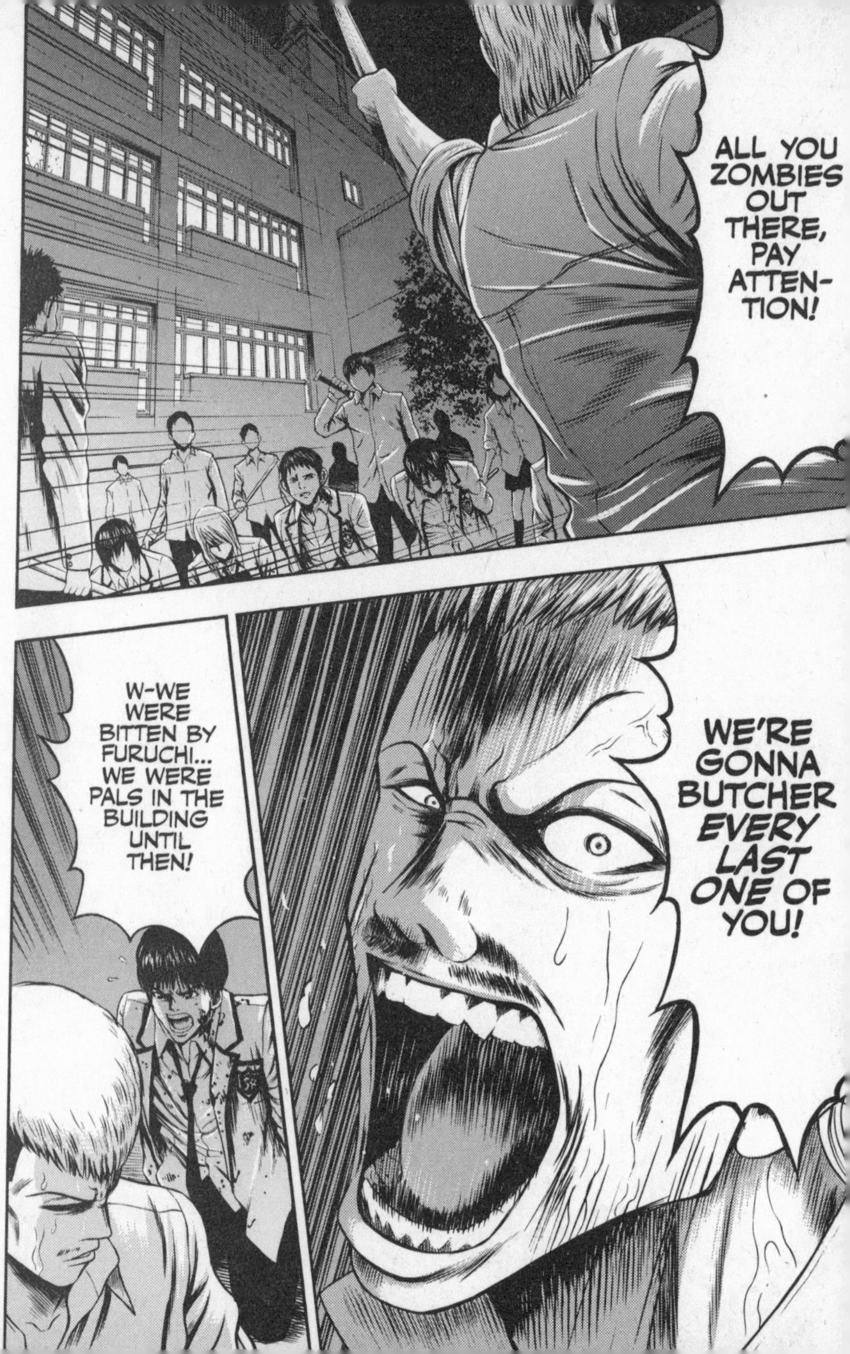
ALL YOU ZOMBIES OUT THERE, PAY ATTENTION!
WE'RE GONNA BUTCHER *EVERY LAST ONE* OF YOU!
W-WE WERE BITTEN BY FURUCHI... WE WERE PALS IN THE BUILDING UNTIL THEN!

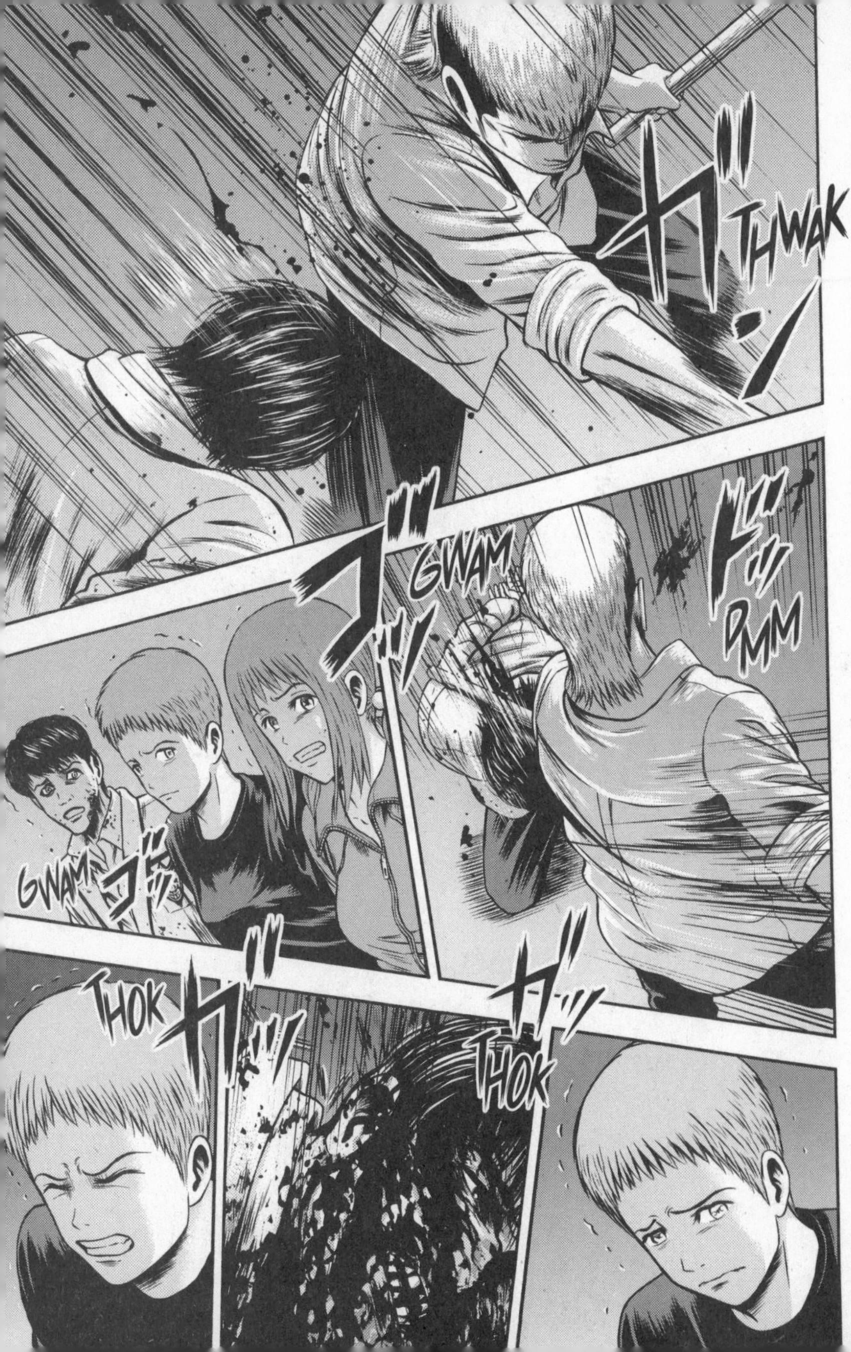
ガッ
THWAK
ドッ
DMM
ゴッ
GWAM
ゴッ
GWAM
ガッ
THOK
ガッ
THOK

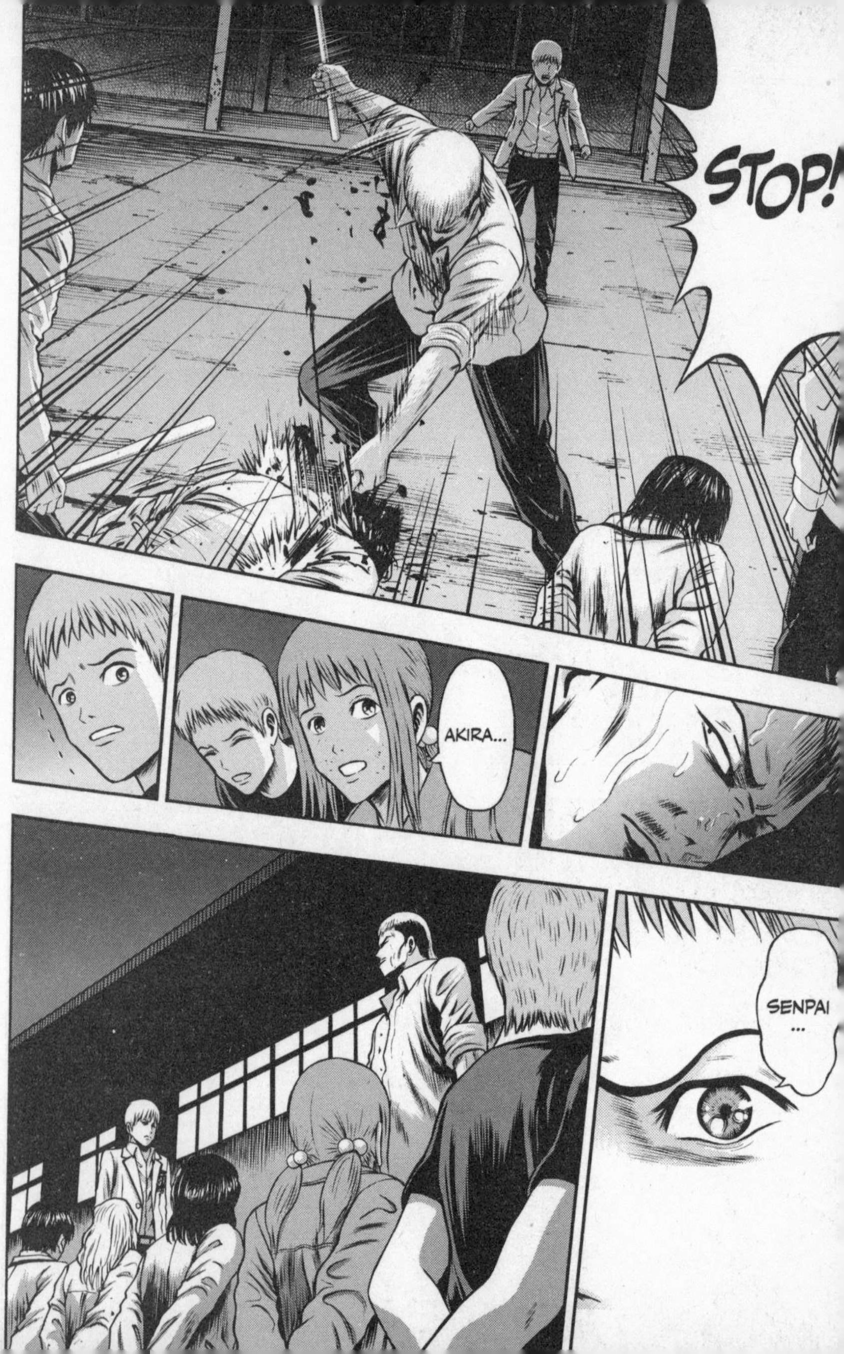
STOP!
AKIRA...
SENPAI ...

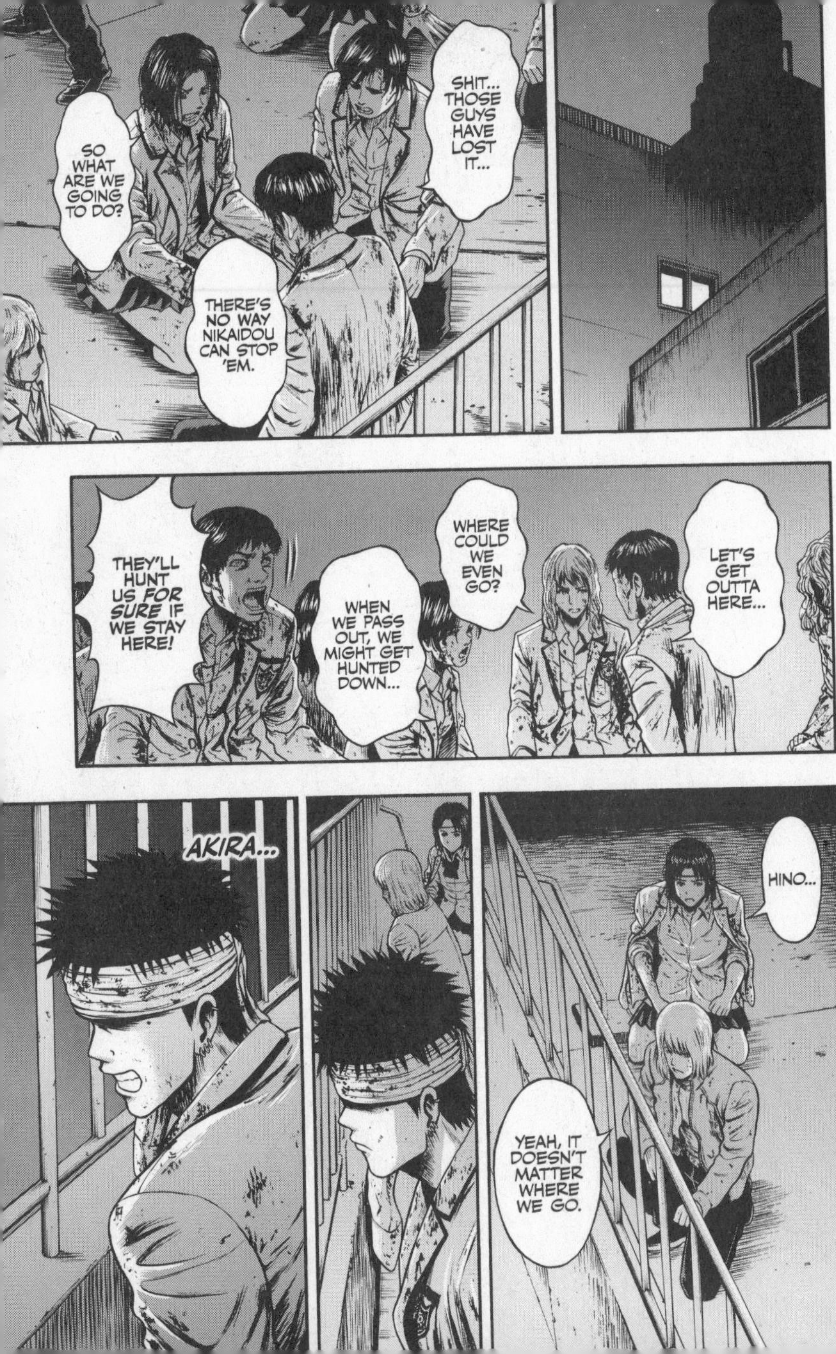
SHIT... THOSE GUYS HAVE LOST IT...
SO WHAT ARE WE GOING TO DO?
THERE'S NO WAY NIKAIDOU CAN STOP 'EM.
LET'S GET OUTTA HERE...
WHERE COULD WE EVEN GO?
WHEN WE PASS OUT, WE MIGHT GET HUNTED DOWN...
THEY'LL HUNT US *FOR SURE* IF WE STAY HERE!
HINO...
YEAH, IT DOESN'T MATTER WHERE WE GO.
AKIRA...

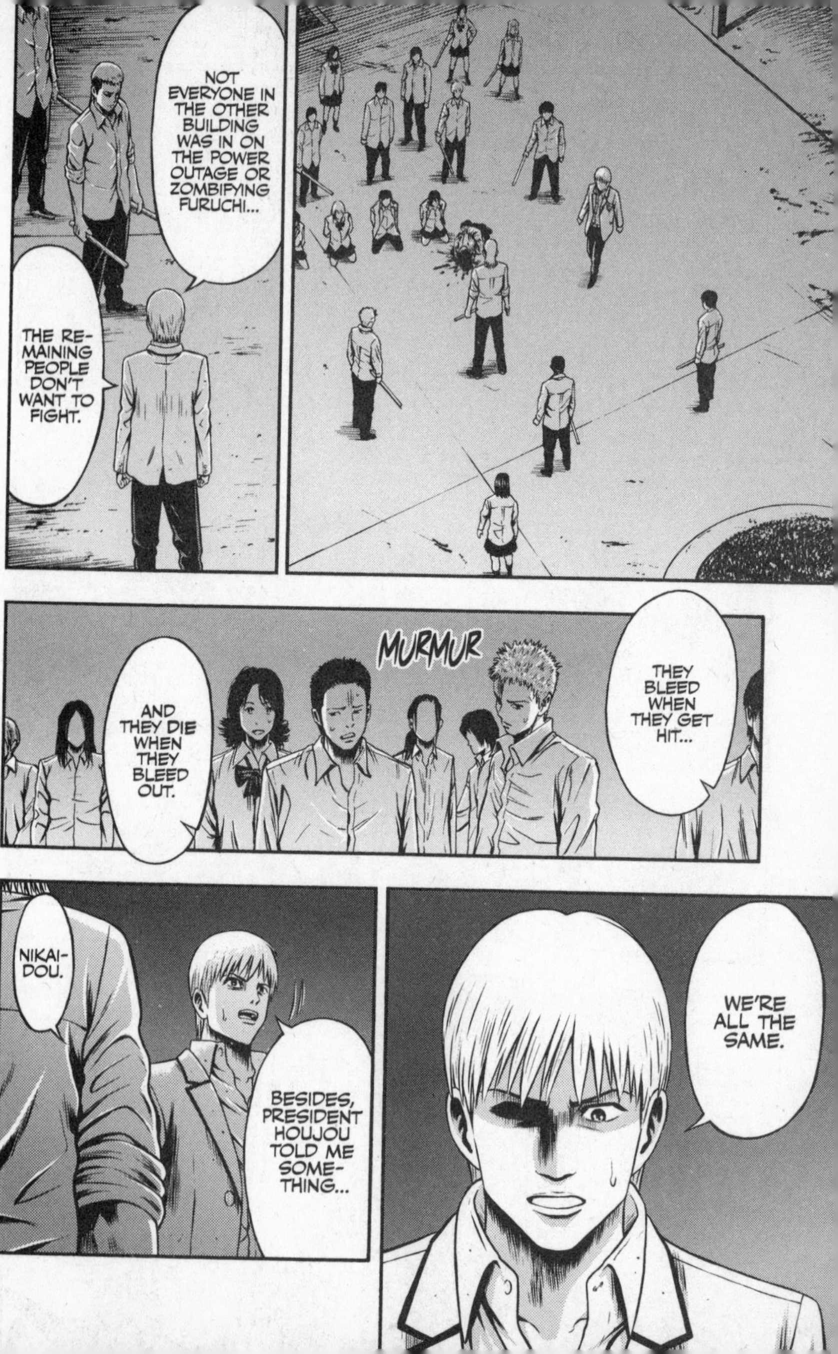
NOT EVERYONE IN THE OTHER BUILDING WAS IN ON THE POWER OUTAGE OR ZOMBIFYING FURUCHI...
THE RE-MAINING PEOPLE DON'T WANT TO FIGHT.
THEY BLEED WHEN THEY GET HIT...
MURMUR
AND THEY DIE WHEN THEY BLEED OUT.
WE'RE ALL THE SAME.
NIKAI-DOU.
BESIDES, PRESIDENT HOUJOU TOLD ME SOME-THING...

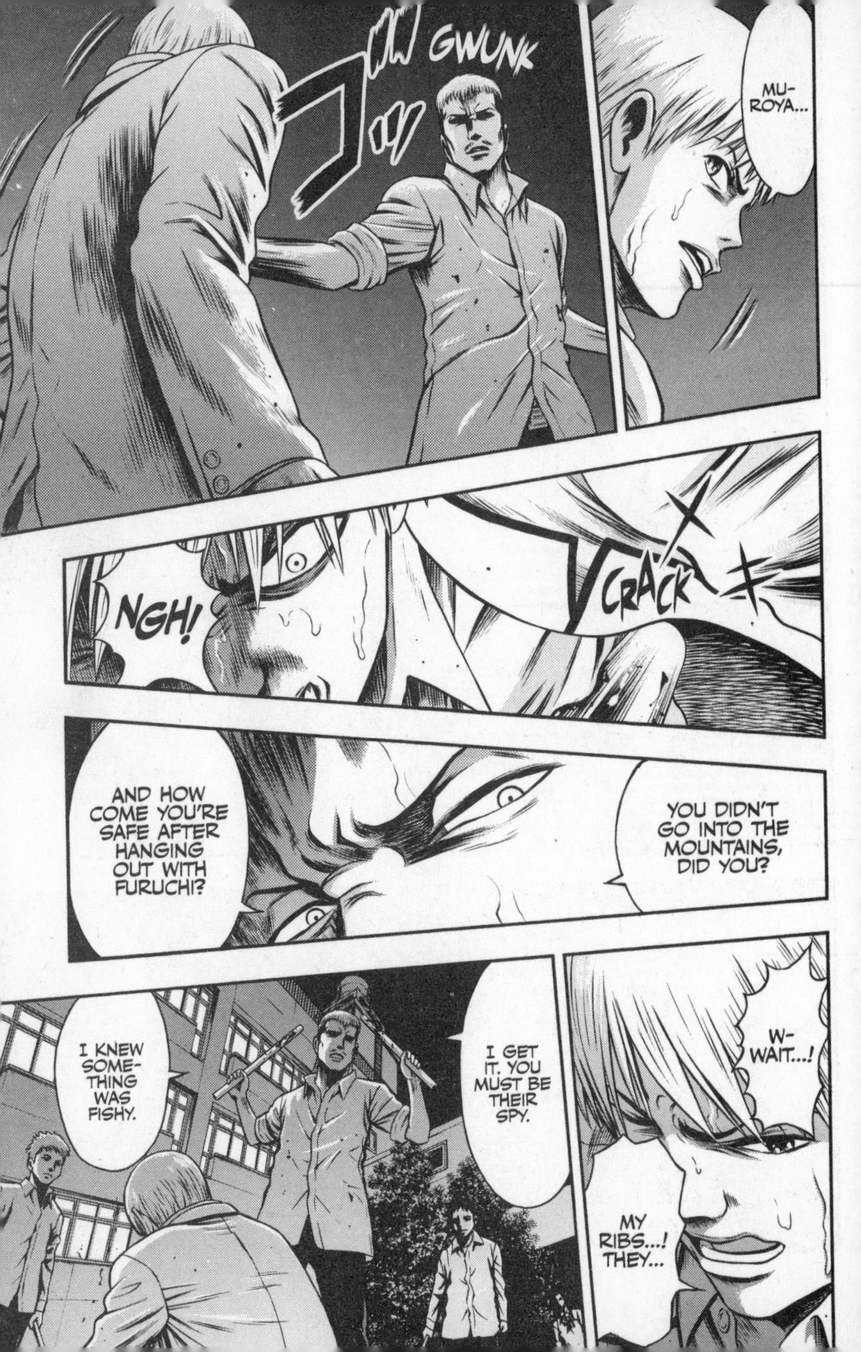
MU-ROYA...
GWUNK
CRACK
NGH!
YOU DIDN'T GO INTO THE MOUNTAINS, DID YOU?
AND HOW COME YOU'RE SAFE AFTER HANGING OUT WITH FURUCHI?
W-WAIT...!
MY RIBS...! THEY...
I GET IT. YOU MUST BE THEIR SPY.
I KNEW SOME-THING WAS FISHY.

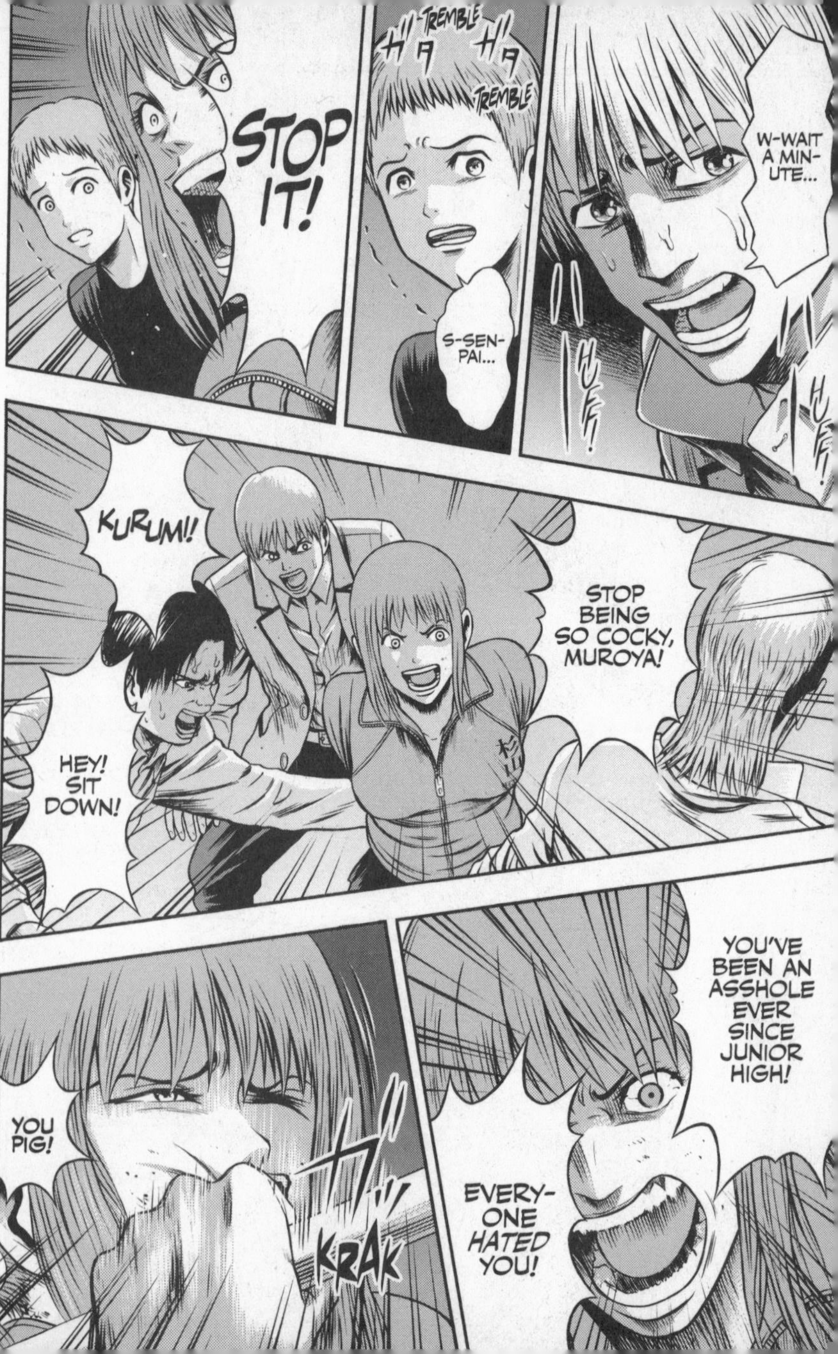
W-WAIT A MIN-UTE...
HUFF!
HUFF!
TREMBLE
TREMBLE
S-SEN-PAI...
STOP IT!
STOP BEING SO COCKY, MUROYA!
KURUMI!!
HEY! SIT DOWN!
YOU'VE BEEN AN ASSHOLE EVER SINCE JUNIOR HIGH!
EVERY-ONE HATED YOU!
YOU PIG!
KRAK

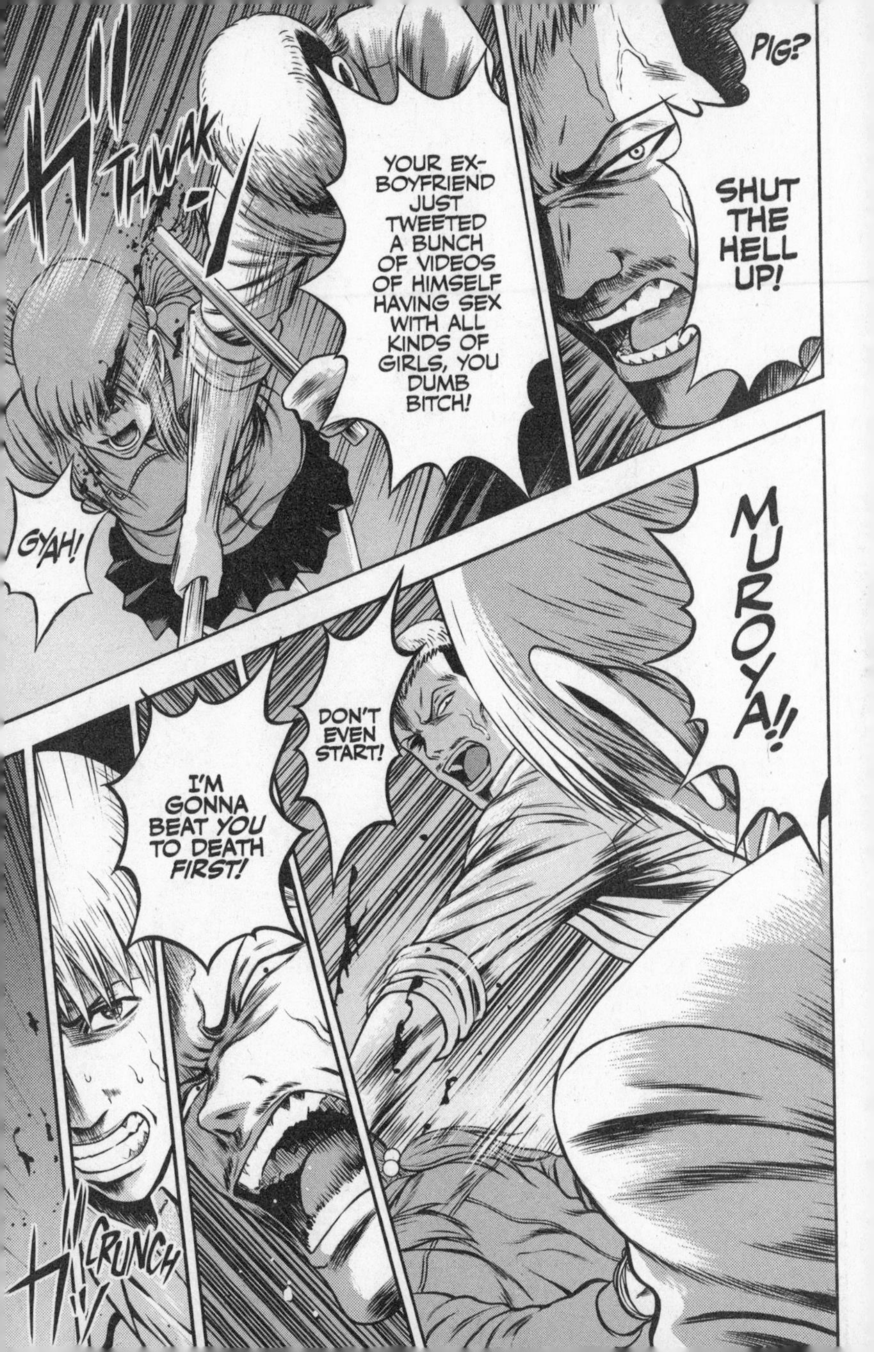
PIG?
SHUT THE HELL UP!
YOUR EX-BOYFRIEND JUST TWEETED A BUNCH OF VIDEOS OF HIMSELF HAVING SEX WITH ALL KINDS OF GIRLS, YOU DUMB BITCH!
THWAK
GYAH!
MUROYA!!
DON'T EVEN START!
I'M GONNA BEAT *YOU* TO DEATH *FIRST!*
CRUNCH

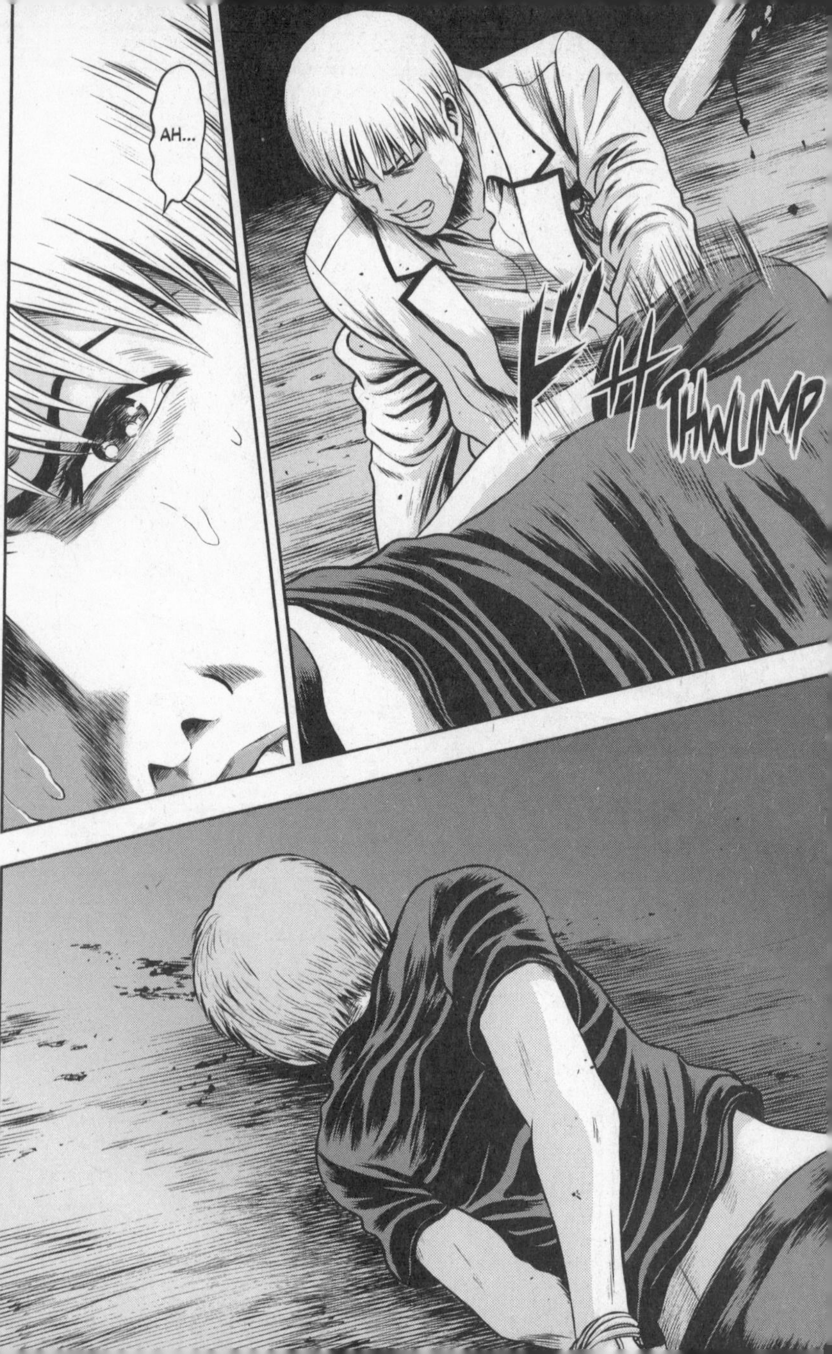
AH...
THWUMP

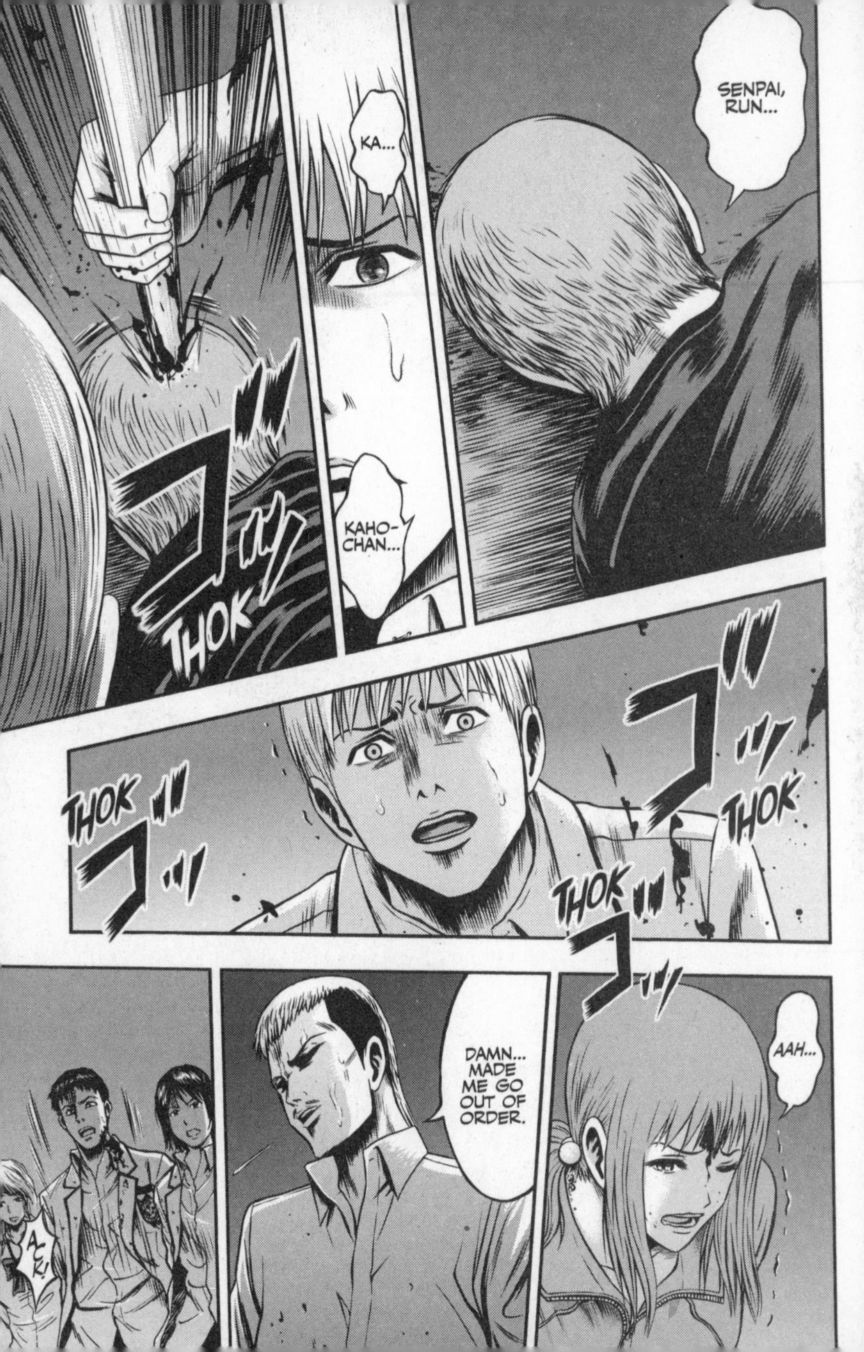
SENPAI, RUN...
KA...
KAHO-CHAN...
ゴッ
THOK
ゴッ
THOK
ゴッ
THOK
ゴッ
THOK
AAH...
DAMN... MADE ME GO OUT OF ORDER.
ACK!

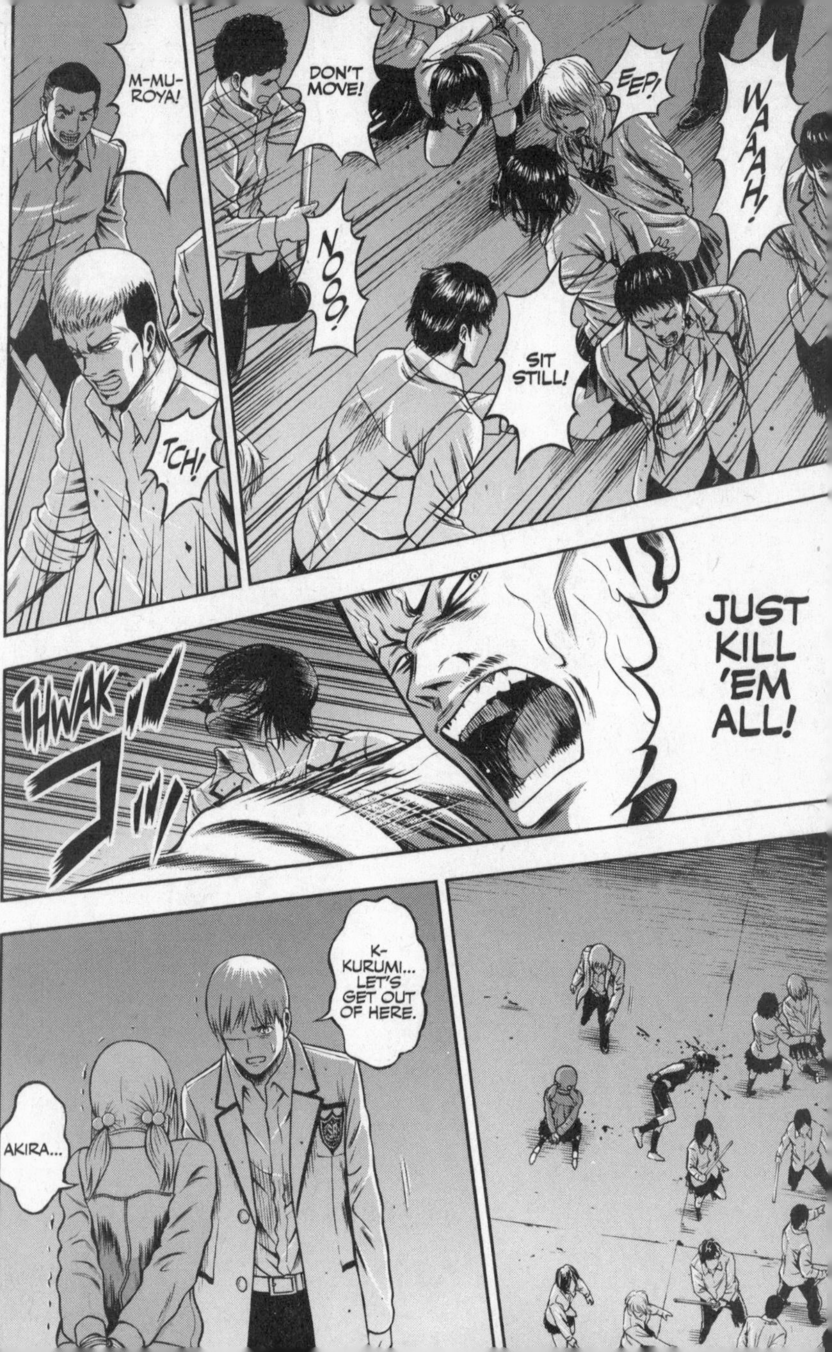
WAAAH!
EEP!
DON'T MOVE!
NOOO!
SIT STILL!
M-MU-ROYA!
TCH!
JUST KILL 'EM ALL!
THWAK
K-KURUMI... LET'S GET OUT OF HERE.
AKIRA...

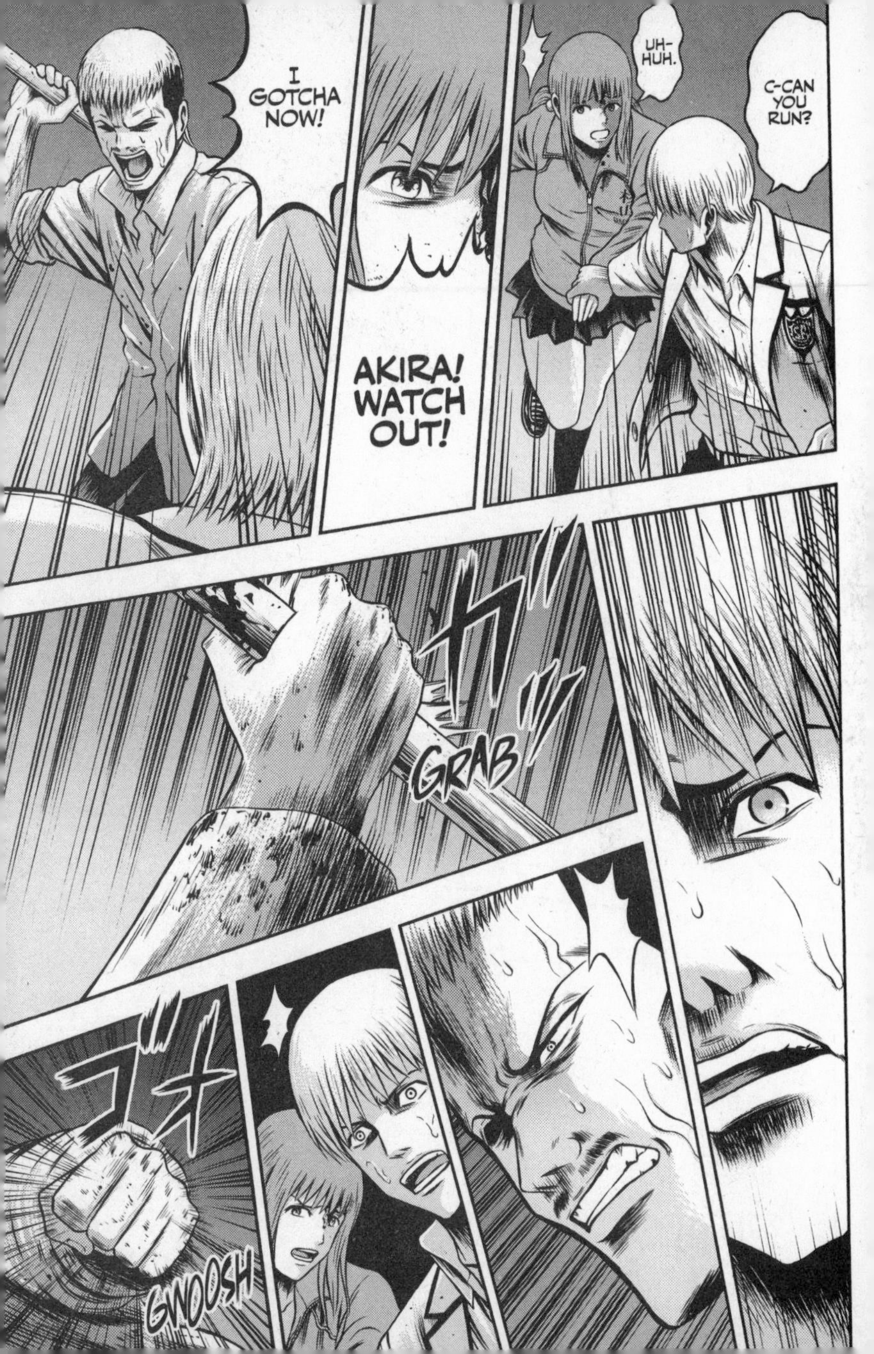
C-CAN YOU RUN?
UH-HUH.
AKIRA! WATCH OUT!
I GOTCHA NOW!
GRAB
GWOOSH

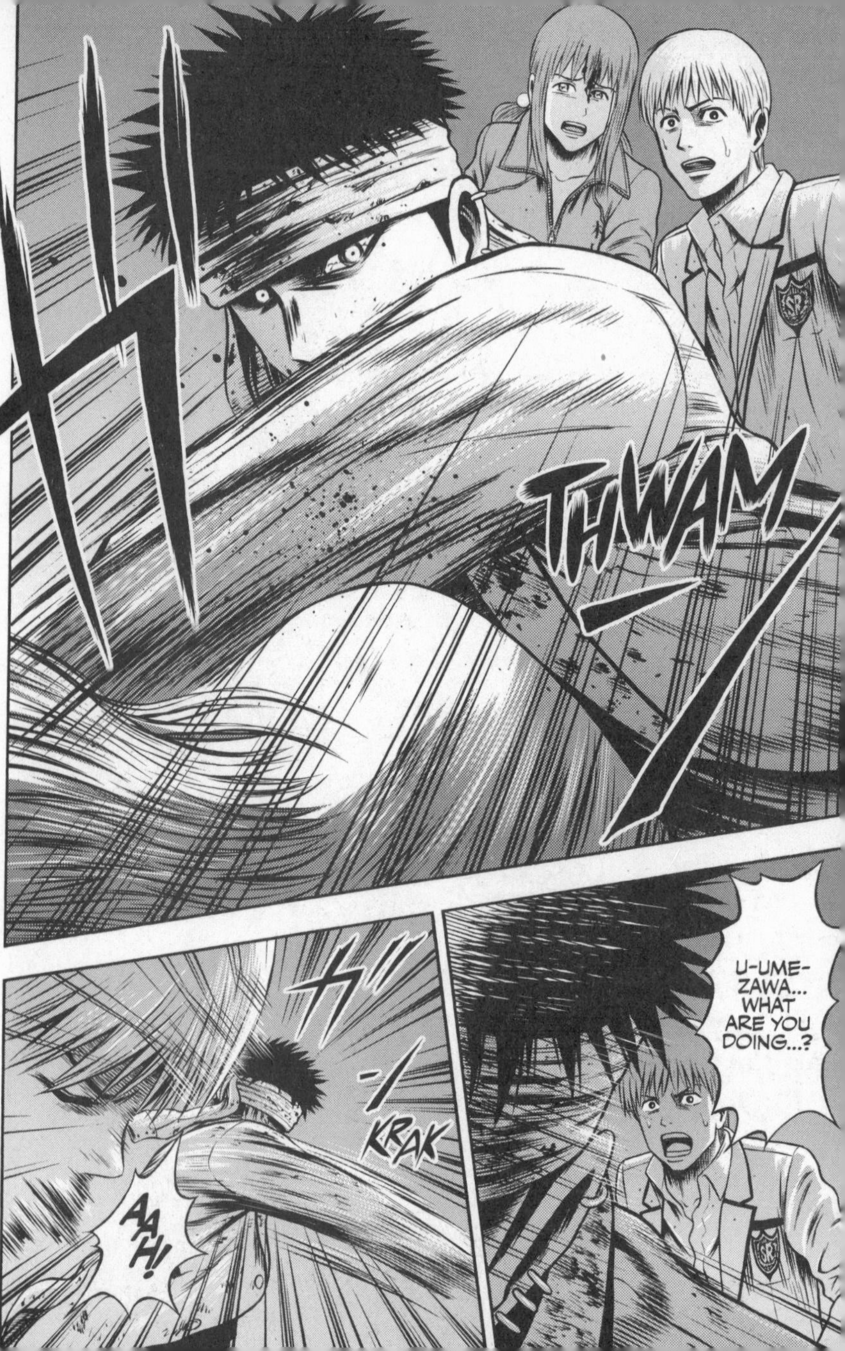
THWAM
U-UME-ZAWA... WHAT ARE YOU DOING...?
KRAK
AAH!

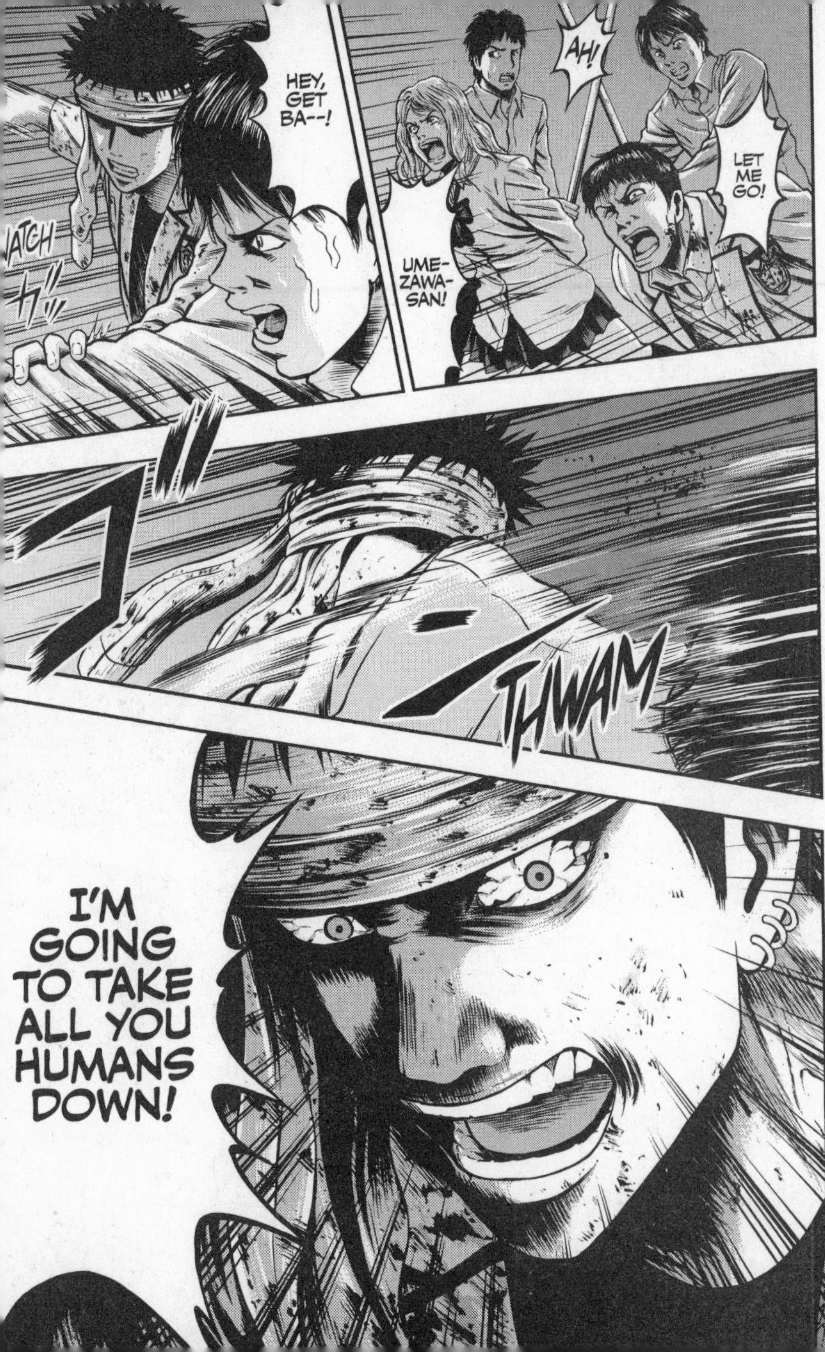
AH!
LET ME GO!
UME-ZAWA-SAN!
HEY, GET BA--!
ATCH
THWAM
I'M GOING TO TAKE ALL YOU HUMANS DOWN!

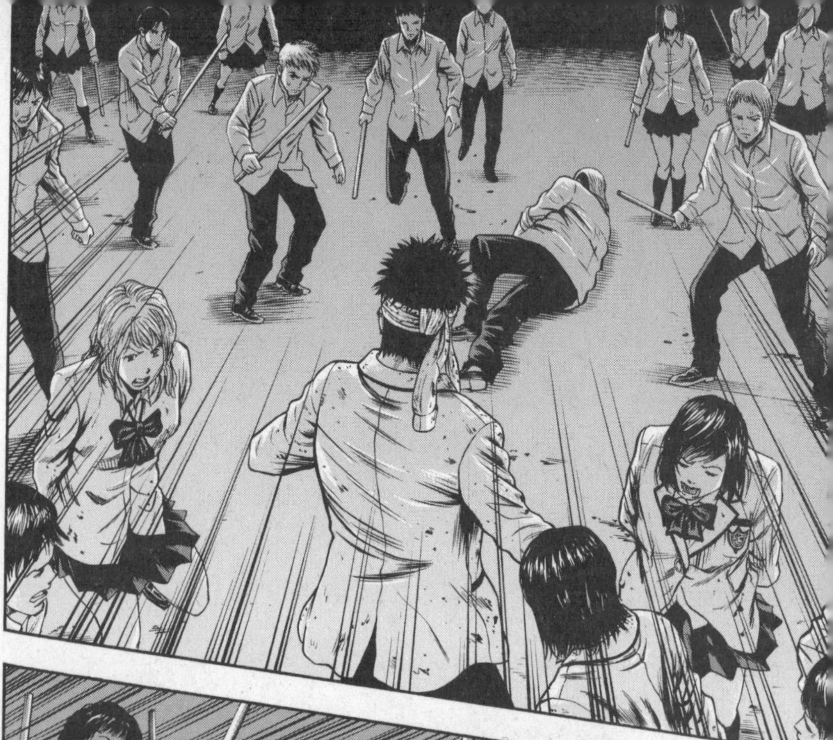
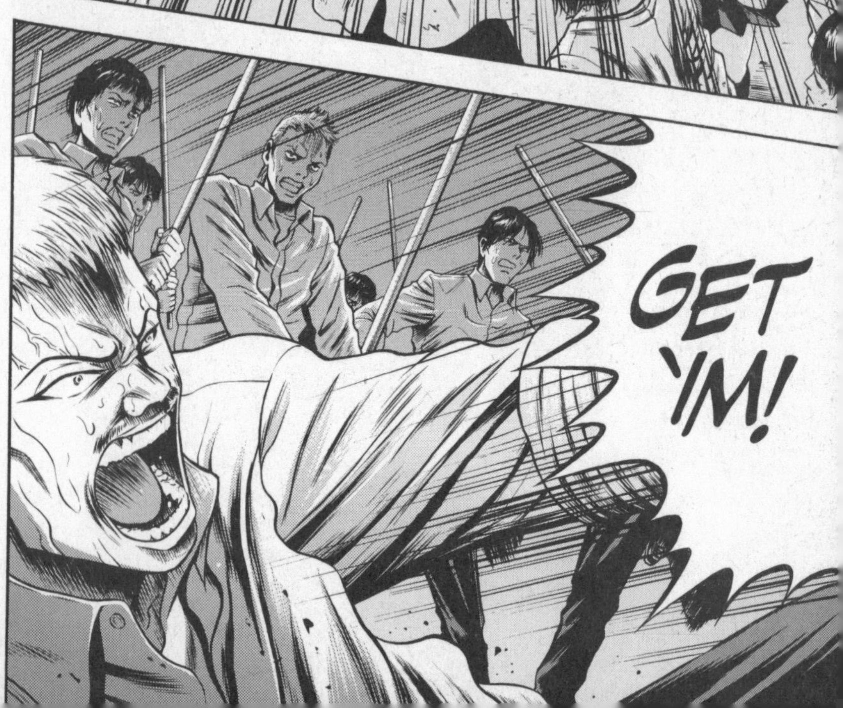
GET 'YM!

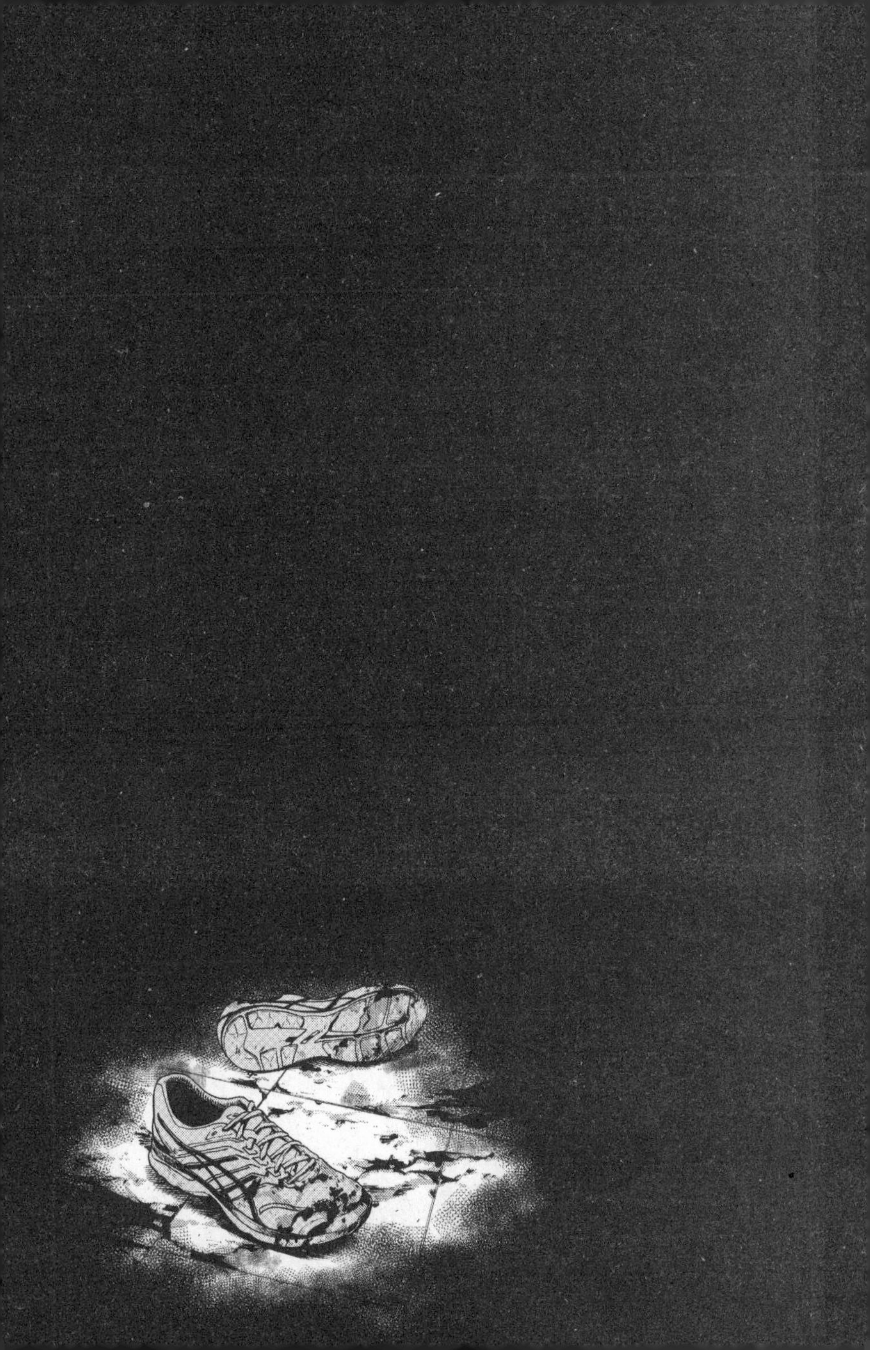

HOUR OF THE ZOMBIE

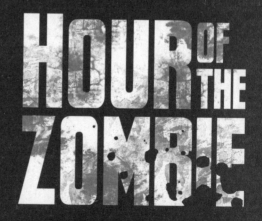

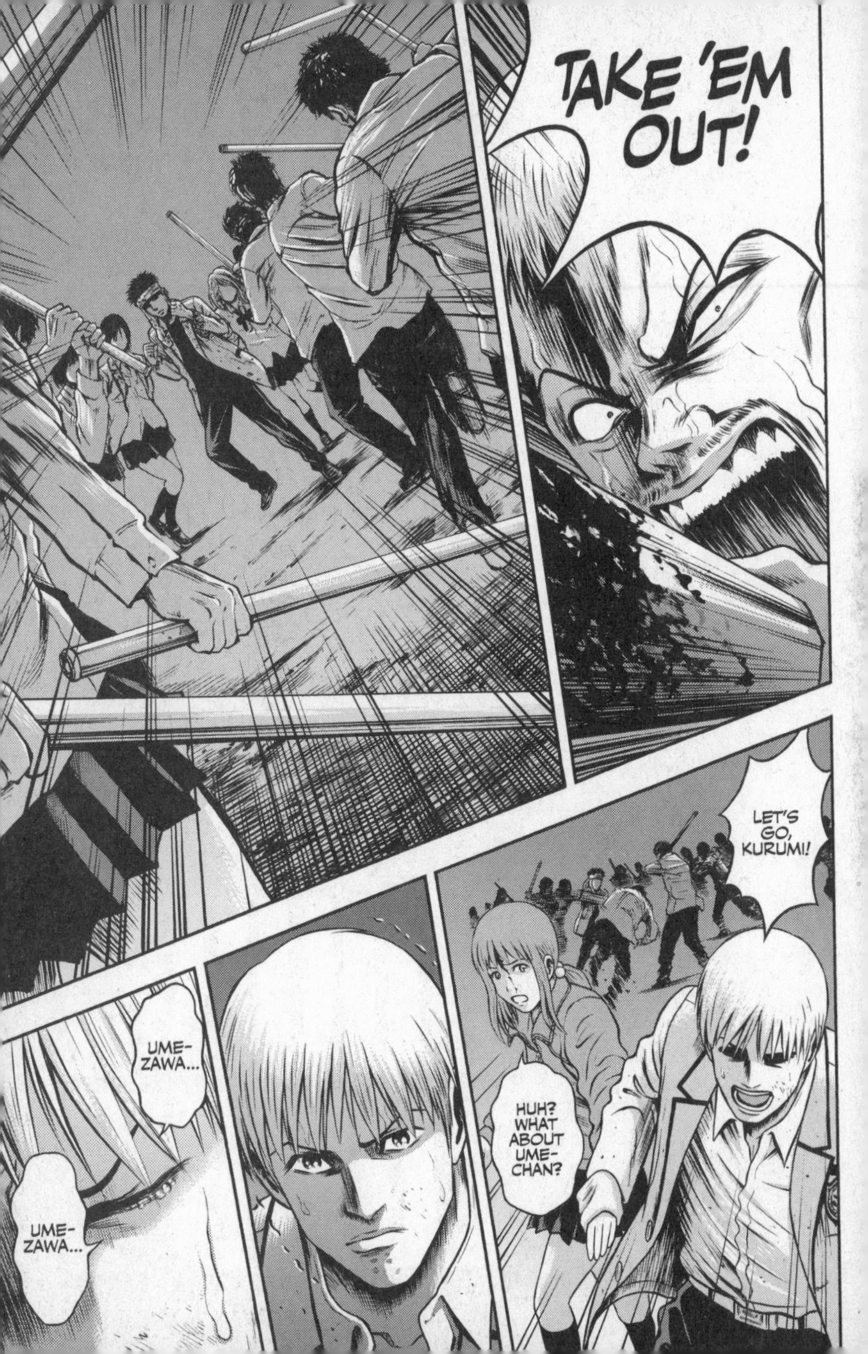
TAKE 'EM OUT!
LET'S GO, KURUMI!
HUH? WHAT ABOUT UME-CHAN?
UME-ZAWA...
UME-ZAWA...

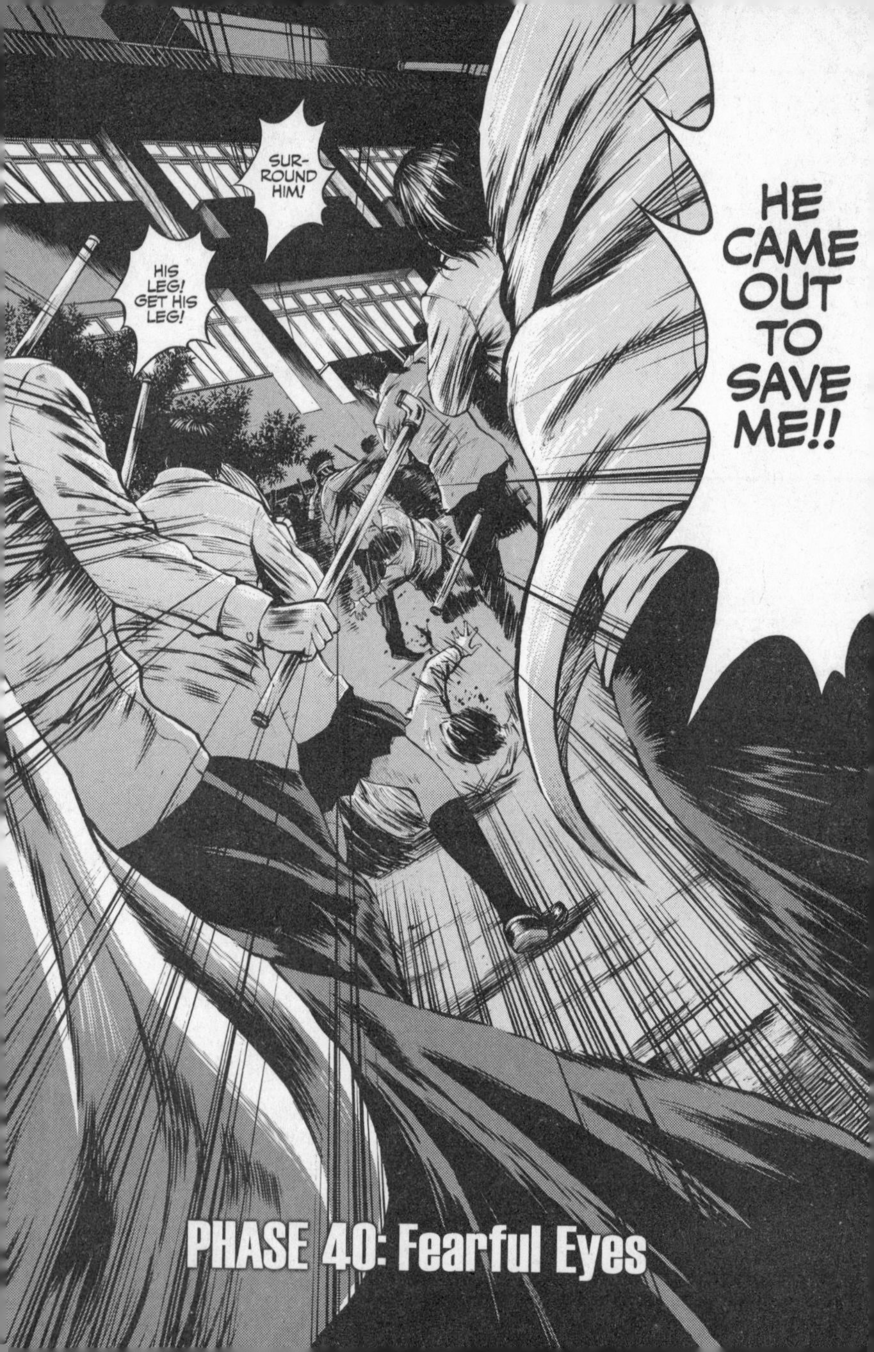
HE CAME OUT TO SAVE ME!!
SUR-ROUND HIM!
HIS LEG! GET HIS LEG!

PHASE 40: Fearful Eyes

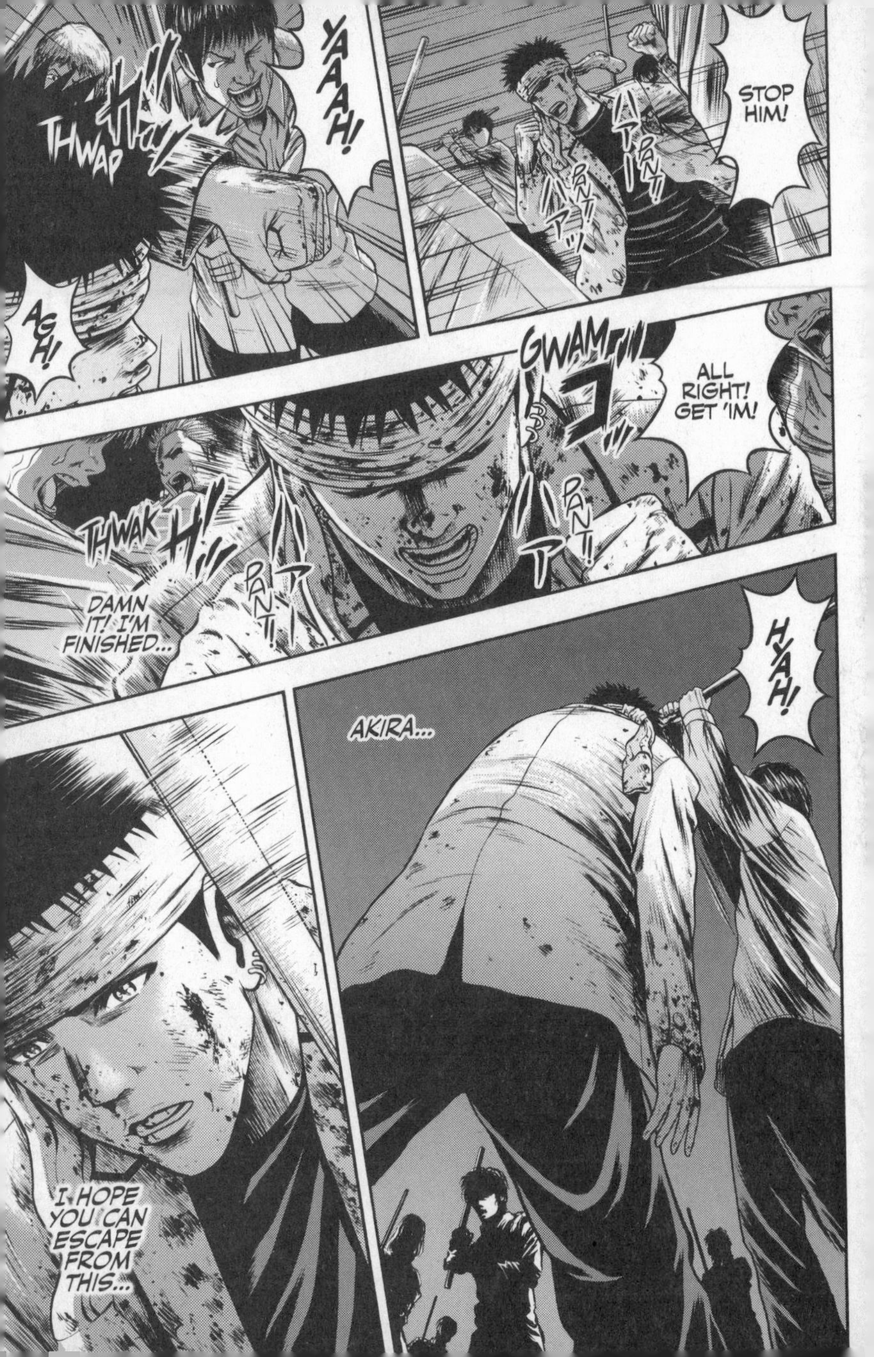
STOP HIM!
PANT! PANT!
YAAAAH!
THWAP
AGH!
ALL RIGHT! GET 'IM!
GWAM
PANT! PANT!
THWAK
PANT!
DAMN IT! I'M FINISHED...
HYAH!
AKIRA...
I HOPE YOU CAN ESCAPE FROM THIS...

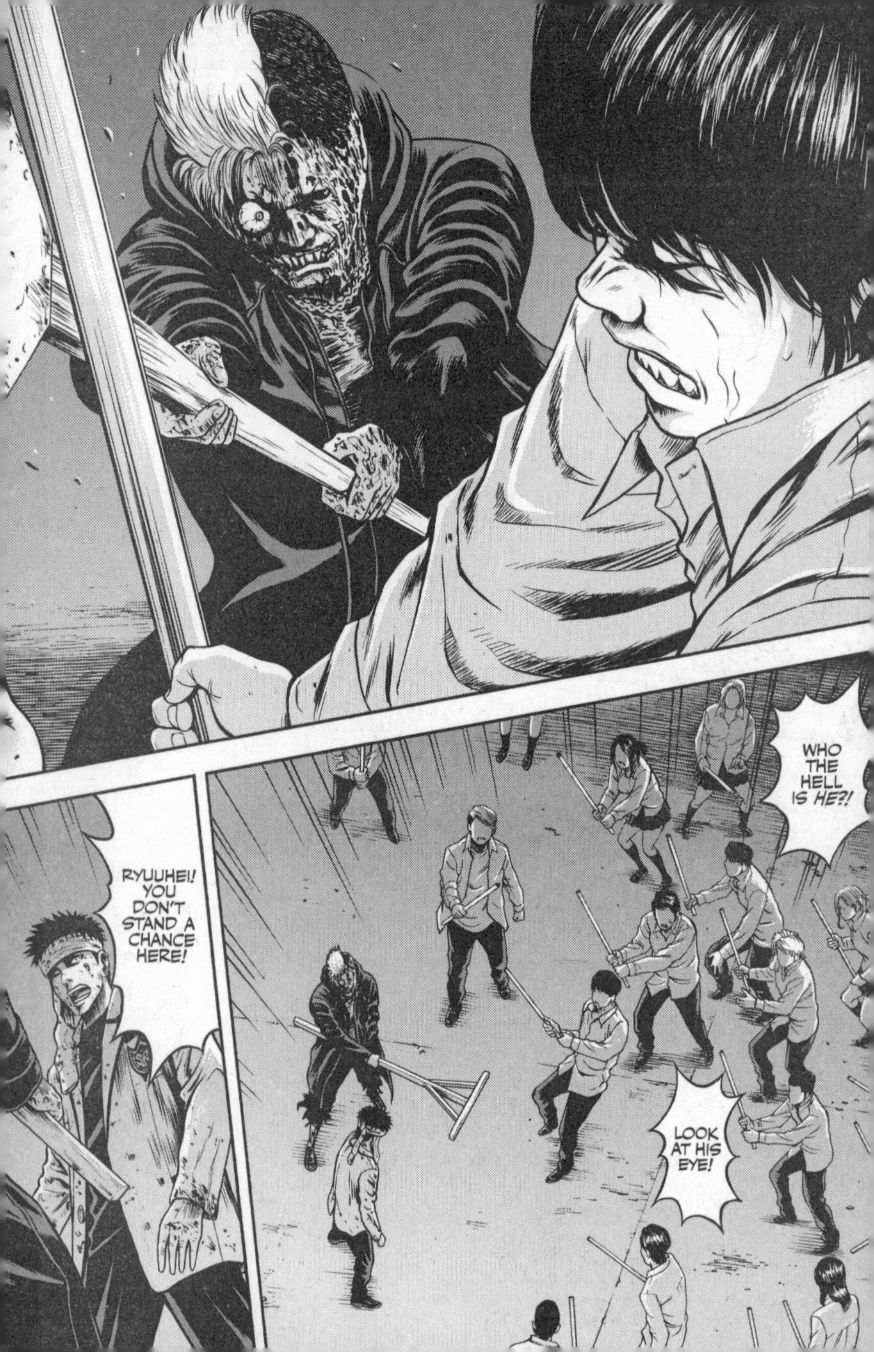
WHO THE HELL IS *HE?!*
LOOK AT HIS EYE!
RYUUHEI! YOU DON'T STAND A CHANCE HERE!

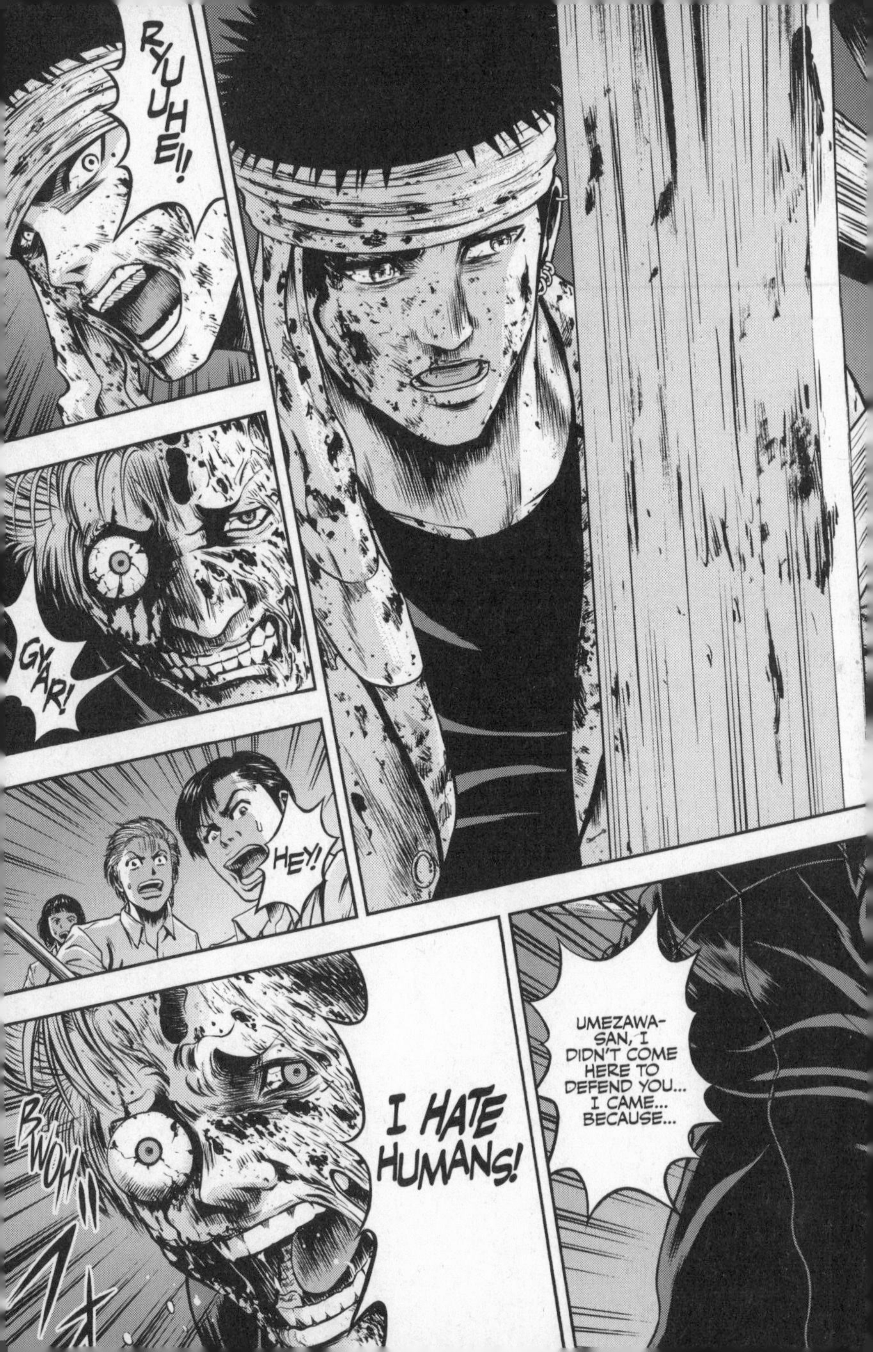
RYUUHEI!
GYAAR!
HEY!
UMEZAWA-SAN, I DIDN'T COME HERE TO DEFEND YOU... I CAME... BECAUSE...
I HATE HUMANS!
BWOH!!

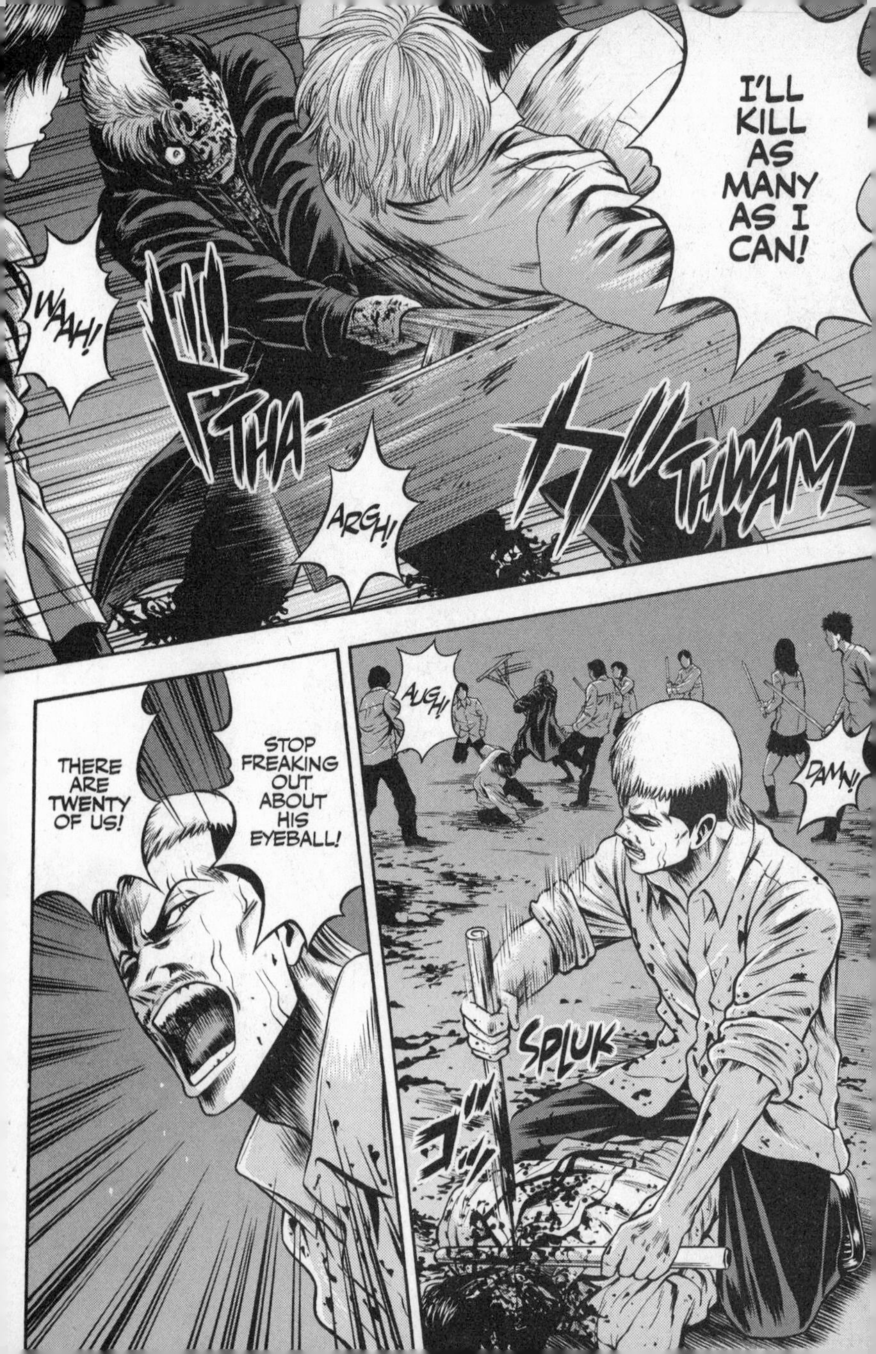
I'LL KILL AS MANY AS I CAN!
WAAH!
THA-
THWAM
ARGH!
AUGH!
DAMN!
SPLUK
STOP FREAKING OUT ABOUT HIS EYEBALL!
THERE ARE TWENTY OF US!

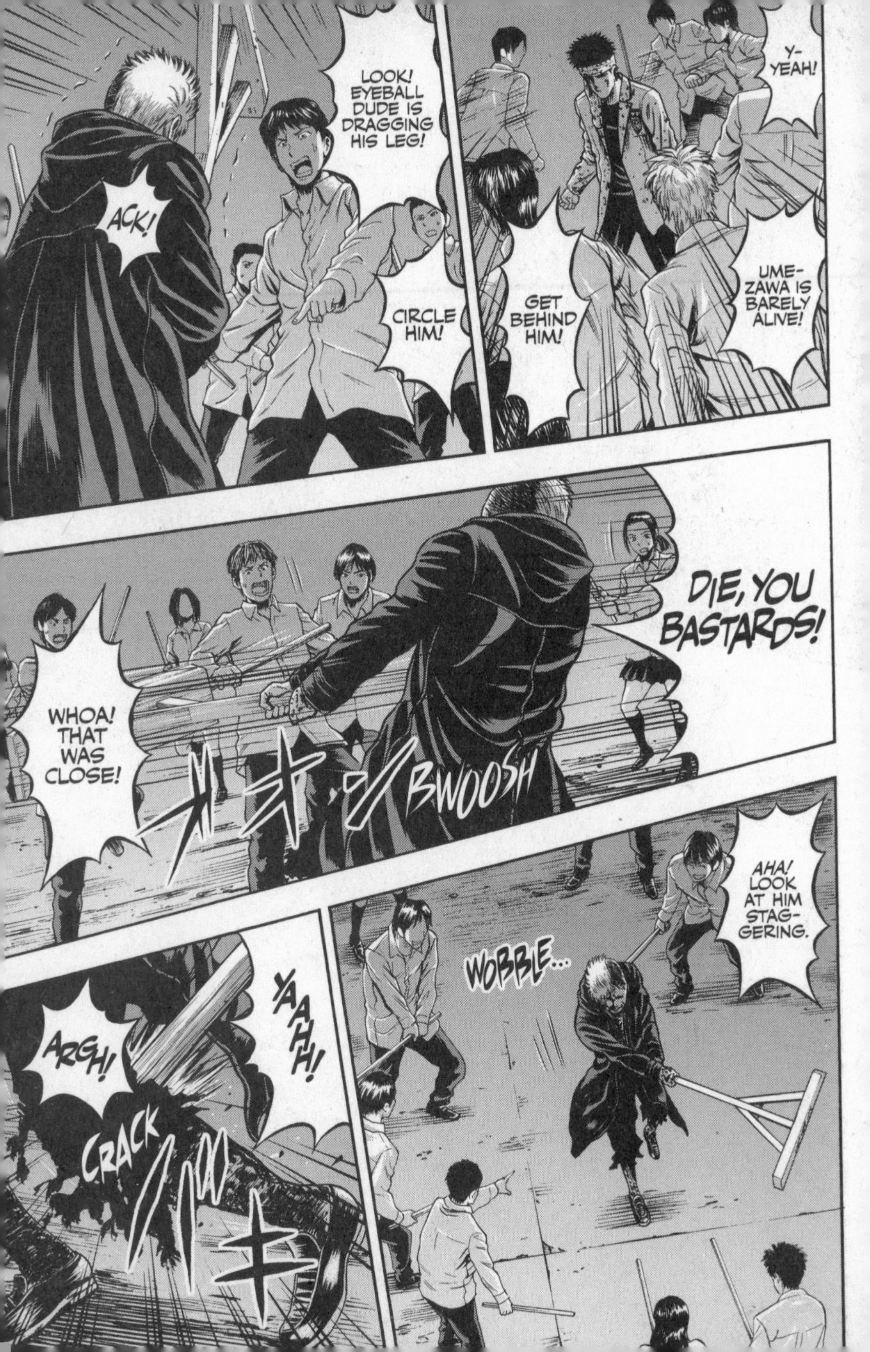
Y-YEAH!
UME-ZAWA IS BARELY ALIVE!
GET BEHIND HIM!
LOOK! EYEBALL DUDE IS DRAGGING HIS LEG!
ACK!
CIRCLE HIM!
DIE, YOU BASTARDS!
BWOOSH
WHOA! THAT WAS CLOSE!
AHA! LOOK AT HIM STAG-GERING.
WOBBLE...
YAAHH!
ARGH!
CRACK

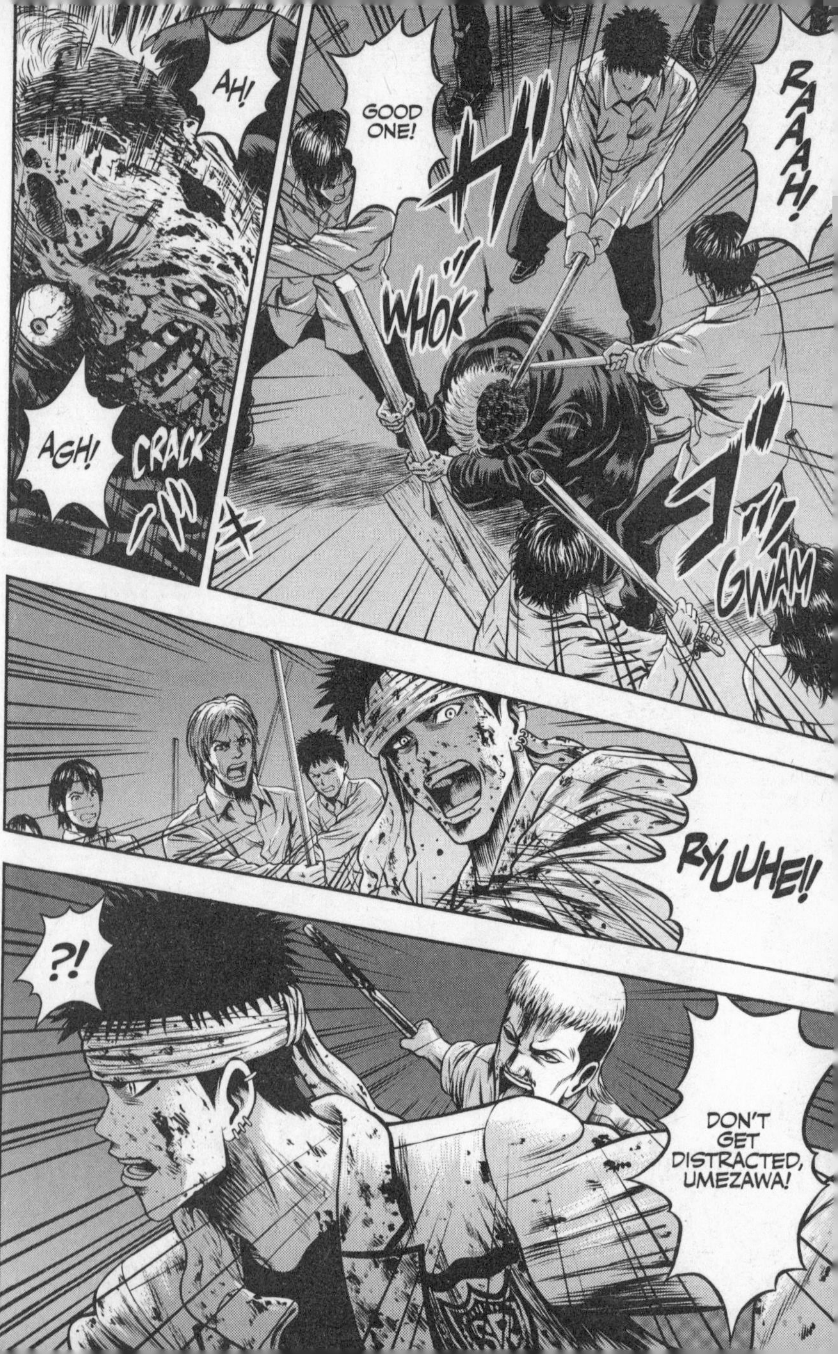
RAAAH!
GOOD ONE!
WHOK
GWAM
AH!
AGH!
CRACK
RYUUHEI!!
?!
DON'T GET DISTRACTED, UMEZAWA!

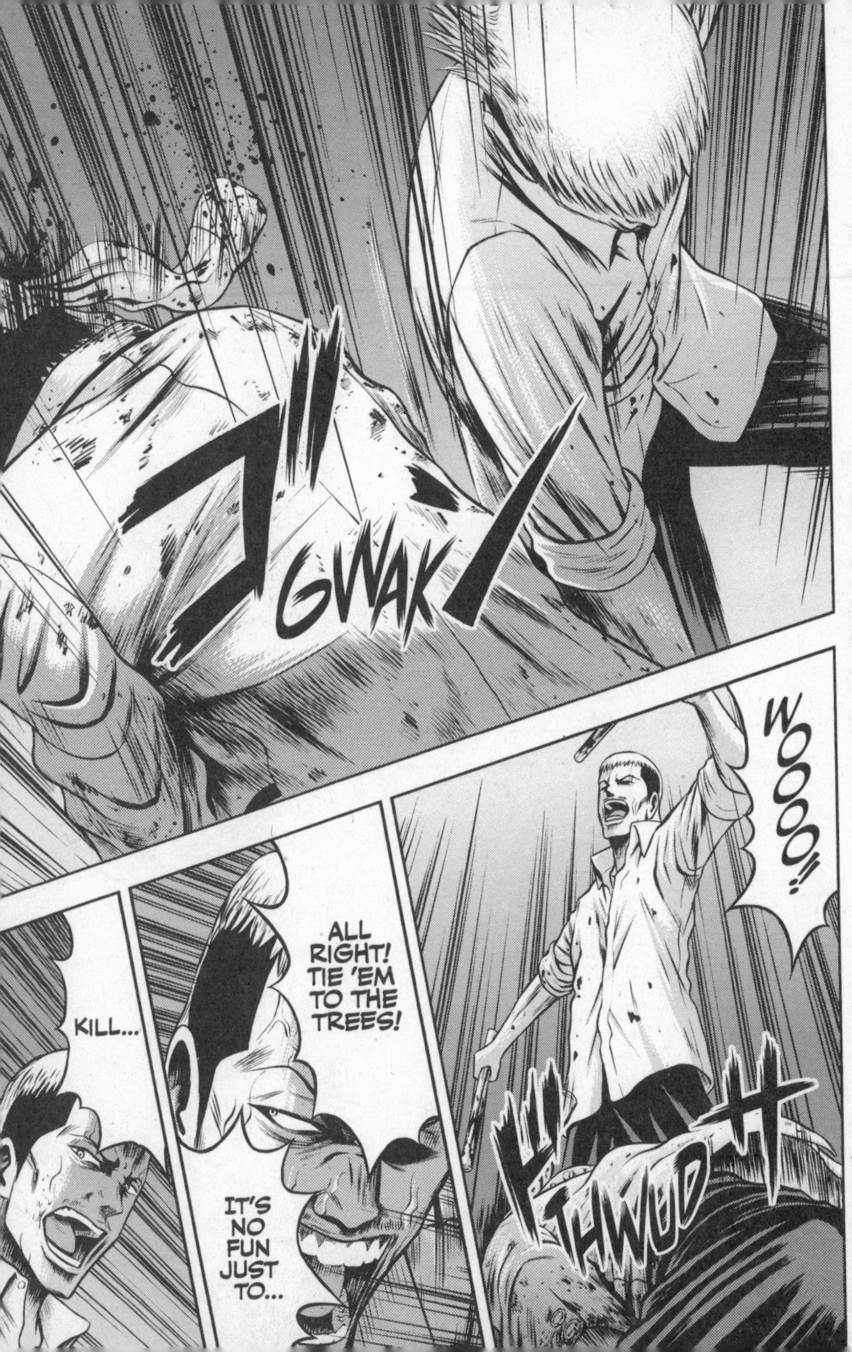
GWAK
WOOOO!!
THWUD
ALL RIGHT! TIE 'EM TO THE TREES!
IT'S NO FUN JUST TO...
KILL...

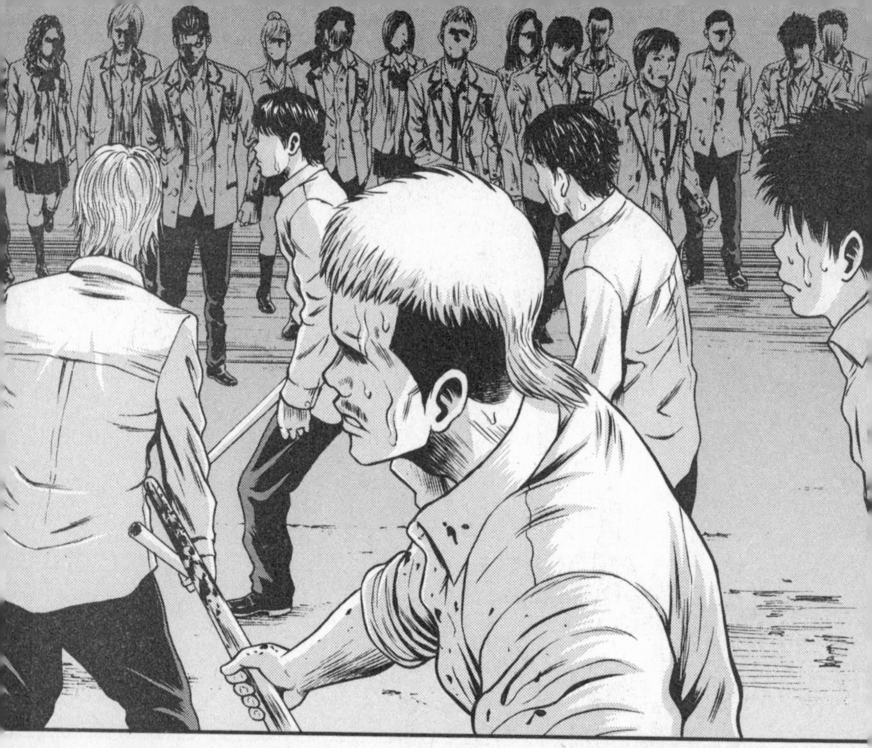
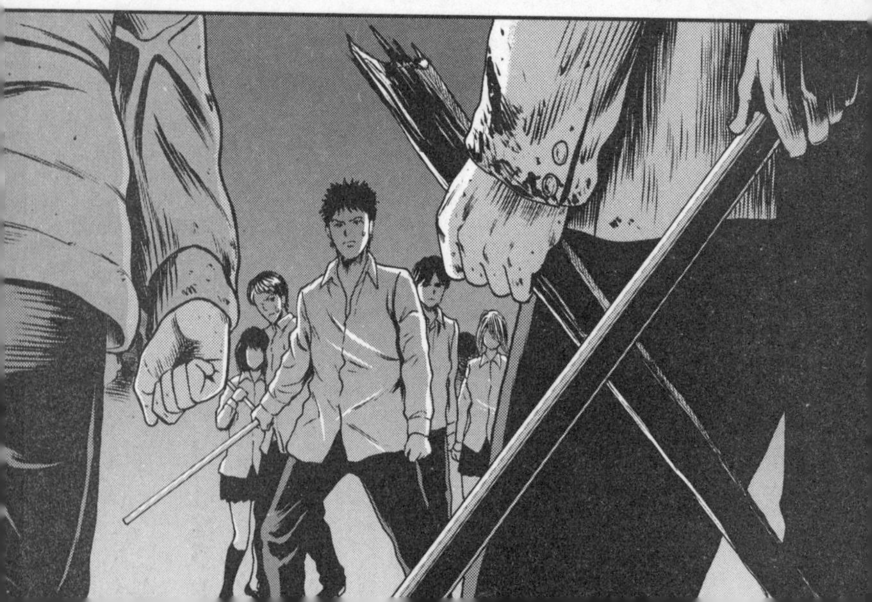

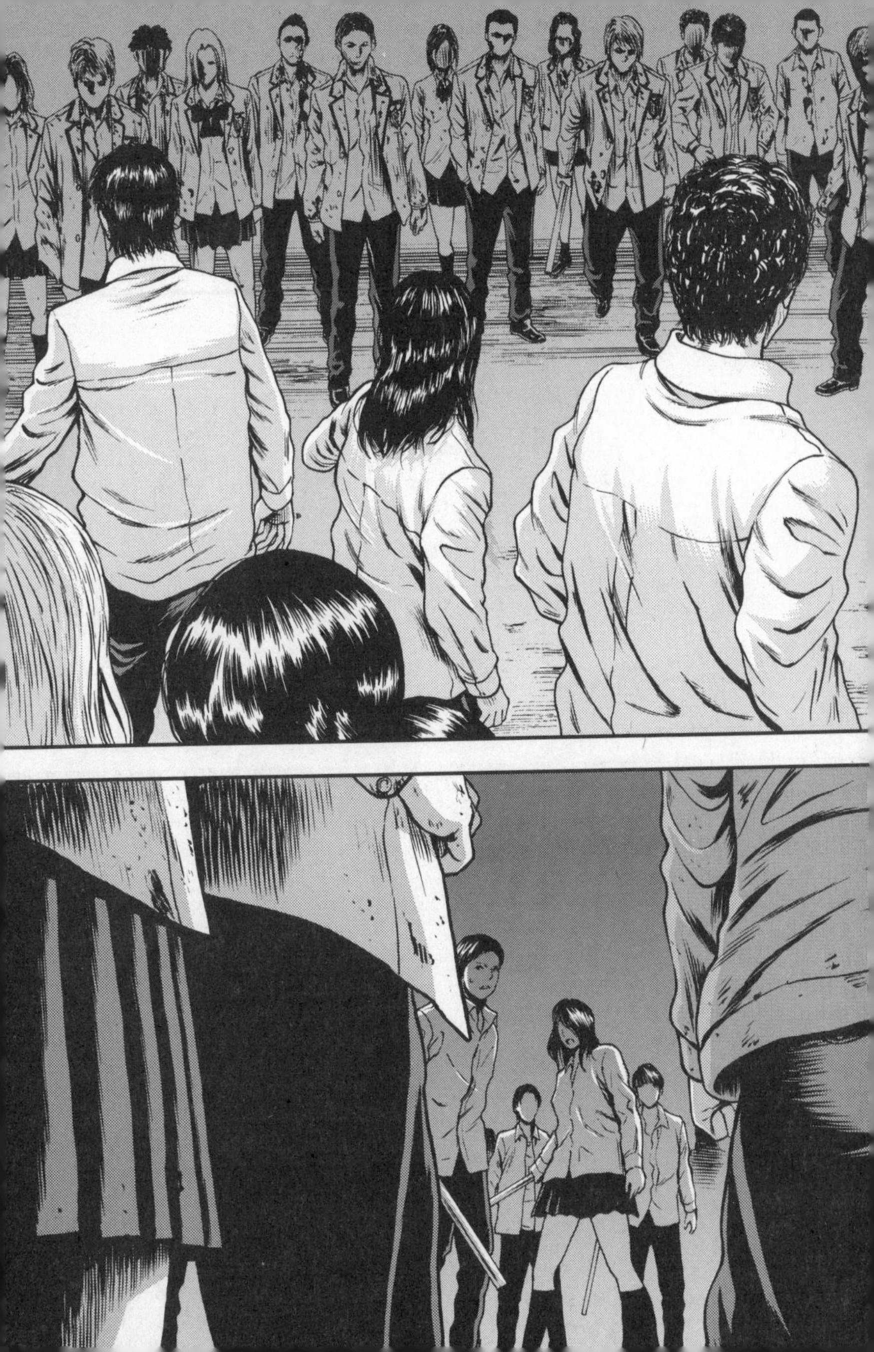

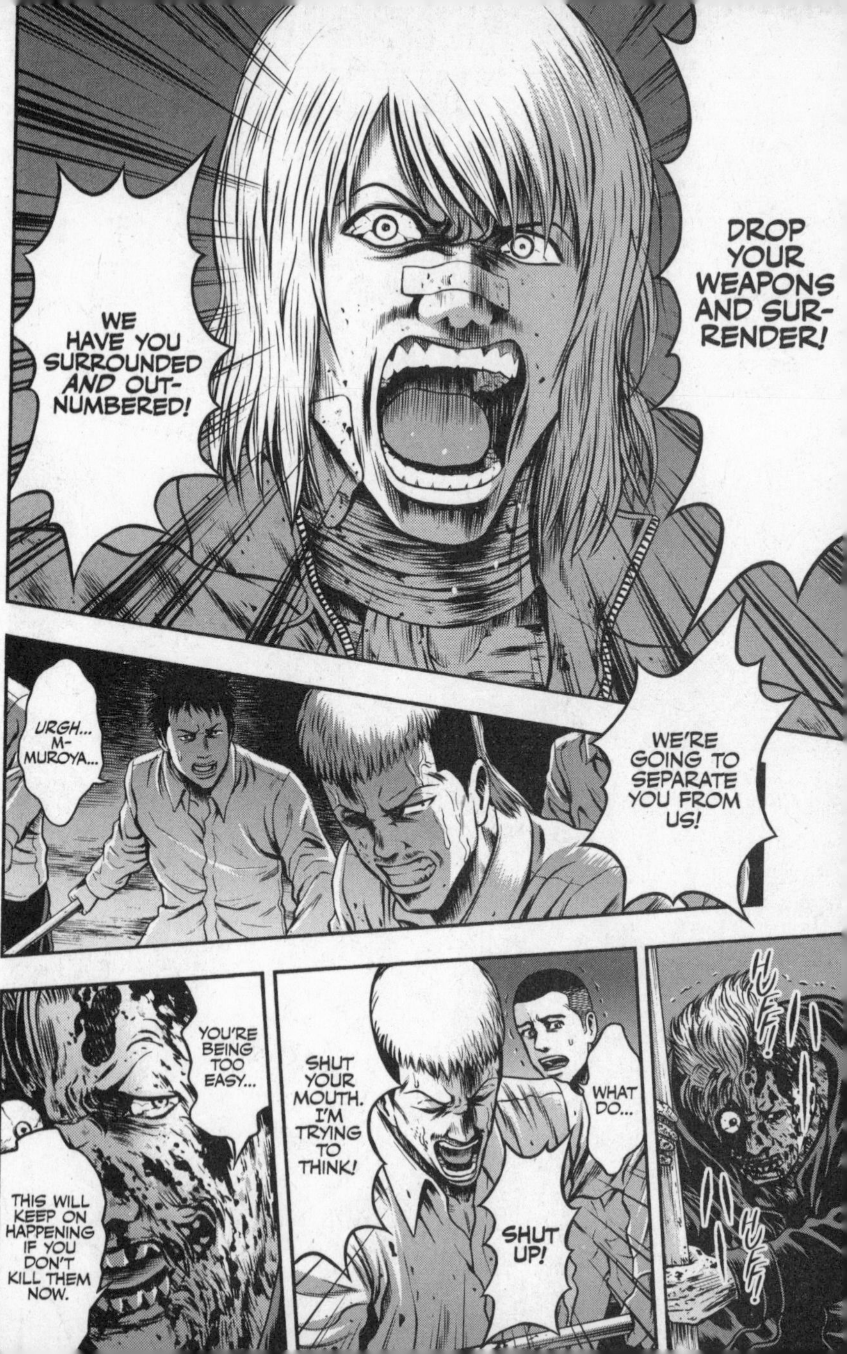
DROP YOUR WEAPONS AND SURRENDER!
WE HAVE YOU SURROUNDED AND OUT-NUMBERED!
WE'RE GOING TO SEPARATE YOU FROM US!
URGH... M-MUROYA...
HUFF!!
HUFF!!
WHAT DO...
SHUT YOUR MOUTH. I'M TRYING TO THINK!
SHUT UP!
YOU'RE BEING TOO EASY...
THIS WILL KEEP ON HAPPENING IF YOU DON'T KILL THEM NOW.

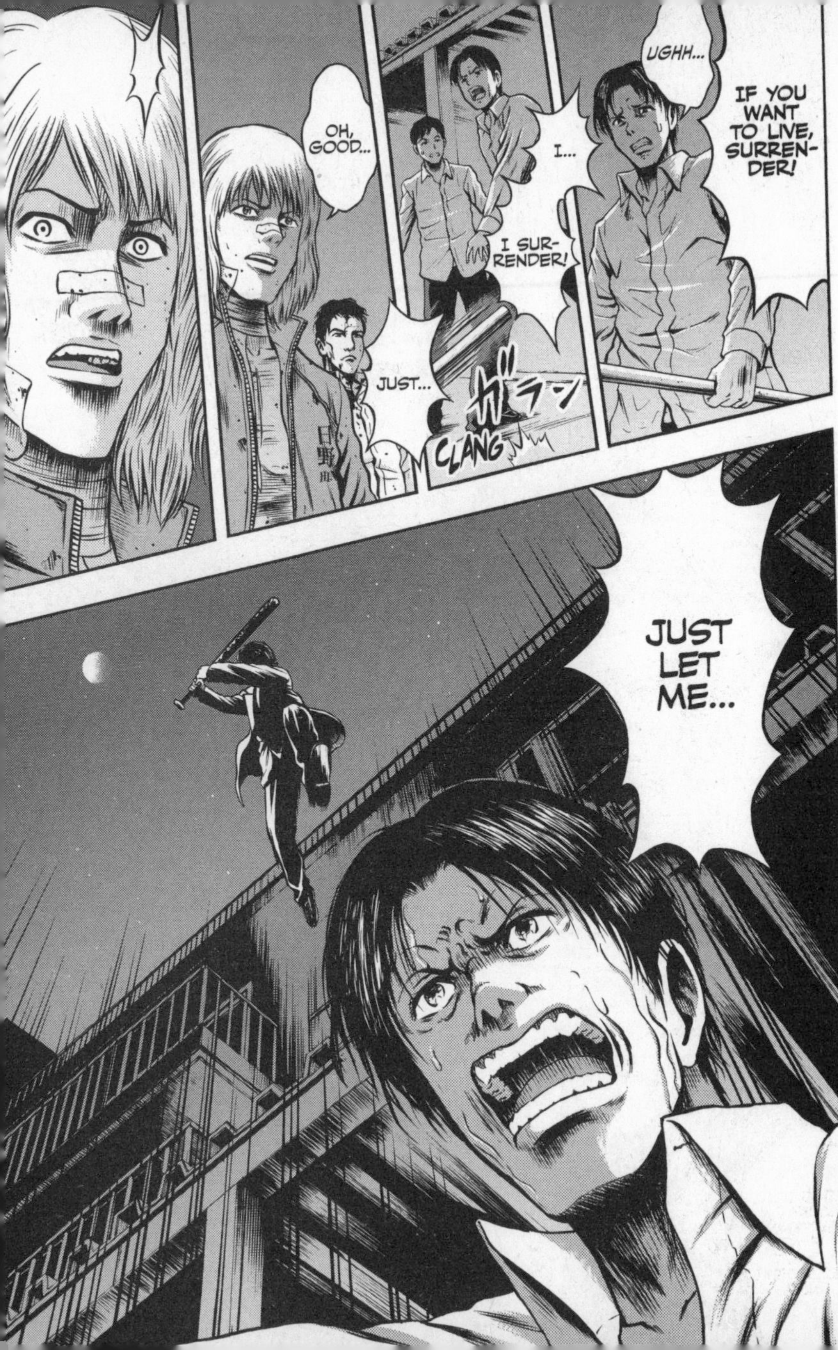
UGHH...
IF YOU WANT TO LIVE, SURRENDER!
I...
I SURRENDER!
ガラン
CLANG
OH, GOOD...
JUST...
JUST LET ME...

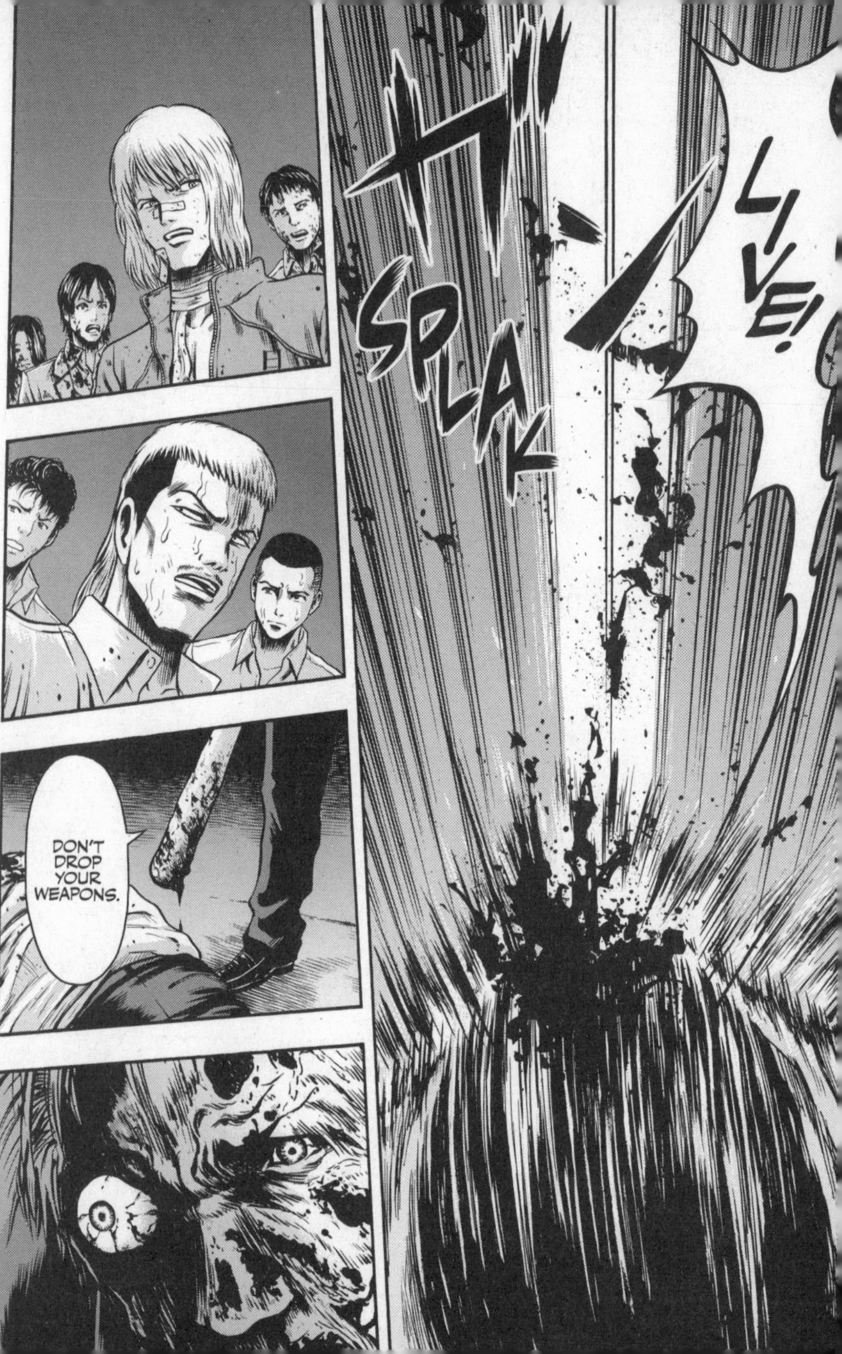
LIVE!
SPLAK
DON'T DROP YOUR WEAPONS.

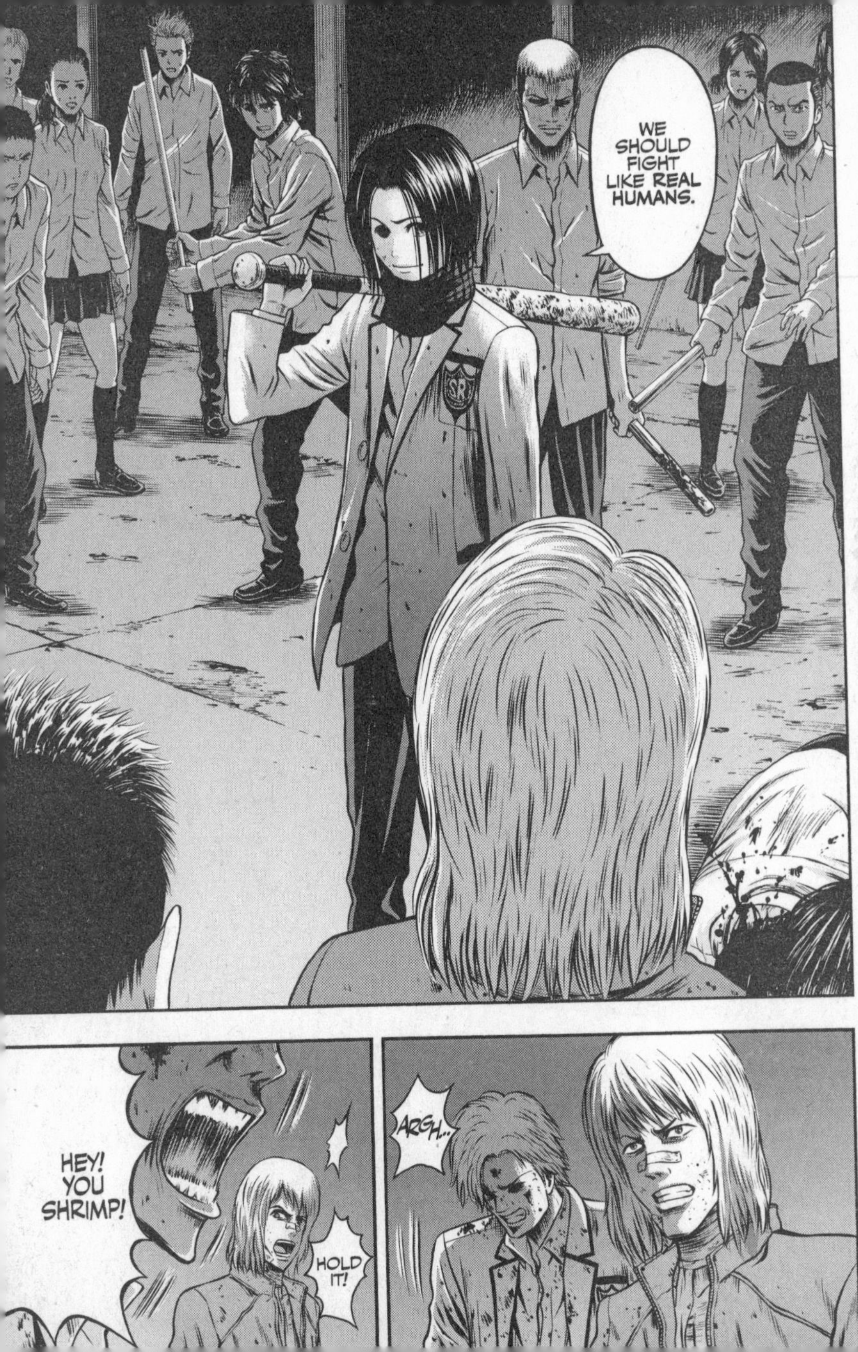
WE SHOULD FIGHT LIKE REAL HUMANS.
ARGH...
HEY! YOU SHRIMP!
HOLD IT!

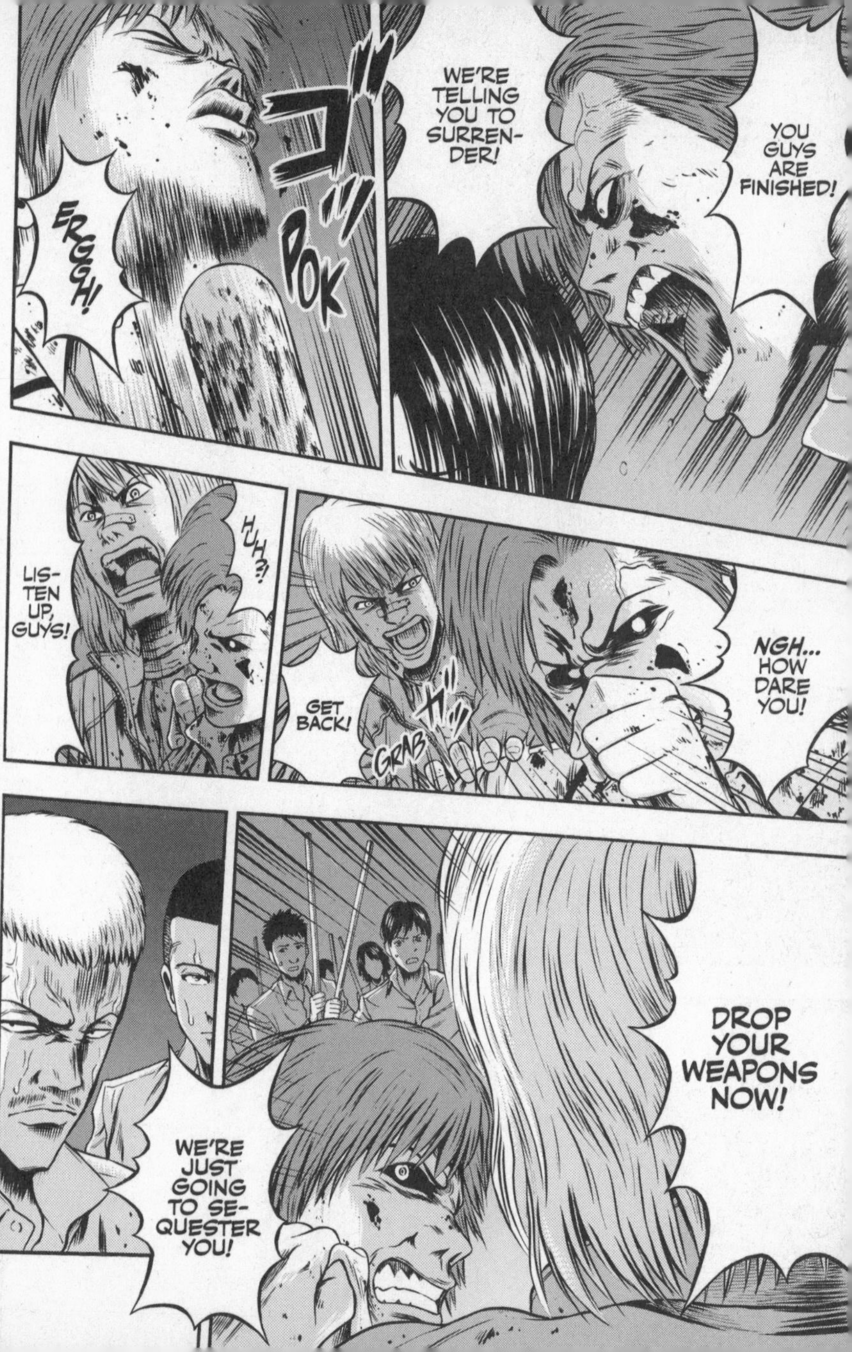
YOU GUYS ARE FINISHED!
WE'RE TELLING YOU TO SURRENDER!
ゴッ
POK
ERGGH!
NGH... HOW DARE YOU!
ガッ
GRAB
GET BACK!
HUH?!
LISTEN UP, GUYS!
DROP YOUR WEAPONS NOW!
WE'RE JUST GOING TO SEQUESTER YOU!

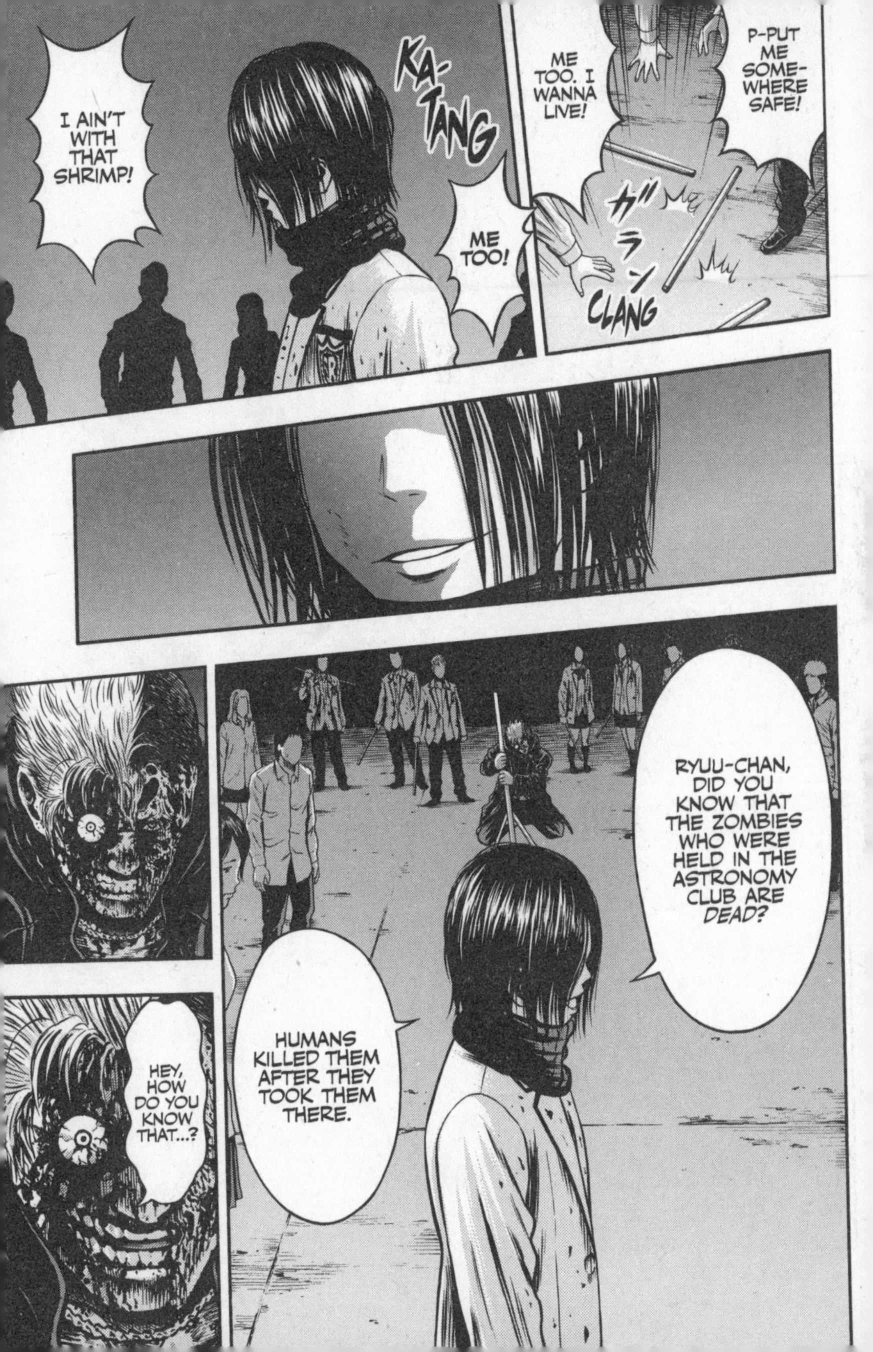
P-PUT ME SOME-WHERE SAFE!
ME TOO. I WANNA LIVE!
ガラン
CLANG
KA-TANG
ME TOO!
I AIN'T WITH THAT SHRIMP!
RYUU-CHAN, DID YOU KNOW THAT THE ZOMBIES WHO WERE HELD IN THE ASTRONOMY CLUB ARE *DEAD?*
HUMANS KILLED THEM AFTER THEY TOOK THEM THERE.
HEY, HOW DO YOU KNOW THAT...?

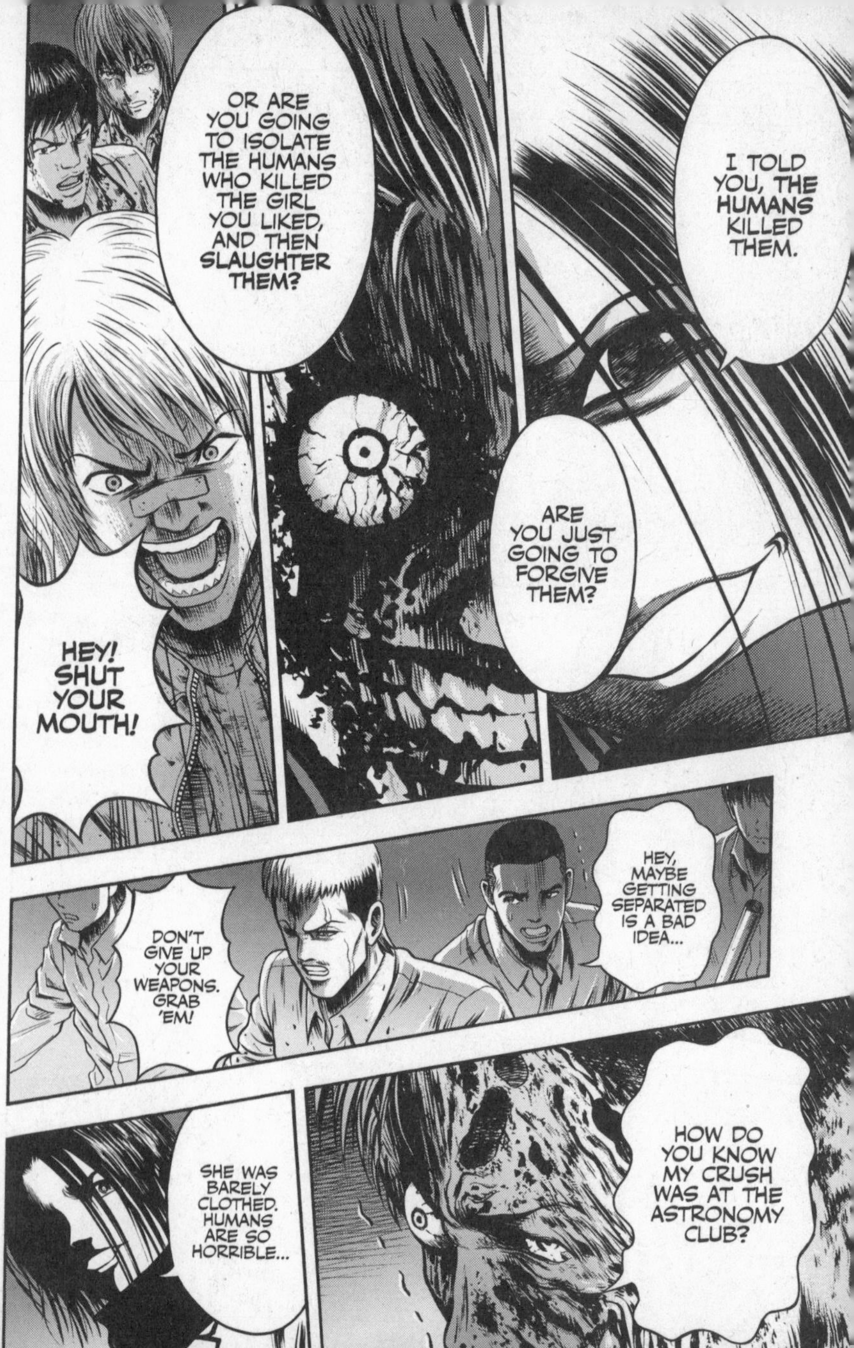
I TOLD YOU, THE HUMANS KILLED THEM.
ARE YOU JUST GOING TO FORGIVE THEM?
OR ARE YOU GOING TO ISOLATE THE HUMANS WHO KILLED THE GIRL YOU LIKED, AND THEN SLAUGHTER THEM?
HEY! SHUT YOUR MOUTH!
HEY, MAYBE GETTING SEPARATED IS A BAD IDEA...
DON'T GIVE UP YOUR WEAPONS. GRAB 'EM!
HOW DO YOU KNOW MY CRUSH WAS AT THE ASTRONOMY CLUB?
SHE WAS BARELY CLOTHED. HUMANS ARE SO HORRIBLE...

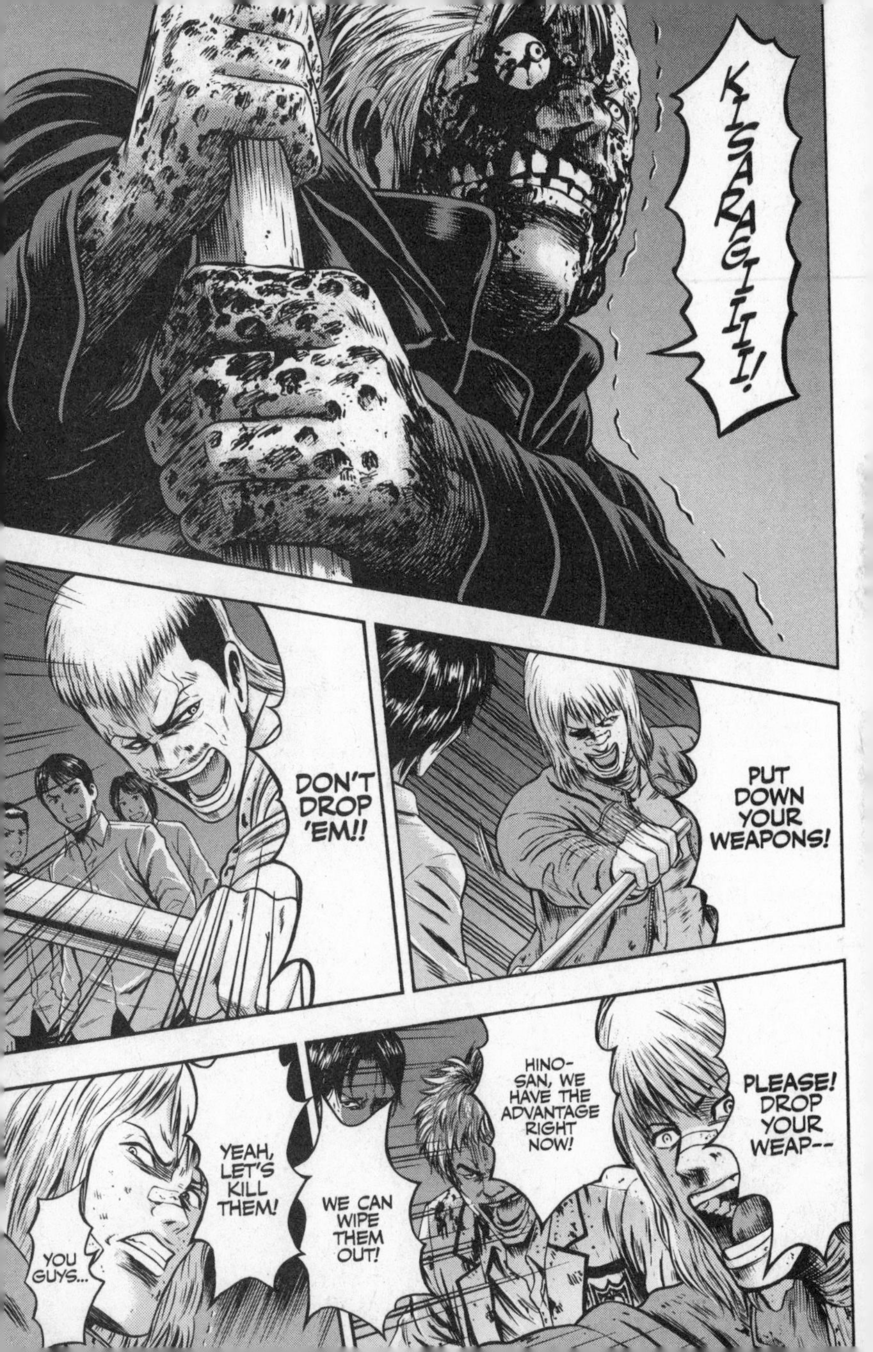
KISARAGIIIII!
PUT DOWN YOUR WEAPONS!
DON'T DROP 'EM!!
PLEASE! DROP YOUR WEAP--
HINO-SAN, WE HAVE THE ADVANTAGE RIGHT NOW!
WE CAN WIPE THEM OUT!
YEAH, LET'S KILL THEM!
YOU GUYS...

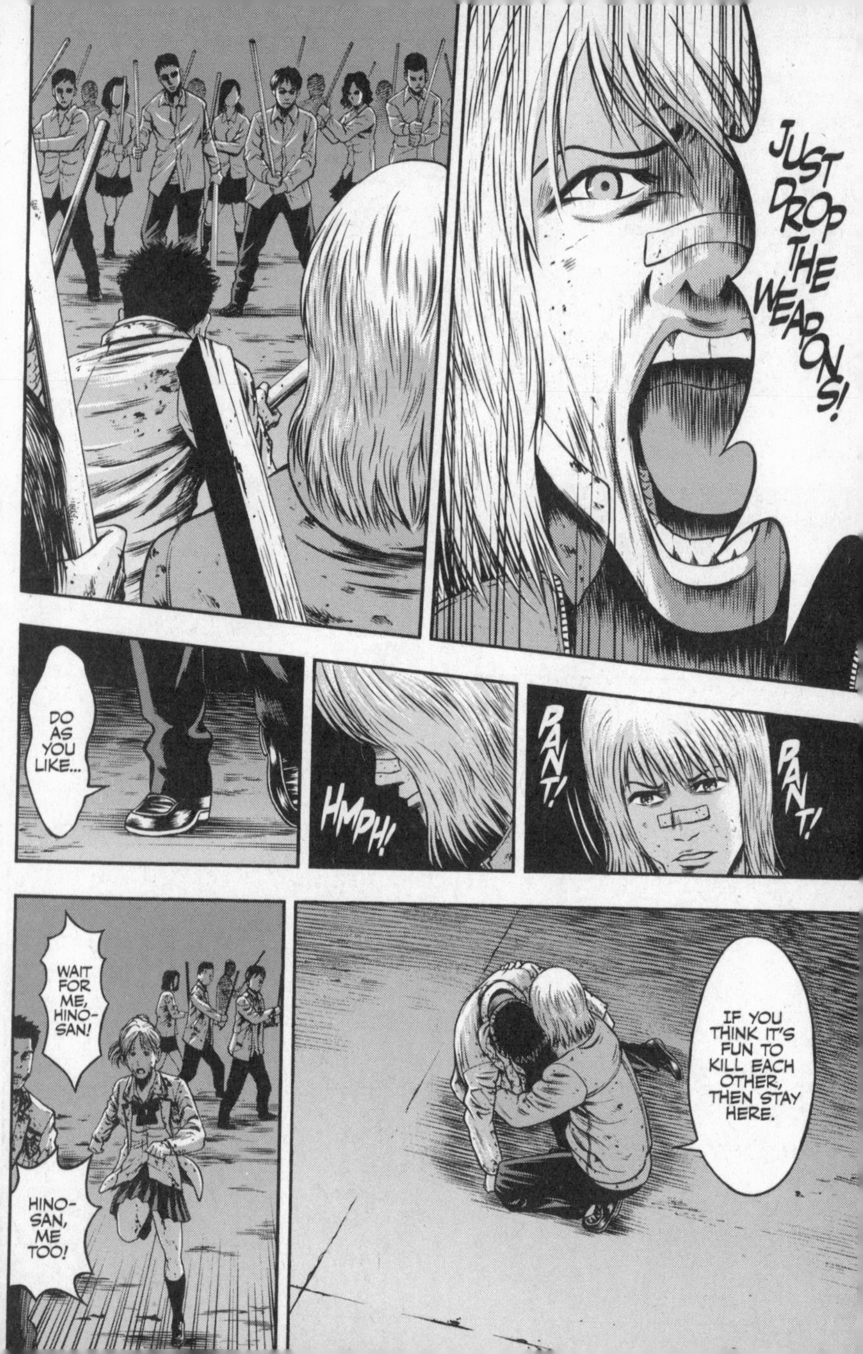
JUST DROP THE WEAPONS!
PANT! PANT!
HMPH!
DO AS YOU LIKE...
IF YOU THINK IT'S FUN TO KILL EACH OTHER, THEN STAY HERE.
WAIT FOR ME, HINO-SAN!
HINO-SAN, ME TOO!

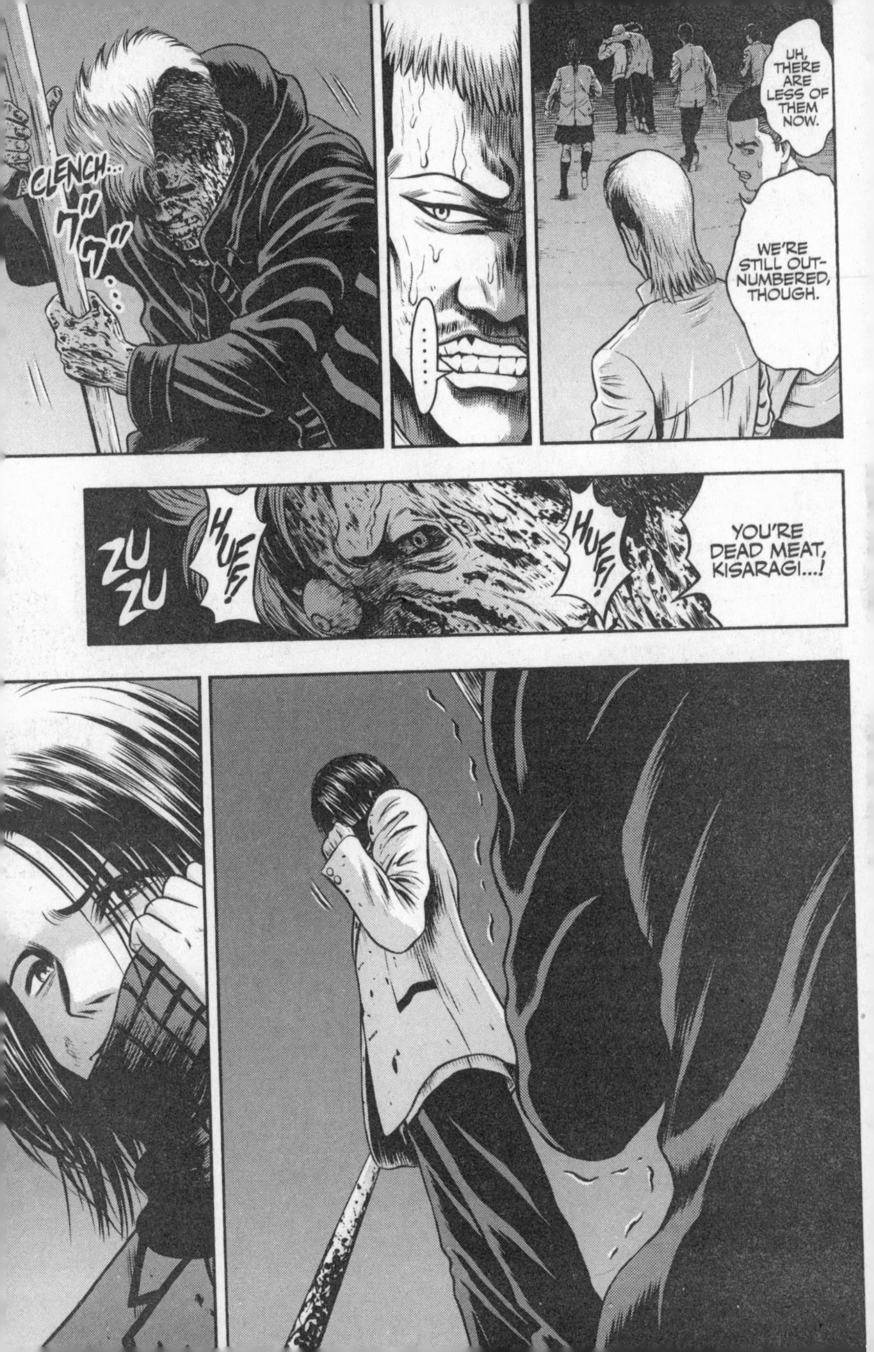
UH, THERE ARE LESS OF THEM NOW.
WE'RE STILL OUT-NUMBERED, THOUGH.
......
CLENCH...
ググ…
YOU'RE DEAD MEAT, KISARAGI...!
HUFF!!
HUFF!!
ZU ZU ZU

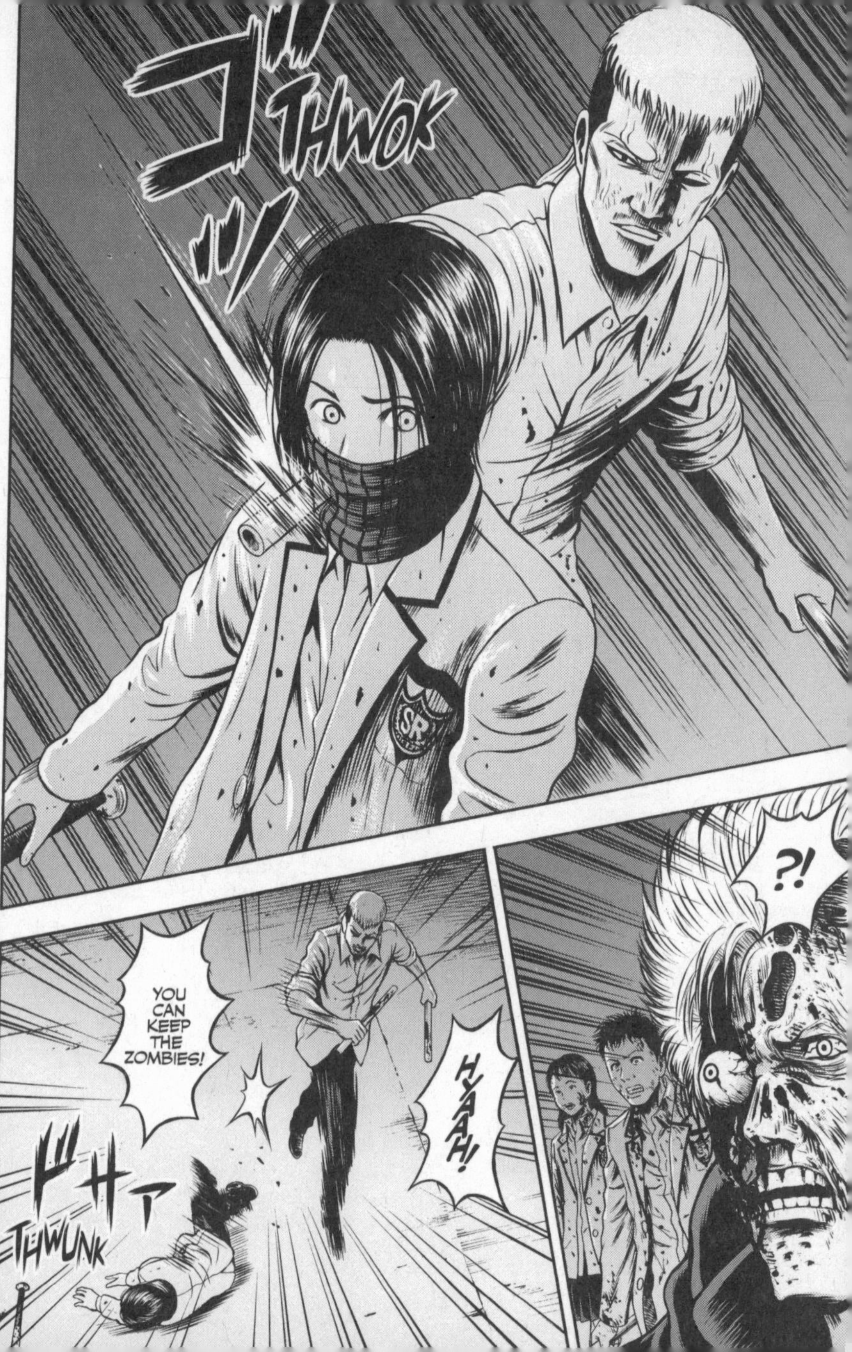
ゴッ
THWOK
?!
YOU CAN KEEP THE ZOMBIES!
HYAAH!
ドサァ
THWUNK

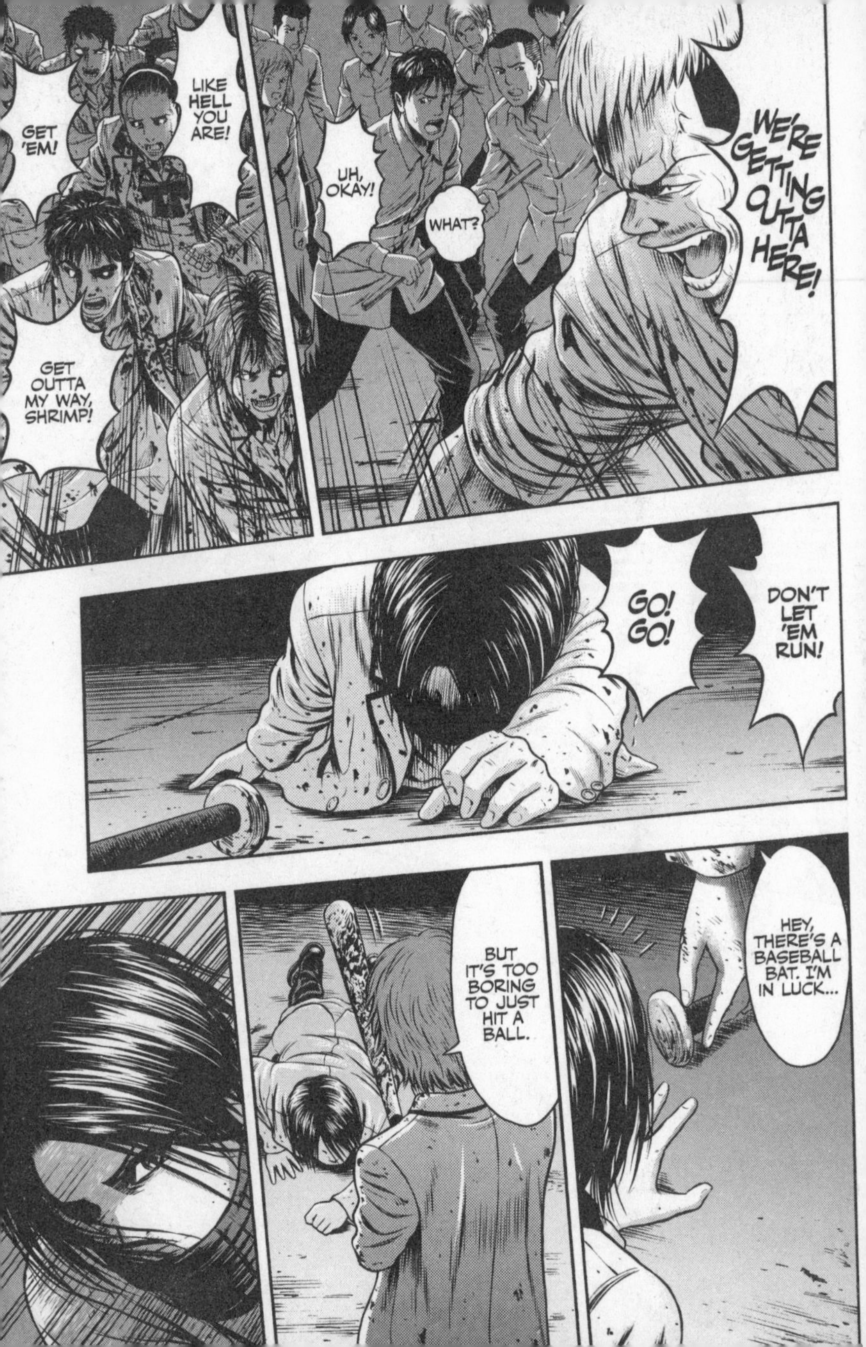
WE'RE GETTING OUTTA HERE!
WHAT?
UH, OKAY!
LIKE HELL YOU ARE!
GET 'EM!
GET OUTTA MY WAY, SHRIMP!
DON'T LET 'EM RUN!
GO! GO!
HEY, THERE'S A BASEBALL BAT. I'M IN LUCK...
BUT IT'S TOO BORING TO JUST HIT A BALL.

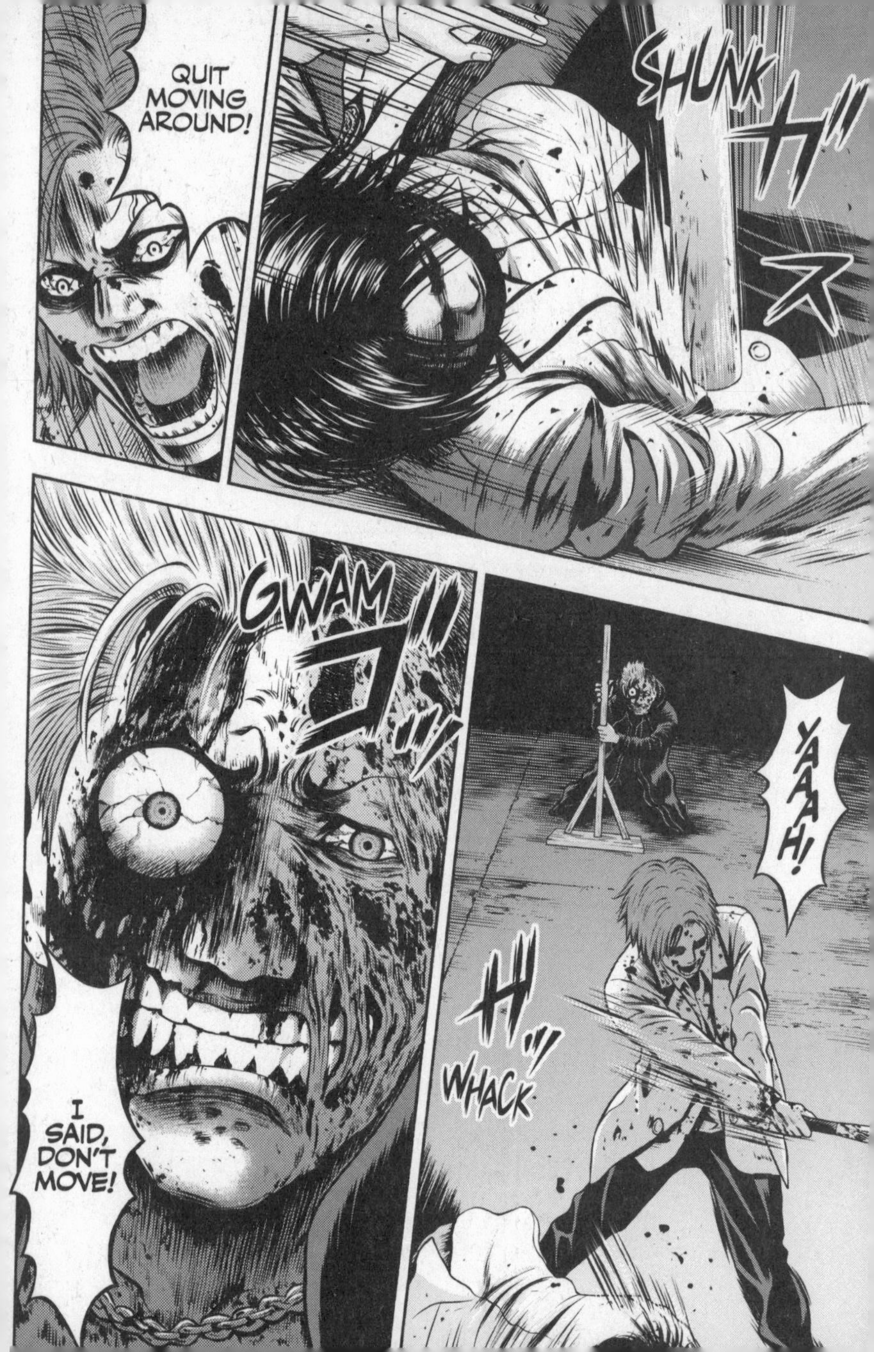
SHUNK
ガズ
QUIT MOVING AROUND!
YAAAH!
ガッ
WHACK
GWAM
ゴッ
I SAID, DON'T MOVE!

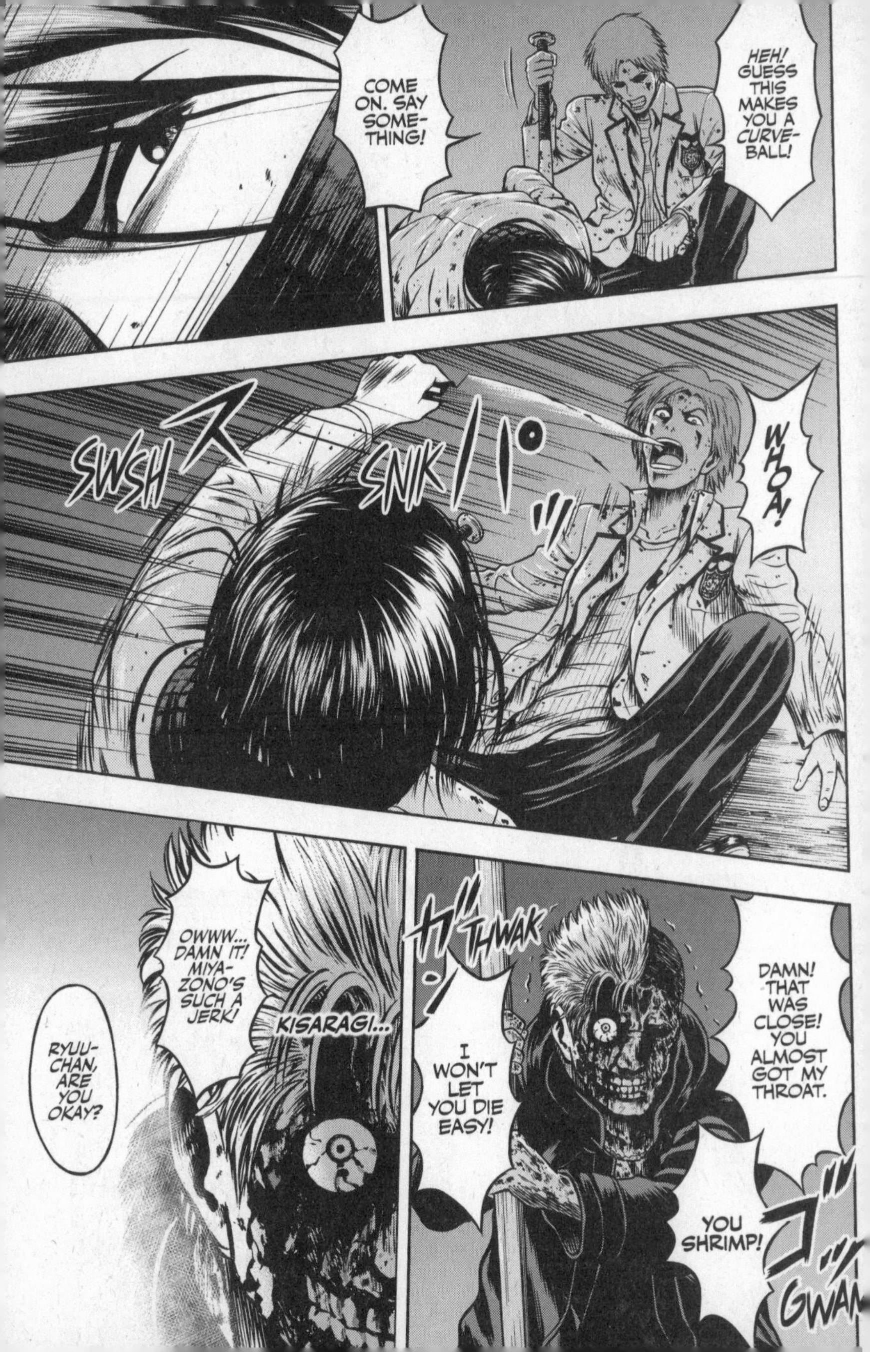
HEH! GUESS THIS MAKES YOU A CURVE-BALL!
COME ON. SAY SOME-THING!
WHOA!
SNIK
SWSH
DAMN! THAT WAS CLOSE! YOU ALMOST GOT MY THROAT.
THWAK
I WON'T LET YOU DIE EASY!
YOU SHRIMP!
GWAM
OWWW... DAMN IT! MIYA-ZONO'S SUCH A JERK!
KISARAGI...
RYUU-CHAN, ARE YOU OKAY?

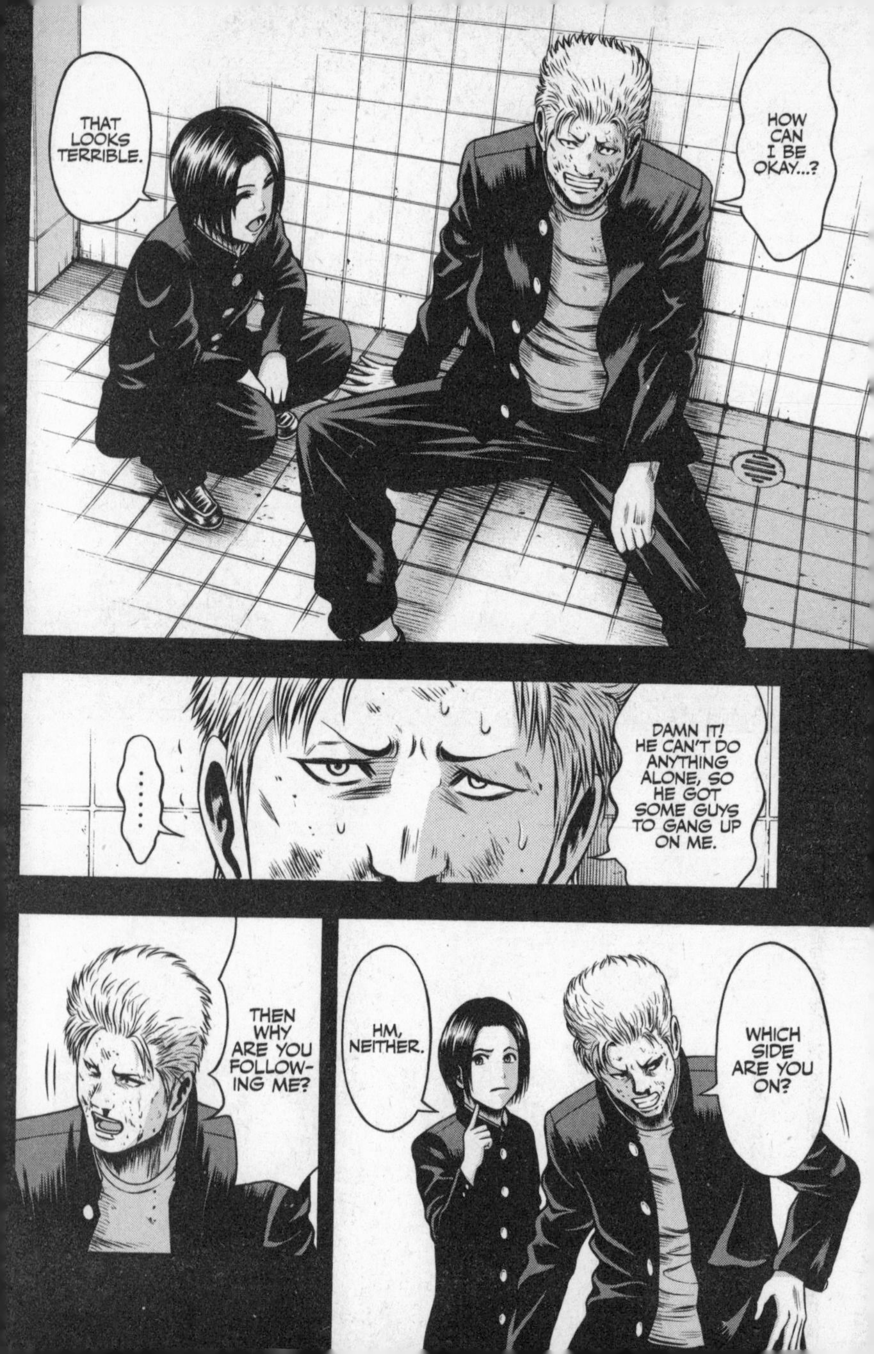
HOW CAN I BE OKAY...?
THAT LOOKS TERRIBLE.
DAMN IT! HE CAN'T DO ANYTHING ALONE, SO HE GOT SOME GUYS TO GANG UP ON ME.
......
WHICH SIDE ARE YOU ON?
HM, NEITHER.
THEN WHY ARE YOU FOLLOWING ME?

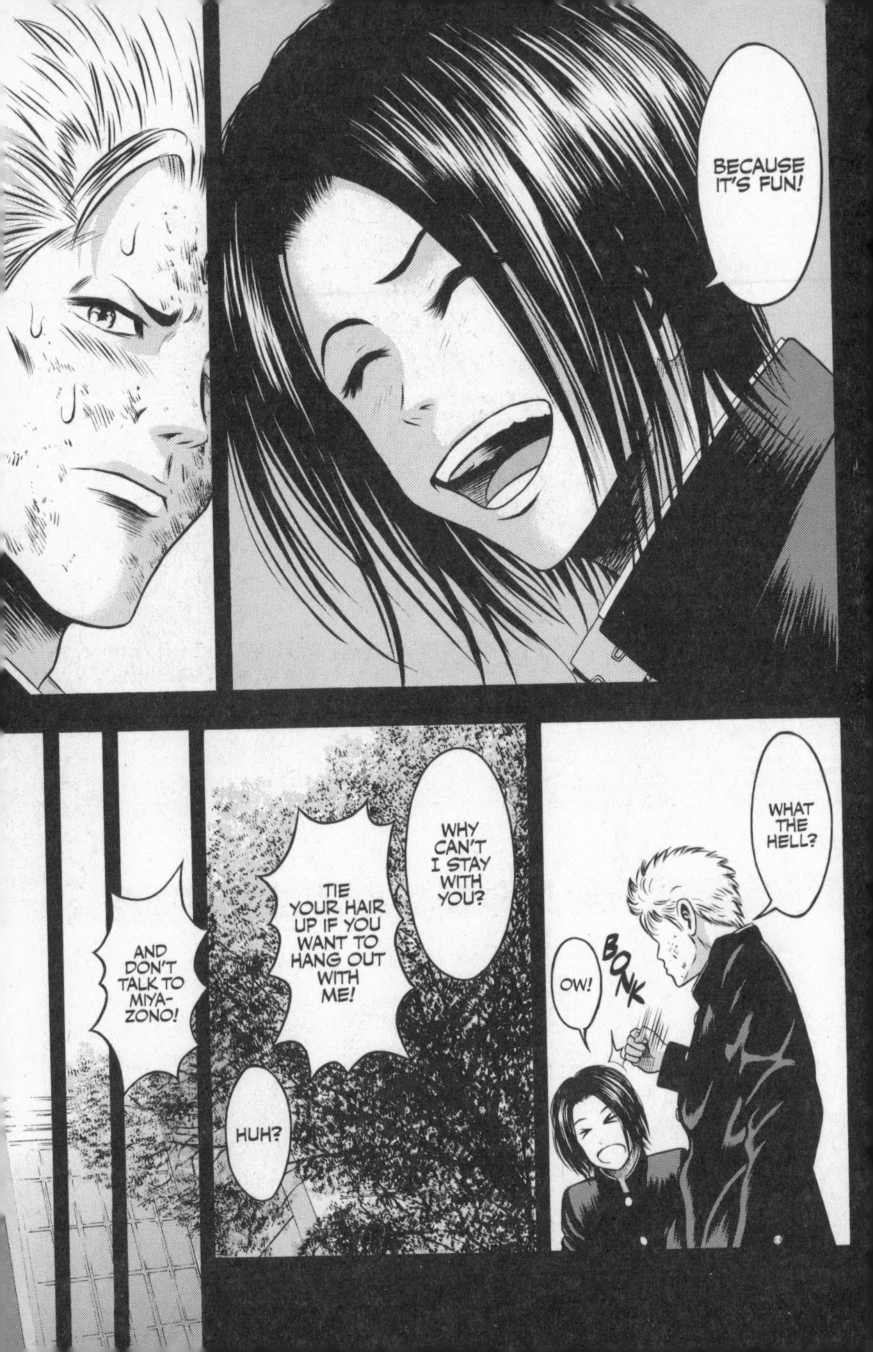
BECAUSE IT'S FUN!
WHAT THE HELL?
BONK
OW!
WHY CAN'T I STAY WITH YOU?
TIE YOUR HAIR UP IF YOU WANT TO HANG OUT WITH ME!
HUH?
AND DON'T TALK TO MIYA-ZONO!

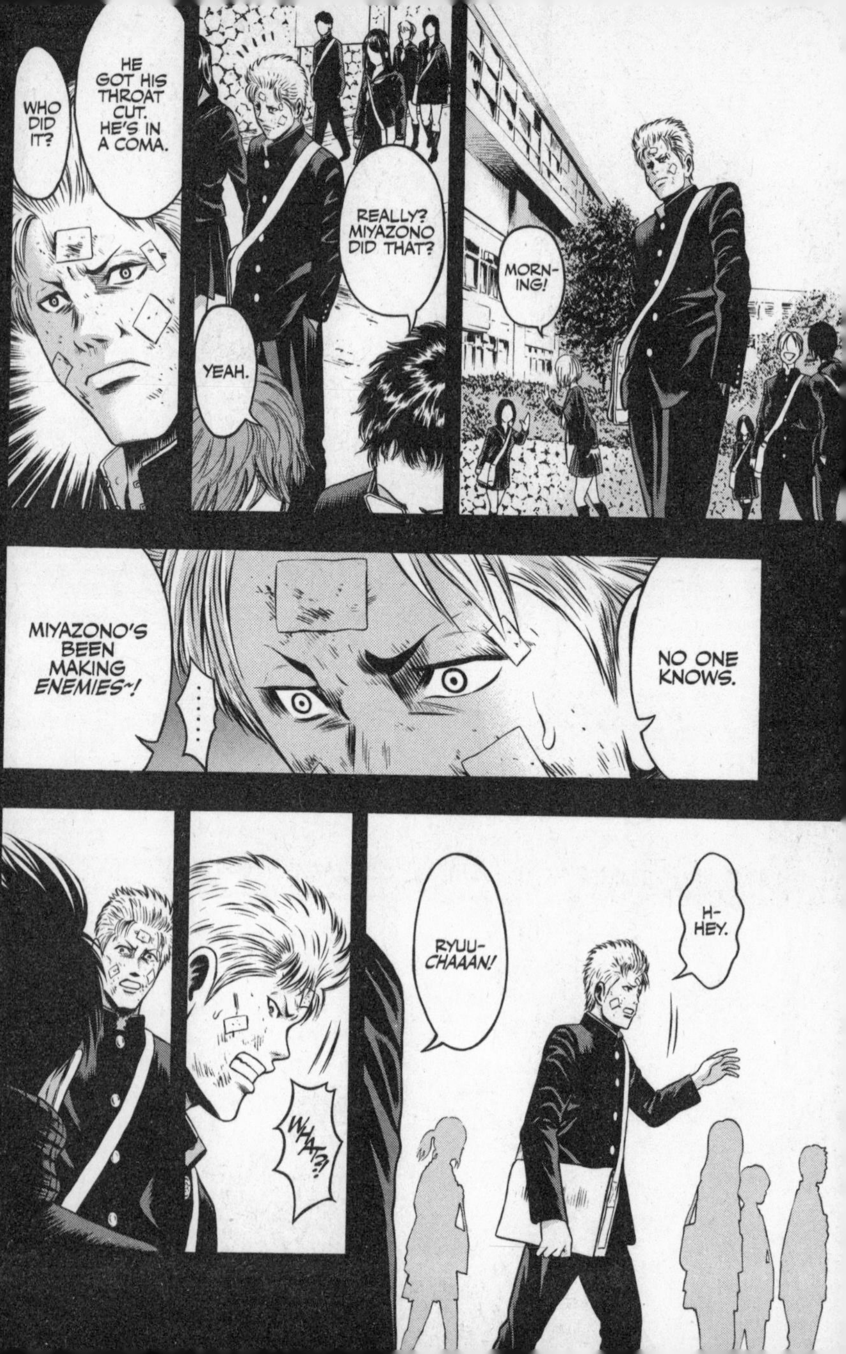
MORNING!
REALLY? MIYAZONO DID THAT?
YEAH.
HE GOT HIS THROAT CUT. HE'S IN A COMA.
WHO DID IT?
NO ONE KNOWS.
......
MIYAZONO'S BEEN MAKING ENEMIES~!
H-HEY.
RYUU-CHAAAN!
WHAT?!

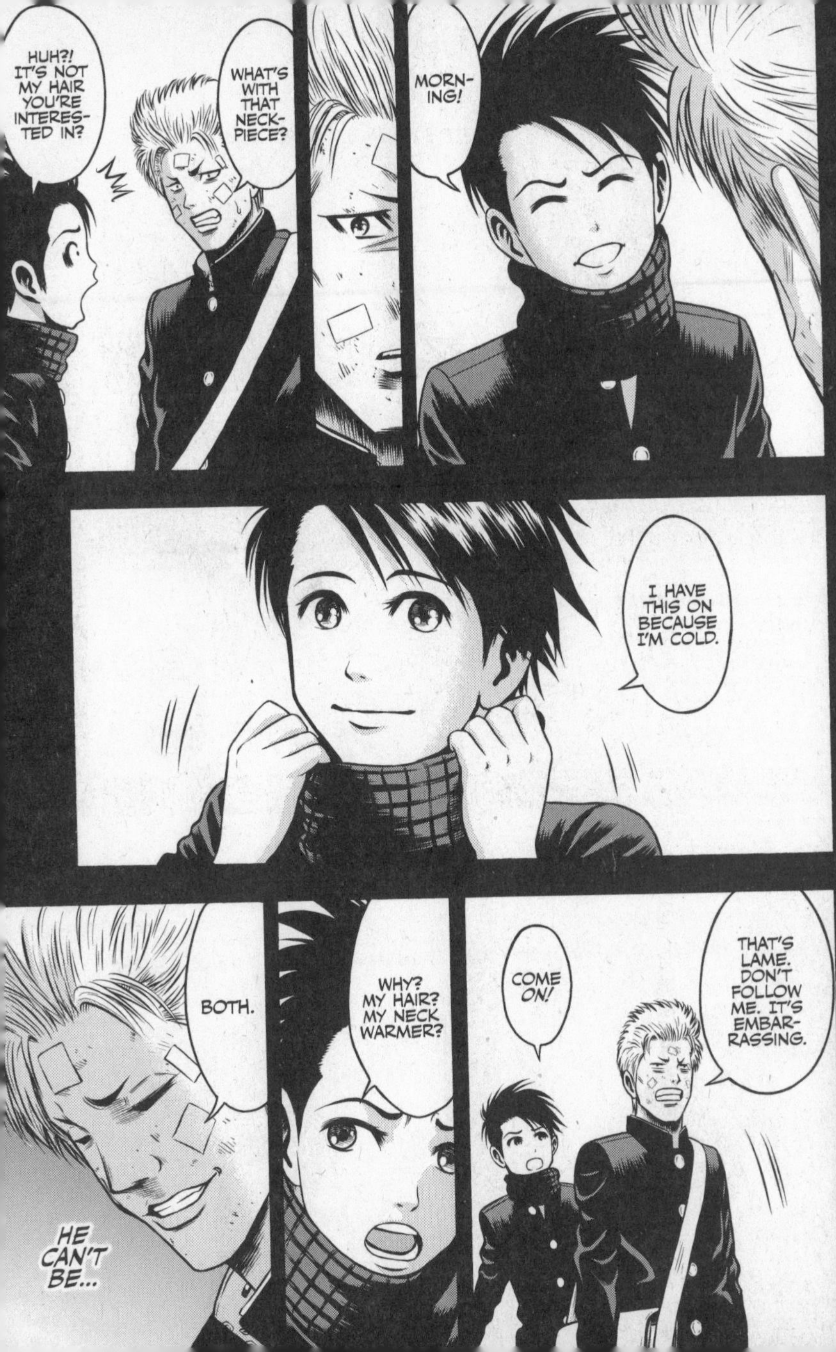
MORNING!
WHAT'S WITH THAT NECKPIECE?
HUH?! IT'S NOT MY HAIR YOU'RE INTERESTED IN?
I HAVE THIS ON BECAUSE I'M COLD.
THAT'S LAME. DON'T FOLLOW ME. IT'S EMBARRASSING.
COME ON!
WHY? MY HAIR? MY NECK WARMER?
BOTH.
HE CAN'T BE...

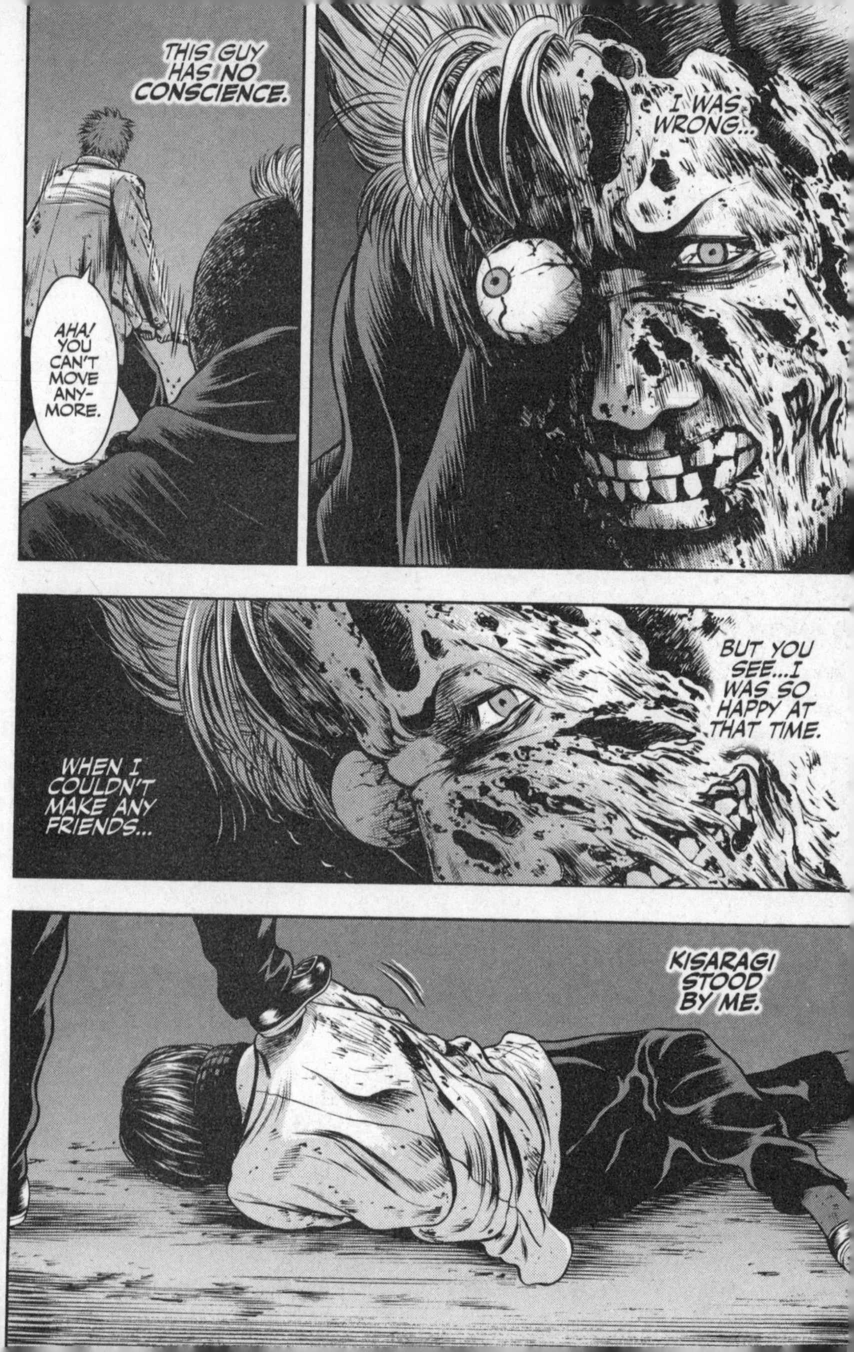
I WAS WRONG...
THIS GUY HAS NO CONSCIENCE.
AHA! YOU CAN'T MOVE ANY-MORE.
BUT YOU SEE...I WAS SO HAPPY AT THAT TIME.
WHEN I COULDN'T MAKE ANY FRIENDS...
KISARAGI STOOD BY ME.

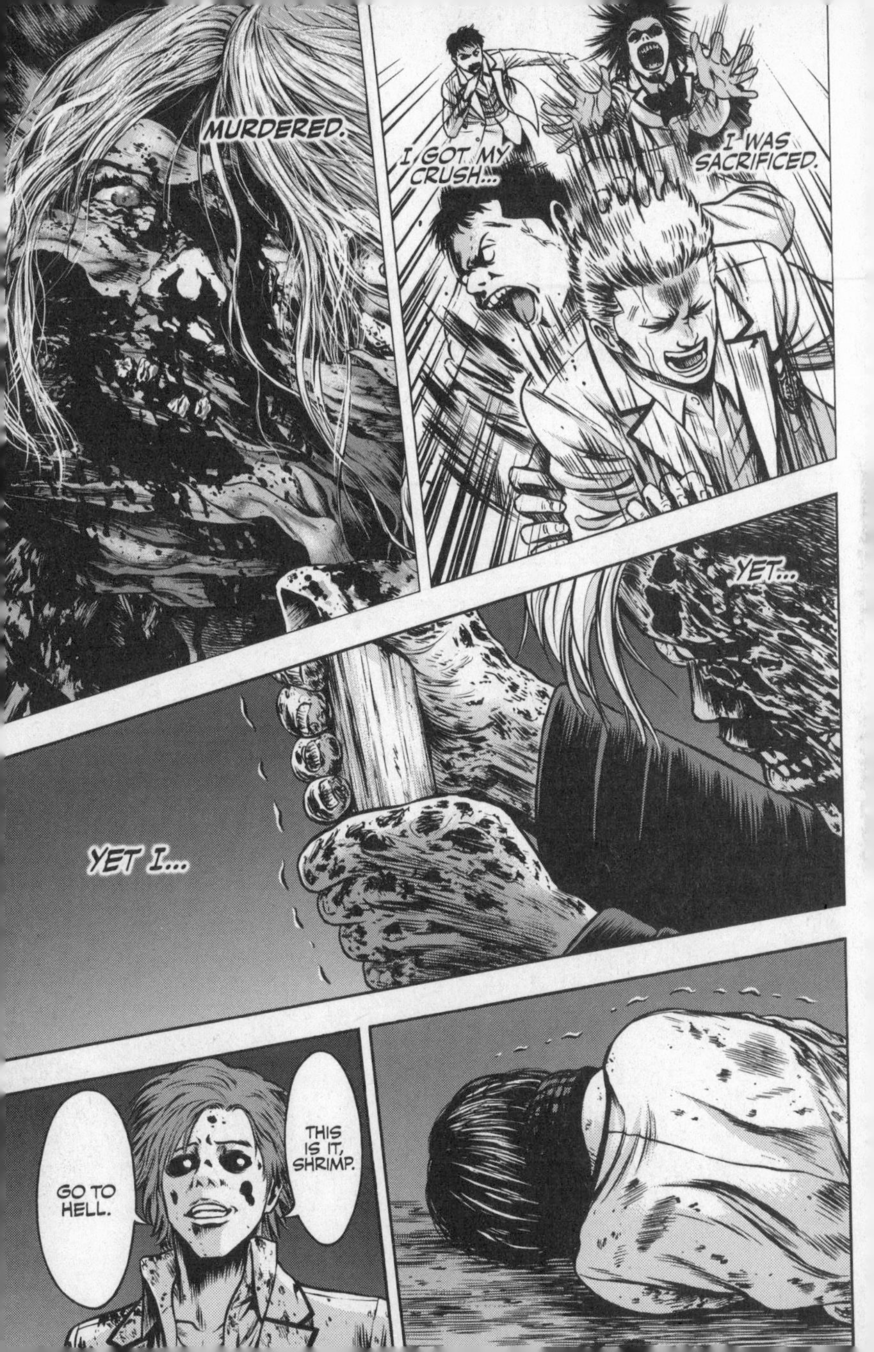
I WAS SACRIFICED.
I GOT MY CRUSH...
MURDERED.
YET...
YET I...
THIS IS IT, SHRIMP.
GO TO HELL.

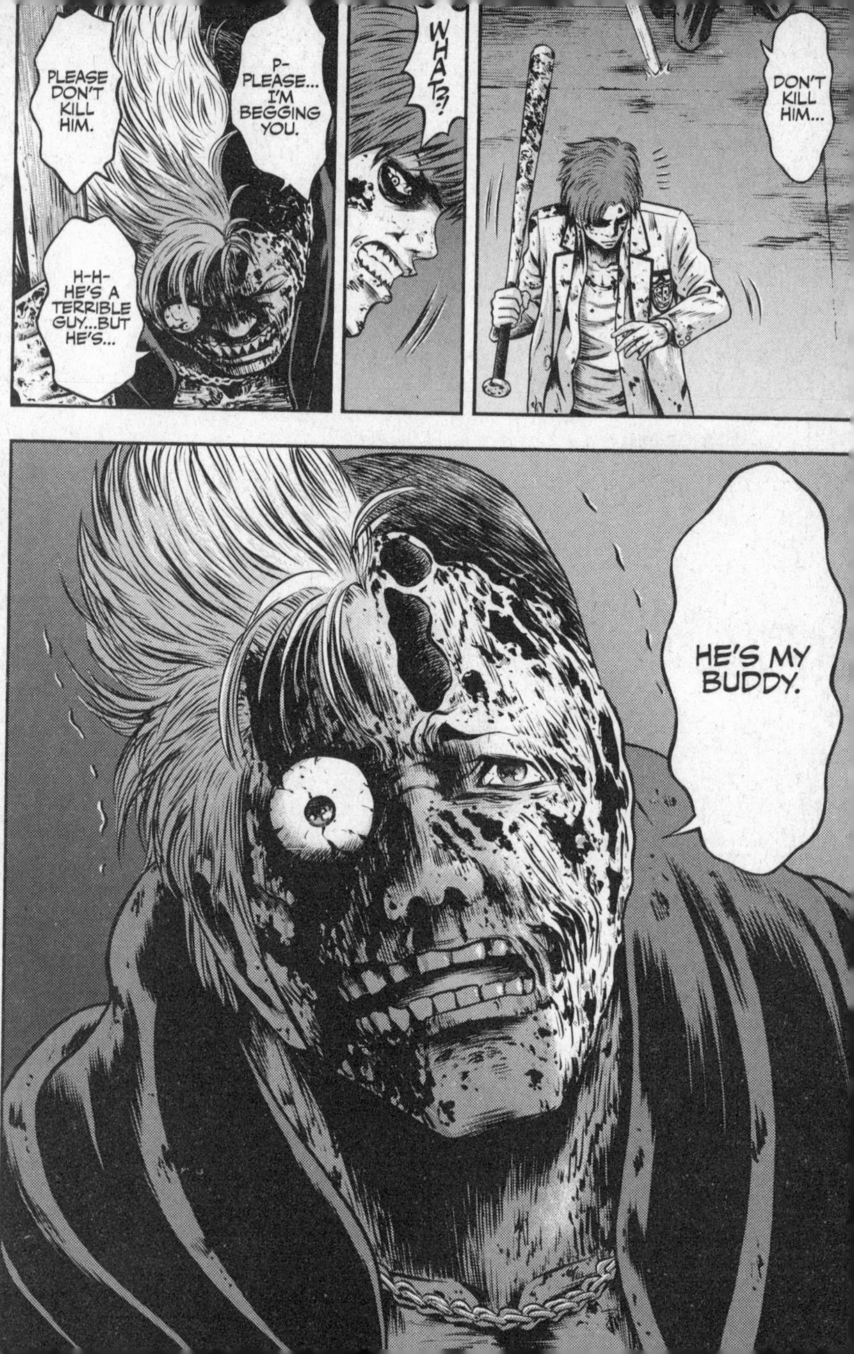
DON'T KILL HIM...
WHAT?!
P-PLEASE... I'M BEGGING YOU.
PLEASE DON'T KILL HIM.
H-H-HE'S A TERRIBLE GUY...BUT HE'S...
HE'S MY BUDDY.

HOUR OF THE ZOMBIE

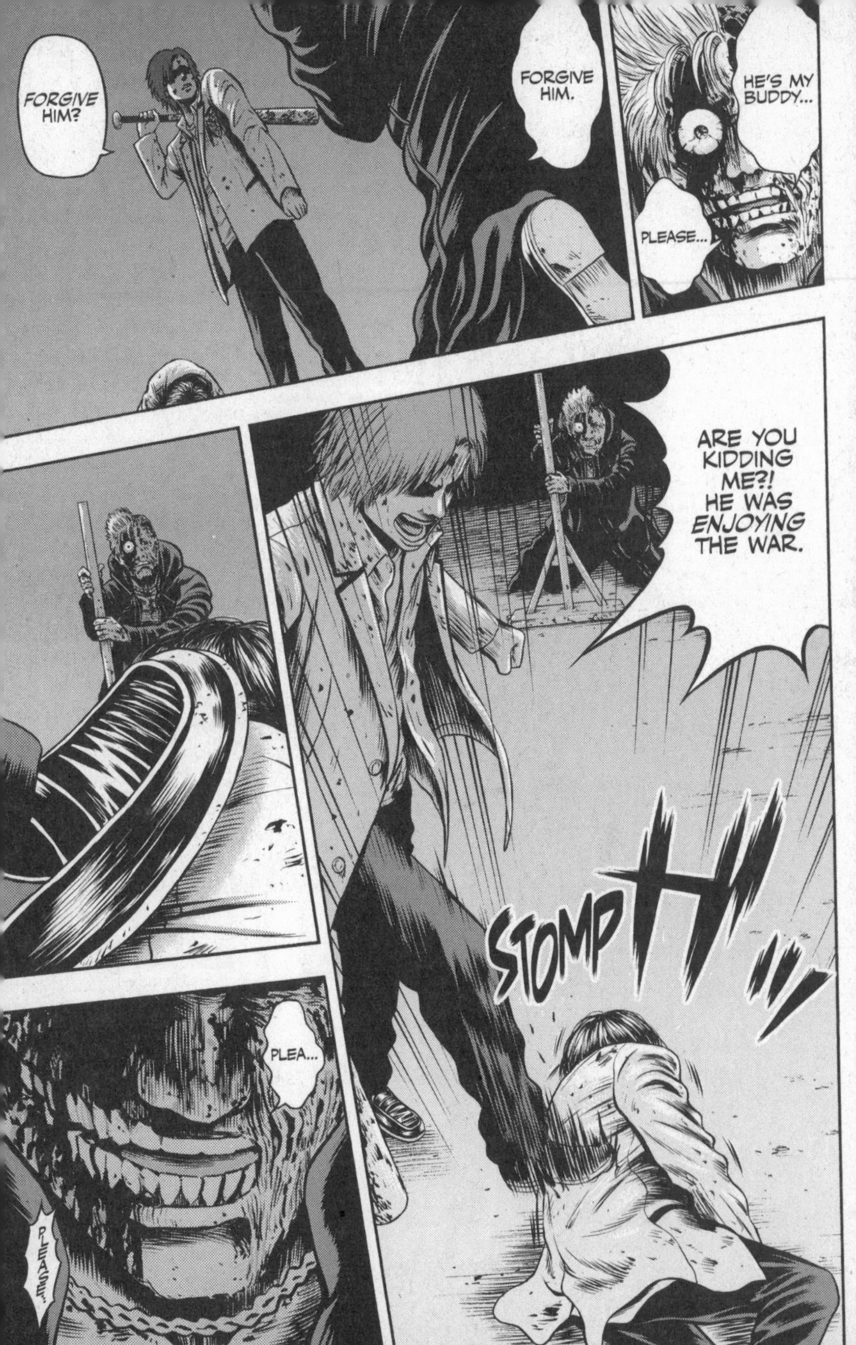
HE'S MY BUDDY...
PLEASE...
FORGIVE HIM.
FORGIVE HIM?
ARE YOU KIDDING ME?! HE WAS *ENJOYING* THE WAR.
STOMP!!
PLEA...
PLEASE...

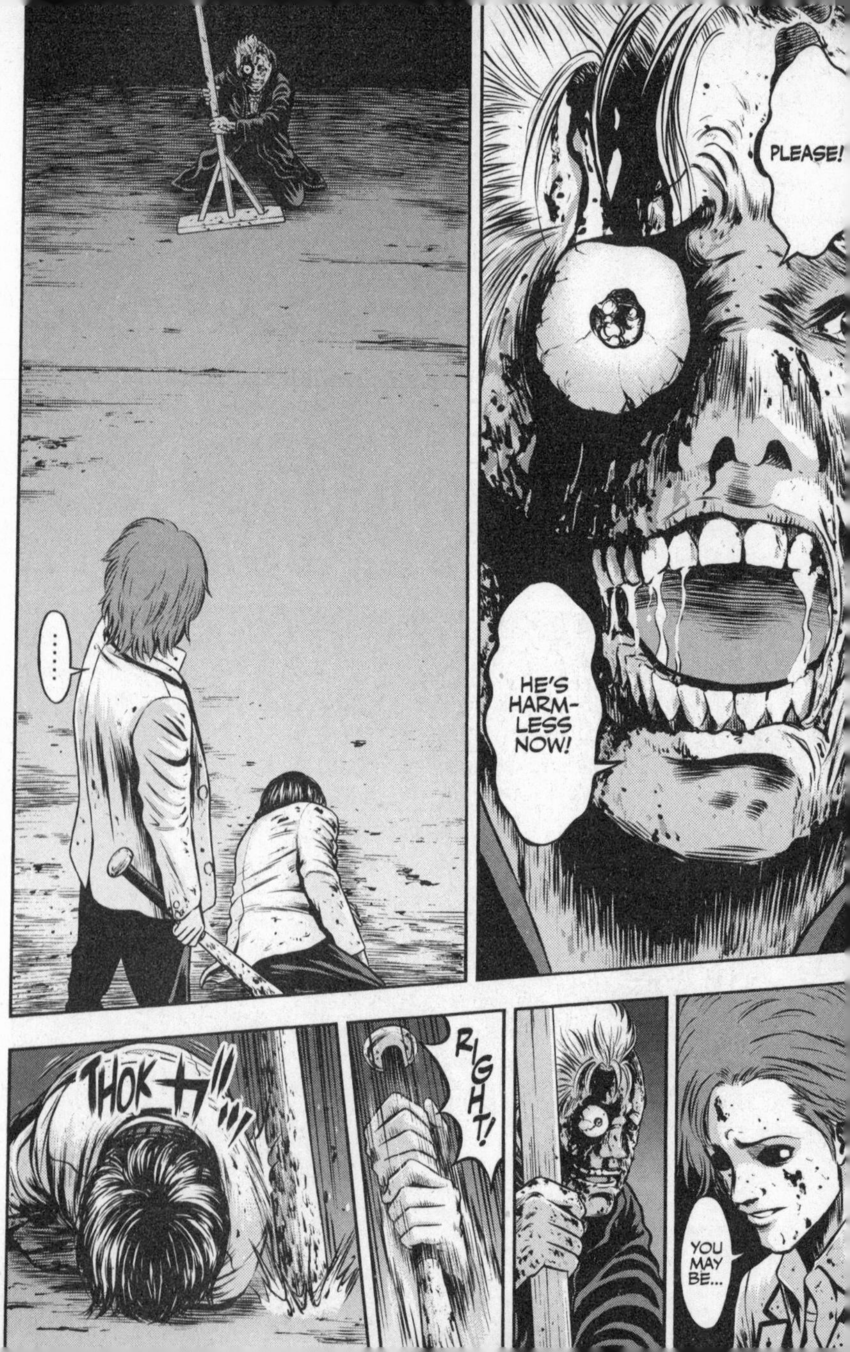
PLEASE!
HE'S HARMLESS NOW!
......
YOU MAY BE...
RIGHT!
THOK!!!

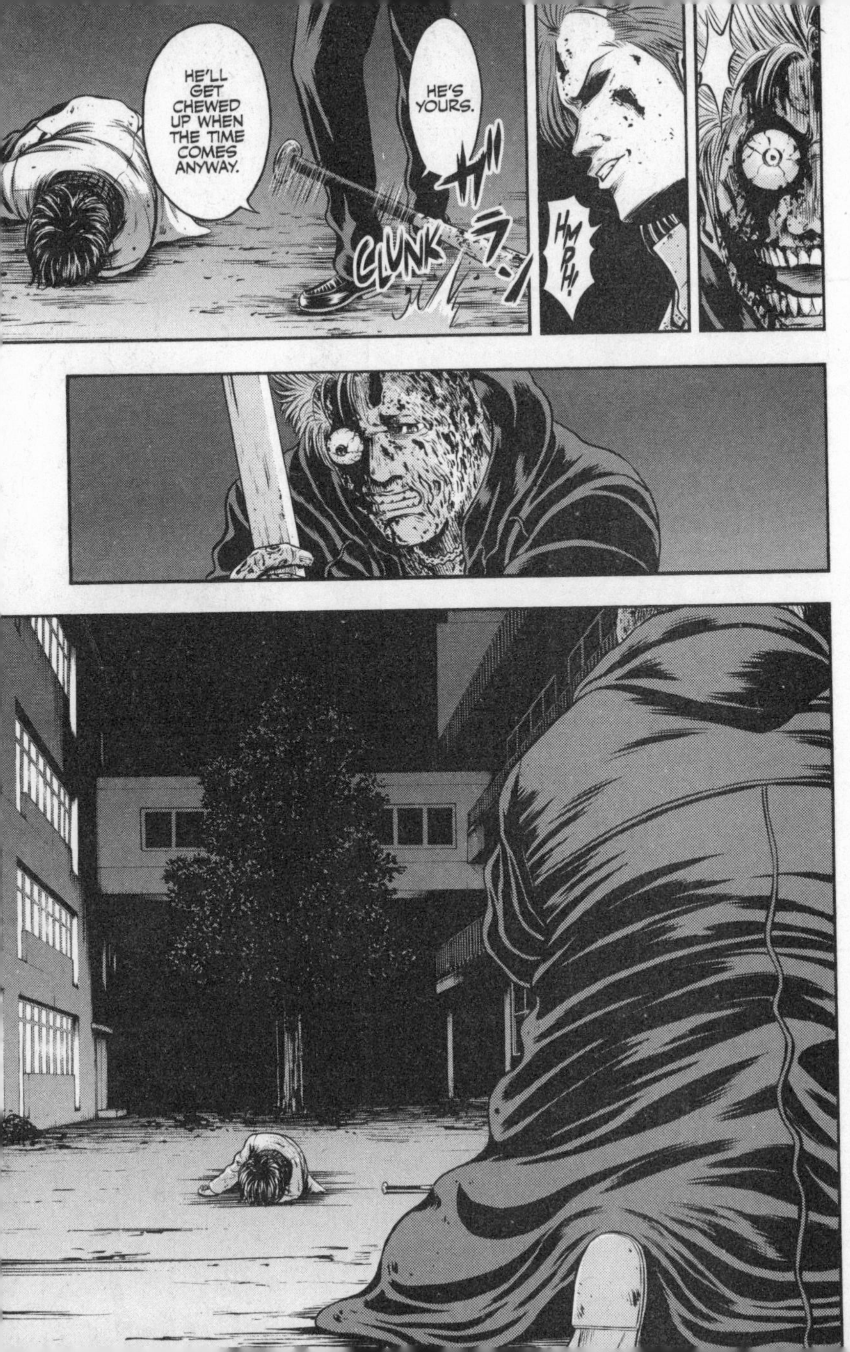
HMPH!
HE'S YOURS.
HE'LL GET CHEWED UP WHEN THE TIME COMES ANYWAY.
CLUNK

PHASE 41: Heaven and Hell

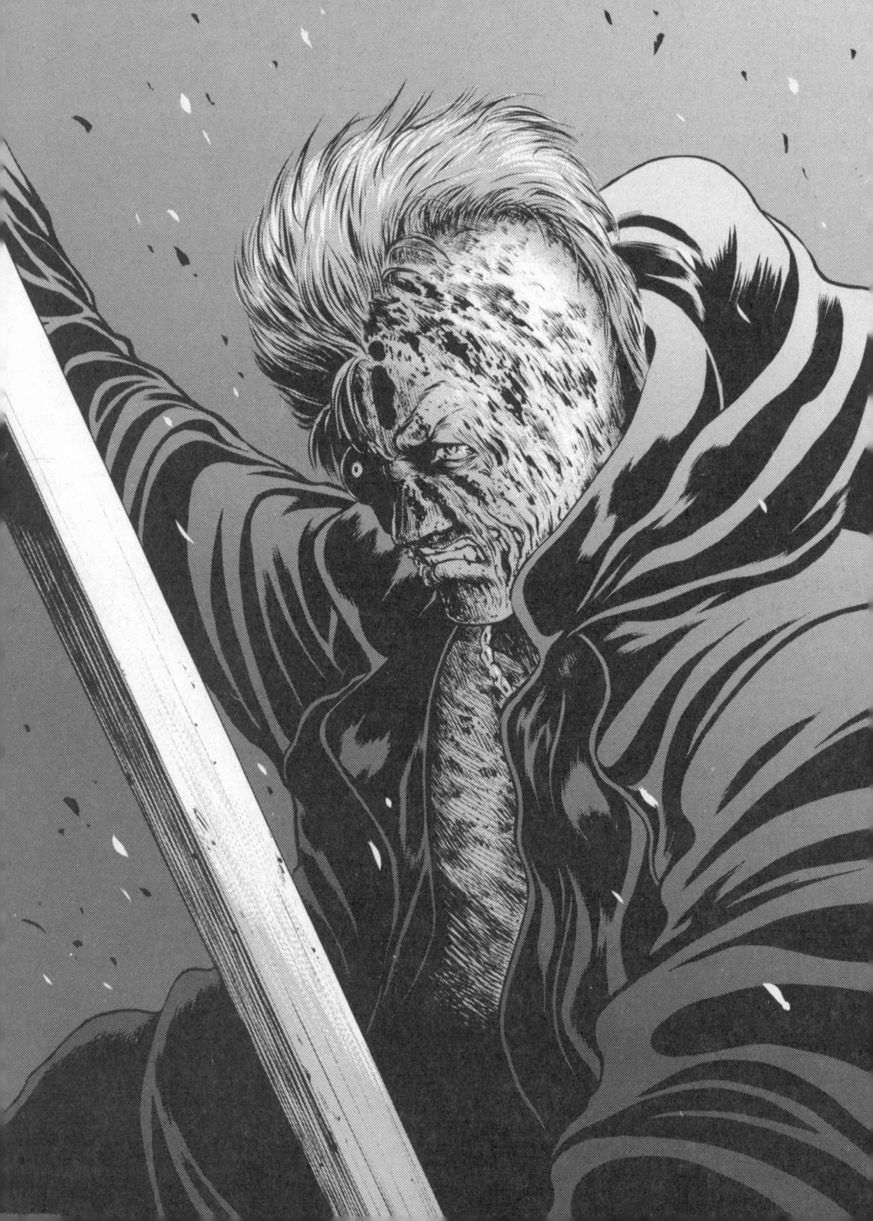

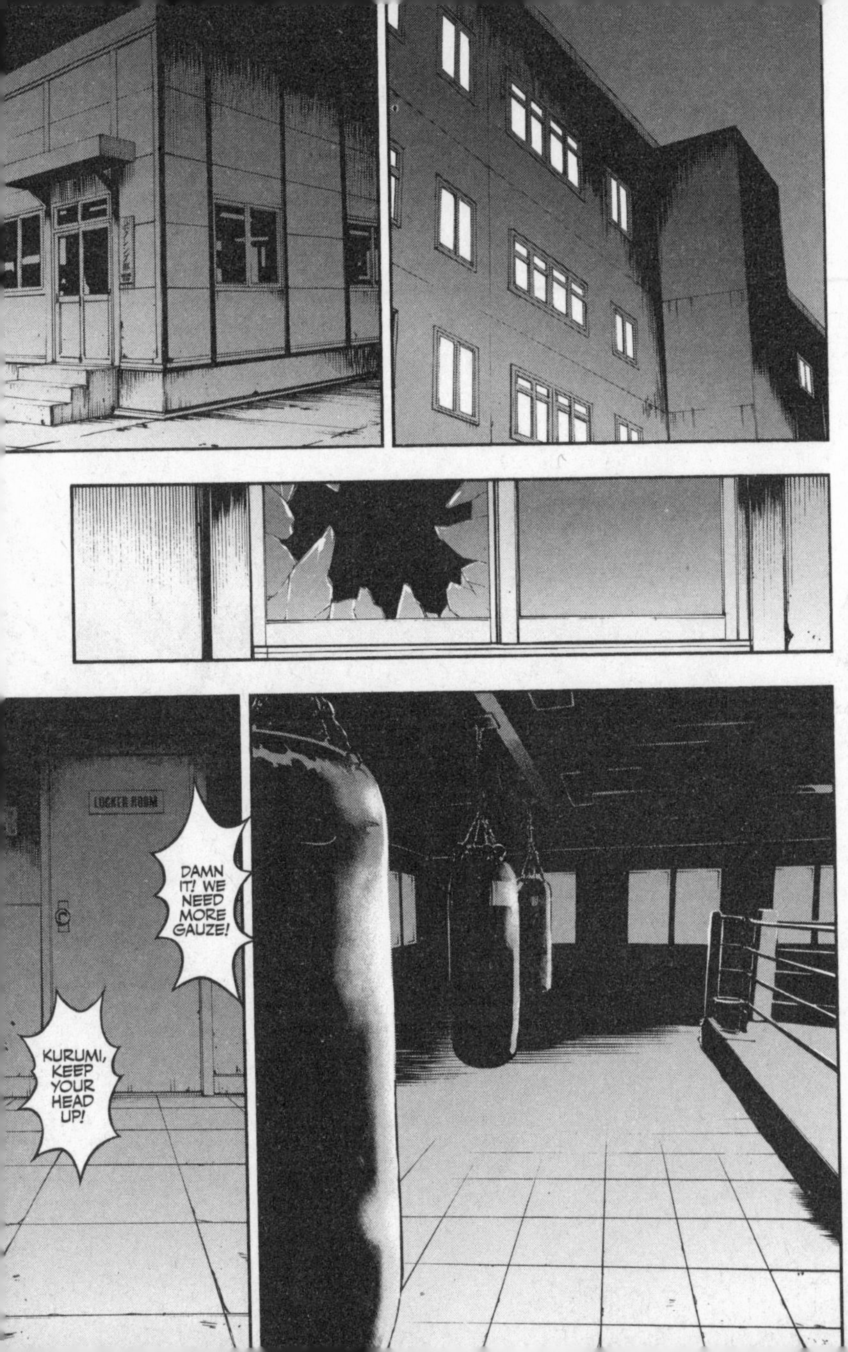
LOCKER ROOM
DAMN IT! WE NEED MORE GAUZE!
KURUMI, KEEP YOUR HEAD UP!

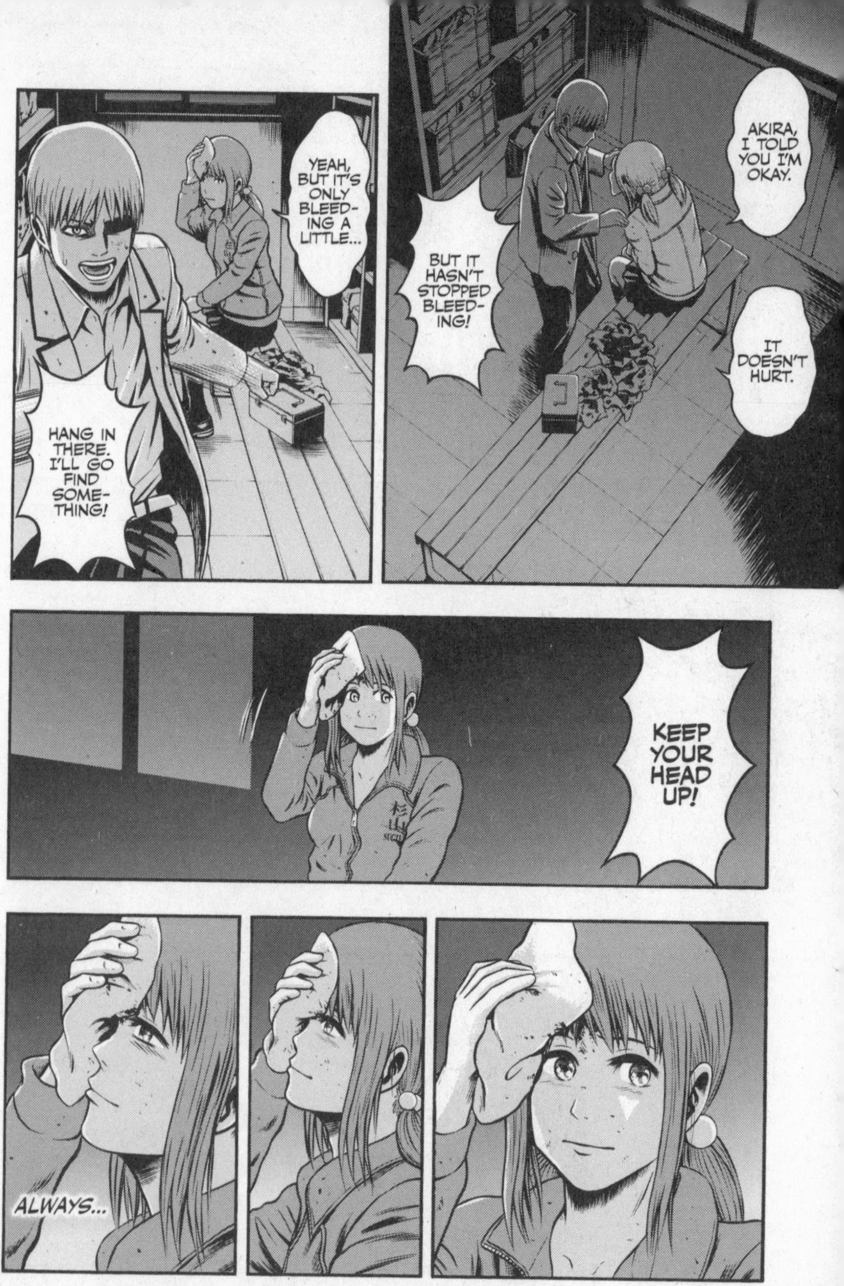
AKIRA, I TOLD YOU I'M OKAY.
BUT IT HASN'T STOPPED BLEEDING!
IT DOESN'T HURT.
YEAH, BUT IT'S ONLY BLEEDING A LITTLE...
HANG IN THERE. I'LL GO FIND SOMETHING!
KEEP YOUR HEAD UP!
ALWAYS...

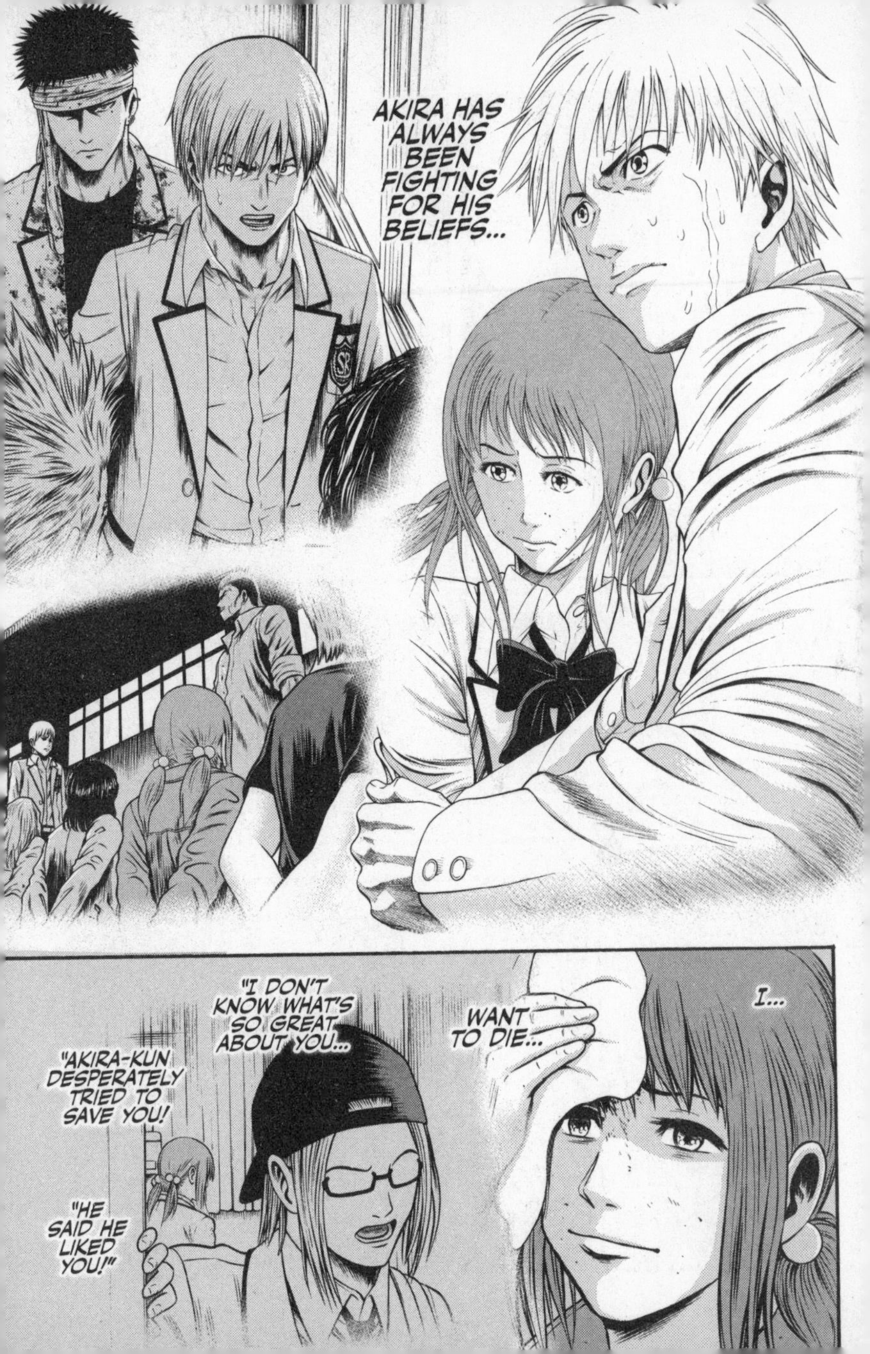
AKIRA HAS ALWAYS BEEN FIGHTING FOR HIS BELIEFS...
I...
WANT TO DIE...
"I DON'T KNOW WHAT'S SO GREAT ABOUT YOU...
"AKIRA-KUN DESPERATELY TRIED TO SAVE YOU!
"HE SAID HE LIKED YOU!"

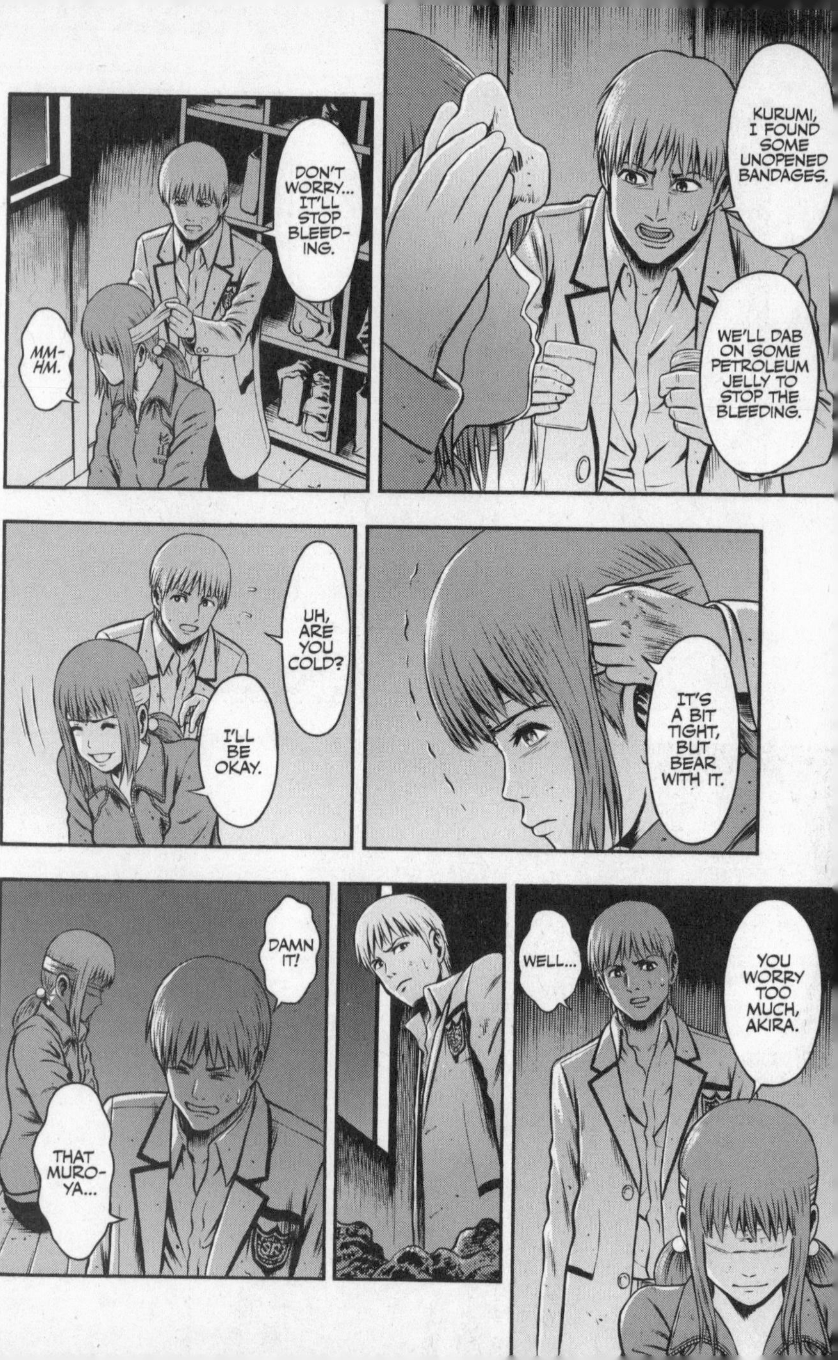
KURUMI, I FOUND SOME UNOPENED BANDAGES.
WE'LL DAB ON SOME PETROLEUM JELLY TO STOP THE BLEEDING.
DON'T WORRY... IT'LL STOP BLEED-ING.
MM-HM.
IT'S A BIT TIGHT, BUT BEAR WITH IT.
UH, ARE YOU COLD?
I'LL BE OKAY.
YOU WORRY TOO MUCH, AKIRA.
WELL...
DAMN IT!
THAT MURO-YA...

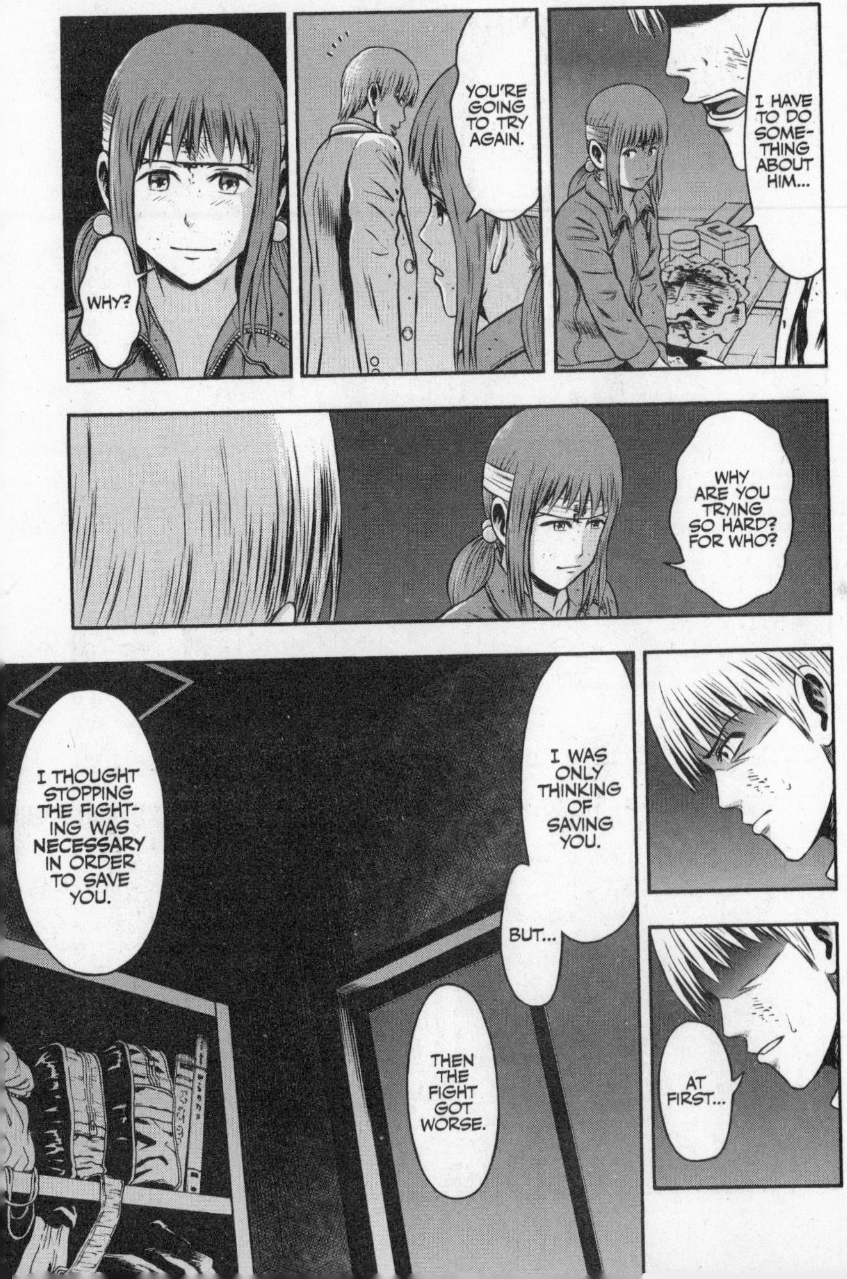
I HAVE TO DO SOME-THING ABOUT HIM...
YOU'RE GOING TO TRY AGAIN.
WHY?
WHY ARE YOU TRYING SO HARD? FOR WHO?
AT FIRST...
I WAS ONLY THINKING OF SAVING YOU.
I THOUGHT STOPPING THE FIGHT-ING WAS NECESSARY IN ORDER TO SAVE YOU.
BUT...
THEN THE FIGHT GOT WORSE.

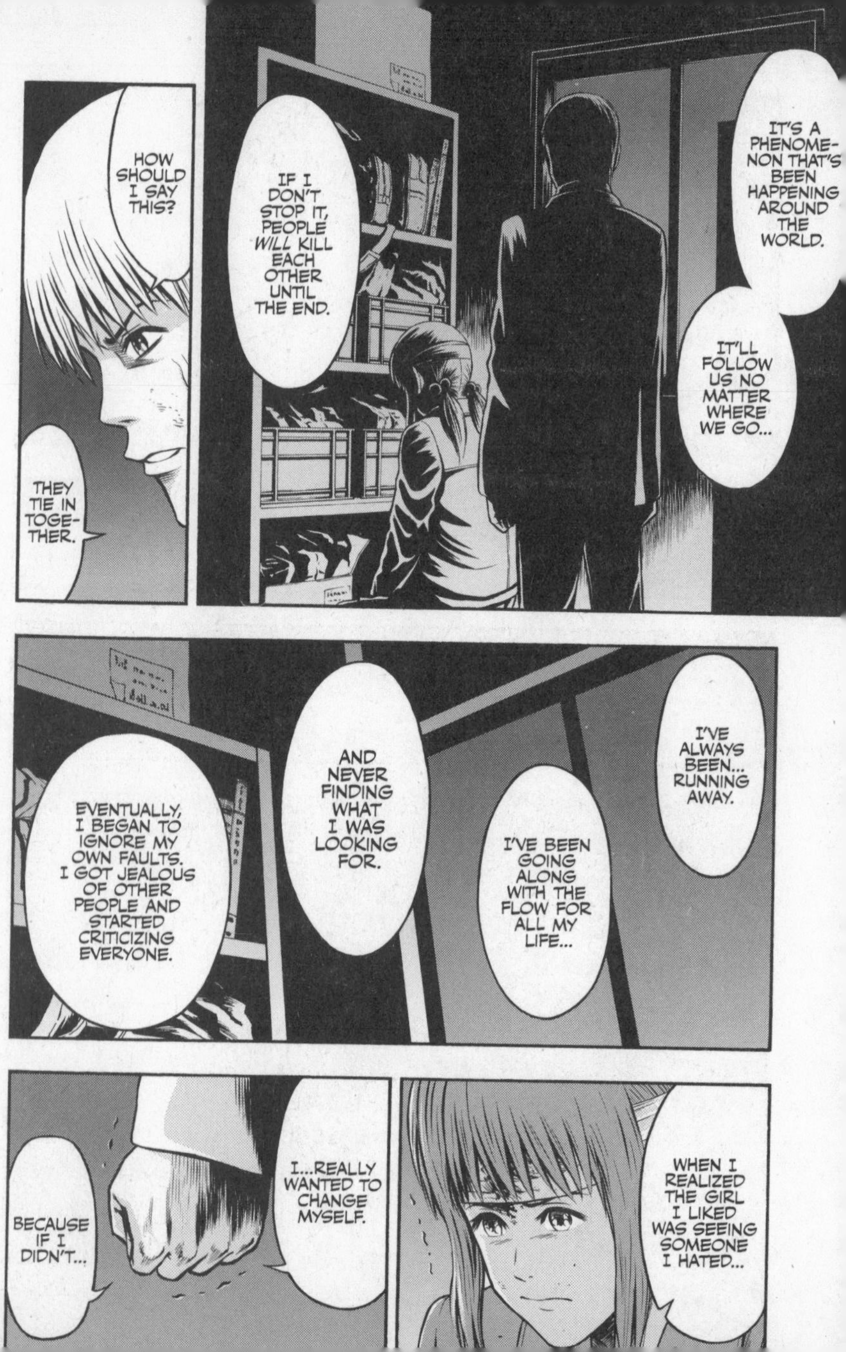
IT'S A PHENOMENON THAT'S BEEN HAPPENING AROUND THE WORLD.
IT'LL FOLLOW US NO MATTER WHERE WE GO...
IF I DON'T STOP IT, PEOPLE *WILL* KILL EACH OTHER UNTIL THE END.
HOW SHOULD I SAY THIS?
THEY TIE IN TOGETHER.
I'VE ALWAYS BEEN... RUNNING AWAY.
I'VE BEEN GOING ALONG WITH THE FLOW FOR ALL MY LIFE...
AND NEVER FINDING WHAT I WAS LOOKING FOR.
EVENTUALLY, I BEGAN TO IGNORE MY OWN FAULTS. I GOT JEALOUS OF OTHER PEOPLE AND STARTED CRITICIZING EVERYONE.
WHEN I REALIZED THE GIRL I LIKED WAS SEEING SOMEONE I HATED...
I...REALLY WANTED TO CHANGE MYSELF.
BECAUSE IF I DIDN'T...

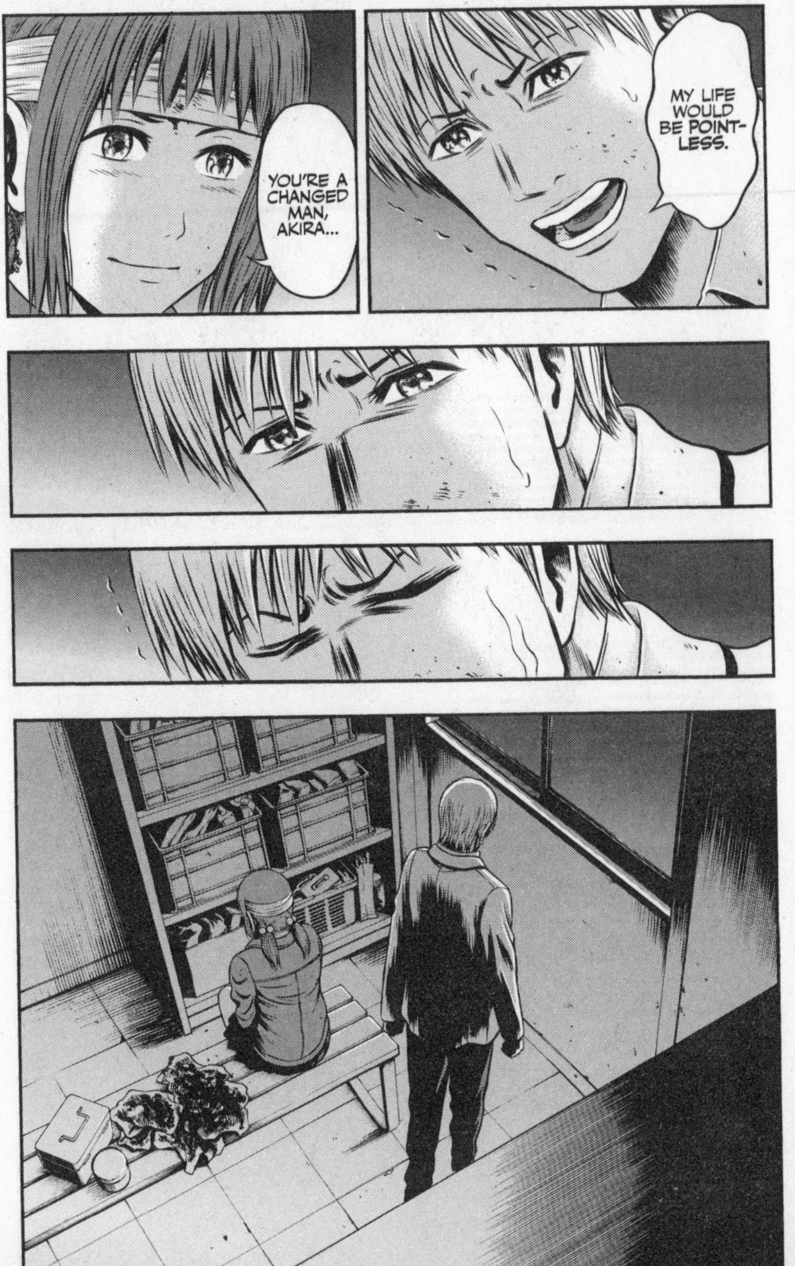
MY LIFE WOULD BE POINTLESS.
YOU'RE A CHANGED MAN, AKIRA...

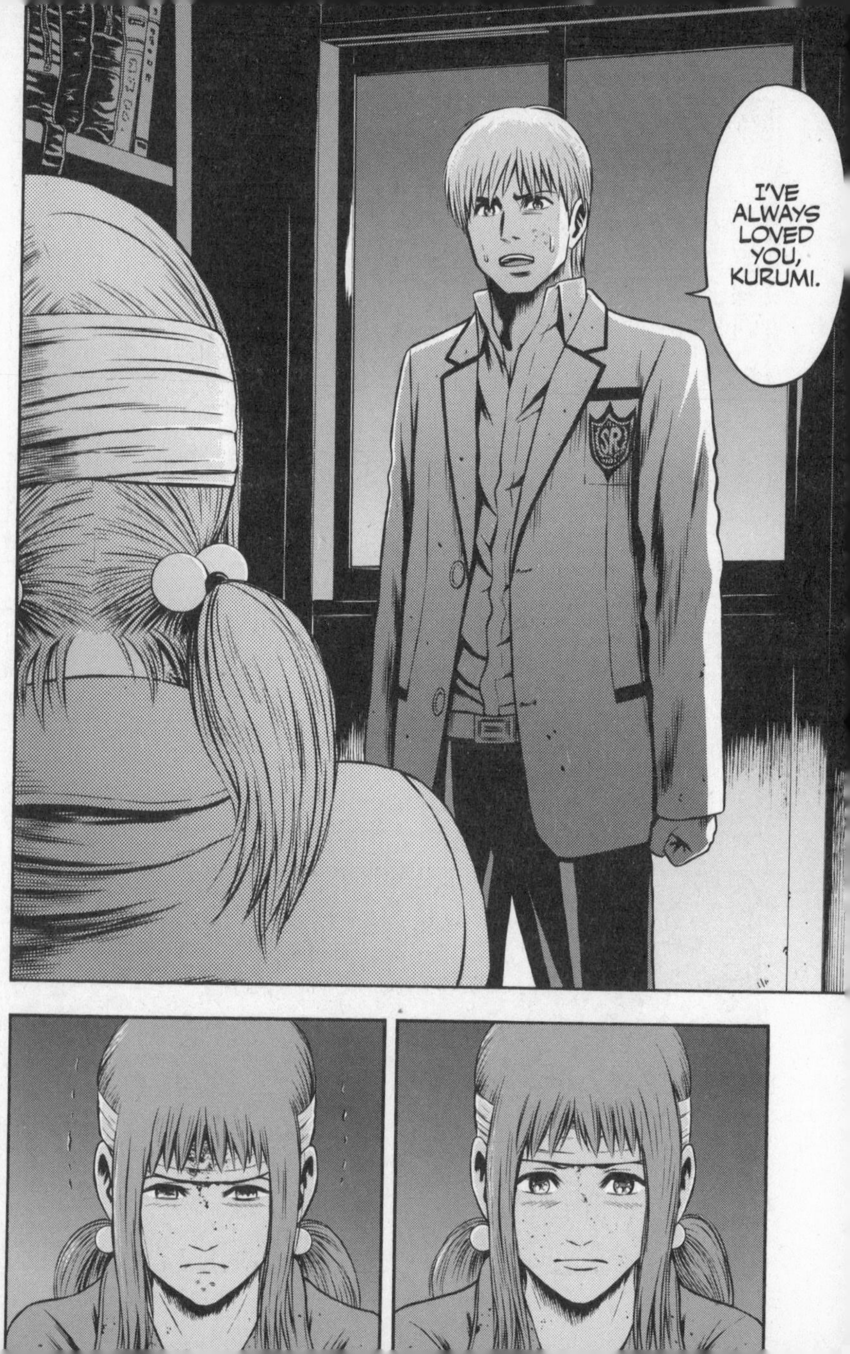
I'VE ALWAYS LOVED YOU, KURUMI.

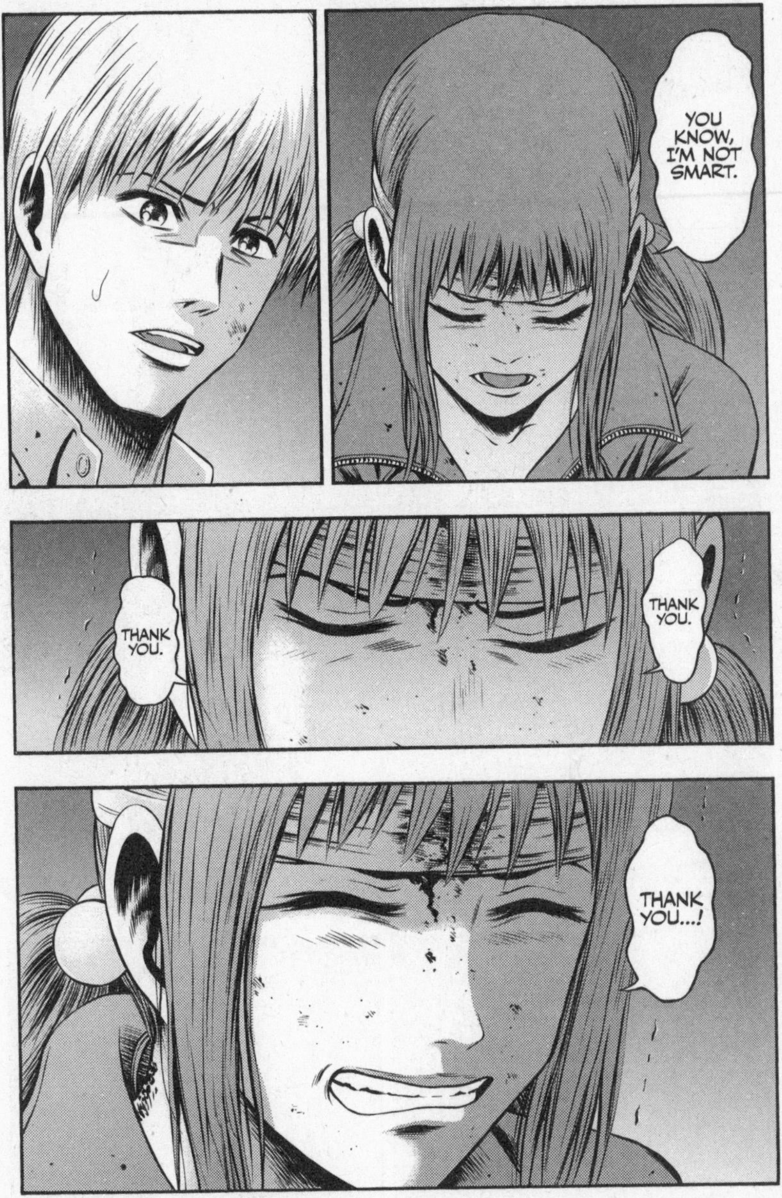
YOU KNOW, I'M NOT SMART.
THANK YOU.
THANK YOU.
THANK YOU...!

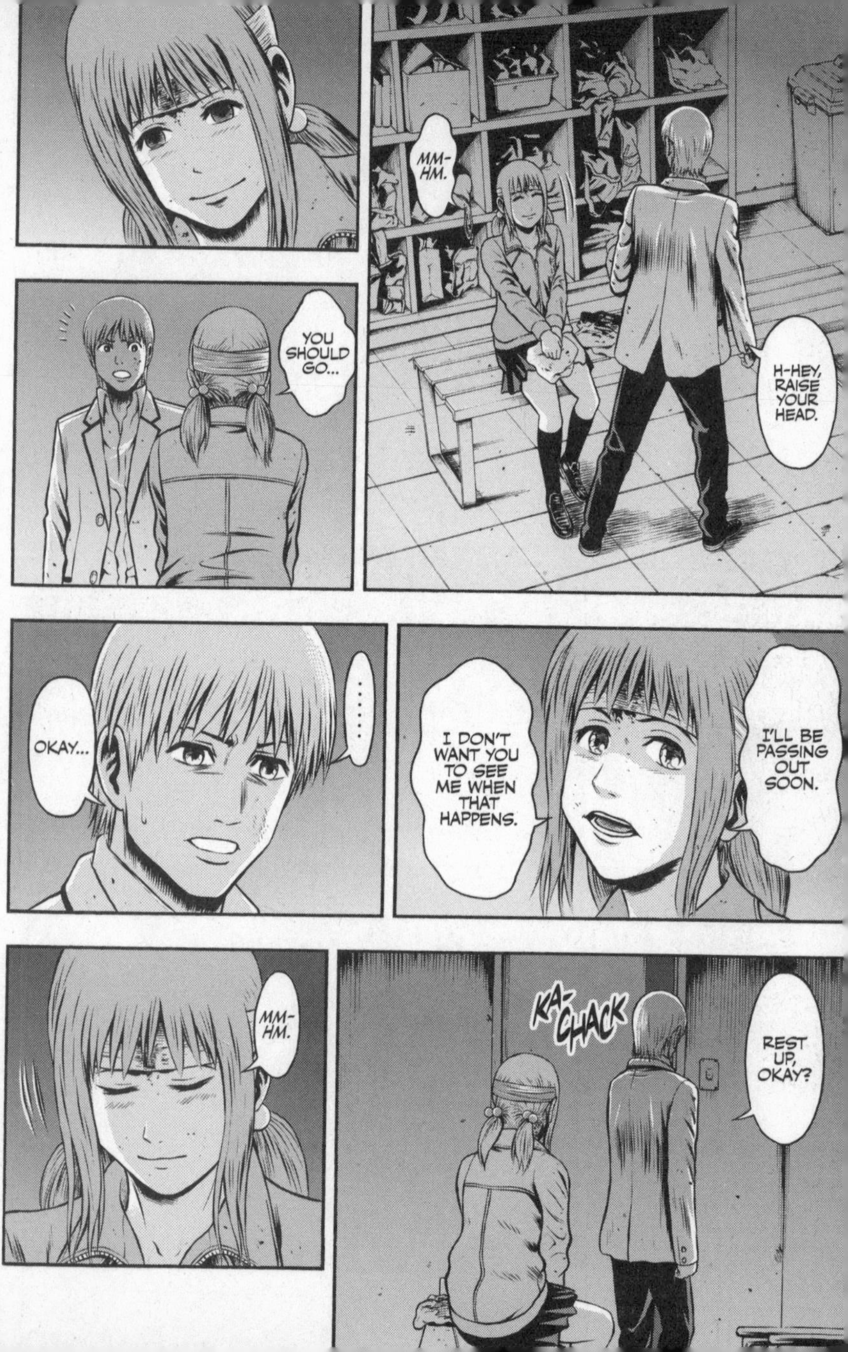
MM-HM.
H-HEY, RAISE YOUR HEAD.
YOU SHOULD GO...
I'LL BE PASSING OUT SOON.
I DON'T WANT YOU TO SEE ME WHEN THAT HAPPENS.
......
OKAY...
KA-CHACK
REST UP, OKAY?
MM-HM.

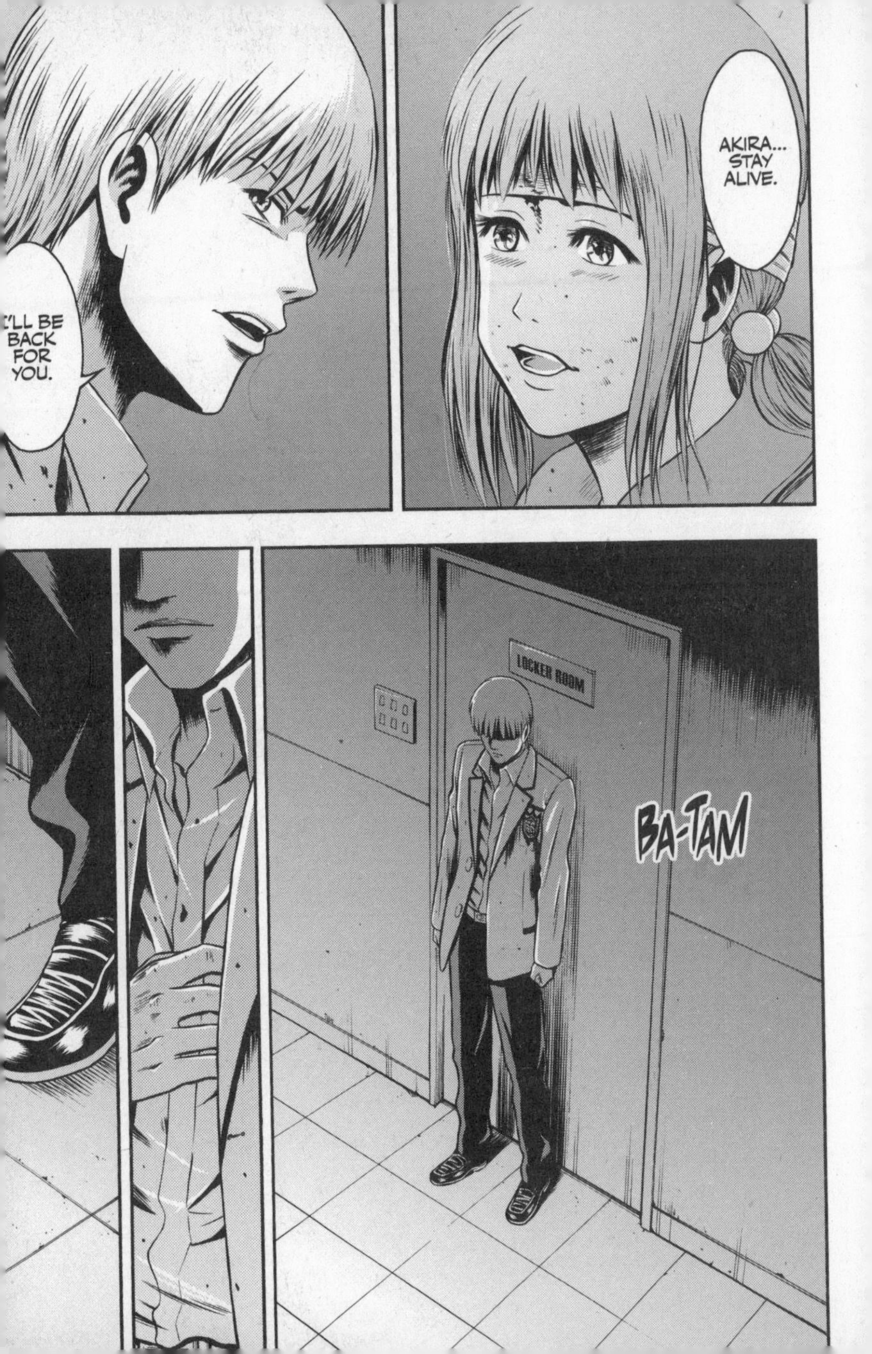

AKIRA... STAY ALIVE.
I'LL BE BACK FOR YOU.
LOCKER ROOM
BA-TAM

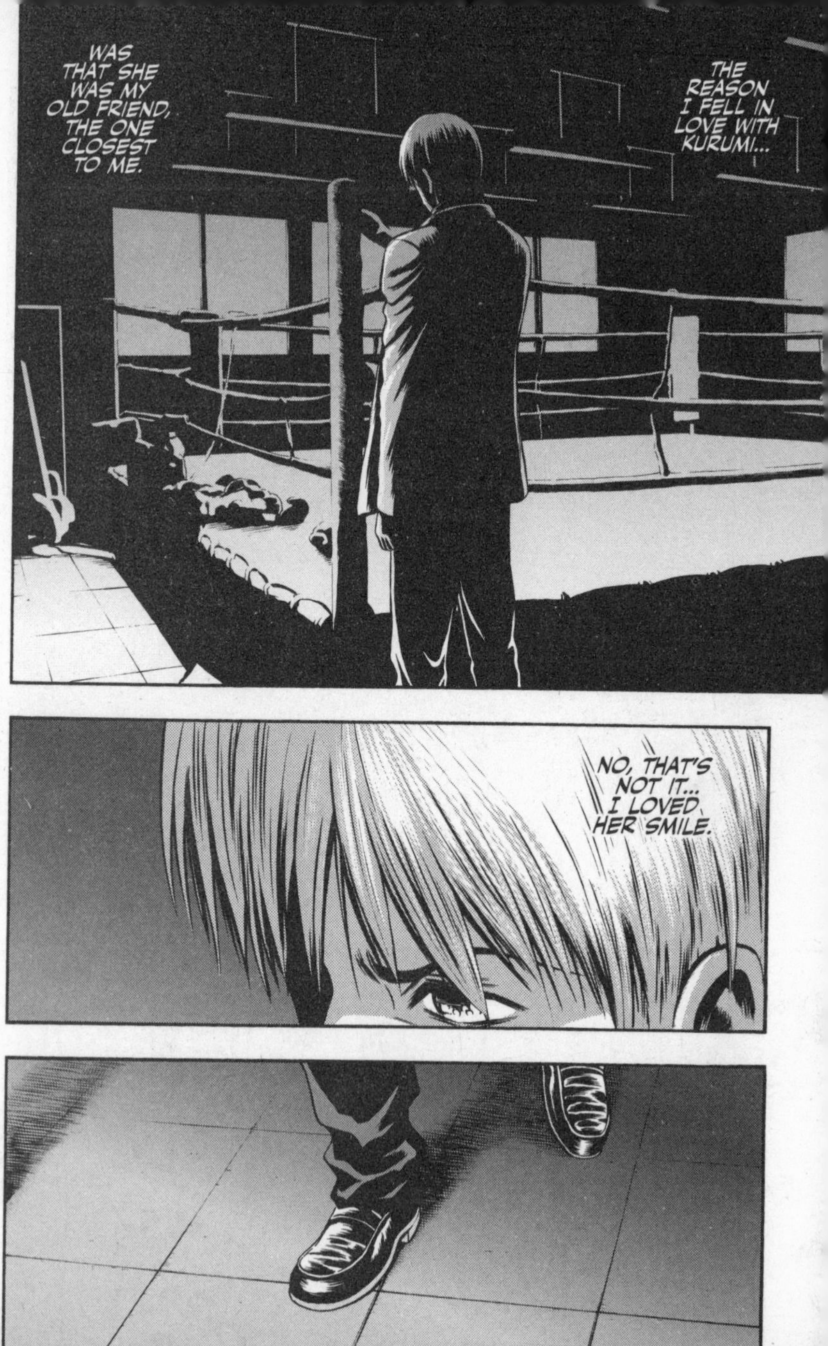
THE REASON I FELL IN LOVE WITH KURUMI...
WAS THAT SHE WAS MY OLD FRIEND, THE ONE CLOSEST TO ME.
NO, THAT'S NOT IT... I LOVED HER SMILE.

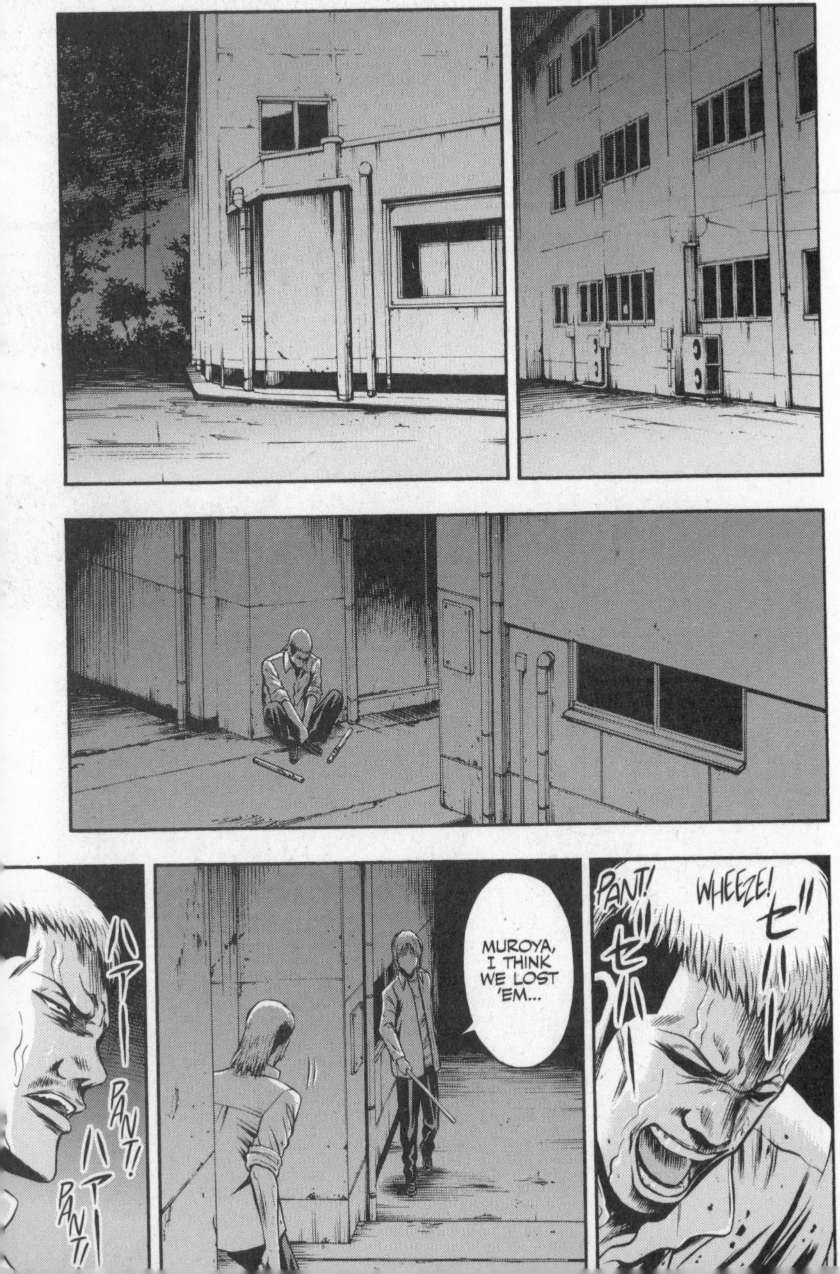
PANT!
WHEEZE!
MUROYA, I THINK WE LOST 'EM...
PANT!
PANT!

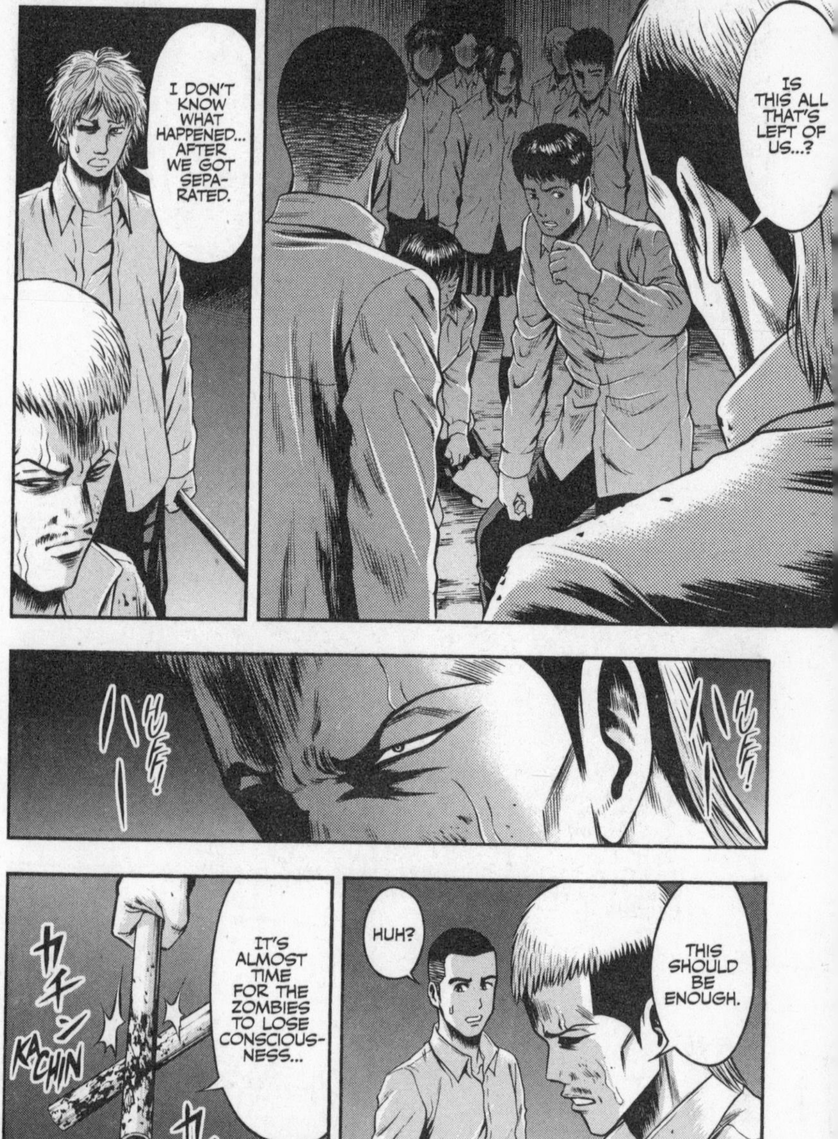
IS THIS ALL THAT'S LEFT OF US...?
I DON'T KNOW WHAT HAPPENED... AFTER WE GOT SEPA-RATED.
HUFF!
HUFF!
THIS SHOULD BE ENOUGH.
HUH?
IT'S ALMOST TIME FOR THE ZOMBIES TO LOSE CONSCIOUS-NESS...
KACHIN
KACHIN

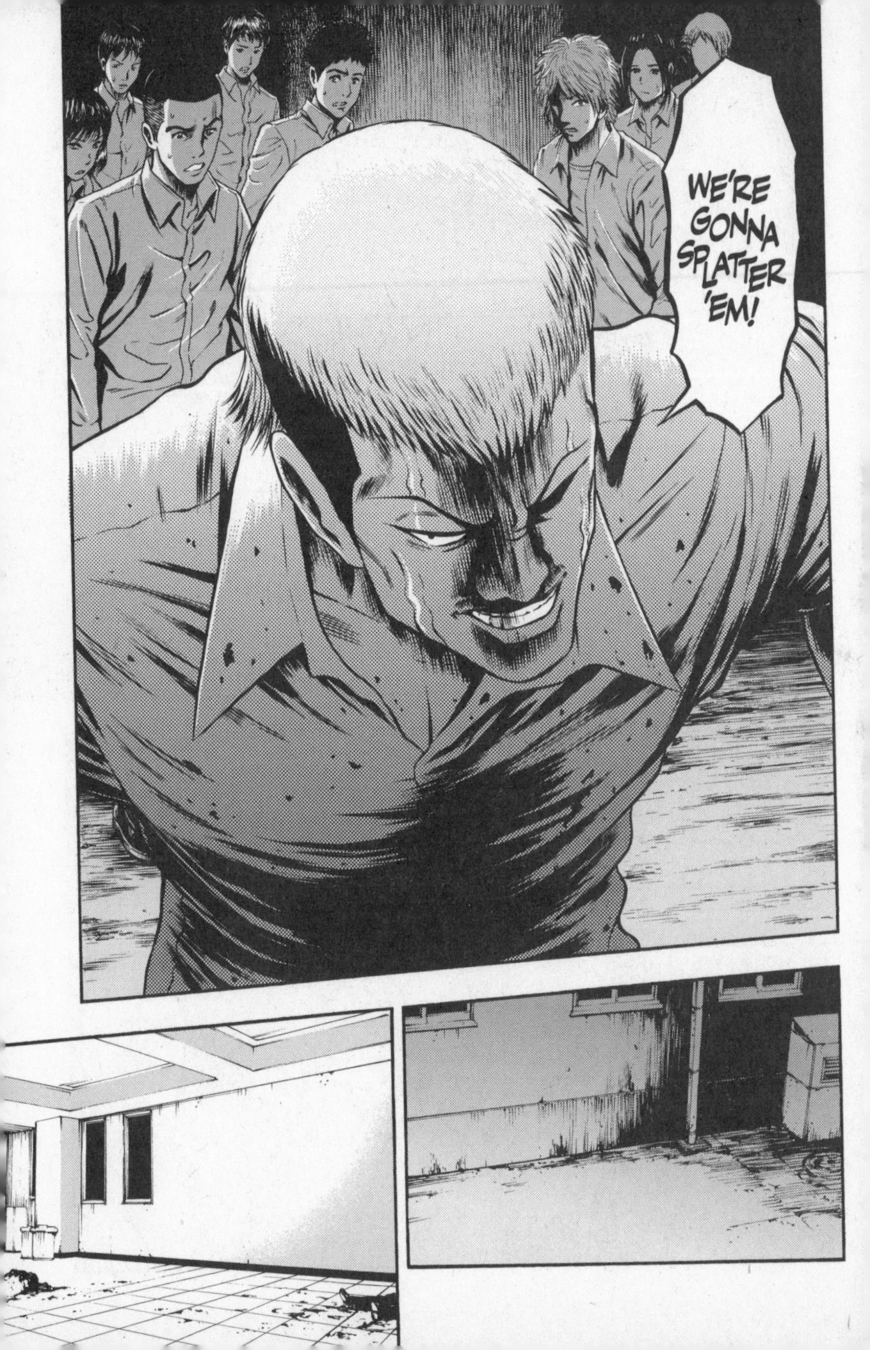
WE'RE GONNA SPLATTER 'EM!

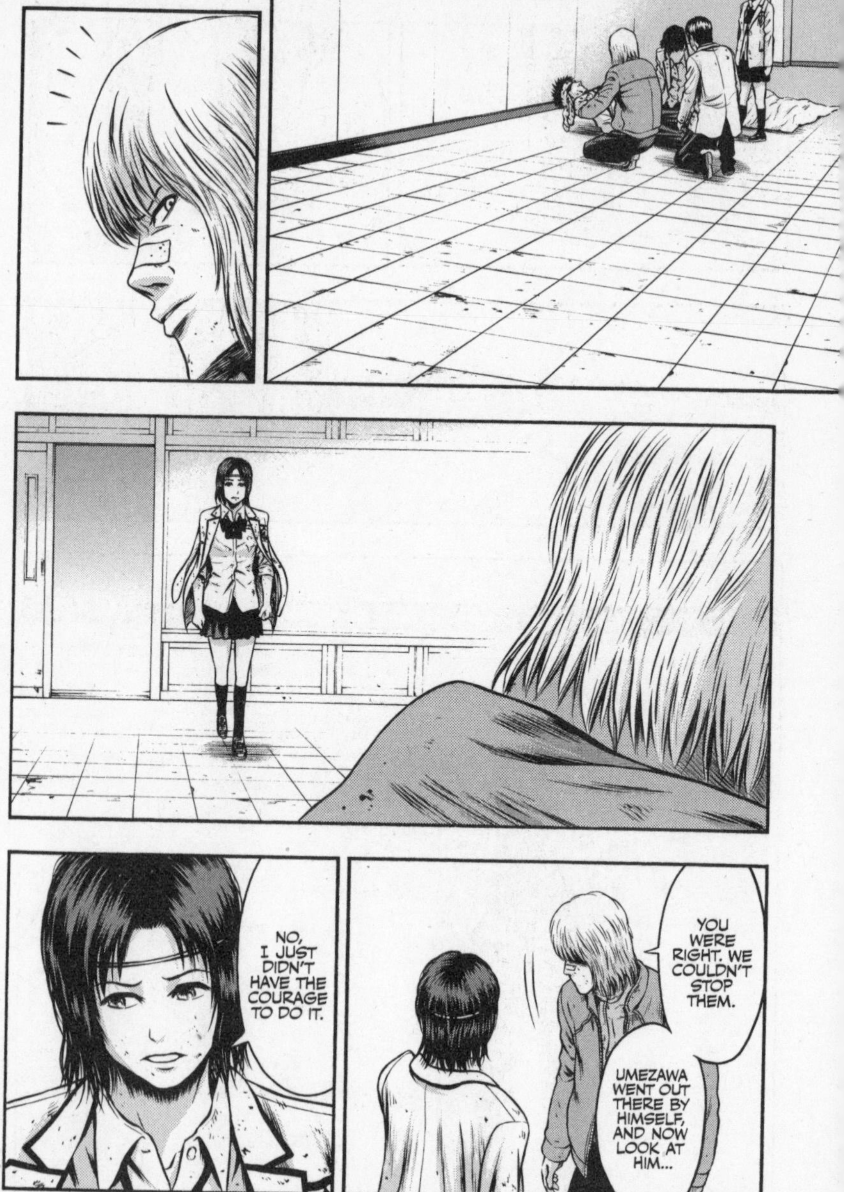
YOU WERE RIGHT. WE COULDN'T STOP THEM.
UMEZAWA WENT OUT THERE BY HIMSELF, AND NOW LOOK AT HIM...
NO, I JUST DIDN'T HAVE THE COURAGE TO DO IT.

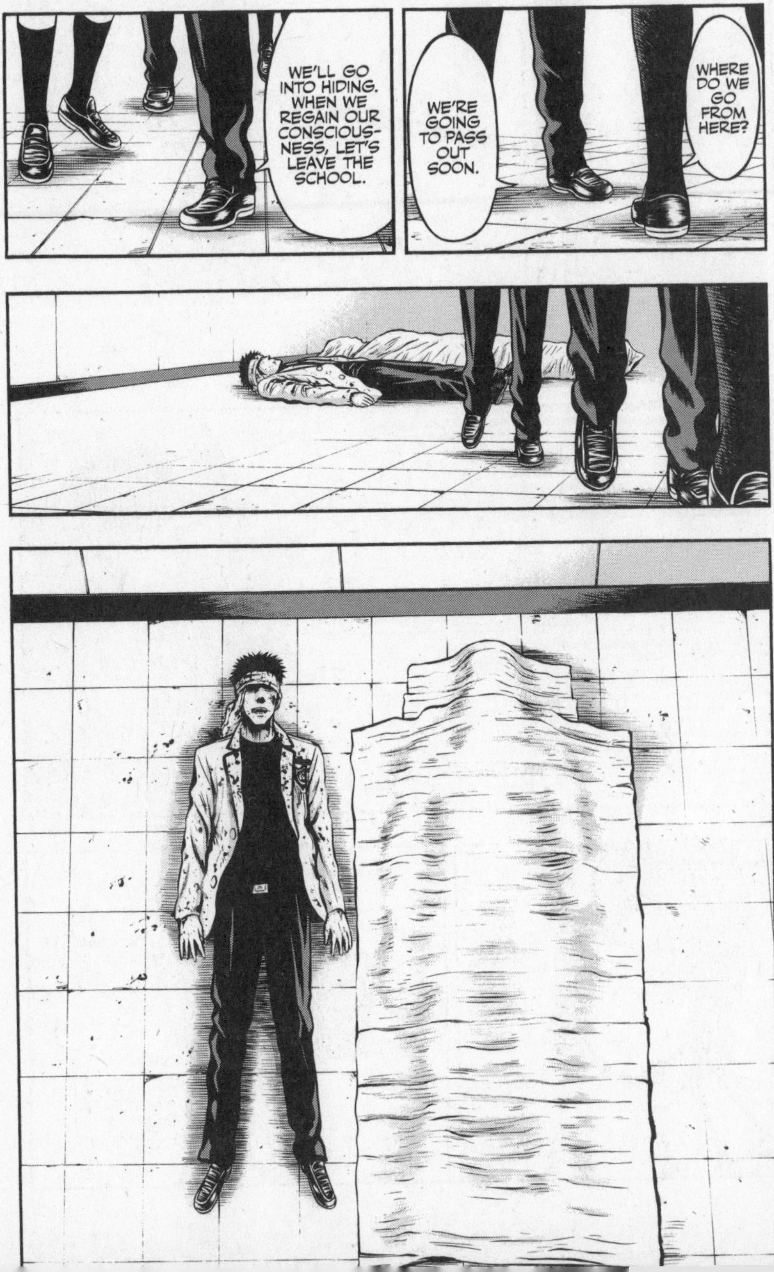
WHERE DO WE GO FROM HERE?
WE'RE GOING TO PASS OUT SOON.
WE'LL GO INTO HIDING. WHEN WE REGAIN OUR CONSCIOUS-NESS, LET'S LEAVE THE SCHOOL.

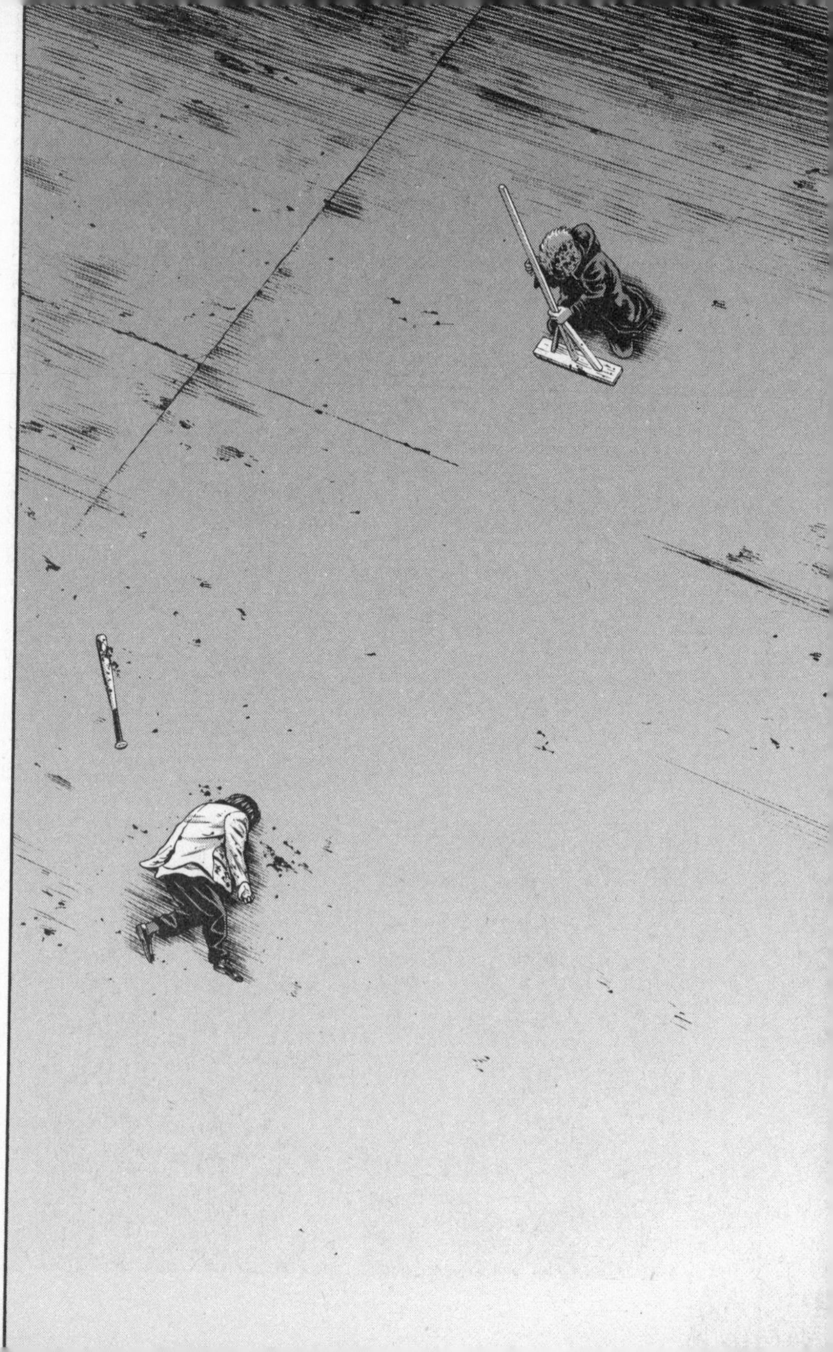

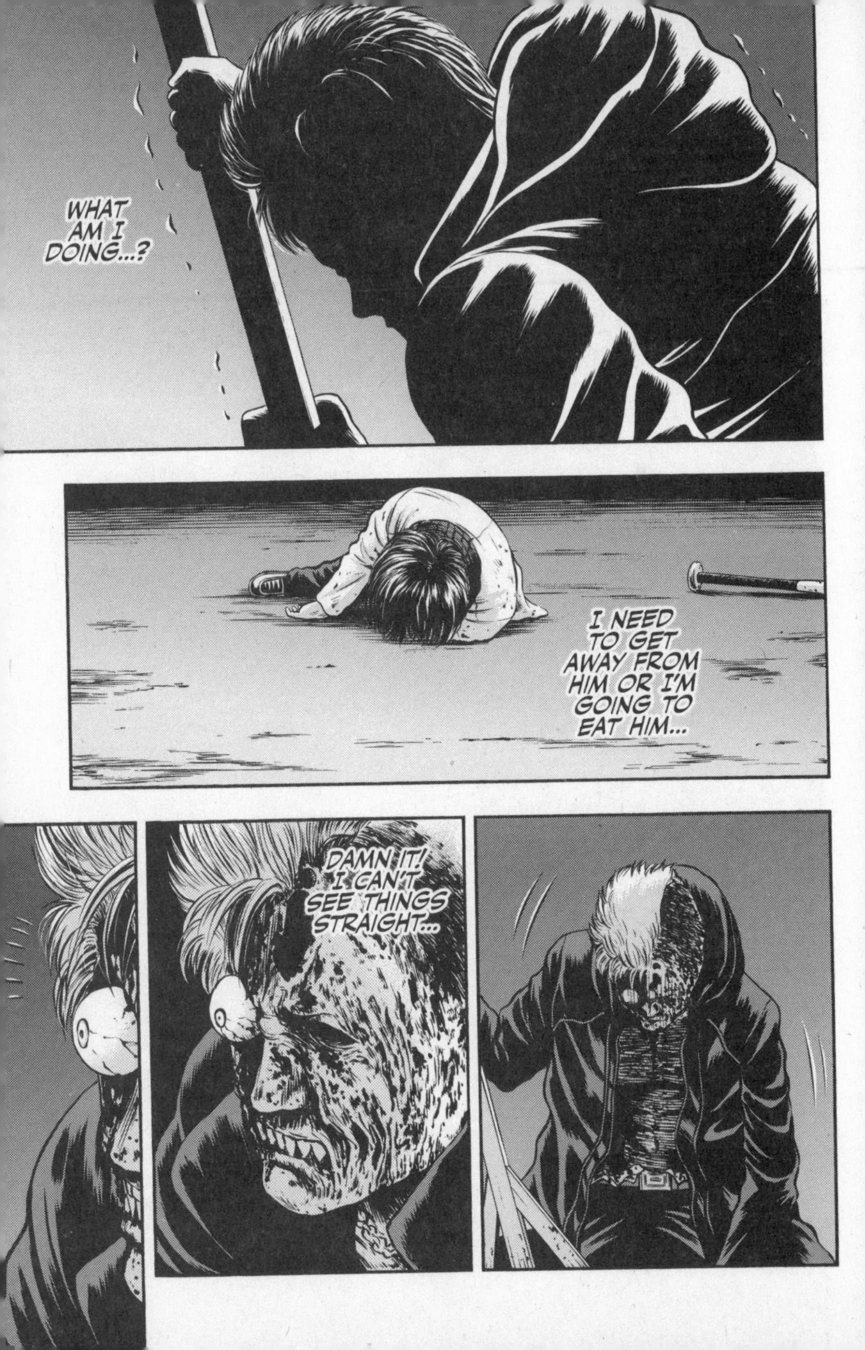
WHAT AM I DOING...?
I NEED TO GET AWAY FROM HIM OR I'M GOING TO EAT HIM...
DAMN IT! I CAN'T SEE THINGS STRAIGHT...

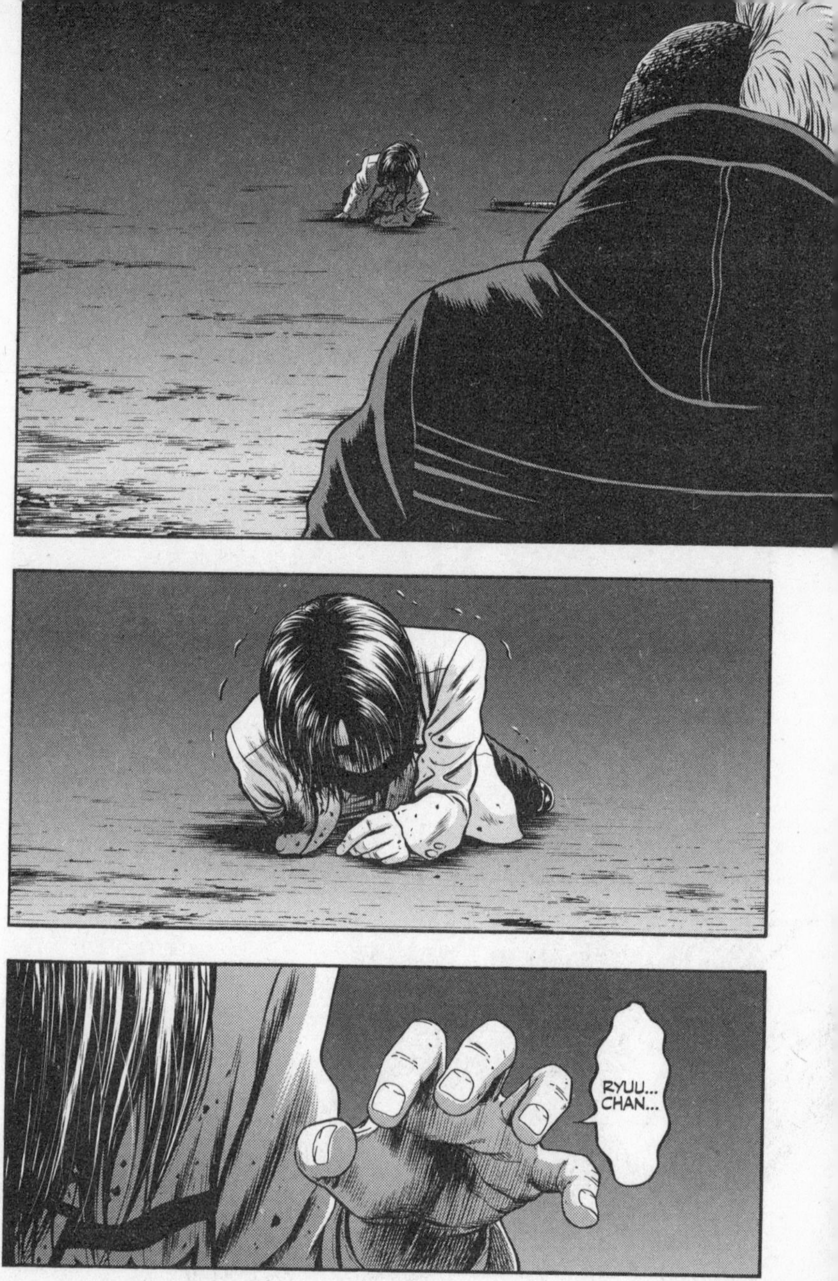
RYUU... CHAN...

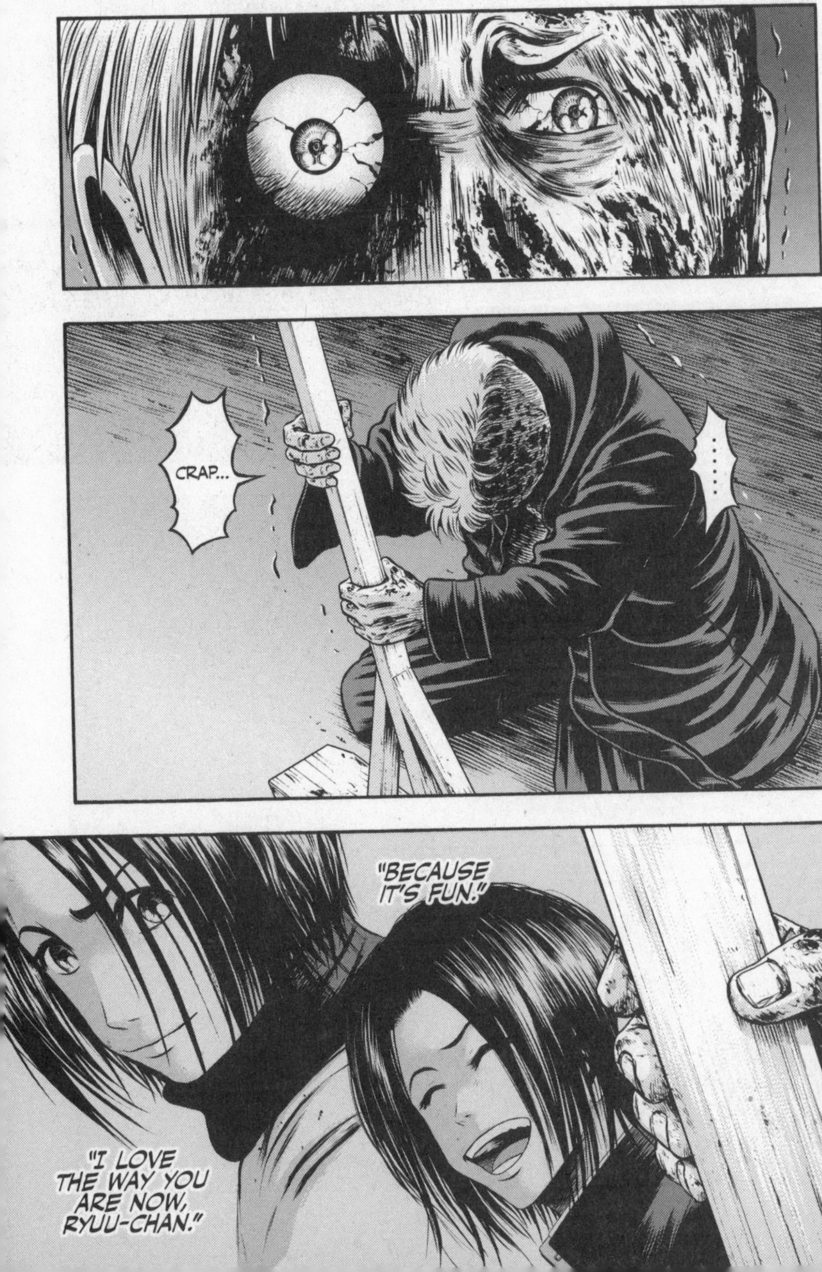
......
CRAP...
"BECAUSE IT'S FUN."
"I LOVE THE WAY YOU ARE NOW, RYUU-CHAN."

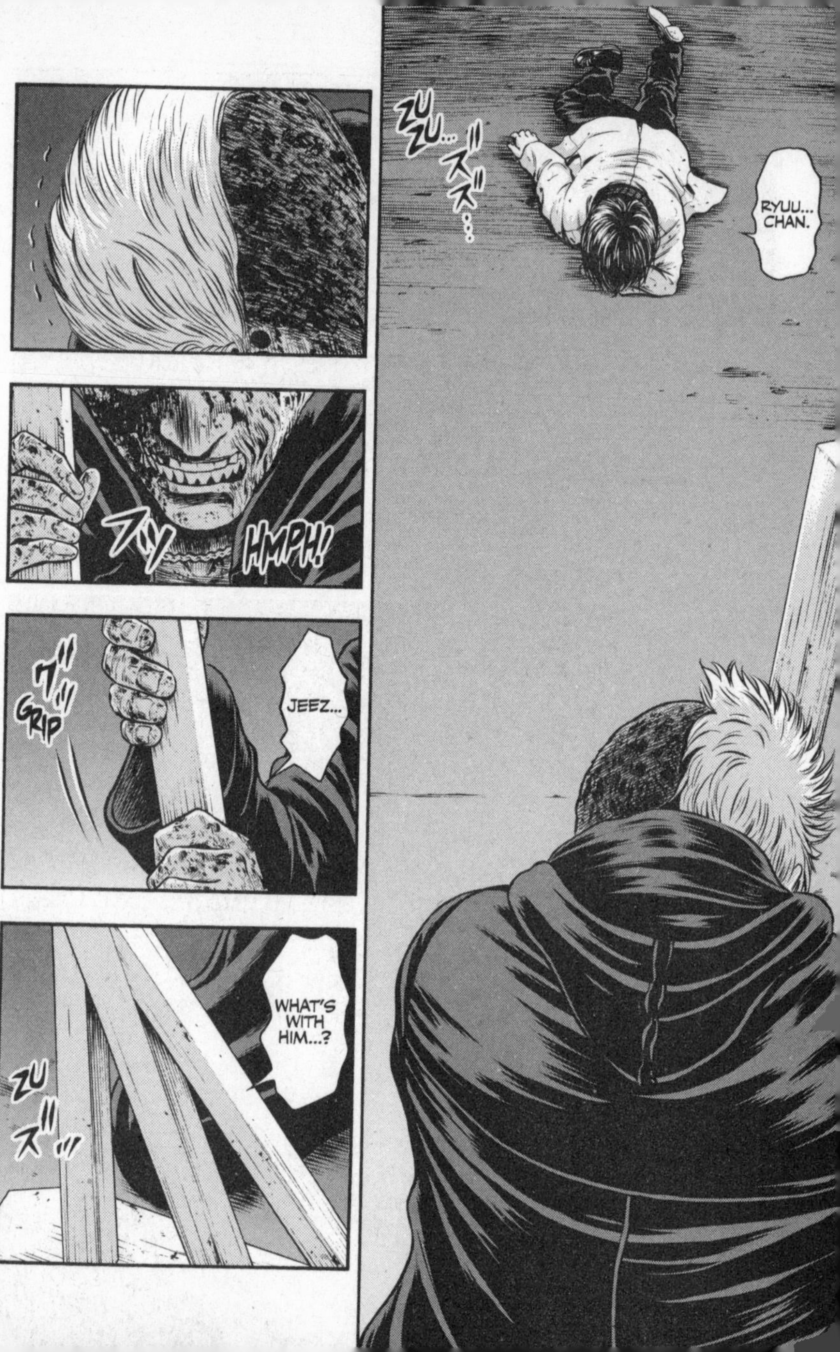
RYUU... CHAN.
ZUZU... ズズ...
フッ HMPH!
ヴッ GRIP
JEEZ...
WHAT'S WITH HIM...?
ZU ズッ

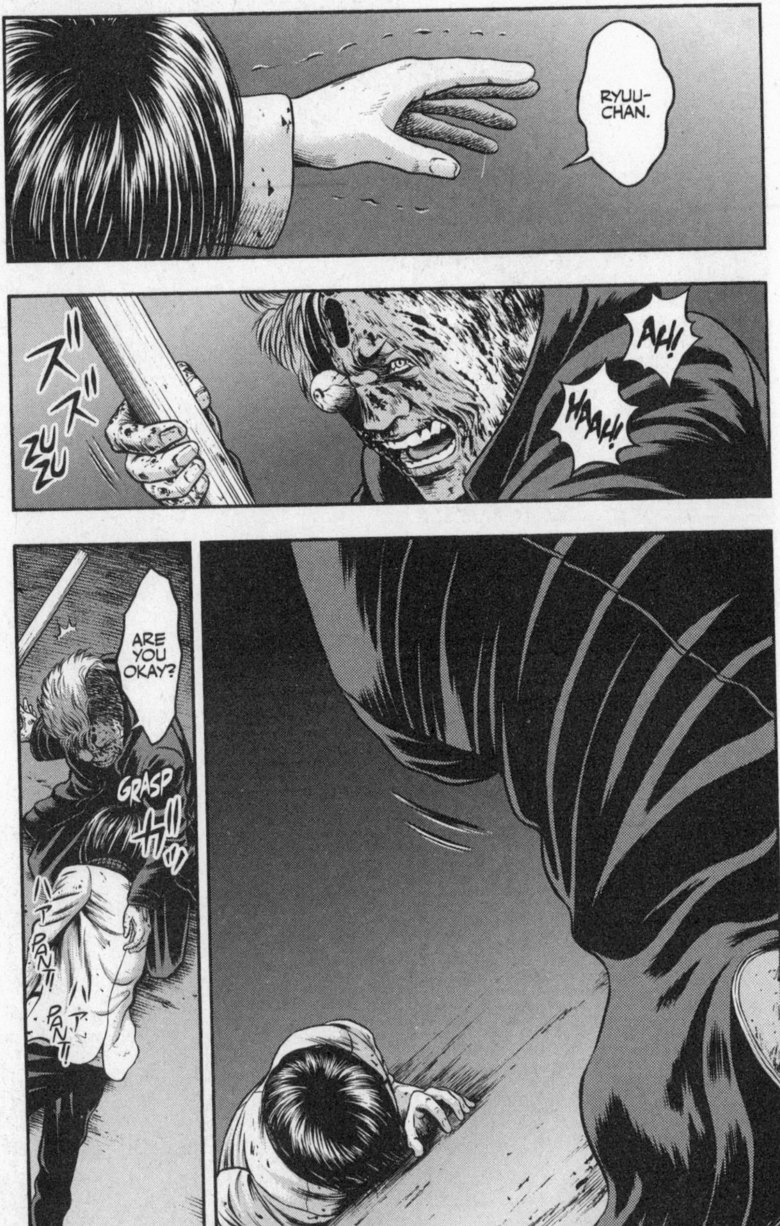
RYUU-CHAN.
AH!
HAAAH!
ズズ
ZUZU
ARE YOU OKAY?
GRASP
PANT!
PANT!

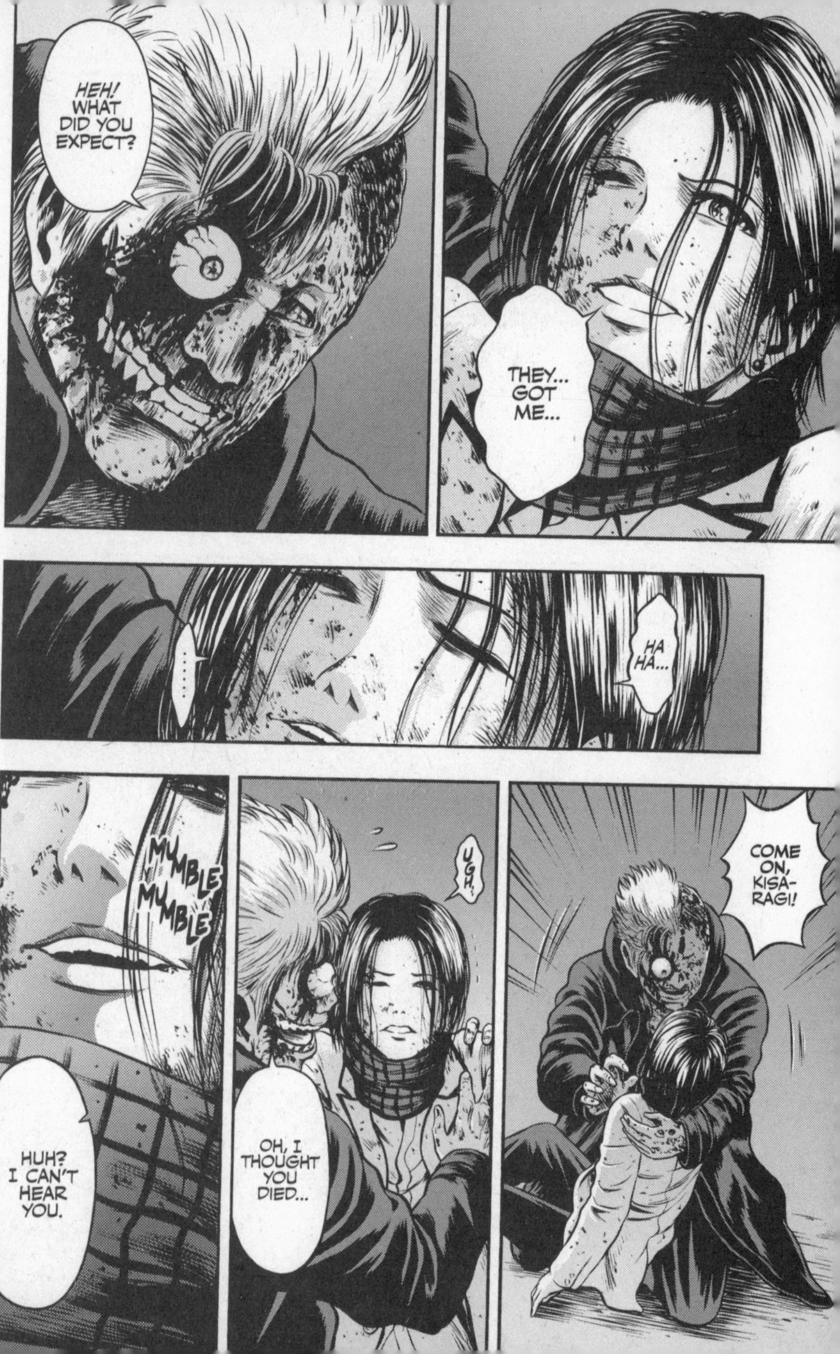
THEY... GOT ME...
HEH! WHAT DID YOU EXPECT?
HA HA...
...
COME ON, KISA-RAGI!
UGH.
OH, I THOUGHT YOU DIED...
MUMBLE MUMBLE
HUH? I CAN'T HEAR YOU.

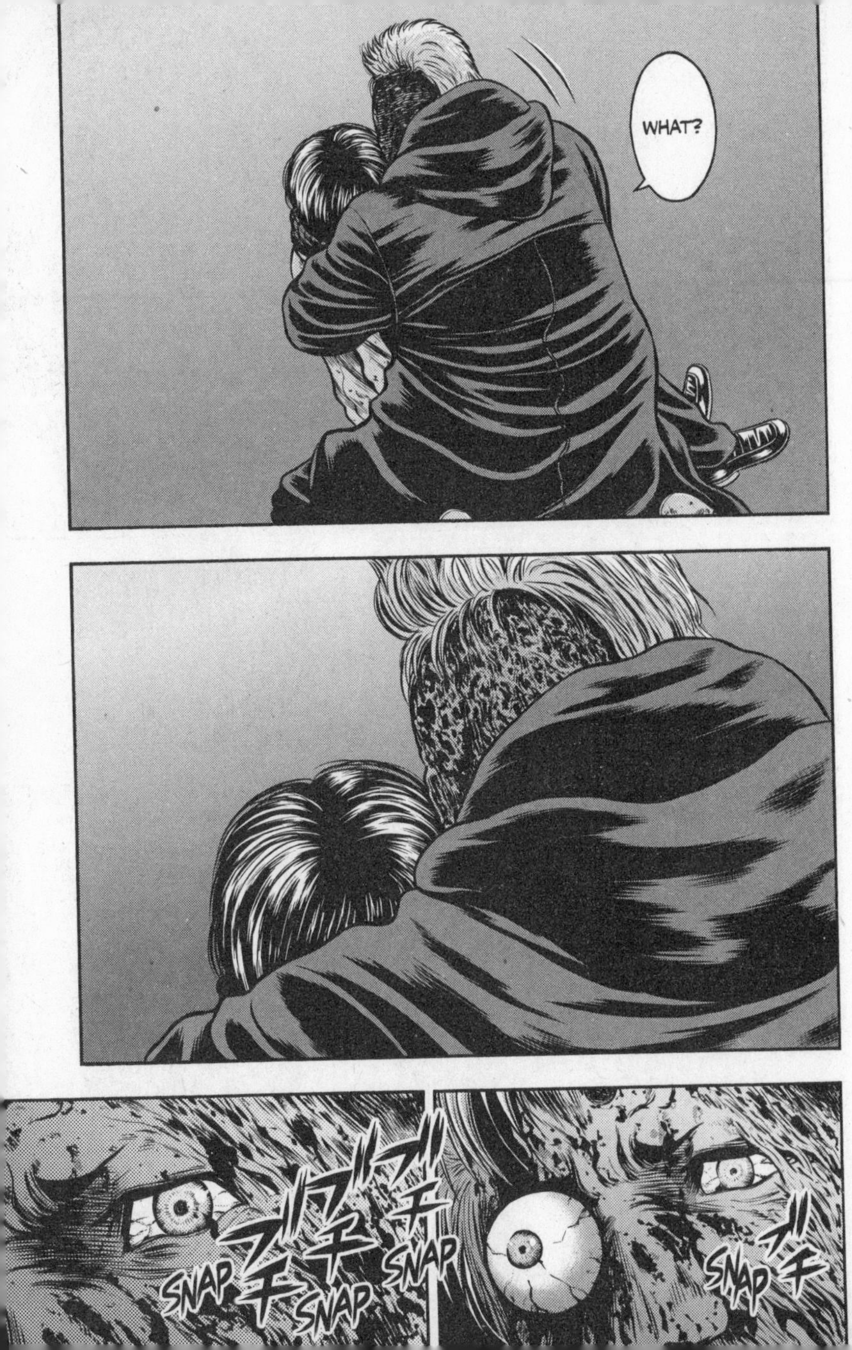
WHAT?
SNAP
SNAP
SNAP
SNAP

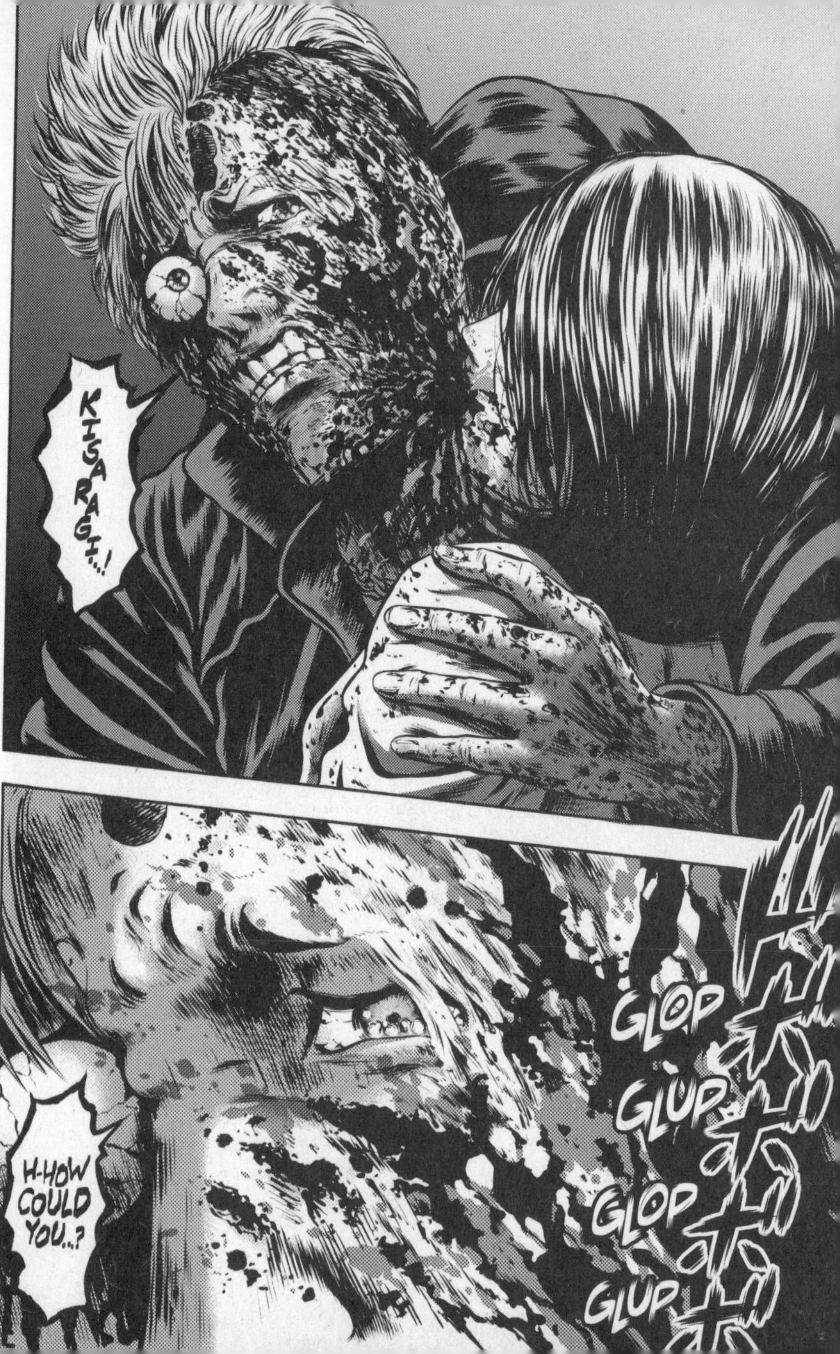
KISARAGI...!
GLOP
GLUP
GLOP
GLUP
H-HOW COULD YOU...?

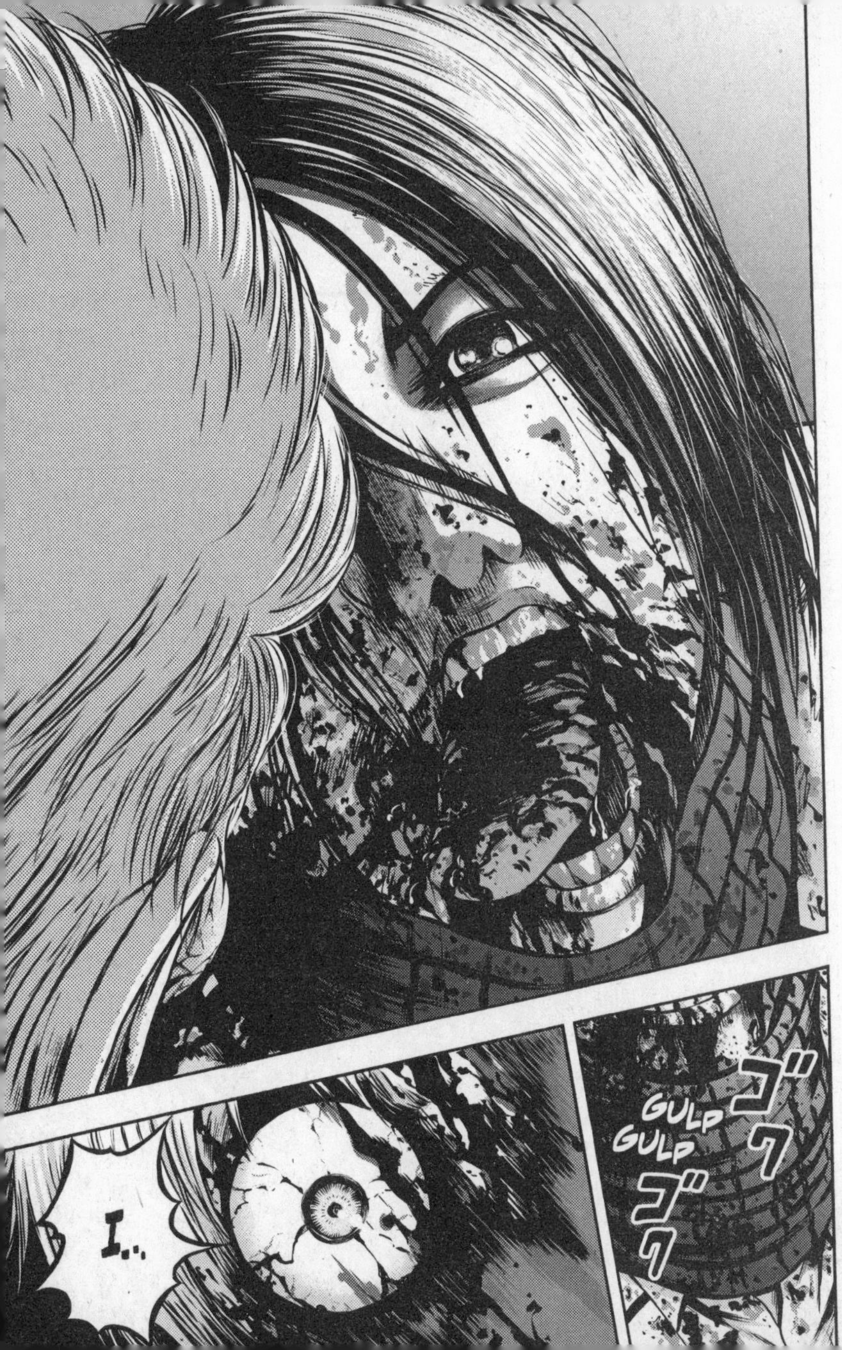
ゴクゴク
GULP GULP
I...

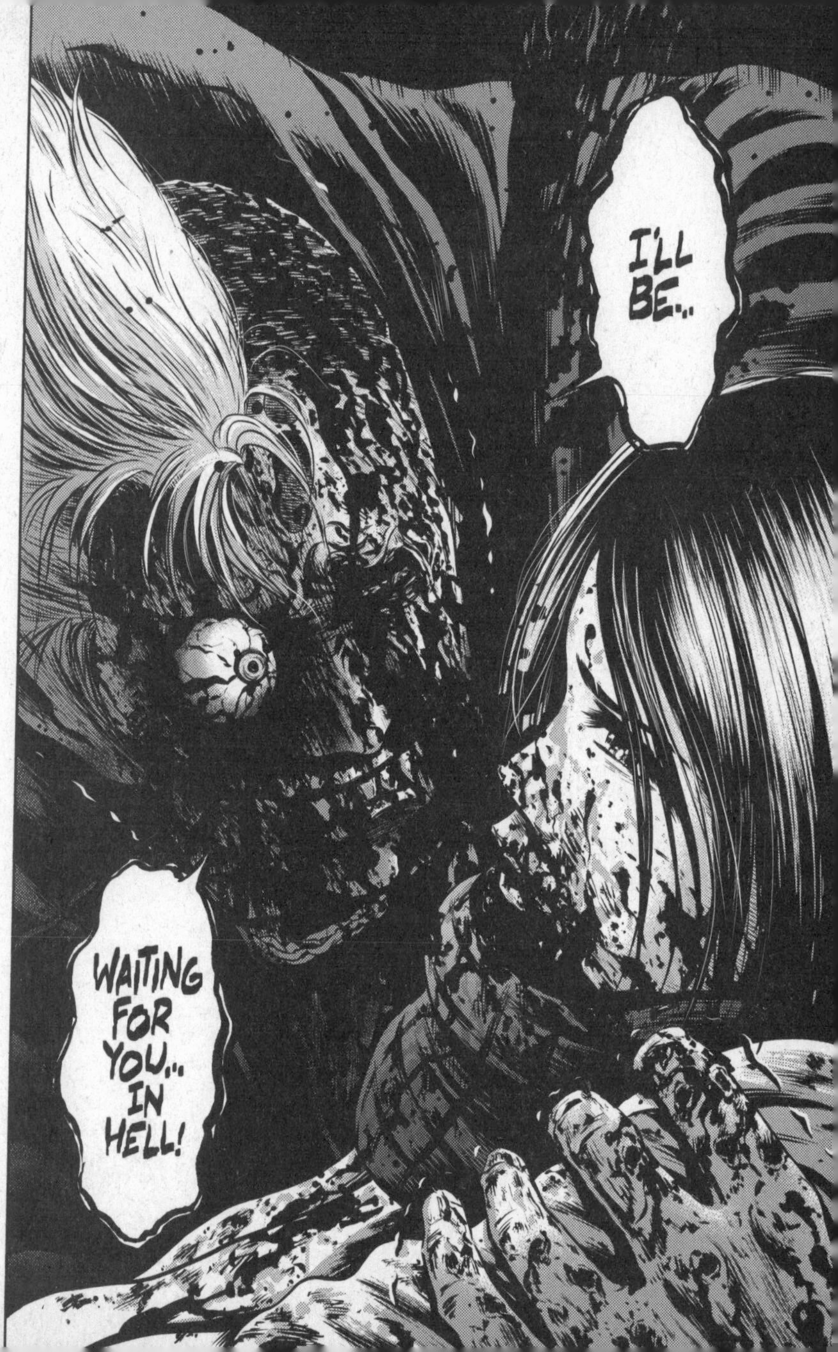
I'LL BE...
WAITING FOR YOU... IN HELL!

HOUR OF THE ZOMBIE

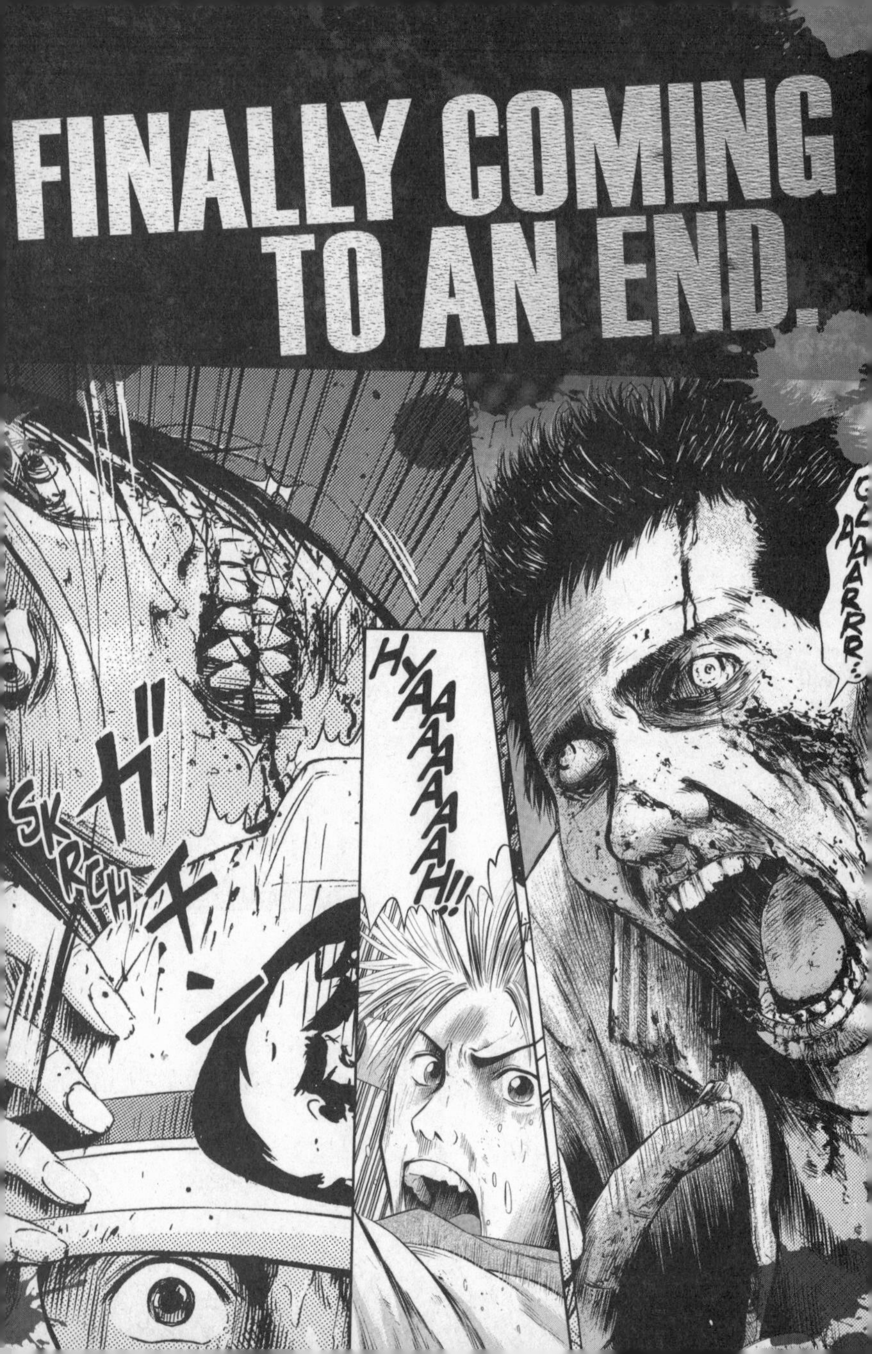
FINALLY COMING TO AN END.
GUAAARRR..
HYAAAAAAAH!!
SKRCH